THE EUROPEAN U[...]

General Editors: Neill Nugent, William E. Paterson, Vincent Wright

The European Union series is designed to provide an authoritative library on the European Union, ranging from general introductory texts to definitive assessments of key institutions and actors, policies and policy processes, and the role of member states.

Book[...]
the n[...]
acces[...] ers, and
intere[...]
• Gen[...] main areas of policy
• The[...] · The member states and the Union

The s[...]ssor of Politics a[...] M[...] Professor of European [...]egration, Manchester Metropolitan Universit[...] Director of the Institute of German Studies, University o[...]

Their co-editor until his death in July 1999, **Vincent Wrig[...]** College, Oxford University. He played an immensely valu[...] development of *The European Union Series* and is greatl[...]

Feedback on the series and book proposals are always we[...] Steven Kennedy, Palgrave Macmillan, Houndmills, Basingstoke, Hampshire RG21 6XS, UK or by e-mail to s.kennedy@palgrave.com

---

General textbooks

Published

Desmond Dinan **Encyclopedia of the European Union**
[Rights: Europe only]

Desmond Dinan **Europe Recast: a History of European Union**
[Rights: Europe only]

Desmond Dinan **Ever Closer Union: An Introduction to European Integration (2nd edn)**
[Rights: World excluding North and South America, Philippines and Japan]

Simon Hix **The Political System of the European Union**

John McCormick **Understanding the European Union: A Concise Introduction (2nd edn)**

Brent F Nelsen and Alexander Stubb **The European Union: Readings on the Theory and Practice of European Integration (3rd edn)**
[Rights: Europe only]

Neill Nugent **The Government and Politics of the European Union (5th edn)**
[Rights: World excluding USA and dependencies and Canada]

John Peterson and Elizabeth Bomberg **Decision-making in the European Union**

Ben Rosamond **Theories of European Integration**

Forthcoming

Laurie Buonanno and Neill Nugent **Policies and Policy Processes of the European Union**

Neill Nugent (ed) **European Union Enlargement**

Andrew Scott **The Political Economy of the European Union**

Philippa Sherrington **Understanding European Union Governance**

The major institutions and actors

Published

Renaud Dehousse **The European Court of Justice**

The major institutions and actors
(continued)

Justin Greenwood **Interest Representation in the European Union**

Fiona Hayes-Renshaw and Helen Wallace **The Council of Ministers**

Simon Hix and Christopher Lord **Political Parties in the European Union**

David Judge and David Earnshaw **The European Parliament**

Neill Nugent **The European Commission**

Anne Stevens with Handley Stevens **Brussels Bureaucrats?: The Administration of the European Union**

Forthcoming

Derek Beach **The Dynamics of European Integration: Why and When EU Institutions Matter**

Simon Bulmer and Wolfgang Wessels **The European Council**

Thomas Christiansen and Christine Reh **Constitutionalising the European Union**

The main areas of policy
Published

Michelle Cini and Lee McGowan **Competition Policy in the European Union**

Wyn Grant **The Common Agricultural Policy**

Martin Holland **The European Union and the Third World**

Brigid Laffan **The Finances of the European Union**

Malcolm Levitt and Christopher Lord **The Political Economy of Monetary Union**

Janne Haaland Matláry **Energy Policy in the European Union**

John McCormick **Environmental Policy in the European Union**

John Peterson and Margaret Sharp **Technology Policy in the European Union**

Handley Stevens **Transport Policy in the European Union**

Forthcoming

David Allen and Geoffrey Edwards **The External Economic Relations of the European Union**

Laura Cram **Social Policy in the European Union**

Steven McGuire and Michael Smith **The USA and the European Union**

Anand Menon **Defence Policy and the European Union**

James Mitchell and Paul McAleavey **Regionalism and Regional Policy in the European Union**

Jörg Monar **Justice and Home Affairs in the European Union**

John Vogler and Charlotte Bretherton **The External Policies of the European Union**

Also planned

Political Union

The member states and the Union
Published

Carlos Closa and Paul Heywood **Spain and the European Union**

Alain Guyomarch, Howard Machin and Ella Ritchie **France in the European Union**

Forthcoming

Simon Bulmer and William E. Paterson **Germany and the European Union**

Phil Daniels and Ella Ritchie **Britain and the European Union**

Robert Ladrech **Europeanization and National Politics**

Brigid Laffan **The European Union and its Member States**

Luisa Perrotti **Italy and the European Union**

Series Standing Order (outside North America only)
ISBN 0–333–71695–7 hardcover
ISBN 0–333–69352–3 paperback
Full details from www.palgrave.com

EUROPE RECAST

A History of European Union

Desmond Dinan

palgrave
macmillan

First published in Europe 2004 by
PALGRAVE MACMILLAN
Houndmills, Basingstoke, Hampshire RG21 6XS

PALGRAVE MACMILLAN is the global academic imprint of the Palgrave
Macmillan division of St. Martin's Press, LLC and of Palgrave Macmillan Ltd.
Macmillan® is a registered trademark in the United States, United Kingdom
and other countries. Palgrave is a registered trademark in the European
Union and other countries.

ISBN 0–333–98733–0 hardback
ISBN 0–333–98734–9 paperback

This book is printed on paper suitable for recycling and
made from fully managed and sustained forest sources.

A catalogue record for this book is available from the British Library.

10   9   8   7   6   5   4   3   2
12   11   10   09   08   07   06   05   04

Printed and bound in Great Britain

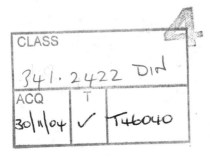

To Denis Smyth,
mentor and friend

Contents

Illustrations

▧ Maps

▧ Photographs

Preface

I t seems appropriate to publish a history of the European Union (EU) in the spring of 2004, on the eve of an epochal enlargement. The accession of ten new member states, eight from the former Soviet bloc in Central and Eastern Europe, surely signifies the resilience and appeal of the highly institutionalized form of integration epitomized by the EU. By their own admission, the new member states are not only joining the EU but also rejoining Europe. The EU, therefore, would appear to symbolize European unity: the triumph of voluntarily shared sovereignty over excessive nationalism, ideological division, and imperial ambition.

The reality is less clear-cut and more complicated. As the outcome of the Brussels summit in December 2003 showed, member states (and prospective member states) are motivated not by nebulous visions of European unity, but by concrete calculations of national advantage. Failure to reach agreement on a new system for qualified majority voting in the Council of Ministers scuttled the proposed constitutional treaty, at least temporarily. Clearly, the protagonists in the unsuccessful summit based the negotiations on a narrow appraisal of their national interests rather than an idealistic presumption of the European interest.

That was always the way in EU history. The difference now is that national interests are often undisguised and generally harder to reconcile. The EU today has a plethora of important issues on the agenda, far higher political stakes, a cumbersome policymaking apparatus that has evolved over the years, and four times as many national governments as originally sat around the table. Inevitably, the EU is increasingly difficult to manage.

Undoubtedly the EU is in a period of flux. Challenges of globalization, Europeanization (the growing intermingling of EU and national politics and policymaking), and Euroskepticism are buffeting it from all sides. Nevertheless, the EU remains remarkably adaptable and durable. The outcome of the Brussels summit is hardly a decisive turning point. A new treaty would be an important development in a long tradition of constitutional advances, rather than a radical departure. Similarly, the current round of enlargement may change the face of the EU, but the accession of many new and different member states is only the latest stage in a process that began more than a decade ago. Inasmuch as this book serves as a guide to the future, the lesson probably is that European integration will rumble along and the EU will muddle through, in some shape or form, whatever challenges lie ahead.

I have wanted to write a history of the EU for some time. Although my textbook, *Ever Closer Union,* contains a sizable section on EU history, *Europe Recast* goes well beyond that general overview in both depth and detail. This book is not only about the EU but also about the idea of European union that surrounded the establishment of the European Communities in the 1950s. I am grateful to Lynne Rienner and Steven Kennedy, my publishers, for encouraging me to write this book. I am also thankful for the astute advice of John Moore, my father-in-law, who read the final draft to give me a layman's view, and of Mary Cleary, a former graduate student, who approached the draft from the viewpoint of a reader with a sound knowledge of the EU. Both made extremely helpful suggestions. Mary also drew on her expertise as an editor in Washington, D.C., to help me select and get permissions for the maps and images sprinkled throughout the text.

A note on style. It is difficult to write elegantly about the EU, a subject replete with abbreviations, acronyms, jargon, and excessive use of capital letters. I tried to improve the flow of the narrative by keeping these encumbrances to a minimum. For instance, I have not capitalized *member states, common foreign and security policy, justice and home affairs, intergovernmental conference,* and the like. I managed to keep the list of abbreviations and acronyms to less than a page, surely a great achievement in a book on the EU. I use "national leaders" instead of "heads of state and government," and "EU leaders" to refer to members of the European Council, the EU's most powerful political body. And I could not bear to use the dreadful term *acquis communautaire,* which purists like to claim cannot be translated accurately into English. Instead I wrote "body or corpus of EU rules and regulations."

Finally, a note on nomenclature. First, the uninitiated invariably confuse the *European Council* and the *Council of Ministers.* The European Council, consisting of national leaders plus the Commission president, meets about four times a year to direct the EU and resolve difficult political problems. The Council of Ministers consists of ordinary government ministers. It meets regularly in a number of formations, such as the foreign ministers, finance ministers, and agriculture ministers, to enact legislation and make policy for the EU. The name *Council,* used by itself, always refers to the Council of Ministers, never to the European Council. Second, the EU officially came into existence only in November 1993. Nevertheless I sometimes use the term EU when referring to the European Community (EC) before that time. In general, however, I refer to the EC until the early 1990s and the EU thereafter. Over-all, I tried to avoid pedantry without sacrificing accuracy, not an easy thing to do when speaking, teaching, or writing about the EU.

—Desmond Dinan

EUROPE RECAST

Introduction

The idea of a united Europe is a recurring theme in the long and often violent history of the continent. The Holy Roman Emperors, Napoleon, Hitler, and others all sought, in sometimes horrifying ways, to achieve a continental unity based variously on princely alliances, ethnic cohesion, ideology, or raw power. Ever since the emergence of the modern state, philosophers and political thinkers have also imagined a united Europe triumphing over narrow national interests and allegiances. Today's European Union (EU) is unique among these competing visions. Tempering the nationalist ethos that had become the ruling principle of European political development, the countries that formed the European Communities, the basis of the European Union, chose to limit (but not eliminate) their own sovereignty, the hallmark of a modern nation-state, in favor of collective peace, economic integration, and supranational governance.

Their reasons for doing so were rooted in the disastrous decades of the early twentieth century. The miserable legacy of heroic European nationalism—two world wars, countless millions dead, and economic ruin—was not lost on the people of Europe, who generally supported economic and political integration after World War II. Eurofederalism was popular. European politicians wanted above all to end international strife, foster social harmony, and promote economic well-being. They sought to build a better world, free of the hatreds and rivalries that had destroyed their countries in recent years. For their generation, European integration became synonymous with peace and prosperity.

Yet, there was nothing inevitable about the emergence of European integration in the form with which we are now familiar. European politicians were (and still are) instinctively averse to sharing national sovereignty, despite rhetorical flourishes to the contrary. National leaders decided to share sovereignty in supranational organizations primarily because they perceived that it was in their countries' (and therefore their own) interests to do so. Ideas, intellectual fashion, opportunity, chance, conviction, calculation, personal predilection, and ambition all played a part. Ultimately, however, European integration emerged as it did because of a rational response by politicians, businesspeople, and other key actors to changing economic, political, and strategic circumstances, ranging from Germany's postwar recovery, to the fall of the Berlin Wall, to the acceleration of globalization. Despite growing public concern about the process and politics of European integration, Europeans generally acquiesced because the outcome seemed worthwhile and the alternatives less attractive.

■ The Interwar Experience

The Great War (later called World War I), fought mostly in Europe, ended in November 1918 after more than four years of frightful slaughter. U.S. intervention on the side of the western allies tipped the balance against Germany, which had earlier forced the newly established Soviet Union to capitulate. The Versailles Treaty of 1919 imposed hefty war reparations on Germany and severely limited its sovereignty. John Maynard Keynes, the brilliant English economist, denounced the financial provisions of the treaty in a best-selling book, *The Economic Consequences of the Peace*, published in 1920.[1] As Keynes predicted, reparations became a huge drain on the German economy, a major irritant in Franco-German relations, and a rallying cry for ardent German nationalists who denounced the democratic Weimar regime for having signed the treaty.

Persistent, virulent nationalism in western Europe between the wars was hardly conducive to visions of European integration. In the east, new nation states, jealous of their sovereignty, emerged from the wreckage of the Russian, Austro-Hungarian, and Ottoman empires. Because the Soviet Union, weakened by civil war, did not pose a serious threat to international security, other European countries were not inclined to unite "against" it. The absence of a Soviet threat accounted in part for the relative aloofness of the United States, which refused to become entangled in European affairs or even to join the League of Nations, the new international security organization. Nor, resentful though they were of the U.S. rise to global power, were the Europeans inclined to unite "against" the United States, a major market and potential ally.

The horrors of the Great War and uncertainty of the early postwar period nevertheless spawned a movement for European union: the Pan-Europa pressure group of Richard Coudenhove-Kalergi, a count of the old Holy Roman Empire. In his influential book *Pan-Europa*, published in 1923, Coudenhove-Kalergi called for a federal union of European states centered on France and Germany, but excluding the Soviet Union (because of its communism and foothold in Asia) and Britain (because of its imperial interests).[2] An aristocrat and elitist, Coudenhove-Kalergi initially sought the support of Italy's dictator, Benito Mussolini. Growing public interest in the idea of Pan-Europa, and Mussolini's rejection of it, led Coudenhove-Kalergi to appreciate the importance of democracy in building European union.

Although it generated chapters in most European continental countries, Pan-Europa was an ephemeral political movement. Nevertheless, two of its members, Edouard Herriot and Aristide Briand, were leading French politicians who sought a rapprochement with Germany. Briand, foreign minister in the mid-1920s, worked with Gustav Stresemann, his German counterpart, to save Franco-German relations from the wreckage of the war and France's punitive policy toward Germany immediately afterward. Together with Britain's foreign minister, Austen Chamberlain, they were instrumental in concluding the Locarno Treaty of October 1925, which guaranteed the borders of western Europe and paved the way for Germany's entry into the League of Nations (for which all three received the Nobel Peace Prize). The "spirit of Locarno" hovered over the "years of hope" (1925–1929), when it seemed as if western Europe was finally on the road to a better future.[3]

Briand and Stresemann had a celebrated summit meeting over a lengthy lunch in the small village of Thoiry, across the French border from Geneva, in September 1926. There they addressed a number of contentious issues in hopes of paving the way for a Franco-German entente. France desperately wanted Germany to make good on its promise to pay reparations; Germany desperately wanted the allies to end their military occupation of the Rhineland, on which France took a hard line. Despite good relations between Briand and Stresemann, Germany and France were too suspicious of each other to follow the Thoiry summit with detailed negotiations and a diplomatic breakthrough. The years of hope gradually gave way to despair as extreme nationalists in both countries entrenched their positions. Stresemann's death in October 1929 symbolized the death also of incipient Franco-German accord.[4]

In his last speech to the League of Nations, in September 1929, Stresemann advocated European integration and even raised the possibility of a common currency.[5] He followed in the footsteps of French prime minister Herriot who, as early as 1925, spoke publicly about a United States of Europe. Briand was another leading proponent of Pan-Europa. Like Stresemann, he extolled the virtues of European integration in a speech to the League in September 1929. Spurred in part by Stresemann's untimely death, Briand followed up with a famous memorandum in May 1930 calling for an association of European states, subordinate to the League, to coordinate economic policies and promote political union. Although far-reaching by the standards of the time, Briand's initiative did not propose that governments share national sovereignty. Even so, it was too radical for most European countries, including Briand's own. The League established a Committee of Enquiry on the European Union, which held a number of sessions in the early 1930s and from which nothing more was heard about the Briand memorandum.[6]

Germany and Austria used the language of European integration to float a proposal in March 1931 for a customs union open to other countries as well. The idea of an Austro-German customs union jogged historical memories of the Zollverein of 1834, the customs union among German states that presaged the rise of Prussia and unification of Germany in 1871. Many Europeans, who ascribed the continent's current ills to German unification, feared that an Austro-German customs union would lead inevitably to an Austro-German *anschluss* (political union). France blocked the proposal, heightening international tension and exacerbating the worsening economic crisis. Once Hitler came to power, any prospect of Franco-German reconciliation and voluntary European integration abruptly came to an end.

The 1930s was a dismal decade in Europe, bracketed by economic recession at the beginning and the outbreak of war at the end. Fascism seemed unstoppable in Germany, Spain, and the faltering democracies of central and eastern Europe, having already taken root in Italy. Emboldened by Anglo-French weakness and U.S. detachment, Hitler scored one foreign policy triumph after another, until his invasion of Poland in September 1939 triggered an Anglo-French declaration of war. In August 1940 Coudenhove-Kalergi fled Europe for the United States, his Pan-Europa movement almost forgotten.[7]

The approach of war triggered a revival of interest in federalism as a way to bolster the democratic nations in the face of fascist aggression. Federal ideas had flourished in Britain in the interwar years. Leading intellectuals such as Lionel Curtis, Philip Kerr (later Lord Lothian), and Harold Laski championed them. These and other federalists joined a new group, Federal Union, established in November 1938, which attracted several thousand members. *Union Now*, a book by the U.S. academic Clarence Streit, calling for a transatlantic union of democratic states, had a big impact on British opinion.[8] As World War II ground on, British federalists produced a steady stream of books and pamphlets advocating the establishment of a federal system of European states in the postwar period. In September 1944 Federal Union adopted as "[an] immediate aim the promotion of a democratic federation of Europe as part of the postwar settlement."[9]

Britain was home during the war to many exiled continental politicians, who both imbibed and shaped such federalist ideas. British federalism also influenced the non-Communist resistance movements throughout occupied Europe, especially in Italy. There Altiero Spinelli and other democratic socialists, detained on the island of Ventotene, smuggled out a Manifesto for a Free and United Europe in July 1941 (it later appeared as an underground publication in Nazi-occupied Rome).[10] Drawing on a tradition of Italian federalism dating from the nineteenth century, the manifesto called for a postwar federation, including Germany, to ensure peace in Europe. Inspired by the Ventotene Manifesto, Italian federalists conferred with the representatives of resistance movements from seven other countries during a clandestine conference in Geneva in spring 1944; the result was the International Federalist Declaration. Like underground literature in the Soviet Union, the declaration circulated secretly throughout Nazi Europe.

At the same time, driven by a malevolent racial nationalism, the Nazis integrated Europe militarily. Yet Albert Speer, Hitler's young economic czar, speculated about a postwar European economic community based on voluntary cooperation rather than coercion. Referring to a meeting in September 1943 with Jean Bichelonne, the like-minded French minister of production, Speer told an interviewer decades later: "We agreed that in the future we would avoid the mistakes of the First World War generation, who were now at the helm. Irrespective of national frontiers, Europe had to be economically integrated."[11] According to his military liaison officer, Speer believed strongly in shared economic sovereignty: "He was certain that the only way towards a better and peaceful future, not only for Germany but for all of Europe, was if Germany could eventually be part of an economic European entity."[12]

■ Toward European Union

Speer never thought that the war would end in Germany's total annihilation. That outcome, together with the emergence of the Soviet Union as the liberator and then the occupier of Central and Eastern Europe, completely changed the geopolitical configuration of the Continent. Eager to establish a new, open, international economic system and protect Western Europe from internal Communist subversion or external Soviet aggression, the United States became deeply embroiled in postwar European affairs. Mindful of the mistakes of the past but fearful as ever of eventual German resurgence, France sought a successful security strategy in the emerging Cold War world. There was a flurry of interest in federalist ideas throughout liberated Europe. Finally, the circumstances seemed propitious for European integration based on shared sovereignty and the rule of law. The Cold War ensured that such integration, instead of being pan-European in scope, however, would be confined to Western Europe.

The intellectual movement for European integration, chronicled in great detail by the German historian Walter Lipgens, reemerged in the aftermath of World War II and reached its apogee in 1949 in the Council of Europe.[13] The Schuman Declaration of 1950, which gave rise to the European Coal and Steel Community (ECSC), originated not in the ferment of the European movement but in the narrow confines of the French planning office. It was an imaginative response to the challenge of rapid German economic recovery at a time of worsening East-West conflict, satisfying differing U.S., French, and German needs and objectives. For leading French and German politicians at the time, the coalescence of European and national interests made sharing sovereignty irresistible and set in train a lengthy, unpredictable, and intriguing process of economic and political integration.

The founding fathers of the EU were not utopian idealists. They did not seek to subsume the nation-state in a new, supranational political entity but to adapt the nation-state to a set of specific historical circumstances. Facing unprecedented economic and strategic challenges, statesmen such as Konrad Adenauer of Germany, Alcide de Gasperi of Italy, and Robert Schuman of France agreed to share sovereignty in specific fields. According to the influential historian Alan Milward, the founding fathers "recognized or stumbled upon the need for . . . limited surrenders of national sovereignty through which the nation state and [the European Community] were jointly strengthened, not as separate and opposed entities, but within a process of mutual reinforcement."[14] The launch of the European Community (EC) and the consolidation of the nation-state were compatible, not contradictory, developments.

In his famous article "The End of History?" Francis Fukuyama referred derisively to "those flabby, prosperous, self-satisfied, inward-looking, weak-willed states whose grandest project was nothing more heroic than the creation of the Common Market."[15] The six countries that launched the European Community in the 1950s were far from flabby, prosperous, self-satisfied, or inward looking. Nor were they weak willed. Despite Fukuyama's disgust for a vision devoid of color and heroic derring-do, it took a leap of faith and rare political courage for most of those countries to turn their backs on traditional nation-state aspirations and agree to exercise some of their powers in common. For France, in particular, accepting the EC meant abandoning decades of protectionism, overcoming deep distrust of Germany, and embracing economic modernization—a drastic revision of the country's long-standing self-image as a great power. For Germany, utterly destroyed at the end of the war, European integration offered salvation and international rehabilitation.

Plans for a European Defense Community (EDC), to be organized along lines similar to the Coal and Steel Community, collapsed because of French fear of German rearmament, apparently poisoning prospects for further formal integration. Yet the European Economic Community (EEC) emerged soon afterward not because of the kind of spillover predicted by Ernst Haas in *The Uniting of Europe*, his path-breaking book on the Coal and Steel Community, but because of the appeal of deeper economic integration at a time of intensifying intra-European trade.[16] Member states built the EC on a solid foundation of informal economic integration stretching back to the late nineteenth century, which they now shaped in particular geographical and functional directions.

Britain stayed outside the Communities because its national interests, or at least the government's perception of its national interests, pointed in a different direction. By the time Britain changed course and applied to join in the early 1960s, French president Charles de Gaulle saw British membership as a threat to France and promptly thwarted it. De Gaulle embraced the EC as an economic entity, not least because of its bountiful agricultural policy, but rejected its political pretensions. His espousal of an intergovernmental political union and dismissal of Commission president Walter Hallstein's federal ambitions brought European integration back to economic basics.

French opposition to British accession ended after de Gaulle's resignation in 1969 and in light of Germany's growing economic power. Unfortunately, British membership in the EC coincided with international financial instability and the oil crisis of the early 1970s. The enlarged EC struggled through a decade of brutal economic conditions: sluggish growth, rampant inflation, and rising unemployment. The recession reinforced British ambivalence toward the EC. Regular meetings of EC leaders, institutionalized in the European Council, helped hold the Community together. The chancellor of Germany and the president of France used the EC as a hook upon which to hang a mechanism for monetary policy cooperation in the late 1970s. Otherwise the EC seemed moribund, the butt of jokes about agricultural surpluses and excessive harmonization of industrial product standards.

The EC sprang back to life in the mid-1980s, rediscovered as the answer to the problems of Eurosclerosis and the lethargy of the previous decade and as a vehicle to confront together the challenges of global economic competition. Commission president Jacques Delors deftly capitalized on the member states' determination to accelerate market integration. He leveraged the single market program to win substantial spending on the so-called structural funds to promote economic development in poorer member states, including recent entrants Portugal and Spain. The Single European Act, the first major treaty reform in the EC's history, facilitated decisionmaking by qualified majority voting in the Council of Ministers in order to accelerate implementation of the single market program.

If legitimacy depends on success, then the EC enjoyed strong legitimacy in the late 1980s. The single market program proved popular with elites and ordinary Europeans alike. Delors reveled in the EC's newfound popularity. France and Germany returned to the driver's seat of European integration, their leaders calling for the ambitious, seemingly improbable goal of monetary union to consolidate the single market and strengthen Europe's political cohesion in the face of dissolution of the old order in Central and Eastern Europe. Increasingly alienated by moves toward monetary union and other forms of integration, British prime minister Margaret Thatcher warned that the EC risked becoming a "superstate." She and Delors had radically different visions of Europe: his federalist, hers fervently antifederalist.

Popular support for European integration helped return Helmut Kohl of Germany, François Mitterrand of France, and Felipe González of Spain to power, and helped topple Thatcher from power, in the late 1980s. Driven by perceived national interests and a presumed European interest, Kohl and Mitterrand pushed forward with plans for monetary union. Rapid reform in Central and Eastern Europe, culminating in the imminent prospect of German unification, helped Kohl overcome the domestic resistance to giving up the cherished deutschemark. The end of the Cold War also emboldened member states to develop a common foreign and security policy, which, together with

Economic and Monetary Union (EMU), became the centerpiece of intergovernmental negotiations in 1991 that resulted in the Maastricht Treaty. A new face of Europe was emerging: that of an aspiring global power, trying to achieve the unified political clout to match its rising economic weight.

But exaggerated claims of the single market's success and a severe economic downturn soured the public mood in the early 1990s. The Maastricht Treaty, which launched the new European Union, fanned popular unease about the pace of European integration. Responding to a near-fatal backlash against the treaty's scope and content, a chastened political establishment struggled to make the EU more open and accountable and responsive to citizen concerns. Member states stressed the notion of subsidiarity—a principle of decentralization and quasi-federalism—to reassure a restive public. Despite these efforts, the EU failed to win widespread acceptance as it struggled to be effective in a difficult international environment.

The newly proclaimed EU faced formidable challenges. The road to monetary union was rocky, obliging member states to make hard economic choices in order to participate. Enlargement reemerged on the EU's agenda with the end of the Cold War. First, the European neutrals (plus Norway), then the newly independent countries of Central and Eastern Europe (plus Cyprus, Malta, and Turkey) sought membership. The European neutrals (minus Norway) joined without fuss in 1995. Primarily because of their low economic level and poor administrative capacity, the second group of countries faced huge obstacles to membership. Turkey was a special case: geographically distant, strategically important, economically impoverished, politically unstable, and predominantly Muslim. The Turkish occupation of the northern part of Cyprus complicated the Mediterranean island's otherwise straightforward membership application.

Enlargement on such a large scale was bound to change the EU. Having avoided major institutional reform during previous enlargements, the EU tried, but largely failed, to overhaul its institutional structure and decision-making procedures in order to cope with the new round of enlargement. The Nice Treaty of 2001, intended to prepare the EU institutionally for enlargement, was patently inadequate. Impelled by imminent enlargement and pervasive public alienation from the EU, national governments launched a Convention on the Future of Europe in 2002 to consider far-reaching reform, including the promulgation of a constitution. Representatives of EU and national institutions struggled in the convention to close the growing gap between "Brussels" and ordinary Europeans.

The emerging EU is very different from the European Communities of the 1950s. Yet certain features endure: the logic of economic integration; French fear of falling behind; general concern about Germany's predominance; the potential for Franco-German leadership; British skepticism; and the small country syndrome (small member states' fear of hegemony). Like the European Community before it, the European Union is mostly about economic integration. Although the common foreign and security policy, a possible defense policy, and cooperation on policing often grab the headlines, the EU is concerned primarily with managing the European marketplace. Economic integration is unglamorous but important. By eliminating barriers to trade and facilitating movement across borders, such integration benefits the people of Europe directly but often imperceptibly.

The EU also operates in an international environment that has changed dramatically since the birth of the original European institutions. Some of the early proponents of European integration wanted Europe to assert itself internationally, seeing the EC as a possible "third force" alongside the United States and the Soviet Union. The Cold War put an end to their dream and to de Gaulle's efforts in the early 1960s to establish a European political union independent of the United States. The end of the Cold War provided an opening for the EU to emerge not as a third force but, because of the disappearance of the Soviet Union, as a second force alongside the United States. By then the EU was a global economic power; becoming a global political and military power proved more difficult. The fallout from the terrorist attacks on the United States in September 2001, and the war in Iraq in 2003, have greatly complicated the EU's efforts to match its economic power with diplomatic and military might.

■ Purpose and Organization of the Book

History is a growth industry in the study of the European Union. Serious historical inquiry into European integration began in the 1970s, as the relevant archives of most member states became accessible to researchers. A major contribution emerged ten years later: Alan Milward's *The Reconstruction of Western Europe, 1945–1951*, a massive work of postwar diplomatic and economic history that explained European integration almost exclusively in terms of national interests. Milward followed up in the early 1990s, as the European Community metamorphosed into the European Union, with *The European Rescue of the Nation State*, a book that made an even more explicit link between the defense of the nation-state, the pursuit of national interests, and the acceleration of European integration. John Gillingham's *Coal, Steel and the Rebirth of Europe, 1945–1955*, a brilliant study of the integration of European heavy industry culminating in the establishment of the European Coal and Steel Community, appeared at about the same time.[17]

A host of "micro" histories of European integration preceded and succeeded these publications, some country-specific, others issue-specific. In keeping with Milward's contribution to European integration theory in *The European Rescue of the Nation State* and a later book, *The Frontier of National Sovereignty: History and Theory, 1945–1992*, Andrew Moravcsik, a political scientist, based liberal intergovernmentalism, his theory of European integration, on detailed historical case studies. In *The Choice for Europe: Social Purpose and State Power from Messina to Maastricht*, Moravcsik sought to show that key developments in the history of European integration depended almost entirely on the preferences of Britain, France, and Germany, which in turn depended almost entirely on commercial interests.[18] The persuasiveness of liberal intergovernmentalism and popularity of *The Choice for Europe* intensified interest among political scientists and other scholars of European integration in the history of the EU.

Yet, for a long time, Derek Urwin's *Community of Europe: A History of European Integration Since 1945* was the only comprehensive overview in English of the history of European integration in the postwar period. Urwin's near monopoly ended in 2003 with the publication of a new survey of contemporary European integration: Mark Gilbert's *Surpassing Realism: The Politics of European Integration Since 1945*.[19] John Gillingham's outstanding *European Integration, 1950–2002*, appeared in the same year. Far from merely reviewing the development of the EU, Gillingham produced an ambitious work of history and theory that explains integration as a struggle between the state and the market, with "the market principle . . . gradually supplant[ing] that of the state in Europe's long march from the economy of war to that of peace."[20]

By contrast, *Europe Recast* focuses specifically on the European Communities' and later the European Union's institutional and policy development in the context of changing economic and political fortunes and a fluctuating global situation. Drawing on original accounts of the establishment of the European Communities and a wealth of scholarship in a range of disciplines, *Europe Recast* seeks to explain and describe the development of European integration as comprehensively as possible within a manageable length, hoping to avoid "Euro-fatigue" on the part of the reader. Because it lacks conventional heroics, the history of the EU often seems dull and dry. The so-called empty chair crisis of the mid-1960s, when French representatives refused to take their seats in the Council of Ministers, is the most exciting political conflict in EU history—hardly on a par with the siege of Vienna or the Napoleonic campaigns. Yet, as this book shows, the making of the EU combines idealism and ideological struggles, the initiative and political entrepreneurship of strong individuals, national interests and international relations, and institutional design and bureaucratic intrigue.

The story of European integration is worth telling not only because of its intrinsic interest but also because of its importance. Having begun as one of a number of competing European projects, economic integration quickly eclipsed all others and soon claimed center stage. As a result, the European Union is a regional integration organization unlike any other, with unprecedented economic and political authority. Understanding the EU is fundamen-

tal to understanding Europe today, and understanding EU history is fundamental to understanding the EU.

While arguing that national interests rather than Euro-idealism accounted
for the emergence of the European Coal and Steel Community and that
national preferences were often paramount as well in later stages of European
integration, this book acknowledges the sometimes pivotal importance of
other influences and factors. Although political pragmatism may explain the
scope and shape of the European Communities, a felicitous combination of
idealism and national self-interest characterized the early years of European
integration. The architects of the new Europe appreciated the popular appeal
as well as the political necessity of pooling national sovereignty. But European integration could not have flourished and Euro-idealism would have
foundered if the undertaking had not worked to the ultimate advantage of the
countries concerned.

Although the ideas that led to the founding of the European Communities
reach back into the nineteenth century, the end of World War II is the critical
point of departure for the story of contemporary European integration, and
therefore for this book. Thus Chapter 1 covers the immediate postwar period.
Chapter 2 examines the emergence of the three Communities in the 1950s, as
well as the failure of the proposed defense community. Chapter 3 covers the
construction of the EC, including the epic constitutional battle provoked by de
Gaulle. Chapter 4 assesses the reversal in the EC's fortunes during the economic upheavals of the mid-1970s. Chapter 5 explains the EC's gradual recovery in the late 1970s and early 1980s, due to changing domestic and international circumstances. Chapter 6 discusses the acceleration of integration in
the late 1980s, focusing on the Single European Act and the single market program. Chapter 7 describes the achievement of European Union in the early
1990s. Chapter 8 reviews the challenges confronting the new European
Union. Chapter 9, the conclusion, returns to key points in the preceding narrative, highlighting the substance of the European idea that survives each new
reinvention and expansion to keep the original vision alive.

■ Notes

1. John Maynard Keynes, *The Economic Consequences of the Peace* (New York:
Harcourt, Brace, and Howe, 1920).

2. R. N. Coudenhove-Kalergi, *Pan-Europa* (Vienna: Pan-Europa-verlag, 1923);
translated as *Pan-Europa* (New York: A. A. Knopf, 1926).

3. See Raymond J. Sontag, *A Broken World: 1919–1939* (New York: Harper and
Row, 1971), p. 127.

4. See Jon Jacobson and John T. Walker, "The Impulse for a Franco-German
Entente: The Origins of the Thoiry Conference, 1926," *Journal of Contemporary History* 10, no. 1 (January 1975), pp. 157–181.

5. On Stresemann's contribution to European integration, see Jonathan Wright, *Gustav Stresemann: Weimar's Greatest Statesman* (Oxford: Oxford University Press, 2002).

6. See Francis Deak, "Can Europe Unite?" *Political Science Quarterly* 46, no. 3 (September 1931), pp. 424–433.

7. On Coudenhove-Kalergi's exile in the United States and return to Europe after the war, see Arnold J. Zurcher, *The Struggle to Unite Europe* (Westport, CT: Greenwood Press, 1958), pp. 10–27. Coudenhove-Kalergi received the first Charlemagne Prize, awarded annually by the city of Aachen for service to the cause of European union.

8. Clarence Streit, *Union Now: A Proposal for a Federal Union in the Democracies of the North Atlantic* (New York: Harper and Brothers, 1939).

9. Michael Burgess, *The British Tradition of Federalism* (London: Leicester University Press, 1995), p. 146.

10. See Charles F. Delzell, "The European Federalist Movement in Italy: First Phase, 1918–1947," *Journal of Modern History* 32, no. 3 (September 1960), pp. 244–245.

11. Quoted in Gita Sereny, *Albert Speer: His Battle with Truth* (New York: Alfred A. Knopf, 1995), pp. 386–387.

12. Ibid., p. 554.

13. Walter Lipgens, ed., *Documents on the History of European Integration,* Vols. 1–3 (Berlin: Walter de Gruyter, 1986–1988). Vol. 3 edited with Wilfried Loth.

14. Alan S. Milward, *The European Rescue of the Nation State*, 2nd ed. (London: Routledge, 2000), p. 319.

15. Francis Fukuyama, "The End of History?" *The National Interest*, no. 16 (Summer 1989), p. 8.

16. Ernst Haas, *The Uniting of Europe: Political, Social, and Economic Forces* (Stanford, CA: Stanford University Press, 1958).

17. Alan Milward, *The Reconstruction of Western Europe, 1945–1951* (Berkeley: University of California Press, 1984); Milward, *The European Rescue of the Nation State* (Berkeley: University of California Press, 1992); John Gillingham, *Coal, Steel, and the Rebirth of Europe, 1945–1955* (Cambridge: Cambridge University Press, 1991).

18. Alan Milward, *The Frontier of National Sovereignty: History and Theory, 1945–1992* (London: Routledge, 1993); Andrew Moravcsik, *The Choice for Europe: Social Purpose and State Power from Messina to Maastricht* (Ithaca, NY: Cornell University Press, 1998).

19. Derek Urwin, *Community of Europe: A History of European Integration Since 1945*, 2nd ed. (London: Longman, 1995); Mark Gilbert, *Surpassing Realism: The Politics of European Integration Since 1945* (Lanham, MD: Rowman and Littlefield, 2003).

20. John Gillingham, *European Integration, 1950–2002: Superstate or New Market Economy?* (Cambridge: Cambridge University Press, 2003), p. xii.

1

What Kind of Union?

The 1940s in Europe saw the end of one war and the beginning of another. World War II ended in 1945; the Cold War began almost immediately afterward. The Cold War was not inevitable but occurred as a result of deep-rooted antagonism, intense mistrust, and happenstance. It gelled in the late 1940s, dividing Europe into two armed camps. Western Europe gratefully accepted U.S. protection from a seemingly messianic and expansionist Soviet Union. Eastern Europe lay under Soviet control, as the Red Army turned from a liberating to an occupying force. The main fault line between East and West ran through Germany, the geopolitical fulcrum of twentieth-century Europe.

World War II changed Europe completely. Germany was defeated, destroyed, and divided into four zones of occupation. Soviet-controlled Communist parties came to power throughout Eastern Europe, establishing dictatorial governments, seizing private property, and imposing command economies. Coping with the consequences of the war and an emerging threat from the East, Western European countries desperately sought economic recovery, political stability, and military security. The United States made it possible for them to achieve all three.

The United States promoted economic interdependence through free trade and unrestricted financial flows. Europe, truncated by the Cold War into Western Europe, was an important element in the U.S.-inspired global system. But Western Europe was too weak economically and financially to participate fully in the emerging international order immediately after the war. The United States came to the rescue with the Marshall Plan to expedite economic recovery and the European Payments Union to facilitate currency convertibility. The North Atlantic Treaty, signed in Washington in April 1949, provided a security umbrella for Western Europe in the form of the U.S.-dominated North Atlantic Treaty Organization (NATO).

This chapter examines the early years of European integration in the context of the emerging Cold War. It shows how the United States supported European integration in order to enhance regional security and accelerate economic recovery, although Europeans were ambivalent about sharing national sovereignty. Very few advocated full-fledged federation; most subscribed to a vague notion of solidarity and transnational cooperation. Rhetorical support for integration reached its zenith in the Congress of Europe in May 1948, leading to the establishment of the intergovernmental Council of Europe a year later. Economic integration along supranational lines emerged instead as a solution to a specific problem in postwar Europe: what to do with the new West Germany. The Schuman Declaration of June 1950 was a French initiative to resolve the German question by means of economic integration.

■ From World War to Cold War

By the end of World War II, Germany was thoroughly defeated and utterly devastated. The former Reich was at the mercy of the four occupying powers (Britain, France, the Soviet Union, and the United States). For Germany, 1945 was "year zero" (*Stunde Null*). The country changed shape as Poland and Czechoslovakia regained disputed territory in the east. Hundreds of thousands · of ethnic Germans fled westward. Together with a huge number of displaced persons already in Germany (forced laborers and concentration camp survivors), these impoverished arrivals caused a refugee problem of unprecedented proportions. The official economy collapsed, and a thriving black market emerged. Law and order broke down. This is how Noel Annan, then a young British army officer and later a distinguished academic, described what he witnessed:

> It was not only the displaced persons who were on the move . . . millions of Germans . . . were moving from east to west. . . . The two great canals were blocked. Trains crept over improvised bridges: only 650 of the 8000 miles of track were operating. You drove along roads where every few miles you met a sign "*Umleitung*" [bypass], and you were diverted down tracks and side roads. The devastation of the bombed cities beggared description. Three out of four houses were destroyed, seven out of eight damaged and shattered. Scarcely a city of any size and importance had escaped. In Berlin the trees in the Tiergarten were cut down for firewood, and a familiar sight was of some wizened old man hauling a little cart with a few sticks in it, and of chains of men and women passing chunks of rubble from hand to hand in an attempt to clear a site. The spectacle of misery pervaded one's life.[1]

The situation varied elsewhere in Europe in the summer of 1945 but was generally grim. Many countries in Central and Eastern Europe had suffered grievously under German occupation and were ravaged by the epic battles of 1944 and early 1945 between the German and Soviet armies. The German occupation regime in Western Europe had not been as harsh as in the east, nor had the scale and impact of fighting on the Western Front been as great as on the Eastern Front. Conditions differed markedly within Western Europe, although most countries endured considerable economic privation and social dislocation. Having escaped heavy damage and been liberated before the end of 1944, Belgium was relatively prosperous in 1945. Parts of neighboring Holland, by contrast, were a battlefield almost until the end of the war. Some liberated countries, such as France and Italy, went through short but sharp civil wars at the time of the German army's retreat, as the resistance settled scores against local Fascists and against elements within its own ideologically diverse membership.

Under the leadership of Josef Stalin, the Soviet Union had withstood a series of ferocious German onslaughts since June 1941, suffering enormous physical destruction and loss of life. Having pushed the progressively weaker German army all the way back to Berlin, the Soviet Union emerged from the war as a great power whose armies were encamped in much of Central and Eastern Europe. Thus Stalin was in a position to impose Communist regimes in a region that the United States and Britain, the two leading Western powers, recognized as a Soviet sphere of influence. Initially, Stalin seemed content to allow non-Communist parties to reorganize themselves in Central and Eastern Europe and participate in coalition governments with the Soviet-supported Communist parties. Nevertheless, historical enmity between Russia and most of its neighbors, as well as the generally loutish behavior of Red Army troops, fostered a climate of deep suspicion toward the Soviet Union.

The United States emerged from the war undamaged and more powerful than any of the other protagonists. It had global postwar ambitions and interests. The United States wanted above all to establish an international economic system conducive to free trade and unfettered investment. This required a tripartite institutional structure: the World Bank, the International Monetary Fund, and the International Trade Organization. Only a country as self-confident and influential as the United States at the end of the war could have hatched such a grandiose scheme for global economic management. Ultimately U.S. plans for the postwar world foundered on domestic and foreign resistance and were only partly realized.

Despite profound differences between their political and economic systems, the United States and the Soviet Union hoped to maintain a working relationship after the war. The United Nations (UN) was to have provided an overarching political framework for postwar diplomatic relations among the members of the wartime Grand Alliance (the countries that had fought against Germany). The death in April 1945 of President Franklin Roosevelt jeopardized prospects for close U.S.-Soviet cooperation. Harry Truman, Roosevelt's successor, adopted a more aggressive stance toward the Soviet Union. Sole possession of the atomic bomb by the United States emboldened Truman and deepened Soviet suspicion of the United States. Mutual mistrust, widespread before the war, quickly resurfaced.

Postwar Politics

National governments returned to power in Europe as soon as the German army withdrew. Apart from discredited collaborators who had no political future (in the short term at least), there were two main distinctions between politicians at the end of the war: the party to which they belonged and where they had spent the years of occupation. Some politicians had fled abroad and formed governments in exile; others remained at home and in many cases joined the resistance. Inevitably tension arose between those who stayed and those who left, even within the same party or political tendency. But the main distinction between politicians after the war, as well as before and during it, was ideological orientation and party affiliation. Communists emerged stronger from the war because they had played a leading role in the resistance and had the support of the Soviet Union, a country widely credited with having defeated Hitler. Social Democrats were also popular because of their long-standing opposition to fascism and the appeal of the social market to voters wary of both communism and capitalism. Eager to distance themselves from disgraced right-wing political parties of the prewar period, conservatives recast themselves after the war as Christian Democrats, advocating compassionate capitalism and accepting the welfare state.

Most governments immediately after the war were coalitions of Communist, Socialist, and Christian Democratic parties. Often infused by the resistance ideals of partnership and shared sacrifice, and conscious-stricken by the failure of anti-Fascist Popular Fronts in the 1930s, they attempted to work harmoniously together to build better societies and fairer economic systems. Human frailty, lingering resentments, political ambition, and party rivalry soon drove them apart. Distrust between the Communists and non-Communists ran deep and erupted into the open at the onset of the Cold War. By the late 1940s, Communist parties were leaving or being thrown out of government in Western Europe (as in France and Italy) and were throwing non-Communist parties out of government in Central and Eastern Europe (for instance in Czechoslovakia and Poland). Socialist and Christian Democratic parties, sharing a common antipathy toward the Communists, generally continued to cooperate with each other in Western Europe.

Britain was an exception to the postwar European pattern. For one thing, Britain did not have a significant Communist party. Thanks to a series of political and economic reforms, the vast majority of the British working class had eschewed revolutionary socialism in the nineteenth century. Instead, most British workers supported the nonrevolutionary, social-democratic Labour Party. For another thing, Britain had a two-party system in which one party alone traditionally formed the government. Following the collapse of the Liberal Party early in the twentieth century, Labour and the Conservatives were the two main parties. Although they had formed a national unity government under Winston Churchill during the war, the two parties competed against each other in the first postwar election, in July 1945. Despite their gratitude for Churchill's wartime leadership, most Britons did not trust the Conservatives to provide housing, jobs, and a generous welfare system. Promising comprehensive state care "from the cradle to the grave," Labour won by a landslide and remained in office until 1951.

Britain's situation was particularly important because continental Socialists looked to the Labour Party for leadership and inspiration.[2] Denis Healey, later a leading British government minister, was Labour's international secretary in the late 1940s. He recalled that "among socialists on the Continent, the British Labour Party . . . had a prestige and influence it never enjoyed before or since. Britain was the only big country in Europe where a socialist party had won power on its own, without depending on any coalition partners. Britain had stood out alone against Hitler after the rest of Europe crumbled. And Britain had won."[3] To the great disappointment of fellow Socialists on the Continent, the Labour government pursued a foreign policy that seemed to place European affairs third in line behind relations with the United States and with the Empire and Commonwealth (a collection of former colonies).

Germany was another exception to the postwar continental political norm, but for very different reasons. Politics in postwar Germany initially remained under the strict control of the occupying powers, whose approach to local government varied considerably. True to national form, the Americans were relaxed about it, the Soviets strict, the British condescending, and the French haughty. Britain and France drew on their respective imperial traditions. To quote Noel Annan again: "In true colonial style the British set up nominated councils as the first faltering step on the path to democracy, and a redoubtable former colonial servant, Harold Ingrams, saw to it that the policy was implemented. Ingrams was apt to treat the Germans as if they were a specially intelligent tribe of Bedouins. Discussion in the shady tent was permitted until the Resident Officer struck the ground with his stick and gave his decision. This attitude exasperated the Germans."[4] A U.S. academic later observed that, in their zone of occupation, the French "sought to re-educate and democratize the German people, to make them worthy of a place in the moral and cultural community of Europe, notably by cathartic acquaintance with the best of France's own cultural heritage."[5]

The Four Powers were supposed to have cooperated in governing Germany through the Allied Control Council, consisting of senior U.S., British, French, and Soviet officials, but never managed to do so. Reparations became a major sticking point. The Soviets wanted to get hold of as much plant and material as possible in the more industrialized Western zones. Mindful of the economic mistakes made in Germany after World War I and realizing that it would ultimately have to foot the bill, the United States objected and eventually stopped delivering reparations to the Soviets in May 1946, triggering a

DENMARK

SWEDEN

Baltic Sea

North Sea

POLAND

British Zone

Berlin •

Soviet Zone

NETHERLANDS

• Cologne
• Bonn

BELGIUM

French Zone

• Frankfurt

CZECHOSLOVAKIA

Saar

United States Zone

LUXEMBOURG

Saarbrücken

• Stuttgart

Strasbourg •

• Baden-Baden

FRANCE

AUSTRIA

SWITZERLAND

Germany Under Occupation

Reprinted from *France Restored: Cold War Diplomacy and the Quest for Leadership in Europe, 1944–1954* by William I. Hitchcock. Copyright © 1998 by the University of North Carolina Press. Used by permission of the publisher.

series of events that drove the former allies farther apart. One of the most dramatic of these was the Berlin Blockade of 1948–1949, when the Soviets blocked all rail, road, and water routes between Berlin and the West. The Western powers responded by supplying their beleaguered zones in Berlin with food and other supplies by air, before the Soviets lifted the blockade eleven months later. The Berlin Blockade symbolized the collapse of the Yalta and Potsdam agreements of 1945 among Britain, the United States, and the Soviet Union on Europe's future and the emergence of a bitter confrontation between East and West.[6]

Mindful of the privations of the Great Depression, European electorates wanted their governments to provide economic growth, full employment, and generous social welfare. That was a tall order at the best of times, let alone immediately after the war when disaster relief was the first priority. It was surprising, under the circumstances, that economic recovery proceeded as quickly as it did in postwar Europe. By 1946 a number of smaller countries— Belgium, Denmark, and Norway—attained a level of gross domestic product (GDP) equivalent to that of 1938 (the last year before the outbreak of war). France and Italy followed suit in 1949. Britain, relatively unscathed in the war, continued to improve upon its 1938 level during the war itself, whereas Germany, greatly damaged at the end of the war, attained its 1938 level only in 1951.[7] This recovery took place despite the massive wartime destruction of industrial plant and infrastructure, shortages of skilled manpower in critical economic sectors, and millions of displaced persons. Nor did the weather help: the winter of 1946–1947 was exceptionally cold and wet, and the summers before and after exceptionally hot and dry.

The Marshall Plan

Following the abrupt termination in August 1945 of its wartime Lend Lease program, the United States continued to assist war-damaged Europe through the United Nations Relief and Rehabilitation Administration. That helped European countries to meet pressing demands for food and fuel. As Europe's recovery gathered speed, Europeans looked to the United States for additional supplies of basic commodities as well as for machinery, raw materials, and consumer goods. The cost of imports depleted Europe's precious dollar reserves. Hence the emergence of a "dollar gap": the difference in dollars between what European countries needed and what they could afford to buy in the United States. The gap could have been narrowed by a combination of domestic austerity drives and more intra-European trade. But austerity was unpopular and therefore politically impracticable, especially so soon after the war; at the same time a plethora of restrictions on the movement of goods and capital, together with the hoarding of dollars for dealings with the United States, hobbled intra-European trade. The only alternative was for the United

States to continue giving more dollars to Europe, an unpopular option in Washington.

U.S. officials were well aware of Europe's predicament. Reports of widespread hunger and poverty in Germany in early 1947 intensified State Department efforts to promote Europe's economic recovery. Although Germany's situation was not typical of the Continent's as a whole, the humanitarian motive proved useful when selling to Congress the idea of additional aid, as did the far more compelling argument that an economically buoyant Western Europe would be less susceptible to communism. More than anything else, the consolidation of Soviet control in Central and Eastern Europe and the strength of Communist parties in Western Europe galvanized elite opinion in the United States in favor of a long-term assistance program.

The provision of massive assistance was also in the economic interest of the United States. As William Clayton, undersecretary for economic affairs, informed Secretary of State George Marshall in a memorandum in May 1947:

> Without further prompt and substantial aid from the United States, economic, social and political disintegration will overwhelm Europe. Aside from the awful implications which this would have for the future peace and security of the world, the immediate effects on our domestic economy would be disastrous: markets for our surplus production gone, unemployment, depression, a heavily unbalanced budget on the background of a mountainous war debt. *These things must not happen.*[8]

Based on reports of Germany's plight and more broadly on their assessment of Europe's economic and political situation—the dollar gap and the threat of communism—officials gave Marshall the outline of an idea to assist Europe's recovery through the provision of U.S. assistance, in cash and in kind, for a period of several years. The United States would act in concert with Europe. As Marshall said in his famous speech at Harvard University in June 1947:

> It would be neither fitting nor efficacious for this Government to undertake to draw up unilaterally a program designed to place Europe on its feet economically. This is the business of the Europeans. The initiative, I think, must come from Europe. The role of this country should consist of friendly aid in the drafting of a European program and of later support of such a program so far as it may be practical for us to do so. The program should be a joint one, agreed to by a number, if not all, European nations.[9]

It took a year of intensive negotiations among the Europeans themselves, between the Americans and the Europeans, and especially within the U.S. government before what became known as the Marshall Plan was fully fleshed out and functioning.[10] Its immediate objective was to close the dollar gap while simultaneously promoting intra-European trade by discouraging imports from the United States and facilitating currency convertibility. Its longer-term objectives were to inculcate U.S. business practices and to fashion in Europe a marketplace similar to the one in the United States: large, integrated, and efficient. In U.S. eyes a single market was an essential prerequisite for peace and prosperity in Europe and for Europe's full participation in the global economic system.

Earlier, in March 1947, President Truman announced the doctrine that bore his name, promising military assistance to Greece (then fending off a Communist insurrection thought to be supported by the Soviet Union) and to any other European country that came under Communist attack. The Marshall Plan was the economic flip side of the Truman Doctrine. The Americans were careful not to exclude the Soviet Union explicitly from the Marshall Plan, but Soviet participation was incompatible with the plan's anti-Communist intent. The Soviet foreign minister attended the conference of potential aid recipients in Paris in July 1947, but withdrew after failing to convince the others to reject the U.S. insistence on a joint European request for assistance. Claiming that the Marshall Plan amounted to U.S. interference in domestic affairs, the Soviets forbade the Central and Eastern European countries from participating as well.

Thus the Marshall Plan and the Soviet Union's negative response to it were pivotal events in the early history of the Cold War. For many Western Europeans the Marshall Plan was synonymous with the selflessness and generosity of the United States toward allies and former enemies alike, in marked contrast to the rapaciousness of the Soviet Union in Central and Eastern Europe. The Communist seizure of power in Czechoslovakia in February 1948 and the Berlin Blockade three months later deepened the growing Cold War divide. Like the Marshall Plan, these events were great propaganda coups for the United States.

The Marshall Plan was a great success. Politically, it signaled the intention of the United States to remain engaged in Europe after World War II, in contrast to the country's disastrous disengagement from Europe a generation earlier. Economically, the plan did not "save" Europe, because Europe was already on the road to recovery.[11] Nevertheless, Marshall aid helped close the dollar gap, even though a recession in the United States in 1948–1949 depressed U.S. demand for European goods, causing the gap temporarily to widen again. Through the sale of goods supplied by the plan, recipient governments were able to raise "counterpart funds" (in local currency) with which to pursue national economic objectives such as infrastructural development or debt reduction. According to Charles Maier, a leading historian of the period, "by easing balance-of-payments constraints and freeing key bottlenecks for specific goods, American aid allowed the European economies to generate their own capital more freely, certainly without returning to the deflationary competition of the 1930s. U.S. aid served, in a sense, like the lubri-

"The Way Back" by Daniel Fitzpatrick appeared in the *St. Louis Post Dispatch* on July 20, 1947. Used by permission, State Historical Society of Missouri, Columbia.

cant of an engine—not the fuel—allowing a machine to run that would otherwise buckle and bind."[12]

◼ The European Movement

In May 1948, three years after the end of the war in Europe, nearly one thousand people attended the Congress of Europe in The Hague, the political capital of the Netherlands. They included senior politicians from most European countries and political parties (excluding the Communist Left and the Far Right). All participated in a private capacity. Winston Churchill, the already legendary prime minister of wartime Britain, then the underemployed leader of the opposition Conservative Party, presided over the event.

The Hague Congress was the high point of the postwar European movement.[13] Inspired by appeals throughout the ages for European unity, and appalled by events in the interwar and wartime periods, the movement included several dozen organizations—some nationally based, others transnational—encompassing thousands of individuals in more than twenty countries.[14] Popular support for European unity in the immediate postwar years was widespread and deeply felt. The idea of European integration in the 1940s was not elitist but had broad support and mass appeal.

Although members of the European movement subscribed to the general goal of European union, they disagreed among themselves on what form such union should take. A few were ardent federalists, convinced by the lessons of the recent past that relations between European states needed radical recasting. Some of the more ideological of them, notably Altiero Spinelli, saw federalism as a panacea for Europe's ills, an antidote to the evils of nationalism and the corruption of modern capitalism. His was a "big bang" approach to European union—a conviction that a United States of Europe should immediately and irrevocably replace the existing states system.[15]

By contrast, most of those attending the congress had only a vague vision of Europe's future. Like the vast majority of Europeans, they were either indifferent to federalism or opposed to it. For them, a high degree of intra-European cooperation was desirable or even imperative, but the legitimacy and efficacy of the nation-state were not disputed. The idea of European union had political, economic, and cultural dimensions, without as yet having precise constitutional contours. For all its proponents, however, European union meant an unequivocal commitment to democracy, justice, and human rights. It also acknowledged the need to bring Germany back into the international fold. The rhetoric of European union was pan-European, but the reality of the emerging Cold War meant that concrete initiatives would be restricted to Western Europe and therefore also to West Germany.

The large and influential attendance at the congress reflected the appeal of European union. Yet ringing phrases in the final resolution could not disguise the difficulty within such a heterogeneous group of deciding what steps to take next. There was general agreement to transform the International Committee of the Movement for European Unity, the body that had organized the congress, into an umbrella organization called the European Movement. The new organization was launched in Brussels in October 1948 under the joint presidency of Churchill, Leon Blum (a French Socialist), Alcide de Gasperi (an Italian Christian Democrat), and Paul-Henri Spaak (a Belgian Socialist).

There was general agreement also on establishing a postgraduate institution for the study of European integration (the College of Europe opened its doors in the picturesque city of Bruges, Belgium, in 1950).

On more substantive issues, however, a consensus could not be found. Efforts to establish a European Assembly, a tangible expression of the movement's commitment to democratic principles and responsiveness to public opinion, became the biggest bone of contention. Deep differences quickly surfaced over the assembly's purpose and organization. Federalists wanted a constituent assembly, organized on transnational lines, to draft a European constitution; antifederalists wanted nothing more than a consultative body, organized on national lines and responsible to a ministerial body. The congress agreed to disagree, leaving the precise nature of the proposed assembly for another day's work.

The French government, then groping toward a European policy of rapprochement with Germany, took up the cause of a European Assembly in July 1948, under the aegis of the five-power Brussels group (made up of Britain, France, and the three Benelux countries). The French ran straight into strong British opposition. Although Churchill was the standard-bearer of European union, the governing Labour Party was uninterested in a European Assembly, however anodyne its responsibilities. Churchill himself, for that matter, liked to orate about European union without being either personally or politically committed to it. Churchill's most famous speech on European union, delivered in Zurich in September 1946, in which he called for "a kind of United States of Europe," is often cited as evidence of Euro-enthusiasm. In fact, Churchill was too nationalistic to champion a new European system based on shared sovereignty.

Regardless of what Churchill said or what people wanted him to say, official British policy toward European union was extremely negative. Britain saw itself as a global power whose foreign policy priorities were twofold: relations with the United States and with the Empire and Commonwealth. The idea of Eurofederalism was anathema to Britain, a country proud of its distinctive political institutions and culture and of its recent wartime record. The prevailing view in London was that shared sovereignty was for continental losers, not for British winners.

Eventually the British government agreed to the establishment of a Consultative Assembly, but one that was virtually powerless and that was answerable to an intergovernmental body, the Committee of Ministers. This was the institutional foundation of the Council of Europe, which ten countries—the Brussels powers plus Denmark, Ireland, Italy, Norway, and Sweden—formed when they signed the Statute of Westminster in May 1949. British foreign secretary Ernest Bevin suggested that the Council be located in Strasbourg, a city long disputed between France and Germany and far enough away from national capitals to help ensure the Council's marginalization.

The assembly met for the first time in August 1949. Churchill led the delegation of British Conservatives at the inaugural session and gave a rousing speech in a square in Strasbourg's war-damaged city center. It was vintage Churchill: emotional, entertaining, and enthralling. It also marked the zenith of Churchill's career as the champion of European union. Although the former prime minister presided over the newly launched European Movement and although popular interest in integration remained strong on the Continent, the Council of Europe's obvious weakness sapped political support for similar grandiose schemes.

Enthusiasts for European integration continued to look to the assembly for inspiration and leadership, believing that it could act as a constituent body for a federal union. Spaak, Belgium's foreign minister and the assembly's first president, personified their hopes. His resignation from the assembly's presidency in December 1951, in protest against the Committee of Ministers' opposition to any and all federal initiatives, signaled the end of the road for the Council of Europe as a possible instrument of political integration.

■ Prospects for Economic Integration

A number of international organizations existed in Europe immediately after the war. They aimed to rebuild national economies rather than integrate Europe economically. There were three emergency organizations—the European Coal Organization, the European Central Inland Transport Organization, and the Emergency Economic Committee for Europe—as well as the United Nations Relief and Rehabilitation Administration, which closed down in 1949. The United Nations Economic Commission for Europe subsumed the remaining emergency organizations in May 1947. Walt Rostow, a U.S. official who was special assistant to the Economic Commission's first executive secretary, wrote in 1949 that "the [Economic Commission] appeared a possible realistic first step along the long slow path towards a democratically negotiated, economic unity in Europe."[16]

The onset of the Cold War destroyed whatever potential the organization had to promote European integration. The Soviet Union was content to keep the commission in existence but had no intention of turning it into a forum for economic cooperation along capitalist lines. The United States and the countries of Western Europe focused instead on the Marshall Plan, which, unlike the Economic Commission for Europe, had the financial means to match its economic ambition and, the United States hoped, would promote European integration.

In his memorandum of May 1947 for Secretary Marshall, Undersecretary Clayton urged that the proposed package "be based on a European plan which the principal European nations . . . should work out. Such a plan should be based on a European economic federation on the order of the Belgium-

Netherlands-Luxembourg Customs Union. Europe cannot recover from this war and again become independent if her economy continues to be divided into many small watertight compartments as it is today."[17] Clayton's equation of "economic federation" and "customs union" shows that integration lacked a precise meaning at the time. Charles Kindleberger, then one of Clayton's officials and later an internationally renowned academic economist, noted in 1950 that "at no time was there in existence a single clear idea of what [integration] meant." Thus the Marshall Plan presented an opportunity for the United States "to usher in a new era of European collaboration, cooperation, unification, or integration—to run the polysyllabic gamut."[18]

Michael Hogan, one of the foremost historians of the Marshall Plan, has described the endeavor as "a grand design for remaking the Old World in the likeness of the New."[19] John Killick, another Marshall Plan historian, quotes a resentful British Treasury official complaining that "the Americans want an integrated Europe looking like the United States of America—God's own country."[20] What the Americans really wanted was what eventually happened in Europe not in 1952 but in 1992: a single market involving the free movement of goods, services, and capital. The free movement of people—the "fourth freedom" in the single market program—seemed neither desirable (except for Italy) nor obtainable in the early 1950s and was not fully implemented even in the early 1990s.

The Foreign Assistance Act of April 1948, which enacted the European Recovery Program (as the Marshall Plan was officially called), contained the following "Declaration of Policy":

> Mindful of the advantages which the U.S. has enjoyed through the existence of a large domestic market with no internal trade barriers, and believing that similar advantages can accrue to the countries of Europe, it is declared to be the policy of the people of the U.S. to encourage these countries [receiving Marshall aid] through a joint organization to exert common efforts . . . which will speedily achieve that economic cooperation in Europe which is essential for lasting peace and recovery.[21]

The countries of Western Europe had no objection to submitting to Washington a joint assistance request. Soon after Marshall's speech in June 1947, they formed the Committee on European Economic Cooperation, and upgraded it in April 1948 to the Organization for European Economic Cooperation (OEEC). But they balked at the suggestion that they should integrate their economies into a single European market. In effect, they paid lip service to the idea of economic union as a guiding principle for Europe's future. For instance, the final resolution of the Hague congress contained a commitment to economic and monetary union as essential elements of European union. In reality, Western European governments were jealous of their economic prerogatives. They had striven immediately after the war to restore the proper functioning of their own economies and were still preoccupied with national economic rehabilitation rather than European economic integration. In an uncertain geopolitical, economic, and monetary environment, governments sought maximum national advantage through a plethora of tariff and nontariff barriers. The lessons of the interwar years may have taught otherwise and the rhetoric of the postwar years may have claimed otherwise, but protectionism was deeply entrenched in Europe in the late 1940s.

A cursory examination of various calls at that time for the formation of customs unions bears out the point. Belgium and Luxembourg, which formed an economic union in 1921, agreed with the Netherlands in 1944 to form the Benelux customs union. It came into existence in 1948, but balance-of-payments problems (for the Dutch) and the persistence of nontariff barriers to trade impeded prospects for closer economic integration. Moreover, Benelux was conceived not as a first step toward wider European integration but as a defensive mechanism against possible postwar economic recession and protectionist measures by larger states.

French interest in forming a customs union, first only with Italy and later with a number of countries, was motivated not by a desire to open the European marketplace but by the goal of limiting Germany's economic recovery. A partial Franco-Italian customs union was finally agreed to in March 1949, but France's earlier idea of extending Benelux had little appeal for Belgium and especially for the Netherlands, which—having had close ties to the prewar German economy—was eager to hasten German's postwar recovery. France then proposed a wider European customs union, once again without German participation. A series of negotiations followed in Brussels, under the auspices of the European Customs Union Study Group, from November 1947 to December 1948. Fourteen countries, including Britain, took part in the talks. It soon became clear that each country was jockeying for sectoral advantage rather than seeking to open markets and that concern about sovereignty would preclude Britain from participating even in a customs union. The study group then transformed itself into the Customs Cooperation Council, a standing body that slaved away on tariff nomenclature. Finally, in April 1949, France called for a customs union with Benelux and Italy (to be known as Fritalux). Once again, Dutch insistence on including Germany thwarted the initiative.[22]

The fate of these efforts shows that economic integration was an idea whose time had not yet come. The OEEC was a prototypical organization for European integration. But the British were not about to concede economically to the OEEC what they refused to concede politically to the Council of Europe: a share of national sovereignty. The Americans wanted Spaak, a leading advocate of European union, to become director general of the OEEC; the British successfully objected to the nature of the office and the political preferences of the proposed incumbent.[23] British obstructionism and continental indifference consigned the OEEC to the role of a clearinghouse for economic information, devoid of real decisionmaking power. In effect, the OEEC became a cover for European disregard of U.S. insistence on closer integration in return for Marshall aid. The OEEC gave the impression that Europeans were integrating by providing a collectivist gloss to individual national assistance requests. The Americans were not fooled. They realized the limits of their influence as well as the extent of European resistance to shared sovereignty in economic affairs.

Yet in the long term, as the success of the single European market program showed more than forty years later, the Marshall Plan and related U.S. initiatives had a profound effect on European integration. As Killick observed, "US policy and the Marshall Plan pushed Europe towards an integrated and multilateral future, created mechanisms to transfer the best of US commercial organization, social patterns, and technology, and attempted to create an open and unified international market."[24] Marshall aid had an immediate impact on the growth of intra-European trade through the establishment in 1950 of the European Payments Union, which restored multilateral settlements and paved the way for the introduction of full currency convertibility by the end of the decade. Backed by the United States, the Payments Union allowed its members to run surpluses or deficits with each other without fear of either nonpayment (in gold or dollars) or withdrawal of credits. The launch of the Payments Union coincided with the adoption by the OEEC of a code of trade liberalization, calling for the progressive removal of quantitative restrictions on a nondiscriminatory basis.[25]

The Marshall Plan, the OEEC, and the Payments Union triggered a virtuous cycle by encouraging countries to reduce tariff and nontariff barriers in order to promote cross-border trade. At the same time, participation in the U.S.-sponsored General Agreement on Tariffs and Trade (GATT) set European countries on the long road to global trade liberalization. The gradual abandonment of trade protection facilitated the emergence in the late 1950s of the European Economic Community. Yet the Economic Community could not have come about unless European countries had tackled a residual postwar problem of fundamental political and economic importance. That was the German question.

▪ Tackling the German Question

Political and/or economic integration could not begin in earnest in Western Europe until the question of Germany's status was resolved to the satisfaction of all concerned, including the West Germans themselves. The immediate question was how to realize Germany's huge economic potential without risking a return to German hegemony and a new imbalance of power in Europe. A solution was as pressing for Germany as it was for the United States and for

Germany's neighbors in Europe. The United States had long since abandoned the wartime Morgenthau Plan that called for Germany to be politically and economically emasculated for a lengthy postwar period. By the late 1940s the United States wanted an economically strong Germany, particularly in the context of the worsening Cold War. U.S. thinking was clear and comprehensible: a weak Germany meant a weak Europe, and a weak Europe meant a weak Atlantic alliance.

Britain underwent a similar change in its approach to Germany after the war. So did France, but only up to a point, and certainly not to the point in 1949 of countenancing German remilitarization, as Britain and the United States were inclined to do. In the meantime, France was far more reluctant than either Britain or the United States to allow unfettered German industrial revival. The difference in allied thinking about Germany was due in part to geography: France was much closer to Germany than was either Britain or, more obviously, the United States. It was also due to history: since the industrial age France had been economically weaker than Germany; Germany's greater economic strength had either caused or contributed to nearly a century of Franco-German conflict. Tackling the German question therefore amounted to allaying French security concerns about Germany's economic recovery. Properly speaking, the German question was the Franco-German question, or perhaps even the French question.

By contrast, there was no "Italian question"; no feeling of French insecurity toward Italy after the war. Although Italy, like Germany, had united late in the nineteenth century and fought against France in World War II, Italy's existence did not threaten France. Compared to Germany and even France, Italy had limited economic potential. Moreover, Italy was burdened by an impoverished and overpopulated south. France and Italy made amends soon after the war, signing a peace treaty in February 1947. Italy's main postwar problem was political instability due to limited economic opportunity and the existence of a powerful Communist party. Alcide de Gasperi, the Italian Christian Democratic leader, used the threat of indigenous communism and the influence of Italian immigrants in the United States to maximize U.S. economic assistance. This, in turn, helped the Christian Democrats to defeat the Communists in the decisive general election in 1948.[26]

France also faced political uncertainty immediately after the war. Charles de Gaulle, leader of the wartime Free French Movement, formed the first government of liberated France (it lasted from August 1944 until January 1946). Despite pressing domestic problems, de Gaulle was keenly interested in foreign affairs. The foreign policy that he pursued then, and later as president of the Fifth Republic between 1958 and 1968, is often described as one of *grandeur* (greatness). It took for granted that France was a great power with global interests. Not only that, but France was a *victorious* great power, having redeemed the defeat of 1940 with the participation of French forces in the allied victory of 1945. But France was not invited to attend the two conferences with the Big Three powers (Britain, the Soviet Union, and the United States), held in Yalta in February 1945 and Potsdam in July–August 1945, where the fate of Germany and Eastern Europe was broadly decided. De Gaulle despised the Yalta and Potsdam settlements and abided by their terms only when it suited him to do so. For instance, he rejected the implicit acceptance by Britain and the United States of a Soviet sphere of influence in Eastern Europe but accepted the decision at Potsdam to give France a small zone of occupation in Germany. In de Gaulle's view, France had every right to occupy part of Germany and have an equal say with Britain, the Soviet Union, and the United States in deciding the country's future.

Yet de Gaulle was not so unrealistic as to think that other countries would take France at face value. France's economic weakness, stretching back a century or more, was as apparent to de Gaulle as it was to other allied leaders. Hence, despite his supposed disdain for the dismal science, in 1945 de Gaulle devoted considerable attention not only to France's immediate economic needs but also to its long-term economic resurgence. France's immediate needs would be met in part by exacting reparations from defeated Germany; France's long-term goal would be met in part by capitalizing on Germany's economic demise. Despite his willingness to confront unpleasant facts of economic life, de Gaulle shied away for political reasons from undertaking thoroughgoing monetary reform of the kind advocated by Pierre Mendès-France, de Gaulle's economics minister. French economic recovery, no matter how impressive, would therefore rest on a rickety financial foundation.

The Monnet Plan

Jean Monnet, a senior civil servant, advocated a modernization plan for France that held out the prospect of achieving economic recovery and long-term security. Monnet did not approach de Gaulle directly—Monnet rarely approached key decisionmakers directly—but hooked de Gaulle on his plan by first winning over one of the general's closest advisers. Monnet was wary of de Gaulle in any case because of their previous dealings with each other. Like de Gaulle, Monnet was in London in June 1940 at the time of the French military collapse. But Monnet chose not to join de Gaulle's Free French Movement, opting instead to work on allied economic policy in Washington, where he was attached to the British embassy. Monnet and de Gaulle met again in Algiers in 1943, where de Gaulle was fighting (politically) to wrest control of the provisional government-in-waiting from Henri Giraud, a senior French general who enjoyed Roosevelt's support. Roosevelt asked Monnet, whom he knew in Washington, to intercede in Algiers on Giraud's behalf. Once in Algiers, Monnet quietly switched sides and supported de Gaulle, who clearly was more qualified to lead the Free French than was the bumbling and undemocratic Giraud.

De Gaulle should have been grateful to Monnet. But gratitude was not in the general's nature. Instead de Gaulle resented Monnet for a variety of reasons, including Monnet's refusal to serve under him in London in 1940, his subsequent service in the British embassy in Washington, his cultivation there of influential U.S. policymakers, and his cosmopolitanism and internationalism. Nevertheless, de Gaulle appreciated Monnet's skill and experience as an economic planner. Monnet also had a major virtue that, for the moment at least, canceled out his obvious vices: he was not a member of any political party. De Gaulle hated political parties, especially those that had sprung back to life in France after the liberation. He craved strong presidential power. De Gaulle was hamstrung as president of the provisional government by what he saw as the machinations of small-minded political parties and their leaders. Those politicians prevailed over de Gaulle in the struggle for the constitution of the new Fourth Republic, which incorporated a parliamentary rather than a presidential system of government. Accordingly, in January 1946, de Gaulle resigned in a huff, but not before he had approved the appointment of Jean Monnet to head the national planning commission (Commissariat Général du Plan), a government agency independent of the giant finance and economics departments.

Monnet spent the next few years absorbed in French economic affairs. He and his small staff oversaw the work of numerous sectoral committees that brought together representatives of all sides in industry, setting guidelines for resource allocation and production levels in order to meet domestic demand and fill foreign markets. For the moment France depended far more on imports than exports for its economic survival. Clearly, international developments held the key to future French and European prosperity.[27] Monnet paid particular attention to the United States, the country at the center of the emerging international economic system and the source of desperately needed dollars.

French planning was not at all like planning in the Soviet Union, which had a command economy. Monnet was not a Socialist, let alone a Communist. Having grown up in the brandy business and spent many years as an international financier before the war, he was a bona fide capitalist. Yet he personified the consensus in postwar France that capitalism could best be served by judicious government direction of key economic activities. This view was not anathema to Washington, where a number of New Dealers were still influential in government. The promulgation of the Marshall Plan, although very different from the Monnet Plan, showed that Washington also accepted the idea that market mechanisms alone would not suffice to get the European economy fully going again.

The Marshall Plan was a mixed blessing for France. It presented both an opportunity and a threat. The opportunity was the prospect of funding the

Monnet Plan's strategy of investment in French industrial modernization. Counterpart funds from the sale of goods supplied to European governments were not supposed to have been used to implement national economic planning. But the Americans made an exception for Monnet, who had a host of influential friends in Washington. For that reason, historians often say that the Marshall Plan saved the Monnet Plan.

France Under Pressure

Yet the Marshall Plan also posed a threat to the Monnet Plan and to French security in general. Whereas the Marshall Plan sought German economic recovery as an integral part of European economic recovery, the Monnet Plan sought French economic recovery at the expense of German economic weakness. This was especially true of the coal and steel sectors, the basis of industrial power in mid-twentieth-century Europe. Historically, France's lack of coking coal, which Germany had in abundance, notably in the Ruhr region in the west of the country, hobbled French steel production. Monnet based his plan to modernize the French steel industry on the assumption that, with Germany on the ropes economically, France would have unlimited access to Ruhr coal and could exploit postwar markets previously filled by German producers. As François Duchêne, Monnet's biographer, put it, France would develop its steel industry "on a diet of Ruhr coke till it largely replaced German steel."[28] Because of the nature of Germany's prewar and wartime military-industrial complex, the Ruhr was synonymous in France with militarism and the rise of Nazism. Controlling the Ruhr was therefore a vital French interest, economically and strategically.

By signaling through the Marshall Plan its intention to allow Germany to revive economically, the United States challenged France's Ruhr policy and stoked French security concerns. Sensitive to France's situation, the United States sought somehow to reconcile French interests with its own determination, for economic and strategic reasons, to reconstitute Germany. As the terms of the Marshall Plan indicated, the Americans believed that European integration could provide the solution. Rather than impose a particular scheme, however, the United States wanted the Europeans themselves to come up with a proposal for economic and, ultimately, political integration. Because French interests were so directly affected by the rapidity of German economic recovery and because the United States strongly supported France, Washington looked primarily to Paris for leadership on the German question.

The ensuing swing from repression to rapprochement in French policy toward Germany, in response to pressure from the United States, is a key theme in the history of European integration in the late 1940s and early 1950s. Robert Marjolin, a Monnet planner, recorded in his autobiography that,

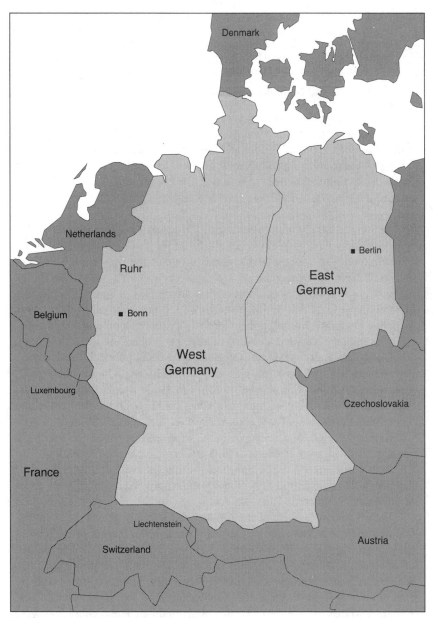

The Ruhr: Germany's industrial heartland

despite the violence of my feelings towards the Germans before and during the war, I had rapidly convinced myself after the hostilities ended that Europe could not recover unless Germany were rebuilt and became once again a great industrial country. . . . I did [not] believe in the dismemberment of western Germany, from which the Rhineland and the Ruhr, for example, would have been separated. That would have sown the seed for future wars. I was therefore quite ready to include the Germans in European cooperation.[29]

Marjolin was ahead of most French people in his attitude toward Germany so soon after the war. The French government, let alone most French people, was not inclined to ease up on Germany. Thus France refused to merge its zone of occupation with those of Britain and the United States and acquiesce in the raising of Germany's allied-approved levels of industrial production. France found itself fighting a rearguard action as Britain and the United States merged their zones in 1947 and raised Germany's production levels regardless.

As long as the Communists were still in government, France was unable to work closely with its Western allies. The removal of the Communists from office in May 1947, an inevitable consequence of the deepening Cold War, increased the French government's freedom of maneuver vis-à-vis the United States but closed the door on cooperation with the Soviet Union. The intensification of the Cold War in turn intensified U.S. pressure on France to relax its policy toward Germany so that Germany's economic potential (and eventually its military potential as well) could be put at the disposal of the West.

France gradually yielded as Germany rebounded politically sooner than any of the allies had expected. Germany's Socialist and Communist parties, proscribed since the Nazi seizure of power in 1933, were reconstituted relatively quickly after the war, and a new Christian Democratic Party came into being. With the Communists predominant in the east, the Socialists and Christian Democrats vied for ascendancy in the west. Konrad Adenauer, a wily old conservative with impeccable anti-Nazi credentials, emerged as leader of the Christian Democrats. Kurt Schumacher, an implacable Socialist and ardent nationalist (but a bitter foe of National Socialism), was the undisputed leader of the Social Democratic Party.

In the London Accords of June 1948, France finally agreed to the formation of the Federal Republic of Germany through the merger of its zone of occupation with the previously merged U.S. and British zones. France insisted on a federal, decentralized Germany and on maintaining control of the Saar, a coal-rich region in southwest Germany. France also hoped to thwart German control of the Ruhr through the establishment of the International Ruhr Authority to oversee coal production and distribution. These conditions were enshrined in the Occupation Statute of April 1949, which regulated relations between Germany and the Western allies. The narrowness of the French Assembly's approval of the London Accords indicated the depth of French distrust toward Germany despite the distance that France had traveled from its initial postwar position.[30]

Under the aegis of the London Accords and the Occupation Statute and of a Basic Law (constitution) drawn up by representatives of Germany's regional authorities, the Federal Republic came into existence in May 1949. Based on the results of national elections that had taken place some weeks earlier, the Bundestag (lower house of parliament) chose Adenauer to become chancellor by a single vote. The Christian Democrats and the small Liberal Party formed the first West German government. The Communists monopolized power in East Germany, which duly became the German Democratic Republic.

The sovereignty of the new West German state was limited, especially in the fields of foreign policy (including foreign economic policy) and defense. Understandably Adenauer sought to restore to Germany as much sovereignty as possible.[31] Adenauer especially resented the International Ruhr Authority that, though largely ineffectual, symbolized Germany's continued economic subjugation. The Ruhr Authority's ineffectualness irked France perhaps even more than the authority's existence irked Germany. Once again, French policy toward the Ruhr seemed unavailing.

Accepting the Inevitable

The United States continued to press Paris to propose an alternative scheme that would allay French concerns about the Ruhr without engendering German resentment and therefore endangering Germany's economic and political rehabilitation. U.S. pressure intensified under Dean Acheson, the new secretary of state. The solution, Acheson told his ambassadors in Europe, lay "in French hands."[32] On October 30, 1949, Acheson sent Robert Schuman, his French counterpart, a forceful message: "I believe that our policy in Germany . . . depends on the assumption by your country of leadership in Europe on these problems."[33] Acheson gave Schuman a deadline—a meeting of allied foreign ministers in London in May 1950—to propose something new.

As the United States and France edged toward a resolution of the German question, Britain stood on the sidelines.[34] Britain's behavior in the OEEC and in the Council of Europe convinced many continental Europeans that Britain was uninterested in contributing much to European integration, through which a solution to the German question would have to be found. A Labour Party pamphlet of 1948, "Feet on the Ground," emphasized Britain's opposition to integration based on a supposedly more pragmatic foreign policy approach.[35] The message was clear: Britain's continental neighbors would have to take further initiatives by themselves. Yet the idea of acting without Britain was unimaginable for most Europeans. After all, Britain was at the pinnacle of its postwar power and prestige. Britain's economic and military strength were formidable by European standards (although not by the standards of the United States and the Soviet Union).

If the experience of the OEEC and the Council of Europe implied that the continentals would have to go it alone, another development, in April 1949, suggested that they *could* proceed without Britain. This was the signing in Washington of the North Atlantic Treaty. As the contractual basis for the future North Atlantic Treaty Organization, the Washington treaty signaled the unequivocal commitment of the United States to Western Europe's defense, which had hitherto rested on the Brussels Pact of March 1947 between Britain, France, and the Benelux countries. Built around Britain, the Brussels Pact was originally intended to guard against a revanchist Germany. With the onset of the Cold War, the Soviet Union replaced Germany as a much more plausible security threat, and NATO replaced the Brussels Pact as a much more effective military alliance. With the United States now committed to Western Europe's defense, continental Europeans were less dependent militarily on Britain. Although NATO's organizational structure was not fleshed out until the end of 1950, the North Atlantic Treaty gave France more security than the Brussels Pact vis-à-vis Germany and Russia and more confidence to take diplomatic initiatives in Europe without fear of offending or possibly alienating Britain.

Yet the political situation in France did not seem conducive to a bold foreign policy initiative. The country was in almost constant flux. Governments followed each other in quick succession, often with the same cast of characters playing ministerial musical chairs. Prime ministers came and went, but two people, Georges Bidault and Robert Schuman, occupied the foreign ministry for most of the Fourth Republic's relatively short life (1946–1958). Bidault, foreign minister for much of the earlier period, was witty, outgoing, and frequently inebriated. Schuman, his successor, was solemn, saintly, and always sober. Yet, Bidault has a historical reputation for obduracy and Schuman for imagination. That is because Bidault is associated with a policy of hostility toward Germany, whereas Schuman is associated with a policy of reconciliation.

Yet, Bidault was moving toward a rapprochement with Germany when he left office in 1948, and Schuman supported a punitive policy toward Germany before replacing Bidault as foreign minister. As de Gaulle's foreign minister immediately after the war, Bidault was obliged to implement a harsh policy toward Germany. Even after de Gaulle's departure, public and official opinion in Paris did not countenance a thaw in relations with Germany for some time to come. When the thaw began in late 1948, it was Schuman's good fortune to be foreign minister. Undoubtedly Schuman favored a new departure with Germany and genuinely supported European union. Unlike Bidault, he quickly grasped the significance of a supranational solution to the problem of the Ruhr and soon personified not only Franco-German rapprochement, but Franco-German reconciliation as well.

Coming from the disputed borderland of Lorraine, speaking French with a German accent and German without a French accent, and wearing his Catholicism on his sleeve, Schuman became the living embodiment of Franco-German amity after generations of Franco-German enmity. He could easily have gone down in history the other way around, however. Had it been politically imperative to do so, Schuman might well have used his borderland background and experiences in Lorraine before 1919 to perpetuate distrust of Germany. Schuman's Catholicism and personality may have predisposed him to seek reconciliation with Germany, but political necessity ultimately determined his course of action. Fortunately for Schuman, a reappraisal of French policy toward Germany made it possible for him to combine personal predilections and political preferences and give his name to a declaration that symbolized a radical new departure by France. The declaration contained a proposal to pool sovereignty in the coal and steel sectors under a supranational High Authority, thereby reconciling U.S., German, and French interests without going too far down the road toward political union.

■ The Schuman Declaration

The announcement of the Schuman Declaration took place at a hastily convened press conference late in the afternoon of May 9, 1950, in the ornate Salon de l'Horloge (clock room) of the French foreign ministry. Schuman proposed both a specific solution to the problem of the Ruhr (a supranational coal and steel organization) and a general solution to the German question (implicit equality and nondiscrimination in the context of European union). It was an approach that combined economic, political, and social objectives. The immediate goal was to ensure "the modernization of production and the improvement of its quality; the supply of coal and steel on equal terms to the French and German markets . . . [and] to those of the [other] member countries; and the equalization as well as the improvement in the living standards and working conditions in those industries." Schuman linked this to the greater goal of European integration, for which strong emotional support still existed despite the Council of Europe's disappointing development. Thus the coal and steel pool would "lay the first concrete foundation for a European Federation which is so indispensable to the preservation of peace."[36]

The immediate background to the declaration was equally dramatic. By his own account, which historians have not disputed, Monnet developed the idea while on one of his periodic hiking holidays in the Alps, in April 1950. After returning to Paris, Monnet instructed key people in his planning office to work out the details. Having gone through various drafts, Monnet sent the final version first to Prime Minister Bidault, who did not respond, then to Foreign Minister Schuman, who did. Monnet also contacted Adenauer through an intermediary. Aware of Adenauer's approval of it, Schuman slipped the proposal through a cabinet meeting on the morning on May 9, hours before the famous press conference.[37]

Monnet's account may be correct, but the manner of its telling, without adequate reference to the evolution of French foreign policy during the previous two years, gives the declaration a heroic quality to which early scholars of European integration eagerly subscribed. William Diebold, author of one of the first books on the Schuman Plan, wrote breathlessly about

> a foreign minister who took a major foreign policy initiative with little or no consultation with his own ministry; a rapid elaboration of the final version of the plan in great secrecy by a tiny group of people; only the briefest discussion before the Cabinet; . . . a measure that went well beyond foreign policy and would have a major effect on the defense and economy of France; almost immediate public announcement with only the shortest notice to allies and others on whose assent success would depend.[38]

Some historians of a later generation, notably Alan Milward, gleefully debunked the myth of May 9.[39] Monnet was certainly imaginative and farsighted. But he did not conjure the proposed community out of nowhere. Ideas about a coal and steel association of some kind or other had been floating around France and Germany, in government and private circles, for several years; some could even be traced back to the interwar period.[40] Thinking along such lines had intensified as France came under mounting pressure in 1949 and early 1950 to adopt a radically new approach toward Germany. Monnet was more imaginative and astute than most: the idea of a High Authority as the supranational instrument of sectoral integration was novel and timely. Yet even François Duchêne, Monnet's former collaborator and biographer, admits that the Schuman Declaration "may have been a lucky strike when other prospectors had given up."[41]

Nor was it surprising that Monnet devoted so much thought to a prospective coal and steel community. After all, it was Monnet who bore the brunt of U.S. pressure for a new French policy toward Germany. Monnet was the main conduit for U.S.-French relations in the late 1940s and early 1950s. He was in almost daily contact with the highest representatives of the United States in France. Monnet knew how badly Washington wanted Paris to launch a new initiative and how desperately Schuman wanted to oblige. Moreover, the future of the Monnet Plan was at stake. Economic modernization in France could not be realized without a resolution of the Ruhr problem. "Internationalization"—the maintenance of French control through the International Ruhr Authority—had failed; "Europeanization," through the creation of a supranational community, might succeed. France's policy options were limited.

Monnet was in his element when under pressure. He was an opportunist who thrived on crises (even his marriage involved elopement and intrigue); he was the right man (a fixer, a close friend of the Americans) in the right place (head of the national planning commission) at the right time (when France needed to come to terms with Germany's resurgence). With the Schuman Declaration, he delivered the goods and saved his own skin. Not only did the Marshall Plan save the Monnet Plan but also, in Milward's memorable phrase, "the Schuman Plan was invented to safeguard the Monnet Plan."[42]

The Schuman initiative bore all the hallmarks of Monnet's approach to economic development. As outlined in the declaration, the High Authority would be an international version of the French planning office. Just as the planning office consisted of technocrats acting independently of government ministries, the High Authority would consist of technocrats acting independently of member state governments. The High Authority would not be overtly *dirigiste*, but would provide overall direction and arbitrate disputes between vested interests. As for the greater goal of European union, the declaration reflected Monnet's preferred approach of sectoral economic integration, what Charles Kindleberger described in a State Department memorandum as a way of moving "crabwise through technical cooperation in economic matters."[43]

Monnet may have hatched the plan, but Schuman took the political risk (Bidault was disinclined to do so). Most members of the French cabinet were still too resentful of Germany and fearful of the future to embrace a bold initiative. Hence Schuman's subterfuge, talking the initiative down in the cabinet and up at the press conference. Only after the press reported favorably on the declaration did the cabinet grudgingly accept a fait accompli. It is often said that Monnet, the architect, deserved to have had the declaration called after him. The name of the declaration accurately indicates, however, where the political credit belongs.[44]

Diebold was half-right when he remarked that France's allies had received only "the shortest notice" of the declaration. Britain received no notice at all because of Schuman's concern that London would again obstruct a major European initiative. Understandably, the British were furious at not having been consulted, let alone notified in advance. Supposedly the United States was informed only on May 7, when Acheson visited Paris en route to the foreign ministers' meeting in London. In fact, U.S. support was too crucial to have been left to chance. Monnet let his U.S. interlocutors in Paris, as well as John J. McCloy, his friend the U.S. high commissioner in Bonn, know that a major initiative was in the offing. Once assured that Schuman was not proposing an international cartel, Acheson was delighted with the declaration. Although the proposal was a lot smaller in scope than what the United States had called for in the Marshall Plan, Washington immediately recognized the declaration's political importance.[45]

Adenauer's response was equally positive. The chancellor wanted a resolution of the German question as much as the allies did. Chafing under the restrictions of the Occupation Statute and the International Ruhr Authority, inevitably Adenauer embraced an initiative based on the principles of equality and nondiscrimination. Fulfilling the promise of the Schuman Declaration became a key element of Adenauer's Westpolitik, which sought to maximize German sovereignty, integrate Germany into the Atlantic system, and bring about a rapprochement with France. The Schuman Declaration was grist to Adenauer's mill (for Germany, shared sovereignty was better than limited sovereignty).[46]

Ironically, the Schuman Declaration came at a time when Adenauer's relations with France were under strain. France's virtual annexation of the Saar under the terms of a convention agreed on in Paris in March 1950 by the French government and the French-sponsored government of the formerly German region inflamed German opinion. A purported goodwill visit by Schuman to Bonn in February 1950 ended on a sour note when Adenauer vehemently protested French policy in the Saar.

Adenauer then floated an idea that may have been sincere but seemed jarring under the circumstances. In an interview with a U.S. journalist on March 9, the chancellor proposed a Franco-German union, complete with a joint parliament.[47] Official reaction across the Rhine was far from favorable: victorious France, not defeated Germany, should make daring overtures. Two months later, with the Schuman Declaration, France took such a step on a less ambitious but more realistic basis. With the declaration coming on the heels of his own trial balloon, and eager to ease Franco-German tension, Adenauer enthusiastically endorsed the declaration at a press conference in Bonn several hours after Schuman's press conference in Paris.

Adenauer was often criticized at home for being subservient to the former occupying powers. Schumacher, leader of the opposition Socialist Party, famously called him the "Chancellor of the Allies."[48] Having stood up to the allies on a number of issues during the previous few months, Adenauer was less vulnerable to charges of complicity with them on the question of the Schuman Declaration. Nevertheless, the declaration became a major domestic political issue. The Socialists disliked the proposed coal and steel organization for ideological reasons (Schumacher dismissed it as "France, Germany, Inc.") and because they thought that it would perpetuate the division of Germany.[49] Adenauer conceded that a rapprochement with the West was incompatible at that time with an opening to the East, but countered that European integration would lead ultimately to German unification, with an economically weak East Germany eventually gravitating toward an economically strong West Germany. "The stronger the Federal Republic of Germany becomes, economically and politically," Adenauer claimed, " . . . the better it will be for Berlin and the German east."[50]

The Schuman Declaration is now hailed as a major turning point in Franco-German relations and in contemporary European history. Those who heard or read Schuman's words at the time could not have foreseen the future and rendered such a verdict, but most grasped that something new was in the air. French and German leaders were now on the same wavelength, public opinion was generally on their side, and the United States stood squarely behind them. Only ardent nationalists, Communists, and doctrinaire Socialists in France and Germany strongly opposed the Schuman Declaration. Vested interests in the coal and steel industries were unenthusiastic about it, fearing a government sellout. France and Germany's prospective partners faced a similar set of domestic circumstances. Realization of the Schuman Plan, in the form of the European Coal and Steel Community, would therefore be tricky.

▨ Notes

1. Noel Annan, *Changing Enemies: The Defeat and Regeneration of Germany* (Ithaca, NY: Cornell University Press, 1997), p. 149.

2. See Clemens A. Wurm, "Britain, Western Europe and European Integration, 1945–1957: The View from the Continent," *Revue Européenne d'Histoire* 6, no. 2 (Autumn 1999), pp. 235–249; and Oliver J. Daddow, *Britain and Europe Since 1945: Historiographical Perspectives on Unification* (Manchester: Manchester University Press, 2003).

3. Denis Healey, *The Time of My Life* (London: Penguin Books, 1990), p. 76. Alan Milward disagreed: "It is not true that the United Kingdom had a fund of goodwill in Europe arising from its wartime role on which it could have traded to lead Europe in support of shared common interests. Europe was not asking to be led." Alan Milward, *The UK and the European Community,* Vol. 1: *The Rise and Fall of a National Strategy, 1945–1963* (London: Whitehall History Publishing in association with Frank Cass, 2002), p. 3. A. J. P. Taylor, the famous British diplomatic historian, wrote in 1971: "How much easier the situation in Europe would be today if the Labour government had followed [Harold] Laski's advice in 1945 and put itself at the head of European social democracy." A. J. P. Taylor, *From the Boer War to the Cold War: Essays on Twentieth-Century Europe* (London: Penguin Books, 1995), p. 329.

4. Annan, *Changing Enemies*, p. 157.

5. F. Roy Willis, *France, Germany and the New Europe, 1945–1963* (Stanford, CA: Stanford University Press, 1965), p. 132.

6. On the outbreak of the Cold War, see John Lewis Gaddis, *We Now Know: Rethinking Cold War History* (Oxford: Clarendon Press, 1997); Arnold A. Offner, *Another Such Victory: President Truman and the Cold War, 1945–1953* (Stanford, CA: Stanford University Press, 2002); Seán Greenwood, *Britain and the Cold War, 1945–1951* (New York: St. Martin's Press, 2000); Charles S. Maier, ed., *The Cold War in Europe: Era of a Divided Continent*, 3rd updated and expanded ed. (Princeton, NJ: Markus Wiener, 1996); Antonio Varsori and Elena Calandri, eds., *The Failure of Peace in Europe, 1943–1948* (Basingstoke: Palgrave, 2002).

7. See Tim Geiger, "Reconstruction and the Beginnings of European Integration," in *Western Europe: Economic and Social Change Since 1945,* ed. Max-Stephan Schulze (London: Longman, 1999), pp. 23–41.

8. William L. Clayton, "GATT, the Marshall Plan, and OECD," *Political Science Quarterly* 78, no. 4 (December 1963), p. 497. Emphasis in the original.

9. The text of the Marshall speech is available at http://www.let.leidenuniv.nl/history/rtg/res1/marshall.htm.

10. On the Marshall Plan, see Gérard Bossuat, *La France, l'aide américaine et la construction européenne, 1944–1954*, 2 vols. (Paris: Comité pour l'Histoire

economique et financière de la France, 1992); Gérard Bossuat, *L'Europe occidentale à l'heure américaine: Le Plan Marshall et l'unité européenne, 1945–52* (Paris: Editions Complexe, 1992); Michael Hogan, *The Marshall Plan: America, Britain, and the Reconstruction of Western Europe, 1947–1952* (Cambridge: Cambridge University Press, 1987); Charles P. Kindleberger, *Marshall Plan Days* (Boston: Allen and Unwin, 1987); John Killick, *The United States and European Reconstruction, 1945–1960* (Edinburgh: Keele University Press, 1997); Immanuel Wexler, *The Marshall Plan Revisited* (Westport, CT: Greenwood Press, 1983); Martin Schain, ed., *The Marshall Plan: Fifty Years After* (Basingstoke: Palgrave, 2001); Alan Milward, *The Reconstruction of Western Europe, 1945–51* (Berkeley: University of California Press, 1984), pp. 56–125.

11. Alan Milward made this point in *Reconstruction of Western Europe*, pp. 56–61.

12. Charles S. Maier, "The Two Postwar Eras and the Conditions for Stability in Twentieth Century Western Europe," *American Historical Review* 86, no. 2 (April 1981), p. 342.

13. See Hendrik Brugmans, *L'Idée européenne, 1918–1965*, 2nd ed. (Bruges: De Temple, 1966); René Courtin, "French Views on European Union," *International Affairs* 25, no. 1 (January 1949), pp. 8–22; John Grantham, "British Labour and the Hague 'Congress of Europe': National Sovereignty Defended," *The Historical Journal* 24, no. 2 (1981), pp. 443–452; A. Loveday, "The European Movement," *International Organization* 3, no. 4 (November 1949), pp. 620–632; Frederick L. Schuman, "The Council of Europe," *The American Political Science Review* 45, no. 3 (September 1951), pp. 724–740.

14. See Walter Lipgens, *A History of European Integration*, Vol. 1: *1945–1947: The Formation of the European Unity Movement* (Oxford: Clarendon Press, 1982); and Pierre Gerbet, *La construction de l'Europe*, rev. ed. (Paris: Imprimerie Nationale, 1994).

15. See Altiero Spinelli, "The Growth of the European Movement Since World War II," in *European Integration,* ed. C. Grove Haines (Baltimore: Johns Hopkins University Press, 1957), pp. 37–63.

16. Walt W. Rostow, "The Economic Commission for Europe," *International Organization* 3, no. 2 (May 1949), p. 255.

17. Clayton, "GATT, the Marshall Plan, and OECD," p. 498.

18. Charles P. Kindleberger, "Memo for the Files: Origins of the Marshall Plan, July 1948," quoted in Kindleberger, *Marshall Plan Days*, pp. 27, 48.

19. Hogan, *Marshall Plan*, p. 53.

20. Killick, *United States and European Reconstruction*, p. 167.

21. The text of the act is available at http://www.let.leidenuniv.nl/history/rtg/res1/marshall.htm.

22. See Wendy Asbeek Brusse, *Tariffs, Trade and European Integration, 1947–1957: From Study Group to Common Market* (New York: St. Martin's Press, 1997), pp. 52–63.

23. See Maier, "Two Postwar Eras," pp. 66–69.

24. Killick, *United States and European Reconstruction*, p. 185.

25. On the European Payments Union and related developments, see Barry Eichengreen, *Globalizing Capital: A History of the International Monetary System* (Princeton, NJ: Princeton University Press, 1996), pp. 93–128; Jacob J. Kaplan and Günther Schleiminger, *The European Payments Union: Financial Diplomacy in the 1950s* (Oxford: Clarendon Press, 1989); Robert Triffin, *The Future of the European*

Payments System (Stockholm: Almquist and Wiksell, 1958); and Wexler, *Marshall Plan Revisited.*

26. See John Lamberton Harper, *America and the Reconstruction of Italy, 1945–1948* (Cambridge: Cambridge University Press, 1986); and James Edward Miller, *The United States and Italy, 1940–1950: The Politics and Diplomacy of Stabilization* (Chapel Hill: University of North Carolina Press, 1986).

27. On postwar French economic planning and recovery, see Bossuat, *La France, l'aide américaine et la construction européenne*; François Bloch-Laine and Jean Bouvier, *La France restaurée, 1944–1954: Dialogue sur les choix d'une modernisation* (Paris: Fayard, 1986); François Duchêne, *Jean Monnet: The First Statesman of Interdependence* (New York: Norton, 1994), pp. 147–180; Richard Kuisel, *Capitalism and the State in Modern France: Renovation and Economic Management in the Twentieth Century* (Cambridge: Cambridge University Press, 1981); Sylvie Lefèvre, *Les Relations économiques franco-allemandes de 1945 a 1955: De l'occupation à la coopération* (Paris: Comité pour l'histoire économique et financière de la France, 1998); and Frances M.B. Lynch, *France and the International Economy: From Vichy to the Treaty of Rome* (London: Routledge, 1997).

28. Duchêne, *Monnet*, p. 156.

29. Robert Marjolin, *Memoirs, 1911–1986: Architect of European Unity* (London: Weidenfeld and Nicolson, 1986), p.186.

30. See William Hitchcock, *France Restored: Cold War Diplomacy and the Quest for Leadership in Europe, 1944–1954* (Chapel Hill: University of North Carolina Press, 1998), pp. 93–97.

31. See Hans-Peter Schwarz, *Konrad Adenauer: A German Politician and Statesman in a Period of War, Revolution and Reconstruction*, Vol. 1: *From the German Empire to the Federal Republic, 1876–1952* (Oxford: Berghahn Books, 1995), pp. 475–502.

32. U.S. Department of State, *Foreign Relations of the United States [FRUS], 1949*, Vol. 4 (Washington, DC: Department of State, 1986) p. 470.

33. *FRUS, 1949*, Vol. 3, pp. 624–625.

34. On Britain's position, see Milward, *The UK and the European Community*, Vol. 1, pp. 10–47.

35. Labour Party, "Feet on the Ground: A Study of Western Union" (1948).

36. Robert Schuman, "Declaration of 9 May 1950," in *The Origins and Development of European Integration: A Reader and Commentary,* ed. Peter M.R. Stirk and David Weigall (London: Pinter, 1999), p. 76. For the text of the Schuman Declaration, see pp. 75–76 in Stirk and Weigall, *The Origins and Development of European Integration.*

37. Jean Monnet, *Memoirs* (Garden City, NY: Doubleday, 1978). On the origins of the Schuman Plan, see Duchêne, *Monnet*, pp. 181–225; Raymond Poidevin, *Histoire des débuts de la construction européenne, mars 1948–mai 1950: Actes du Colloque de Strasbourg 28–30 novembre 1984* (Brussels: Byuylant, 1986); Raymond Poidevin, *Robert Schuman, Homme d'État, 1886–1963* (Paris: Imprimerie nationale, 1986), pp. 244–269; P. Gerbet, "La Genèse du plan Schuman. Des origines à la déclaration du 9 mai, 1950," *Revue Française de Sciences Politiques* 6, no. 3 (1956), pp. 525–553; Matthias Kipping, *Zwischen Kartellen und Konkurrenz: Der Schuman-Plan und die Ursprünge der Europäischen Einigung, 1944–1952* (Berlin: Duncker and Humblot, 1996).

38. William Diebold Jr., *The Schuman Plan: A Study in Economic Cooperation, 1950–1959* (New York: Praeger, 1959).

39. Milward, *Reconstruction of Western Europe,* pp. 395–397; and Milward, *The European Rescue of the Nation State*, 2nd ed. (London: Routledge, 2000), pp. 318–344.

40. See John Gillingham, *Coal, Steel and the Rebirth of Europe, 1945–1955* (Cambridge: Cambridge University Press, 1991).

41. Duchêne, *Monnet*, p. 189.

42. Milward, *Reconstruction of Western Europe*, p. 395.

43. Kindleberger, "Memo for the Files," p. 27.

44. For an account of Schuman's contribution to the declaration and surrounding events, see Poidevin, *Schuman*, pp. 244–269.

45. On U.S. knowledge of the Schuman Declaration see James Chace, *Acheson: The Secretary of State Who Created the American World* (Cambridge: Harvard University Press, 1998), pp. 241–254; Thomas Alan Schwartz, *America's Germany: John J. McCloy and the Federal Republic of Germany* (Cambridge: Cambridge University Press, 1991).

46. On Adenauer's emerging Westpolitik and relations with the French, see Schwarz, *Adenauer*, Vol. 1, pp. 475–516.

47. See Ibid., pp. 493–494.

48. See Alfred Grosser, "France, Germany in the Atlantic Community," *International Organization* 17, no. 3 (Summer 1963), p. 556.

49. Quoted in Willis, *France, Germany*, p. 67.

50. Quoted in Schwarz, *Adenauer*, Vol. 1, p. 507.

2

Europe of the Communities

The Cold War hung like a dark cloud over Europe in the 1950s. The decade began with the Korean War, a possible harbinger of hostilities in Europe, and ended with a Soviet-American standoff over Berlin. International tension eased after Stalin's death in March 1953 but rose again when the Soviets violently suppressed workers' demonstrations in East Berlin in June 1953 and broader reform movements in Poland and Hungary in 1956. West German remilitarization in the mid-1950s kept the Soviet Union on edge. In response, the Soviets launched a number of diplomatic initiatives. One of the most dramatic of them resulted in a treaty in 1955 for the establishment of a united, sovereign, neutral Austria, divided between East and West since the end of World War II. The Soviets wanted the Austrian treaty to serve as a model for Germany, but German chancellor Konrad Adenauer feared that a united, neutral Germany would succumb to internal Communist subversion and external Soviet pressure. Soviet overtures to Adenauer and the Western allies ended in late 1955. Thereafter the German question seemed set in stone.

The 1950s also saw the acceleration of decolonization as former dependencies of European countries, mostly Britain and France, gained independence. The process of decolonization was traumatic for France, which became embroiled in large-scale colonial conflicts, first in Indochina (Vietnam), where the French lost decisively in 1954, then in North Africa, where the increasingly brutal war in Algeria caused the collapse of the French Fourth Republic in 1958. Britain and France intervened militarily in Egypt in 1956 following Egypt's nationalization of the Suez Canal. The latter-day act of gunboat diplomacy ended when the Soviet Union threatened to come to Egypt's assistance and the United States refused to support Britain and France. Humiliated and distrusting each other, Britain and France withdrew with their tails between their legs.

Those colonial and postcolonial adventures drained French resources and compounded prevailing pessimism about the country's prospects. Foreign observers dismissed France as the "sick man of Europe," an epithet applied in the late nineteenth century to Turkey. Despite enjoying unprecedented growth,

France seemed merely to be making up ground lost during and before the war, not entering into a new stage of dynamic development. A few far-sighted French officials and politicians, centered on Prime Minister Guy Mollet, advocated liberalization and market integration in the mid-1950s. For them a common market was the key to France's future. They used every economic, political, and ideological argument to make their case, ultimately dragging France into the modern world.

The outlook in Germany was markedly different. By the mid-1950s, the country was prosperous, semisovereign, and, as a NATO member, relatively secure. Despite being unpopular early in his chancellorship, Adenauer won overwhelming election victories in 1953 and 1957. Then in his eighties, he fit the German body politic like a comfortable old shoe. Yet Adenauer's support for the proposed common market divided his own party. Ludwig Erhard, Germany's economics minister, claimed that a common market would promote protectionism in Europe to the detriment of global trade liberalization through the General Agreement on Tariffs and Trade (GATT). The argument in Germany was settled not on economic but on political grounds. Apart from its economic merits, Adenauer saw the common market as an instrument of Franco-German reconciliation and European integration. Politics trumped economics, and the chancellor's view prevailed.

The European Economic Community, which encapsulated the common market, was the fifth initiative for a community of European countries in the 1950s. It accompanied a proposal to establish a European Atomic Energy Community and followed the failure of the European Defense Community and the related European Political Community. The quest for new communities demonstrated an appreciation of increasing interdependence among the countries of Western Europe, a regional manifestation of a global postwar trend. Yet the word *community,* rather than simply *association* or *organization,* connoted common interests that transcended economic goals. This chapter shows how officials and politicians sought to overcome the recent past, forge a better relationship between Germany and its neighbors, and improve Europe's economic prospects through deeper integration. The defense and political communities went too far, too soon after the end of the war. But the functional economic communities were an ideal means of pursuing national strategies in the broader European context.

▪ The European Coal and Steel Community

According to the Schuman Declaration, the proposed coal and steel community, centered on France and Germany, would be "open to the participation of the other European countries." That was a bit disingenuous. Eastern Europe was excluded by virtue of the Cold War; the Scandinavians had rejected supranationalism in the late 1940s; and Spain was isolated because of Gen. Francisco Franco's support for Hitler during World War II. Effectively, the proposal was open to only a small group of countries—Belgium, Luxembourg, the Netherlands, and Italy—tied to France and Germany for economic and strategic reasons. Alcide de Gasperi, Italy's prime minister, embraced the proposal not only because he was a fervent Eurofederalist but also because it might help to strengthen his government's position vis-à-vis the strong Communist opposition. Although well aware of the proposal's strategic significance, most politicians in the Benelux countries were not much inclined toward Eurofederalism (Paul-Henri Spaak of Belgium and Joseph Bech of Luxembourg were notable exceptions). But they knew that their countries could not afford to stay out of a Franco-German economic organization.

Britain's Position

The proposal was open also to Britain. Although Robert Schuman made his declaration without consulting London, he hoped that Britain would overcome its reticence and play a leading role in European affairs. Other prospective members hoped so as well. The Benelux countries especially wanted Britain to act as a counterweight to France and Germany. Yet the British were uninterested in participating. Only a month after the Schuman Declaration, Britain's chancellor of the exchequer (finance minister) torpedoed in the Organization for European Economic Cooperation three relatively limited proposals for closer economic integration (the so-called Stikker, Pella, and Petsch plans).[1] Monnet's insistence that countries accept the principle of supranationalism in order to enter the negotiations precluded British participation in the ensuing intergovernmental conference. As Alan Milward noted in his official history of Britain's involvement with European integration,

> The arguments that weighed in the balance against joining the Schuman Plan negotiations came from the Foreign Office: that by entering into the commitment to supranationality the United Kingdom would be accepting obligations to its European neighbors which would reduce its independence from, and thus its status and influence with, the USA, while at the same time weakening its links with the Commonwealth and thus even further reducing its influence over the USA. The foundations for Britain's post-war national strategy would have been shattered by accepting the concept of supranationality.[2]

Britain's concern about sovereignty was understandable but seemed excessive. The contemporaneous case of the Netherlands is revealing. Although as skeptical of supranationalism as the British, the Dutch reluctantly paid Monnet's price of admission. Despite its small size, in the course of the negotiations the Netherlands managed to dilute Monnet's original supranational idea almost beyond recognition. As the outcome of the negotiations would prove, in practice supranationalism was not nearly as frightening as it

The Six Original Member States

looked in principle. As Monnet himself conceded in July 1950, "the translation of this principle [of supranationality] into reality can be amended and undoubtedly improved."[3]

In a blistering indictment of Britain's reaction to the Schuman Plan, Edmund Dell, a prominent British academic, politician (in the 1960s), and member of the European Commission (in the 1970s), argued that Britain's political and economic circumstances did not preclude participation in the negotiations. Britain could have been "a global power . . . at the center of the Commonwealth and sterling area, and still [have subscribed to] the Schuman Plan."[4] Dell also asserted that Britain never assessed the plan adequately and that "the handling of the issue by the Attlee government and, in particular, by [Foreign Minister] Bevin and the Foreign Office, was governed too much by resentment at lack of consultation by France and too little by attention to the national interest."[5] This is similar to the conclusion of a leading British journalist that "at bottom there was [in Britain] a mysterious visceral hostility [toward European integration] great enough to transcend any amount of cool calculation."[6]

As the title of his book suggests, Dell believed that Britain's rejection of Schuman's proposal amounted to an abdication of leadership in Europe. In fact, Britain had already taken a back seat. For that reason, France launched by itself "a diplomatic revolution in Europe."[7] In political terms, the Schuman Declaration was nothing less than "a dramatic reassertion of French leadership on the Continent."[8] Fearful of Germany's recovery, France finally responded with a creative and courageous initiative. Indifferent to France's plight and complacent about the future, Britain pursued an unimaginative foreign policy. Nor did Britain's position change after the election of October 1951, when the Conservatives replaced Labour in government and Churchill again became prime minister.

Although Britain did not participate in the negotiations, its presence was keenly felt around the table in Paris where the others feared that Britain, for reasons of policy or pride, would attempt to derail the talks. In the event, Britain did not do so, not least because the United States made its interest in the success of the negotiations abundantly clear. If anything, the British helped the negotiations by not floating alternative proposals and by pressuring Adenauer to reach agreement when it seemed in early 1951 that Germany's interest in the plan was waning.[9]

The Intergovernmental Conference

In June 1950, negotiations began among representatives of France, Germany, Italy, and the Benelux countries to flesh out the Schuman Plan and establish what became the European Coal and Steel Community (ECSC).[10] The outbreak of war in Korea overshadowed the negotiations almost immediately.

The question of German remilitarization, already in the background, suddenly leaped to the fore. Adenauer could now link remilitarization, an urgent U.S. objective, to the restoration of full sovereignty, a pressing German objective. France feared that Germany would lose interest in the negotiations, but Adenauer was too sensitive to U.S. and French opinion to shy away from them. The Schuman Plan remained an essential building block of Germany's policy of rapprochement with France and full integration into the West.

The negotiations were the first in a series of intergovernmental conferences—lengthy diplomatic negotiations—in the history of European integration. The Schuman talks set a procedural as well as a political precedent. A delegation of government officials represented each country. Working groups stood on the lowest rung of the conference ladder. Above them, the heads of delegation (most of whom went on to join the High Authority, the ECSC's executive body) met regularly in restricted session. At the top, the foreign ministers (including Adenauer, who was both chancellor and foreign minister of Germany) met occasionally to resolve particularly contentious problems.

Compared to later intergovernmental conferences, the Schuman Plan negotiations were atypical in two important respects. First, because a supranational body did not yet exist, there was no supranational input into the negotiations. Second, whereas foreign ministries dominated the other countries' delegations, the French delegation consisted mostly of Monnet's economic planners in Paris, with Monnet himself at its head. That gave the French delegation considerable flexibility and informality. Nevertheless, Monnet worked closely with Foreign Minister Schuman, who provided overall political direction to the French delegation and to the talks themselves.

Monnet dominated the negotiations. He disliked large meetings, preferring to work directly with delegation heads, either bilaterally or multilaterally. Participants remembered the conference fondly not so much as a set of negotiations but as a series of consultations with Monnet, in which all sides edged amicably toward an agreement. In fact, as in later intergovernmental conferences, there was intensive bargaining and occasional rancor. When things threatened to get out of hand, Schuman would reproach the delegates. Like a kindly uncle addressing unruly children, he would urge them to temper national interests for the sake of European union. Such was France's influence and Schuman's stature that the delegates invariably fell back into line.

Walter Hallstein, a former professor and university administrator and a future Commission president, led the German delegation. In the course of the conference Hallstein became state secretary (director) of Germany's new foreign ministry and one of Adenauer's closest associates. His prestige, confidence, and assertiveness grew accordingly. So did his zeal for European integration.

Although a spirit of reconciliation hovered over the conference, hard bargaining characterized the negotiations themselves. The prospect of European security through limited economic integration, rather than the ideal of European unity, drove the proceedings. As Alan Milward observed of Belgium's approach to the negotiations, "there was no trace of idealism about the wider advantages to mankind of European integration. . . . It was taken for granted that peace between France and Germany was essential for Belgium's security, and that this was the strongest reason for accession to the treaty."[11]

An impatient Monnet thought that the negotiations could be completed in a few weeks. Typically, he wanted to focus on institutional issues to the exclusion of economic arrangements. Monnet's first draft treaty called for a High Authority, a parliamentary assembly, and a court. Monnet wanted to give the High Authority, the repository of shared sovereignty, virtually unfettered powers within its field of competence. As a sop to democratic control, he accepted a provision in the treaty allowing the assembly to dismiss the High Authority by a two-thirds majority. Otherwise the assembly would be relatively powerless.[12]

The major institutional battle in the conference concerned the role of the High Authority. The main protagonist was the Netherlands, a country that, in contrast to its later position in the European Community, deeply distrusted supranationalism and sought to limit the power of the High Authority by means of national control.[13] Hans-Peter Schwarz, Adenauer's biographer, described the Dutch position generally as "an unfortunate mixture of trade calculations, aversion to French or German hegemony, openness to British influence, and deep concern about the prospect of being absorbed into larger units."[14]

Dutch pragmatism irritated Adenauer and infuriated Monnet. But other national leaders, fearful of Franco-German dominance of the High Authority, shared Dutch concerns. Thus Monnet grudgingly acquiesced in the establishment of a Council of Ministers on the grounds that coal and steel questions could not be neatly separated from broader economic issues in which the High Authority lacked competence. The treaty supposedly established a balance between the Council and the High Authority, with the High Authority supreme in certain supranational areas. From the perspective of the original proposal, the institutional outcome represented a setback for supranationalism, as would the operational experience of the ECSC itself.

Just as one small country thwarted Monnet's hopes with regard to institutional design, another small country dug in its heels on economic issues. Belgian industry generally loathed the Schuman Plan. Industry and unions feared the consequences of competition. The Belgian government saw the ECSC as an opportunity to replace national subsidization of the steel sector with European-level subsidization and to undertake painful industrial restructuring. The struggle inside Belgium, and in the negotiations between Belgium and its partners, was a harbinger of struggles within and among future ECSC member states on a wide range of issues. The outcome of the Belgian case was indeed prototypical: a complex regime of transfer payments, concessions, and transitional measures in the treaty to cushion the inevitable economic blow to cosseted national industries.[15]

The plan's overriding economic objective was to create a single market in coal and steel among participating countries. That meant removing a plethora of tariff and nontariff barriers, such as price fixing, turnover and sales taxes, subsidies, and differentiated freight rates, in order to facilitate the free movement of coal and steel across national frontiers. But the single market would not be an unregulated market. Using a variety of instruments and measures, the High Authority and Council of Ministers would try to improve productivity, rationalize distribution, safeguard employment, equalize working conditions, and minimize economic dislocation. The treaty's most innovative provisions were in the area of competition policy. Largely to allay U.S. concern, the treaty included tough measures against restrictive practices and monopolies, including the possibility of fining companies up to 10 percent of their annual turnover. The treaty covered a period of fifty years (the ECSC came to an end in 2002, fifty years after it came into existence).

Outstanding Issues

The treaty was all but wrapped up by December 1950, six months after the negotiations began. Yet it was another four months before the treaty was signed. The reason for the delay was German foot dragging due to French insistence on the deconcentration of the coal and steel industries in the Ruhr. The big Ruhr conglomerates were to have been broken up under the terms of the Potsdam agreement, but the allies had not pressed the point. It was only in early 1951, with the ECSC hanging in the balance, that the French government launched an offensive. Afraid that the conglomerates would prove impervious to the treaty's antitrust provisions and sensitive to growing domestic unrest about the relationship between the Ruhr and German rearmament, France linked deconcentration to a successful conclusion of the negotiations.

France's last-minute insistence on industrial reorganization in the Ruhr aroused additional ill feeling in Germany, where many industrialists saw the Schuman Plan as a French plot to weaken German industry. French action and German reaction placed Adenauer in a dilemma: How could he reconcile economic interests at the national level and political interests at the European level? By backing France wholeheartedly and insisting on deconcentration, the United States resolved the dilemma for him. Even the most recalcitrant Germans acknowledged that Adenauer would have to bow to U.S. pressure. Accordingly, Adenauer reached agreement with U.S. high commissioner John McCloy on the terms of deconcentration at the end of March 1951.[16] This paved the way for the signing of the ECSC treaty in Paris in April.

Adenauer and Schuman decided that the International Ruhr Authority, which Adenauer abhorred, would cease to operate as soon as the ECSC came

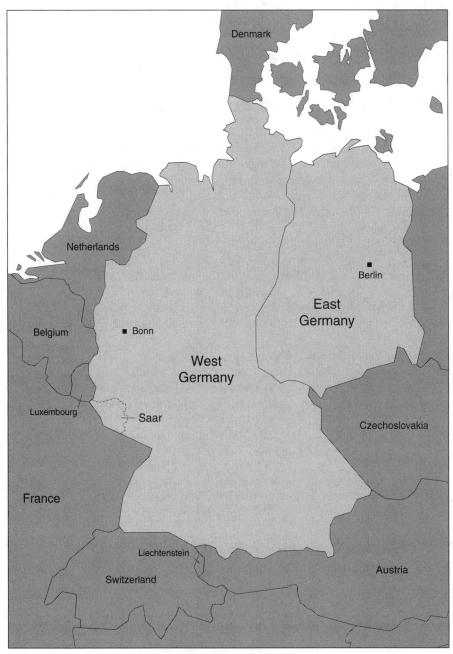

The Saar: A bone of contention between France and Germany

into being. The special status of the Ruhr, a bitter bone of contention in post-war Franco-German relations, would therefore come to an end. Yet the future of the Saar, a region of Germany controlled by France since the war, remained unresolved at the end of the conference. The French-controlled government of the Saar wanted the region to become the ECSC's seventh member state. That was too much even for the French government in Paris, which signed the treaty on behalf of France as well as the Saar. Adenauer insisted that, by signing the treaty, he was not abandoning Germany's determination eventually to reacquire the Saar. He and Schuman attached to the treaty an exchange of letters on the issue, affirming each side's position.

The foreign ministers had to resolve three other difficult issues, of a kind that would recur throughout the history of European integration, before the ECSC became operational. The first concerned the weighting of votes in the Council. Should Germany have more votes because its coal and steel sectors were the largest in the Community? Not surprisingly, France proposed equality of voting weight with Germany. Not surprisingly either, Germany agreed.

The second concerned the language regime in the Community. Speaking in German, the common language of the foreign ministers, Schuman proposed that French be either the sole or the preponderant language of the ECSC.[17] The ministers finally agreed that each country's language would have official status, but French would be the working language within the ECSC's institutions.

The third issue was the hardest to resolve. It concerned the location of the institutions. A protracted row erupted at a foreign ministers' meeting in Paris in July 1952, with each minister insisting on the location of one or more institution in his own country (Adenauer avoided chauvinism by championing the cause of Saarbrucken, the capital of the French-occupied Saar). The row seemed to make a mockery of the underlying purpose of the whole exercise. Dirk Stikker, the Dutch foreign minister, described what happened:

> For many months we had based our discussions on high principles of supra-nationalism and the exclusion of selfish, purely nationalistic interests. . . . The meeting [on the seat of the institutions] began at nine in the morning. . . . Questions of national prestige began to rise in importance. Proposals began to wander ever farther afield. No one was prepared to give way on any point before he had obtained another advantage. Europe was lost sight of. . . . As the confusion grew the discussion dragged on to midnight. At one point I rose in my place, ostensibly in wrath, told my colleagues in no uncertain terms what I thought of their high supranational principles, declared that I renounced any special position for the Netherlands, and walked out. . . . After some hours I returned, but it was still four o'clock [in the morning] before every national desire was satisfied.[18]

The foreign ministers finally agreed to hold meetings of the Council in Brussels, locate the court and High Authority temporarily in Luxembourg, and put the assembly in Strasbourg, where it could share facilities with the assembly of the Council of Europe.

Proceedings to ratify the treaty in the parliaments of the signatory states began in late 1951. Ratification was not a foregone conclusion. Various vested interests deployed a battery of political and economic arguments against the treaty. Anti-ECSC steel producers nearly unseated Schuman in the parliamentary elections of June 1951 (Schuman's constituency was in the steel-producing region of Lorraine). The biggest threat to ratification came not from business interests, which were often divided within and among the coal and steel sectors, but from political parties on the Far Right (nationalists) and Far Left (Communists). West Germany had only a small Communist party and an insignificant Far Right nationalist party. But the Socialists under Kurt Schumacher, who were both Marxist and nationalist, strongly opposed the treaty. In France the Communists and the recently constituted Gaullist Party, the largest party in parliament, tried unsuccessfully to defeat the treaty.

Launching the ECSC

The ECSC began operating in August 1952, at an inauspicious time politically. Adenauer's government was weak and unpopular. The French government was even weaker. The issue of German remilitarization, then at its height, cast European integration in a bad light. The political significance of the ECSC was lost in the bitterness of the controversy over the European Defense Community (EDC) and the relative complexity of the new treaty's institutional and policy provisions. Perhaps it was just as well that the ECSC received only sporadic media attention (including in the United States) and that the new organization had a relatively low public profile. Meetings of the High Authority and the Common Assembly went largely unreported. The ECSC had little impact on the everyday lives of most Europeans.

Behind the scenes the organization got off to a good start, thanks to soaring demand for coal and steel. That was due partly to the continuing Korean War and consequent rearmament in Western Europe and the United States and largely to the beginning of the postwar boom, epitomized by the so-called German miracle. Yet it is doubtful if the ECSC contributed much to Europe's rapid economic growth. The ECSC is barely mentioned in textbooks on national and European economic development in the 1950s.[19] Tariffs and quantitative restrictions were indeed removed in the coal and steel sectors, but nontariff barriers proved more difficult to identify and eradicate. The market remained fragmented, competitiveness did not increase greatly, productivity was not much improved, and cartels crept back into being.

A benign economic climate obviated the necessity for hard decisions by the High Authority, whose nine members and their staff, drawn mostly from national government ministries with a few international civil servants and academics thrown in, settled easily into Luxembourg. There was a great sense of excitement within the High Authority as the ECSC began its work. Despite the mundane reality of setting up a common market for coal and steel, most officials believed that they were serving the higher cause of European union.

Monnet, at the head of the High Authority, missed Paris, but Paris did not miss him. His political shelf life was effectively over. Monnet's main use to the French government was close contacts with the Americans. But U.S. assistance was now less important for France as U.S. influence in Europe gradually diminished. Monnet was no longer needed to direct the modernization plan, and the realization of the Schuman Plan reduced his value as an entrepreneur of European integration. Moreover, because of his authorship of the unpopular defense community idea, Monnet had become a political liability. It was better for the French government to have Monnet far away in Luxembourg at a time when opposition to the EDC was about to boil over in Paris.

As usual, Monnet was indefatigable. Now in his mid-sixties, he worked day and night to put the coal and steel community in place. But he was frustrated and bored: frustrated because the High Authority was too large and bureaucratic for his liking (in fact, it was a relatively small organization); bored because the political action was in Paris, not Luxembourg. It was not surprising that, soon after the EDC collapsed in August 1954, Monnet announced his intention to retire from the High Authority and return to Paris to try to reinvigorate European integration. His staff and fellow commissioners were relieved to see him go. While acknowledging his brilliance and creativity, they had been ground down by his poor management and chaotic work practices. Those with families looked forward to going home at a reasonable hour and staying there without risk of being summoned back to work late at night.

A steady stream of academic visitors had enlivened Monnet's life in Luxembourg. In addition to regulating the coal and steel industries, the ECSC spawned another industry: European union scholarship. The number of books and articles written on the ECSC in the 1950s and early 1960s is astounding. German academics were first on the scene, then French, then American. The three most important books of that epoch in English, by William Diebold, Hans Schmidt, and Ernst Haas, were based in part on lengthy observations of the High Authority in Luxembourg (before and after Monnet's departure).[20] Despite their best efforts, none of the authors was able to show that the community was economically significant. Even Haas, the father of neofunctionalism, later admitted that the ECSC had not had a marked spillover effect.[21]

Significance of the ECSC

Nevertheless the ECSC was important politically and institutionally. The High Authority forged a good working relationship with the Council of Ministers and the member states' permanent representatives. According to Duchêne,

Monnet's initial "narrow, technocratic view of relations between the High Authority and the industries and governments [developed into] a political system, which is substantially that of the Community today [1994]."[22] Thus a blend of supranationalism and intergovernmentalism characterized the functioning of the Community from the beginning.

The ECSC achieved both its immediate goal of resolving the problem of the Ruhr and its long-term objective of overcoming entrenched Franco-German enmity. Robert Marjolin, a contemporary observer who was far from starry-eyed about European integration, described the ECSC as "estimable on two counts. First, it represented a step forward, a new start on the road to a united Europe. Second, it represented a revolution in Franco-German relations. Nearly a century of wars, of attempts at domination, of an antagonism that had come absurdly to be called hereditary, had given way to a will to cooperate on completely equal terms."[23] Milward, the arch-revisionist of European integration, saw the Community's significance as having "ended eighty years of bitter and deadly [Franco-German] dispute and made the reconstruction of Western Europe possible. It did so by avoiding all major questions of war and peace and creating instead a formalized network of institutional economic interdependence. International regulation of the economy was institutionalized as the alternative to the formal diplomatic resolution of major areas of political conflict."[24]

The ECSC set a profound historical precedent. It represented a reversal of Europe's recent misfortunes. John Gillingham, author of one of the best studies of the early years of European integration, characterized the Paris Treaty as a de facto peace treaty between France and Germany:

> This was no grand settlement in the manner of Westphalia or Versailles. The agreement to create a heavy industry pool changed no borders, created no new military alliances, and reduced only a few commercial and financial barriers. It did not even end the occupation of the Federal Republic. . . . By resolving the coal and steel conflicts that had stood between France and Germany since World War II, it did, however, remove the main obstacle to an economic partnership between the two nations.[25]

■ The European Defense Community and the European Political Community

Speaking in a debate in the French National Assembly in July 1949, Robert Schuman made a statement that soon came back to haunt him. The question of Germany's admission to NATO, Schuman said, "cannot come up, either now or even in the future. Germany still has no peace treaty. It has no army, and it must not have one. It has no weapons, and it will have none."[26] Yet in little more than a year the question of Germany's NATO membership *was* on the agenda, thanks to the outbreak of the Korean War. Schuman had sincerely believed what he said in the French assembly in 1949; he could not have fore-seen that events would proceed as swiftly as they did in 1950.

Even before the Korean War, Adenauer wanted German remilitarization. His motive was less political (a quest for full sovereignty) than strategic (a quest for self-defense). Across the as-yet unfortified border between the two Germanys, the East German government, with Soviet support, had established an armed force, the Volkspolizei. Allied occupation forces in West Germany were small and weak. Adenauer feared that West Germany would be easily overrun in the event of an invasion by the Red Army or an incursion by the Volkspolizei. The answer, surely, was to build up allied forces and raise a West German army.

Adenauer knew only too well how controversial this idea was. Following a backlash against a statement about remilitarization that he had made in a newspaper interview in December 1949, Adenauer moved extremely care-fully.[27] Circumstances changed suddenly with the outbreak of war in Korea. If the North Koreans had invaded South Korea, might not the East Germans invade West Germany? Improbable though it now seems, many Europeans feared that war with the Soviet Union was imminent in the summer of 1950. The British and Americans spoke openly about the prospect of German remil-itarization. At a meeting of the Council of Europe's consultative assembly in August 1950, Churchill called for German rearmament in the context of European integration. Matters came to a head at a NATO ministerial meeting in New York in September 1950 when U.S. secretary of state Dean Acheson made it official: the United States wanted German military units to be raised and integrated into NATO forces in Europe.

Schuman cannot have been surprised by Acheson's announcement, but Acheson was surprised by the vehemence of Schuman's reaction to it. France was utterly opposed to German remilitarization in any shape or form. Bring-ing the issue into the open greatly strengthened Adenauer's diplomatic hand. Inevitably, Germany's negotiating position in the coal and steel negotiations hardened. Inevitably also, Adenauer linked Acheson's call for German remil-itarization to Germany's desire for abolition of the Occupation Statute and restoration of full sovereignty. France's policy of controlling Germany's post-war recovery was again endangered.

To protect the Schuman Plan and the overall strategy toward Germany of which it was a part, France needed a new initiative. Monnet provided it in the form of the Pleven Plan of October 1950: a scheme in the name of the French prime minister for a supranational European army, conditional on a successful conclusion of the ECSC negotiations. The difference between the Acheson and Pleven plans for German remilitarization was stark: Acheson wanted Germany to raise large armored units, if necessary as part of a reconstituted German army; Pleven wanted Germany to integrate small infantry units directly into a European army, without forming a German army. The original Pleven Plan was both politically inequitable and militarily infeasible. Acheson rejected it out of hand. Adenauer was more circumspect, protesting the plan's concrete proposals while welcoming its acceptance in principle of German remilitarization. Adenauer also assured Schuman that, despite changing strategic circumstances, Germany remained committed to negotiating the ECSC treaty. Still sensitive to French security concerns, the United States in any case pressured Germany to stick with the ECSC, threatening otherwise not to restore full sovereignty.

The Trauma of the EDC

Thus began a four-year drama that traumatized France politically, tested Franco-German relations to the limit, and deeply alienated France and the United States from each other. In February 1951, the six participants in the concurrent ECSC negotiations began a parallel intergovernmental conference to establish what came to be called the European Defense Community.[28] Ever suspicious of supranationalism, Britain declined to participate.[29] For France and the Benelux countries, this was a serious setback. Britain was the leading military power in Western Europe and a traditional guarantor of the continental balance of power. Britain's membership in the EDC would have helped to allay French and Benelux concerns about Germany's military resurgence. In the hope that Britain might still join the negotiations, the Netherlands postponed its full participation in them until November 1951.

The prospect of German remilitarization reopened deep political wounds in France and energized the Communist and Gaullist opposition. The Gaullists made sweeping gains in the parliamentary elections of June 1951. Opinion in Germany was equally divided, with the Socialists tapping into a groundswell of pacifism epitomized by the slogan *Ohnemich* (without me or, colloquially, count me out). The EDC would not win Adenauer any votes, but the restoration of full sovereignty might. Hence, for domestic political consumption, he linked the negotiations to establish the EDC and rescind the Occupation Statute, the former taking place in Paris, the latter just outside Bonn.

Despite the French government's postelection weakness, the EDC negotiations gathered speed in the fall of 1951. In the preceding months, Monnet had worked his magic on U.S. high commissioner McCloy and Gen. Dwight Eisenhower, the newly arrived NATO supreme commander. In return for French concessions on the size and equipment of German military units, McCloy and Eisenhower, whose influence in Europe was unrivaled, championed a revised version of the Pleven Plan, which they saw as a means of strengthening the European contribution to NATO. Acheson, in Washington, soon fell into line. Adenauer dropped his reservations about the plan's seemingly discriminatory proposals. He and the Americans still wanted the EDC to serve as a vehicle for German entry into NATO, but this was too much for the French. Nevertheless, with wholehearted U.S. support, the negotiators in Paris gradually put the EDC's institutional and organizational elements into place: a nine-member Commission, a Council of Ministers, a parliamentary assembly, German *groupements* (the word *division* was anathema to the French) of 12,500 troops, Germany's contribution not to exceed one-third of the total force, and no German defense ministry or general staff.

A Soviet diplomatic note of March 1952, calling for Four Power talks to conclude a German peace treaty, "burst like a bombshell" into the EDC negotiations.[30] By raising the prospect of German unification and neutrality, the Soviets sought to prevent German remilitarization within the Western alliance. The prospect of German neutrality filled Adenauer with dread. Vulnerable to Communist subversion, a neutral Germany might slip into the Soviet sphere of influence. The Americans were aware of the danger. Accordingly, the Western powers decided to press ahead with the modified Pleven Plan. The six negotiating countries signed the EDC treaty in May 1952, in Paris. On the previous day in Bonn, Britain, France, Germany, and the United States had signed an accord replacing the Occupation Statute with a number of contractual agreements, thereby effectively restoring sovereignty to Germany.

A debate on the EDC in the French National Assembly in February 1952, three months before the treaty was signed, signaled that ratification would be difficult. Changes in the international situation, notably the cease-fire in Korea and the death of Josef Stalin in March 1953, emboldened opponents of the treaty. With a possible thaw in the Cold War, was German remilitarization necessary? Adenauer had no doubts on that score and pushed the treaty through a restive German parliament. The Benelux countries and Italy also ratified the treaty. That left France, the originator of the Pleven Plan, as the sole holdout. Eisenhower, now president of the United States, and John Foster Dulles, his secretary of state, pressed France unrelentingly to ratify. So did Adenauer and Spaak, the zealous Eurofederalist foreign minister of Belgium.

A public debate raged in France on the merits of the treaty. It was likened at the time to the conflict-ridden Dreyfus affair of fifty years earlier, except that divisions over the EDC "were perhaps even more complicated and more irrational."[31] Charles de Gaulle, then in retirement, gave a celebrated press conference in November 1953 denouncing the treaty and Monnet, its unnamed "inspirer."[32] Indifferent to European integration and ambivalent about the EDC, Pierre Mendès-France, one of the most able politicians of the Fourth Republic, decided when he became prime minister in June 1954 to settle the issue. Having just ended France's disastrous involvement in Indochina and brokered an agreement with the nationalist rebels in Tunisia, Mendès-France was in a stronger position than most prime ministers of the hapless Fourth Republic.

The much-awaited parliamentary debate took place at the end of August 1954. Opponents of the treaty appeared less concerned about the fact of German remilitarization than about the implications of the treaty for France itself. Edouard Herriot, an influential old politician and former prime minister, claimed that membership in the EDC would mean "the end of France." Others emphasized the danger to France's two most cherished institutions, the army and the empire. One deputy spoke of "the acute danger that touches the hearts of all of us, the danger that the French Army might disappear, the Army which, through all changes of regime, we know to be the permanent artery of the fatherland." As for the empire, a deputy representing an overseas constituency wondered how a country about to make a large-scale "abandonment of sovereignty" could possibly retain its colonies. Concern about France's future international stature also infused the debate. As one deputy put it, "we are still a nation . . . with rights equal to those of America and Great Britain. . . . The ratification of the EDC would put us on the level of two defeated and three tiny countries." By implication, Britain and the United States were eager to see France reduced in rank, so that they could deal "from now on with world strategy in an Anglo-Saxon tete-à-tete."[33]

It was almost impossible in the face of such emotion to make reasonable arguments in favor of ratification. Pro-EDC *cedistes*—Christian Democrats, centrists, and some Socialists—were outnumbered and shouted down. In a final insult, the treaty was defeated not in a straight vote but on a procedural motion. By a majority of 319 to 264, the French parliament threw out the treaty "in an atmosphere of riot."[34]

Anthony Eden, the British foreign secretary, then suggested turning the old Brussels Treaty Organization (consisting of Britain, France, and the Benelux countries) into the Western European Union by the addition of Germany and Italy. Through the Western European Union, the former Axis powers could join NATO. The idea was fleshed out at a conference in London and reached fruition in the Paris agreement of October 1954. Consisting of a Council of Ministers and an assembly, and covering cultural and educational as well as military issues, the Western European Union was an intergovernmental rather than a supranational organization. That fact, together with the reassurance of British membership in it, won over many French parliamentarians who had voted against the EDC. Nevertheless, it took a vote of confidence (meaning that the government would stand or fall on the result) to get a majority of deputies to back the Western European Union in December 1954. As a result, within a year of the collapse of the EDC, Germany was remilitarized and a member of NATO.

The European Political Community

The collapse of the EDC resulted also in the collapse of a related initiative: the launch of an overarching political community. This originated in a proposal by Italy's fervently federalist prime minister, Alcide de Gasperi, to attach to the EDC treaty a provision (Article 38) calling for the EDC's assembly, within six months of its inauguration, to consider establishing "a permanent organization . . . of a confederal or federal structure."[35] At the urging of the Council of Europe's consultative assembly, the foreign ministers of the EDC's prospective member states agreed in September 1952 to ask an ad hoc assembly to carry out the terms of Article 38 while awaiting ratification of the EDC treaty. Presided over by Spaak, the ad hoc assembly (in effect the assembly of the Coal and Steel Community) adopted in March 1953 a draft treaty to establish the European Political Community.[36]

The Political Community was to have provided an organizational umbrella for the Defense Community and the Coal and Steel Community. Thus the EDC's and ECSC's institutions would have been replaced or superseded by a bicameral parliament (consisting of a directly elected Peoples' Chamber and an indirectly elected Senate), a European Executive Council whose president would be elected by the Senate, a Council of National Ministers, and a Court of Justice. Subject to swift ratification by the six prospective member states, the Political Community would have become operational at the same time as the EDC.

Spaak described the draft treaty as "neither the work of the maximalists nor the minimalists" in the ad hoc assembly. As for the polity he proposed to create, it was "neither federal nor confederal." By quoting George Washington on the draft constitution of the United States, however, Spaak revealed his federalist ambition. Nor can the first sentence of the first article have reassured intergovernmentalists: "The present Treaty sets up a European [Political] Community of a supranational character." Heinrich von Brentano, a leading German politician and chairman of the ad hoc assembly's constitutional committee, which drafted the treaty, enthusiastically described a community that would "be able to take on a more and more precise form . . . until it develops by a natural process into a real Federal State or Confederation. This appears particularly clearly from the fact that the supranational Community possesses one of the attributes of a State: . . . a directly elected Peoples' Chamber."[37]

In the increasingly anti-supranationalist climate of the EDC ratification debate, sentiments such as von Brentano's and aspirations such as Spaak's were both unrealistic and unnerving. Yet the other foreign ministers must have known what to expect when they asked Spaak to preside over the ad hoc assembly. If so, with the exception of Italy's Eurofederalist foreign minister, they could not have intended to take the draft treaty seriously. It was hardly surprising, therefore, that the foreign ministers allowed it to languish procedurally in late 1953 and 1954, until the death of the EDC resulted also in the death of the Political Community. By that time even Italy had lost much of its federalist fervor, de Gasperi having died only twelve days before the French Assembly rejected the EDC.

An Opportunity Lost?

For many proponents of European federalism, the demise of the EDC and the Political Community was the greatest lost opportunity in the history of European integration. Like the revolutionary year of 1848 just over a century earlier, 1954 was a pivotal year, a turning point at which Europe failed to turn. Implementation of the EDC, they argue, would have brought defense policy under supranational control and resolved in the mid-1950s an issue with which the European Union only began to grapple in the late 1990s. Implementation of the Political Community, in turn, would have established an integrative framework for specific industrial sectors and for European defense as well as for a growing array of socioeconomic policies. Yet the bitterness of the EDC debate in France suggests that, even if it had been ratified, the treaty could not have been implemented. Failure to implement the treaty would have left the question of German remilitarization unresolved. As it was, German remilitarization and membership in NATO through the Western European Union settled the issue in a manner acceptable to Germany and France and removed from the agenda of European integration an otherwise intractable problem.

Far from being a historical accident, the defeat of the EDC was, according to one of Mendès-France's closest colleagues, "a historical necessity." In his view, ratification of the treaty would have opened "a permanent civil war in France. Imagine the Sunday ceremonies at the war memorial in every village, with the Gaullists and the Communists united behind every tricolor? The [Gaullist-Communist] alliance institutionalized from that point on would not only have made France ungovernable, it would have put it in a state of uncontrollable effervescence. It was this mortal danger, which . . . perhaps Mendès . . . did not see at the time, that we avoided."[38] Alfred Grosser, an expert on France and Germany, concluded shortly after the event that defeat of the EDC benefited Franco-German relations and European integration. In addition to extremists on the Right and Left, most young people and many moderates in both countries generally opposed the EDC. Accordingly, ratification of the treaty could have alienated a constituency that was vital for the achievement of European integration and eventual Franco-German reconciliation.[39] Far from enriching the movement for European integration, the proposed EDC had muddied the waters. The entire episode fueled fears that integration meant militarization, to the detriment of closer economic cooperation among the six prospective member states.

Although defeat of the EDC seemed at the time to deal a near-fatal blow to prospects for further integration—*supranationalism* was a dirty word, Franco-German relations were soured, and federalist hopes were dashed—it cleared the air and allowed the countries concerned to focus on economic priorities. A key provision in the treaty for the Political Community identified one of those priorities: the establishment of a common market. The Dutch government, which in the early 1950s became the leading proponent of economic integration, insisted on a commitment to establishing a common market in return for its lukewarm support of the EDC. That raised problems for France, then wedded to a policy of commercial protection. The inclusion of the common market clauses in the Political Community treaty suggests that, even if the EDC had been ratified, fundamental economic differences among the signatory states would have delayed or prevented implementation of the Political Community. As it was, it took another three years, including a new intergovernmental conference, before the Six negotiated, signed, and ratified the European Economic Community. The defeat of the EDC helped, not hindered, the road to Rome.

■ The European Economic Community and the European Atomic Energy Community

Andrew Moravcsik opened his masterful study of European integration with a bold assertion. The history of the European Community, he wrote, "begins with a failure." The failure in question was the defeat of the European Defense Community, which "crushed hopes that the European Coal and Steel Community . . . would lead automatically to deeper integration."[40] Regardless of the defeat of the EDC, the ECSC had little chance of leading automatically to deeper integration. The ECSC was politically important and institutionally innovative, but economically insignificant. It set an organizational precedent for postwar relations among the countries of Western Europe, but the peculiarities of the Ruhr problem that gave rise to the ECSC, the unique nature of the coal and steel sectors, and a deep attachment to national sovereignty precluded automatic spillover.

Even the most ardent supporters of further integration must have appreciated the limits of the ECSC well before the defeat of the EDC. There were not many hopes of automatic spillover left to crush when the EDC finally collapsed in August 1954. Although Monnet, the personification of European integration, announced his wish not to be reappointed president of the High Authority in November 1954, three months after the EDC debacle, his disillusionment with the ECSC was long-standing. The collapse of the EDC merely confirmed Monnet in the belief that he could best serve the cause of European integration by promoting a new initiative independently, at the head of an international lobby, rather than by staying in Luxembourg and trying to expand the scope of the ECSC. Oddly enough, Monnet changed his mind in early 1955 about leaving the High Authority following the fall of the Mendès-France government, with which Monnet was out of favor. Monnet's belated request to stay in Luxembourg showed poor judgment: the new government of Edgar Faure did not much like Monnet either. Without the backing of the

French government, even with Adenauer's continued support, Monnet could not have continued to lead the High Authority.[41]

Paradoxically, the EDC debacle contributed to a noticeable improvement in Franco-German relations in 1955 and 1956. Faure wanted to make amends for some of the fiercely anti-German rhetoric that had flowed in France during the national debate on German remilitarization. It is hardly coincidental that a number of government-sanctioned "people-to-people" initiatives, in the cultural, educational, and linguistic fields, got off the ground at that time. The conclusion of a commercial treaty in August 1955 illustrated the extent of the thaw between France and Germany exactly one year after the traumatic collapse of the EDC. Similarly, the opening of a new bridge in September 1956, linking Strasbourg and Kehl across the Rhine, became a celebration of Franco-German rapprochement. Perhaps more than anything else on the political plane, the meeting of Adenauer and his French counterpart Guy Mollet in November 1956, at the height of the Suez crisis, demonstrated a newfound Franco-German willingness to work together.[42]

The improvement in Franco-German relations, and with it the beginning of genuine reconciliation, took place not only in the aftermath of the EDC debacle but also in the context of a new strategic situation. As a result of the Paris agreement to establish the Western European Union, in October 1954, Germany regained almost unrestricted sovereignty. Acceptance into NATO in May 1955 tied Germany firmly into the Western camp. With Germany once again sovereign and remilitarized, the nature of the German question, and therefore of Franco-German relations, changed markedly. France could no longer extract concessions from Britain and the United States by threatening to block Germany's recovery. Increasingly, France would base its policy toward Germany primarily on economic rather than geopolitical calculations.

Nevertheless, Franco-German relations retained a special quality. Given Germany's recent past (conduct in the war) and uncertain future (possible reunification), dealings between Paris and Bonn could not be entirely normal. Adenauer was excessively deferential to French feelings. For sentimental and strategic reasons, he put a premium on maintaining harmonious relations with France. Adenauer's willingness to subordinate economic objectives to supposed strategic necessity irritated many of the chancellor's colleagues and gave France a comparative advantage in international negotiations. This was especially striking in the intergovernmental conference of 1956–1957 that resulted in the Rome Treaty.

The resolution of the Saar problem was the most obvious manifestation of improved Franco-German relations in the mid-1950s. French control of the Saar since the end of World War II had caused deep resentment in Germany. France's proposal in 1954 to "Europeanize" the region under the auspices of the Western European Union failed to mollify German opinion. In an effort to ease tension with Germany and mute international criticism, France made the

proposed change in the Saar's status contingent on the outcome of a referendum there in October 1955. Within the German political establishment only
Adenauer, blinded by Francophilia and enamored of all things European,
advocated a "yes" vote. Far from endorsing the latest French proposal, a large
majority of the Saar's population voted "no" and opted instead to rejoin Germany. Most of the region's residents seemed motivated not by German nationalism but by economic self-interest (postwar Germany was already much
more prosperous than France). Regardless of the population's motives, Paris
and Bonn subsequently negotiated the return of the Saar to Germany in an
atmosphere remarkably free of rancor. The Saar was eventually incorporated
into the Federal Republic in January 1957, shortly before the end of the negotiations on the Rome Treaty.

Messina

The famous meeting of foreign ministers in the Sicilian town of Messina in
June 1955 therefore took place in a climate of growing Franco-German amity.
The Messina meeting looms large in the history of European integration.
Casual accounts of the EU's origins credit Messina with deliberately
relaunching the process of integration after the seemingly fatal setback of the
EDC's defeat. In retrospect, Messina assumed the mantle of a Second Com-
ing, after the initial incarnation of European integration in the Schuman Dec-
laration of May 1950.

The ministers who gathered in Messina in 1955 would have been surprised to learn that the meeting would acquire such a retrospective gloss. The
primary purpose of Messina was much less grandiose than relaunching European integration: it was to appoint a successor to Monnet as president of the
High Authority. France still had a lock on the job. The other member states
endorsed the French government's choice of René Meyer, a former prime
minister (a distinction not uncommon in the French Fourth Republic).
Meyer's selection was announced on the first day of the Messina meeting.

The ministers then discussed proposals for further economic integration.
Two stood out. One, championed by Monnet and strongly supported by Spaak
as a means of reviving the European project, was for an atomic energy community analogous to the coal and steel community. The second was a reitera-
tion of the Beyen Plan (named after the Dutch foreign minister) for an industrial customs union that had originally been incorporated into the draft treaty
for the European Political Community.[43] The failure of the EDC, and with it
the Political Community, left the Beyen Plan in limbo. Because he thought a
customs union too ambitious, Spaak preferred Monnet's atomic energy proposal. Under pressure from Beyen, however, Spaak incorporated the atomic
energy and customs union ideas into a single package, the so-called Benelux
memorandum of May 1955. Spaak and Beyen had different objectives in

mind. Whereas Spaak saw economic integration as a stepping-stone to political union, Beyen was interested mostly in exploiting opportunities for economic growth.

The Netherlands' dependence on international trade explains Beyen's preoccupation with regional economic integration. Trade barriers were stifling the Dutch economy. The Dutch and other members of the so-called Low Tariff Club became fierce advocates of free trade. They were disappointed by the slow pace of tariff reduction in the GATT and especially of quota removal in the Organization for European Economic Cooperation (OEEC). The OEEC's Trade Liberalizing Program, launched in 1949, made little headway. With decisionmaking in the OEEC subject to unanimity, it was easy for sovereignty-conscious and protectionist members to block progress. European free traders soon lost patience with the GATT and faith in the OEEC. Hence their advocacy of a regional organization with real decisionmaking power to establish a common market, which would also increase their leverage to accelerate GATT negotiations for lower tariff barriers.[44]

The release of the Benelux memorandum in May 1955, two weeks before the Messina meeting, intensified political and business interest in the idea of a common market. Lively domestic debates on regional economic integration took place in most ECSC member states throughout 1955. The question in Germany was not whether, but how, to liberalize trade. Should Germany pursue liberalization globally through the GATT or regionally through a European organization? If regionally, was a free trade area or a customs union preferable? Ludwig Erhard, Germany's economics minister, favored a multilateral approach. As a doctrinaire economic liberal, he feared that regional arrangements would hinder rather than help the achievement of global free trade. Of the two regional options, he viewed a customs union as potentially protectionist and therefore undesirable.

Hallstein, in the foreign ministry, advocated a customs union for economic and political reasons. He thought a customs union would afford Germany the economic benefits of market liberalization and the political benefits of deeper European integration. The rift between Erhard and Hallstein was personal, ideological, and bureaucratic. Personally, Erhard and Hallstein disliked each other; ideologically, Erhard disdained Hallstein's Eurofederalism; bureaucratically, their respective foreign and economics ministries vied for leadership in the formulation of trade policy, although a number of senior officials in the economics ministry supported the establishment of a common market.

Adenauer arbitrated the dispute between his two strong-willed ministers. The chancellor's preferences suggested that he would favor Hallstein over Erhard, as indeed he did. But Adenauer proceeded carefully, not least because Monnet pressured him to opt for the atomic energy idea instead of the common market proposal. Also, Erhard was immensely popular in the country (he was known as the father of the economic miracle) and had the backing of influential interest groups. Adenauer wanted to assuage Erhard rather than confront him outright. Erhard suspected that he was fighting a losing battle. He must have known, as one historian put it, that Germany's European policy in the 1950s "was under the primacy of . . . objectives to which national economic interests, even if they found an advocate in the Ministry for the Economy, had largely to be subjected."[45]

Advocates of free trade were in a small minority in France in the mid-1950s. Robert Marjolin, who resigned as head of the OEEC in April 1955 because of the organization's impotence, was one of the few prominent French people to champion market liberalization. Marjolin was not an ideologue. He was less interested in the form than the substance of European integration. Marjolin believed that France could realize its full potential only through membership in a common market. High trade barriers and an overvalued currency were holding France back. Pessimistic about its economic performance, France was in danger of falling farther behind unless it embraced regional economic integration.

French political and business elites were still deeply protectionist. The only European initiative that caught their imagination was the proposed atomic energy community, known as Euratom.[46] Monnet and the French establishment supported Euratom for different reasons. Whereas Monnet saw it as an opportunity to advance supranationalism and relaunch European integration, French leaders championed it on narrow nationalistic grounds. Their main goal was to put European resources at the disposal of the French atomic energy industry for both civil and military purposes. French objectives were so transparent that other countries instinctively recoiled from the idea. Only Monnet's dogged advocacy of it, and French insistence on linking the atomic energy and common market proposals, kept the prospect of Euratom alive.

Contrary to the impression now widely held, governments did not commit themselves at Messina unreservedly to jump-starting European integration. Although most of the ministers present were ardent Europeanists and although prospects for integration were increasingly propitious, a majority of national governments preferred to proceed slowly. Franco-German relations had improved greatly since the collapse of the EDC, but French distrust of German calls for trade liberalization and German distrust of French calls for atomic energy cooperation ran deep. The Benelux countries wondered how protectionism in France and internal divisions in Germany could ever be overcome.

Not wanting the Messina meeting to end inconclusively, the foreign ministers agreed at the last minute to establish an intergovernmental committee to continue work on the atomic energy and common market proposals. Antoine Pinay, the French foreign minister, was the last holdout. Under pressure from his colleagues, Pinay went along with the idea of an intergovernmental committee in order to end the conference on a positive note and save France, once again, from isolation. The decision to keep existing options open, reached reluctantly and at the last minute, marks the real significance of Messina. Understandably, however, the foreign ministers couched the meeting's outcome in verbose language. "The time has come to enter a new phase in the construction of Europe," they declared, ". . . through the development of common institutions, the gradual merger of national economies, the creation of a common market, and increasing harmonization of social policies."[47]

From Messina to Venice

The intergovernmental committee set up after Messina, under Spaak's energetic chairmanship, met in the summer and fall of 1955 without much fanfare. The governments and peoples of France and Germany had more immediate concerns. The question of the Saar and Adenauer's historic visit to Moscow in December 1955 preoccupied Germany while the escalating conflict in Algeria preoccupied France. Whereas the Schuman Declaration and the EDC had been front-page stories, the activities of the Spaak committee were lucky to get an occasional mention in the media.

Relevant government ministries and interest groups nevertheless focused on the committee's work. The stakes were high especially for France, which faced the greatest barrier to establishing a common market. Political instability increased French uncertainty until the election in January 1956 of the pro-European government of Guy Mollet. Even so, France insisted in the Spaak committee on numerous safeguards and special concessions. By working closely at home with various industrial and agricultural interests and in committee meetings in Brussels with sympathetic national delegations, the French government helped fashion a final report that could serve as a basis for an intergovernmental conference to negotiate a treaty establishing a common market.

In October 1955, at the height of the intergovernmental committee's deliberations, Monnet launched the Action Committee for the United States of Europe to lobby for further integration.[48] Monnet invited leading politicians and trade unionists (excluding Communists) to join. Most accepted out of respect for Monnet and because the obligations of membership were not onerous. Initially, Monnet used the committee to push exclusively for Euratom, his new brainchild. Most members of the Action Committee were uninterested in Euratom, preferring the idea of a common market, which Monnet eventually endorsed.

Given that France would not proceed with negotiations on a common market without negotiations also on Euratom and that Germany would not proceed with negotiations on Euratom without negotiations also on a common market, inevitably the Spaak report, presented to the governments of the Six in April 1956, endorsed both options. Nevertheless the report focused mostly on the proposed common market, with a customs union at its core and possibly including agricultural policy, the "harmonization of social and fiscal charges" (due to higher taxation and social benefits in France), the free movement of labor, monetary policy cooperation, a "readaptation fund" to help compensate for job losses, and an investment fund for poorer regions.[49]

The foreign ministers met in Venice in late May 1956, almost a year after Messina, to consider the Spaak report. In the meantime, domestic interests mobilized for and against the proposed common market and Euratom. Opinion in most countries strongly favored the common market, but not Euratom. French opinion strongly favored Euratom, but mostly opposed the common market. The negotiations would not be easy. In addition to their earlier demands, the French insisted in Venice that a final agreement include free access to the proposed common market for products from French colonies. Rather than kicking up a fuss at that stage, Germany agreed to put the latest French demand on the conference agenda. The foreign ministers then gave a green light to launch an intergovernmental conference to establish a common market and an atomic energy community.

Britain Bows Out

Membership in the proposed common market was not formally restricted to the Six. Britain declined to attend the Messina conference and sent a mid-level official to observe the work of the intergovernmental committee. The government recalled him to London in October 1955, fully six months before the committee presented its report. Although Moravcsik asserted that British policy at the time of Messina "constituted a rational, remarkably flexible, even far-sighted defense of enduring British economic interests," Britain's approach to European integration in the mid-1950s suggests instead irrationality, rigidity, and shortsightedness.[50]

Undoubtedly the pattern of British trade differed substantially from that of the Six. Whereas the Six dealt mostly with each other, the bulk of Britain's trade was with countries other than the Six. Moreover, Britain had a special trading relationship with the Commonwealth, involving preferential terms unavailable to other trading partners and incompatible with participation in a European common market. British officials and businesspeople must have known that the tide of British trade was turning away from the Commonwealth and toward Europe. Undoubtedly, it would have been painful politically for Britain to explore the possibility of joining a European common market in the mid-1950s. Yet France, a country with a deep-rooted protectionist streak, was about to take an equally difficult political decision and opt for further integration.

A European free trade area limited to industrial goods would have suited the British. It would have suited Erhard and other economic liberals in Germany too, but was unacceptable to most political leaders in the Six. France wanted an agreement that included agriculture, social protection, and other safeguards; the Six generally wanted a more cohesive and dynamic economic organization than a loose free trade agreement would provide. As it was, by the mid-1950s the Six comprised an informal trading bloc. A customs union, with a common external tariff and a common commercial policy, was more likely than a free trade area to develop the economic potential of such a group of countries.

The British poured scorn on the continentals' efforts to integrate further. The disdain with which British politicians and officials dismissed the move toward a common market is now legendary. It could never happen, they said, because France would not allow it to happen. The idea of a common market was pie in the sky; further evidence of federalist fantasizing. As planning for the common market progressed, the British became even more dismissive. "The possibility that the negotiations might succeed," Moravcsik observed, " . . . instantly transformed Britain's skeptical ennui into virulent hostility."[51] That was hardly sensible behavior on Britain's part.

Concern about the future of the Anglo-American "special relationship" is often cited as a reason for British aloofness from European integration. Yet the United States consistently supported European integration and British participation in it. To the extent that the special relationship existed, it did so despite, not because of, Britain's refusal to join the ECSC and later the EEC. Phrases in the Messina resolution, such as "the construction of Europe" and "the establishment of a united Europe," appealed to the United States. Economically, the United State wanted to ensure that the common market would benefit U.S. investors and exporters.

The Intergovernmental Conference

The intergovernmental conference took place in Brussels, in recognition of Spaak's successful chairmanship of the committee that had prepared it.[52] Egypt's nationalization of the Suez Canal, which culminated in October in a failed Anglo-French military expedition to restore international control of the Canal Zone, dominated the headlines. The coincidence of the two events suggests a link between the negotiation of the Rome Treaty and the end of the Suez debacle. France supposedly reacted to the Suez situation by grasping the strategic importance of European integration and enthusiastically embracing the common market.[53] According to this analysis, Gamal Abdul Nasser, the Egyptian leader, unintentionally became the "federator" of Europe.

If a link existed between Suez and the conference, however, it lay in Mollet's use of Suez as a strategic argument to bolster a policy in Europe to which he was already committed for economic reasons.[54] It also lay in the fact that, with the all-consuming Suez affair out of the way, the French government could devote more attention to the ongoing Brussels negotiations. Nevertheless, by cementing official Franco-German ties (Adenauer wholeheartedly supported the French intervention and went ahead with a previously planned visit to Paris at the height of the crisis, which he could easily have cancelled), Suez contributed in a roundabout way to cementing European integration.

Similarly, developments in the Soviet bloc in October and November 1956 provided a strategic backdrop to the conference without impinging on the negotiations themselves. The failed uprisings in Poland and Hungary heightened Cold War tension but did not directly affect European integration, especially as NATO was already well established. Indirectly, however, the Soviet invasion of Hungary helped European integration because it triggered a popular reaction in Western Europe against local-Communist parties that supported the Soviet intervention. As Communist parties were implacable and influential opponents of European integration, the decline in their fortunes in Western Europe benefited the European movement.

A contemporary observer described the conference as "an intricate mixture of academic exercises in abstruse economic theory and poker games of political skill."[55] The theorizing took place mostly in the two expert groups, one on Euratom and the other on the common market; the poker playing took place in regular meetings of the heads of delegations and occasional meetings of foreign ministers. The heads of government met once toward the end of the conference, along with their foreign ministers, to resolve the most contentious issues. Adenauer and Mollet, who met alone in Paris in November 1956 and at the joint meeting of prime ministers and foreign ministers, also in Paris, in February 1957, were the dealmakers and power brokers. Reflecting the reality of Franco-German hegemony within the Six, the others generally went along with what Adenauer and Mollet decided. Beset by frequent changes of government and economic uncertainty, Italy played a weak hand.

As host of the conference and chair of the heads of delegation committee, Spaak was particularly influential. Taking care not to alarm protectionists in France and economic liberals in Germany, Spaak moderated his usual Euroenthusiasm and assumed the role of honest broker. Perhaps chastened by the EDC experience, Spaak avoided using federalist language during the conference. His closest assistant was Pierre Uri, a French official of the ECSC dispatched to Brussels for the duration of the negotiations. This was the extent of supranational involvement in the conference.

The negotiators in Brussels, as well as the prime ministers and foreign ministers who met occasionally to move the negotiations along, were the tip of the conference iceberg. An array of government officials, parliamentarians, and interest group leaders labored intermittently on the conference in Brussels and the national capitals. Mindful of the EDC debacle, governments sought to form coalitions with opposition parties and interest groups to ensure support for the conference and its outcome. The German Social Democratic Party, then in the course of abandoning doctrinaire anticapitalism, accepted the idea of the common market. Two key parliamentary victories in France, one on Euratom in

July 1956 and the other on the common market in January 1957, cleared the air and strengthened the government's negotiating position in Brussels.

Fear of the future, of the brave new world of market liberalization, nevertheless remained pervasive in France. Mollet's strategy was not to confront opponents of further integration head-on, but to win as many concessions as possible in the negotiations while cultivating key vested interests at home. French foreign minister Christian Pineau and Robert Marjolin, Pineau's special adviser, ably assisted Mollet. Together they conducted a two-front campaign: one in Brussels at the conference; the other at home in the cabinet, parliament, boardrooms, and offices of interest groups (what Marjolin called the "Battle of Paris"[56]). Knowing the fragility of French domestic support, the other five cut France as much slack as possible in order to ensure ratification in the French parliament. Naturally the French delegation turned that to advantage, occasionally exaggerating the extent of domestic opposition in order to win even more favorable terms from the other delegations.

The French got away with this because France was central to the project for deeper integration in a way that Britain, for instance, was not. A large country with great economic potential, France already comprised part of an informal continental trading bloc. It would hardly have been worth it for the Five to form a common market without France. Moreover, for political reasons Germany placed a premium on cooperation with France. Thus France was in a privileged position in the conference, a position that its negotiators exploited to the full.

Nevertheless, there was a limit to what France could demand. The Euratom treaty, in particular, contained far less than France wanted. For instance, France agreed that Euratom could not monopolize the supply of fissionable materials, would not have an assembly separate from that of the ECSC and the EC (thereby precluding selective membership in Euratom by non-ECSC and non-EC member states), and would not be used for military purposes (this was a key demand of Monnet's Action Committee and of the German parliament). The government was able to swallow these compromises and maintain parliamentary support because, as the conference progressed, domestic critics of French concessions on Euratom became increasingly divided on the question of the common market. Many rural, right-wing critics of the Euratom treaty, for instance, supported the EC's agricultural provisions. As Euratom and the EC would stand or fall together, opponents of deeper integration acquiesced in the treaties for the sake of the promised common agricultural policy.

France fared better in the EC than in the Euratom negotiations, although there, too, France often had to give way. But France refused to budge on agriculture. Having experienced severe food shortages during or after the war and having subsidized their agricultural production to some extent, the others disputed not the principle of a common agricultural policy but the practical application of it. Because it had the largest farming sector, France had most at stake in the negotiations politically and economically. Indeed, Marjolin and other advocates of an industrial common market stirred up French enthusiasm for a common agricultural policy partly to generate a powerful domestic lobby in favor of the Rome Treaty. The others eventually agreed to go along with a provision in the treaty endorsing a common agricultural policy, with the details to be negotiated soon after implementation of the treaty.

With Belgian support, France insisted during the conference on associating the member states' overseas territories with the common market. The idea had great emotional appeal in France, where it helped allay concerns that deeper European integration would drive a wedge between France and its colonies (and ex-colonies). Germany wanted nothing to do with the other member states' overseas territories, fearing especially that trade with Latin America would suffer as a result. The issue became one of the most difficult to settle in the conference. Adenauer and Mollet finally agreed to give preferential trade terms to the overseas territories and to establish a special fund for development assistance outside the Community budget, to which Germany, as the largest member state, would contribute the largest share. For the sake of Franco-German friendship Adenauer rammed this concession through a fiercely indignant cabinet, at considerable political cost.

France accepted the Spaak Report's recommendation that the customs union be established over a twelve-year period, in three stages of equal length. Fearful of the impact of international competition, France wanted to make the launch of the second stage subject to a unanimous decision of the member states. That would have given France a veto over implementation of the customs union, which the others refused to countenance. Adenauer and Mollet worked out a compromise at their bilateral summit in November 1956. The treaty would allow a member state to delay transition to the second stage for two years; the member state's objection would then go to arbitration. Thus a member state could delay but not prevent implementation of the customs union. Negotiators presumed in any case that implementation of the customs union would assume an almost unstoppable momentum.

France complained that the cost of providing generous employment benefits—lengthy paid holidays, high rates of overtime pay, and the like—as well as equal pay for men and women would put the country at a competitive disadvantage in the common market. The solution, according to France, was for the other member states to subscribe to the much-vaunted French social model. The demand for social "equalization" or "harmonization" became a mantra of French employers and workers and a rallying cry for opponents of the common market. As the Five were not about to burden themselves financially for France's sake, the issue became a major stumbling block in the conference.

Adenauer and Mollet resolved it in November 1956. Germany agreed to a provision in the treaty promising equal pay for men and women to be included in a section on social policy that paid lip service to "the harmonization of social systems" in the common market. Germany also agreed that a special protocol attached to the treaty would allow France to take "protective measures" in industries affected by "disparities [among member states] in the method of payment for overtime," should such disparities continue to exist after implementation of the first stage of the common market.[57] Otherwise France softened its demand for social equalization in the face of concerted opposition from the Five. By the end of the conference, the economic benefits for France of establishing a common market clearly outweighed the political costs of insisting on social equalization.

It is often said that the common market was a trade-off between France and Germany: an agricultural common market for France in return for an industrial common market for Germany. That was not the case. The French government—more specifically, the prime minister and foreign minister— wanted both and used one (the promise of an agricultural common market) to get the other (an industrial common market). Germany wanted an industrial

Signing of the Rome Treaty, March 25, 1957. Beneath the fresco *The Horatii and Curatii*, leaders of six European countries sign treaties for a European Common Market and European Atomic Pool. Seen here from left are Belgian foreign minister Paul Henri Spaak (extreme left), French foreign minister Christian Pineau (third from left), West German chancellor and foreign minister Konrad Adenauer (center, signing), his undersecretary Walter Hallstein (second from right), and Italian prime minister Antonio Segni.

© Bettmann/CORBIS

common market above all, but accepted an agricultural common market not only as a means of ensuring French participation but also for the sake of its own agricultural sector.

Some of the treaty's signatories, notably Spaak, Hallstein, and Bech, were ideologically committed to European integration. The others saw the EC primarily as a means to meet the challenges and exploit the opportunities of international economic interdependence. Yet this was no ordinary common market. Everyone involved in the negotiations remembered the war vividly. Few of them would have predicted that such an agreement would have been reached among the Six so soon after 1945. The central role of the foreign ministers and, occasionally, the heads of government in the negotiation and subsequent operation of the EC demonstrated that the Community's importance was more than merely commercial.

The Rome Treaties

Member states' prime ministers and foreign ministers signed the EEC and Euratom treaties in Rome on March 25, 1957. Italy, which had not played a big part in the negotiations themselves, organized the elaborate signing ceremony. The symbolism of the occasion moved Adenauer and some of the other signatories, especially as it came so soon after the failure of the EDC. The preamble of the Euratom treaty includes two key words in the lexicon of European integration: *peace* and *prosperity* ("nuclear energy . . . will permit the advancement of the cause of peace," and "a powerful nuclear industry . . . will . . . contribute to the prosperity" of the member states). The preamble of the EEC treaty, by contrast, not only mentioned peace and, by implication, prosperity (member states seek "the constant improvement of the living and working condition of their peoples") but also suggested that the EC was a means to a greater end: "an ever closer union among the peoples of Europe."[58]

The preambles stood in marked contrast to the utilitarian nature of the treaties themselves. The Euratom treaty contained detailed provisions covering the organization's main objectives: promotion of research, dissemination of information, protection of health and safety, facilitation of investment, supply of ores and nuclear fuels, proper use of nuclear materials, and the establishment of a common market "in specialized materials and equipment." Even before it came into existence, however, most member states regarded Euratom as irrelevant. Far from forging deeper integration, Euratom became a clearinghouse for information exchange among the Six. As imported oil was abundant and cheap and as consumer resistance to nuclear energy grew, Euratom languished. Instead, France successfully pursued a national route to atomic energy for both civil and military purposes.

The EEC treaty was by far more important, so much so that the term *Rome Treaty* soon referred exclusively to it. The treaty's provisions ranged from the general to the specific, the mundane to the arcane. Mind-boggling lists of existing tariffs constituted a lengthy annex. Other attachments—lists of overseas territories, the implementing convention on the association of overseas territories, protocols, and a final act consisting of various declarations on specific national interests—ran to many more pages than the treaty itself. Some of the protocols and declarations were for domestic political purposes. Without affecting implementation of the treaty itself, they acknowledged national sensitivities in areas likely to be affected by the common market.

The treaty proper included provisions for a customs union, a common commercial policy, a common transport policy, competition policy, limited monetary policy cooperation, and coordination of macroeconomic policy. A provision on social policy called for the establishment of the European Social Fund to contribute to retraining and other assistance to workers. The treaty also established a European Investment Bank to provide cheap loans for regional development and other modernization projects. The treaty's provisions for the free movement of persons, services, and capital were tentative, reflecting the tension between what was theoretically desirable and politically practicable in the establishment of the common market.

The treaty established an assembly, council, commission, and court. The Commission was the most distinctive new institution. Eager to play down supranationalism, the Six agreed almost by default to use the less controversial name Commission rather than the value-laden name High Authority. Nevertheless the Commission, supposedly independent of national governments, was potentially powerful, notably with respect to upholding Community law and initiating and implementing Community legislation. But the Council of Ministers would be the EC's chief decisionmaking body. Depending on the issue under discussion (in accordance with the relevant treaty article), decisions would be taken by unanimity, simple majority vote, or qualified majority vote. Votes in the Council were allocated according to the member states' size, with Germany and France having equal representation.

One of the treaty's most important articles stated that, in cases where the treaty "has not provided the necessary powers," the Council, acting unanimously, could take "appropriate measures . . . necessary to attain . . . one of the objectives of the Community."[59] In other words, member states could agree to extend integration to areas not specifically mentioned in the treaty. Subject only to unanimity among member states, it amounted to an open-ended instrument for further economic integration.

Ratification

National parliaments ratified the treaties before the end of 1957. Some opponents raised the specter of a European superstate, but the reality of the intergovernmental conference and its outcome was too pedestrian to sustain fantasies of that kind. The old charge of German domination recurred in the French debate, although many Germans, especially economic liberals, saw the treaty as a sellout to France. Gaullists were divided on the EC: some went along with it for economic reasons; others opposed it for political reasons (because it would erode national sovereignty and promote technocracy). De Gaulle himself mostly kept quiet on the issue.

Other objections to the treaty, in France and elsewhere, focused on fears of mass migration and of large-scale job losses. In France, at least, the parliamentary votes of July 1956 (in favor of negotiating Euratom) and January 1957 (in favor of negotiating the common market) had essentially decided the issue. Ratification of the treaty in July 1957, by a margin of almost one hundred votes, was a foregone conclusion. In yet another turn of the French political carousel, Mollet's government collapsed in May 1957, two months after the treaty was signed and two months before it was ratified. But the government's fall had nothing to do with the EC.

Adenauer faced more difficulty over ratification of the treaty than did his French counterpart. Not that ratification was ever in doubt in Germany, as the treaty clearly benefited the Federal Republic economically and politically. The problem lay in Erhard's resentment of Adenauer and dissatisfaction with the direction of Germany's foreign economic policy. Erhard accepted the treaty only grudgingly. He would have preferred to explore Britain's alternative proposal for a wider free trade area limited to industrial products. Erhard never forgave Adenauer for deferring to France. This opened a chasm within the ruling Christian Democratic Party that eventually cost Adenauer the chancellorship of Germany.

Much is made of Monnet's contribution to the treaty's ratification, especially in Germany. According to this line of thought, the membership of prominent German Social Democrats in Monnet's Action Committee helped reconcile the Social Democratic Party to the EC and undermine potential opposition to the treaty in the German parliament.[60] Undoubtedly membership in the Action Committee brought German Social Democrats into contact with supporters of European integration in neighboring countries. But German Social Democrats had tempered their ideological opposition to European integration before Monnet launched his committee in October 1955, and developments in East-West relations in the mid-1950s meant that further European integration would have little immediate bearing on the division of Germany, an issue close to the hearts of many Social Democrats.

Ratification of the treaty in France and Germany presaged swift ratification in the other prospective EC member states. There was a flurry of activity in late 1957 to prepare for the Community's launch in January 1958. One of the most important decisions still to be taken was where to locate the EC's institutions. Luxembourg, home of the High Authority, the assembly's secretariat, and the Court of Justice, was bursting at the seams. Having convened both the intergovernmental committee and the subsequent conference in Brussels, member states decided without much demur to locate the Commission there. In addition to hosting the World's Fair in 1958, Brussels became the headquarters of the new Communities. Memories of the World's Fair soon faded, but playing host to the EC saved Brussels, the declining capital of a declining country, from relative obscurity.

A more crucial political decision was the selection of the Commission's first president. As France, a big country, had the presidency of the High Authority, by common consent it was the turn of a small member state to nominate the Commission president. Belgium, the unofficial leader of the Benelux countries, chose instead to host the Commission in Brussels. That put the ball back in Germany's court. Hallstein seemed a natural choice. A confidant of Adenauer's, he was steeped in the workings of the ECSC and in the negotiations that led to the EC.

Yet the choice of Hallstein was unfortunate. Despite having held high government positions, he had never held elective office. As Commission president Hallstein personified the new institution's lack of direct accountability. Hallstein saw himself and the Commission primarily in political terms. A zealous federalist, he set out to put the EC politically on the map. That ran counter to most member states' view of the organization and set him on a collision course with de Gaulle, who became leader of France soon after the Community came into existence. The unequal struggle between de Gaulle and Hallstein personified the unequal struggle between intergovernmentalism and supranationalism in the development of the European Community in the decade ahead.

▨ Notes

1. As Dutch foreign minister Dirk Stikker observed, these were irreverently called "The St. Pee-Pee Plans." Stikker, *Men of Responsibility* (New York: Harper and Row, 1965), p. 188.

2. Alan S. Milward, *The UK and the European Community*, Vol. 1: *The Rise and Fall of a National Strategy, 1945–1963* (London: Whitehall History Publishing in association with Frank Cass, 2002), p. 75. On Britain's response to the Schuman Declaration, see ibid., pp. 48–77; Edmund Dell, *The Schuman Plan and the British Abdication of Leadership in Europe* (Oxford: Oxford University Press, 1995); G. Warner, "The Labour Governments and the Unity of Western Europe," in *The Foreign Policy of the Labour Governments, 1945–51*, ed. R. Ovendale (Leicester: Leicester University Press, 1984); Christopher Lord, *Absent at the Creation: Britain and the Formation of the European Community, 1950–1952* (Aldershot: Dartmouth, 1996).

3. Quoted in Dirk Spierenburg and Raymond Poidevin, *The History of the High Authority of the European Coal and Steel Community: Supranationality in Operation* (London: Weidenfeld and Nicolson, 1994), p. 17.

4. Dell, *Schuman Plan*, p. 4.

5. Ibid., p. viii.

6. Hugo Young, *This Blessed Plot: Britain and Europe from Churchill to Blair* (Woodstock: Overlook Press, 1999), p. 69.

7. William Hitchcock, *France Restored: Cold War Diplomacy and the Quest for Leadership in Europe, 1944–1954* (Chapel Hill: University of North Carolina Press, 1998), p. 129.

8. Michael Hogan, *The Marshall Plan: America, Britain, and the Reconstruction of Western Europe, 1947–1952* (Cambridge: Cambridge University Press, 1987), p. 367.

9. See Alan Milward, *The Reconstruction of Western Europe, 1945–1951* (Berkeley: University of California Press, 1984), pp. 405–406.

10. On the negotiations that resulted in the European Coal and Steel Community, see John Gillingham, *Coal, Steel and the Rebirth of Europe, 1945–1955* (Cambridge: Cambridge University Press, 1991); Klaus Schwabe, ed., *Die Anfänge des Schuman-Plans, 1950–1951* (Baden-Baden: Nomos, 1988); Raymond Poidevin, *Robert Schuman, Homme d'État, 1886–1963* (Paris: Imprimerie nationale, 1986), pp. 240–274; François Duchêne, *Jean Monnet: The First Statesman of Interdependence* (New York: Norton, 1994), pp. 207–220; Milward, *Reconstruction*, pp. 397–420; Hans-Peter Schwarz, *Konrad Adenauer: A German Politician and Statesman in a Period of War, Revolution and Reconstruction*, Vol. 1: *From the German Empire to the Federal Republic, 1876–1952* (Oxford: Berghahn Books, 1995); Hitchcock, *France Restored*.

11. Alan Milward, *The European Rescue of the Nation-State*, 2nd ed. (London: Routledge, 2000), pp. 82–83.

12. On the institutional architecture of the ECSC, see Paul Reuter, *La Communauté européenne du charbon et de l'acier* (Paris: Librairie général du droit et de la jurisprudence, 1953).

13. On the Dutch position, see Albert Kersten, "A Welcome Surprise? The Netherlands and the Schuman Plan Negotiations," in Schwabe, *Anfänge*.

14. Schwarz, *Adenauer*, Vol. 1, p. 613.

15. On the Belgian case specifically, see Milward, *Rescue*, pp. 64–83; M. Dumoulin, "La Belgique et les débuts du Plan Schuman (mai 1950–février 1952)," in Schwabe, *Anfänge*.

16. On the deconcentration issue, see Gillingham, *Rebirth of Europe*, pp. 255–262, 266–281; A. W. Lovett, "The United States and the Schuman Plan: A Study in French Diplomacy, 1950–1952," *The Historical Journal* 39, no. 2 (1996), pp. 425–455; Thomas Alan Schwartz, *America's Germany: John J. McCloy and the Federal Republic of Germany* (Cambridge: Cambridge University Press, 1991); and Matthias Kipping, *Zwischen Kartellen und Konkurrenz: Der Schuman-Plan und die Ursprünge der Europäischen Einigung, 1944–1952* (Berlin: Duncker and Humblot, 1996).

17. De Gasperi was also a fluent German speaker. Stikker tells the story of de Gasperi's first meeting with Schuman, in Paris. "As the Italian, who had been, just before the First World War, a member of the Austrian Parliament, struggled along in his heavily accented French, [Schuman], educated in Imperial Germany, spoke to him in German. 'Shall we try it in the mother tongue?' asked Schuman." Stikker, *Men of Responsibility*, p. 306.

18. Ibid., pp. 304–305.

19. See, for instance, Alan Kramer, *The West German Economy, 1945–1955* (New York: Berg, 1991).

20. William Diebold Jr., *The Schuman Plan: A Study in Economic Cooperation, 1950–1959* (New York: Praeger, 1959); Ernst Haas, *The Uniting of Europe: Political, Social and Economic Forces, 1950–1957* (Stanford, CA: Stanford University Press, 1958); and Hans A. Schmidt, *The Path to European Union: From the Marshall Plan to the Common Market* (Baton Rouge: Louisiana State University Press, 1962).

21. See Gillingham, *Rebirth of Europe*, p. ix.

22. Duchêne, *Monnet*, p. 214.

23. Robert Marjolin, *Memoirs, 1911–1986: Architect of European Unity* (London: Weidenfeld and Nicolson, 1986), p. 273.

24. Milward, *Reconstruction*, p. 418.

25. Gillingham, *Rebirth of Europe*, pp. 297–298.

26. Quoted in F. Roy Willis, *France, Germany and the New Europe, 1945–1963* (Stanford, CA: Stanford University Press, 1965), p. 130.

27. See Schwarz, *Adenauer*, Vol. 1, p. 522.

28. For an account of the EDC initiative and negotiations, see Edward Fursdon, *The European Defense Community: A History* (New York: St. Martin's Press, 1980); Hitchcock, *France Restored*, pp. 133–202; Daniel Lerner and Raymond Aron, eds., *France Defeats the EDC* (New York: Praeger, 1957); Kevin Ruane, *The Rise and Fall of the European Defense Community: Anglo-American Relations and the Crisis of European Defense, 1950–1955* (Basingstoke: Macmillan, 2000); Irwin M. Wall, *The United States and the Making of Post-War France, 1945–1954* (Cambridge: Cambridge University Press, 1991), pp. 263–274; David Clay Large, *Germans to the Front: West German Rearmament in the Adenauer Era* (Chapel Hill: University of North Carolina Press, 1996); Saki Dockrill, *Britain's Policy for West German Rearmament, 1950–1955* (Cambridge, Cambridge University Press, 1991).

29. On Britain and the EDC, see Milward, *UK and the European Community*, Vol. 1, pp. 78–125.

30. Schwarz, *Adenauer*, Vol. 1, p. 652.

31. Jean Lacouture, *Pierre Mendès-France* (New York: Holmes and Meier, 1984), p. 268.

32. Charles de Gaulle, *Mémoires d'Espoir, suivi d'un choix d'allocutions et messages sur la IVe et la Ve Républiques* (Paris: Plon, 1994), p. 564.

33. The quotations are from Nathan Leites and Christian de la Malene, "Paris from EDC to WEU," *World Politics* 9, no. 2 (January 1957), pp. 193–219.

34. Lacouture, *Mendès-France,* p. 278.

35. See Fursdon, *European Defense Community,* p. 86.

36. On the Political Community, see Richard T. Griffiths, "Europe's First Constitution: The European Political Community, 1952–1954," in *The Construction of Europe,* ed. S. Martin (Dordrecht: Kluwer, 1994), pp. 19–39.

37. These quotations are from Herbert W. Briggs, "The Proposed European Political Community," *The American Journal of International Law* 48, no. 1 (January 1955), pp. 110–122.

38. Quoted in Lacouture, *Mendès-France*, p. 279.

39. Alfred Grosser, "France and Germany: A Confrontation," in Lerner and Aron, *France Defeats the EDC*, pp. 54–70.

40. Andrew Moravcsik, *The Choice for Europe: Social Purpose and State Power from Messina to Maastricht* (Ithaca, NY: Cornell University Press, 1998), p. 86.

41. Spierenburg and Poidevin, *History of the High Authority*, pp. 228–229.

42. See Schwarz, *Adenauer*, Vol. 2, pp. 243–245.

43. See Richard T. Griffiths, "The Beyen Plan," in *The Netherlands and the Integration of Europe, 1945–1957* (Amsterdam: NEHA, 1990), pp. 165–182.

44. See Wendy Asbeek Brusse, *Tariffs, Trade and European Integration, 1947–1957: From Study Group to Common Market* (New York: St. Martin's Press, 1997), pp. 143–184.

45. Werner Abelshauer, "Integration à la Carte: The Primacy of Politics and the Integration of Europe in the 1950s," in *The Construction of Europe*, ed. S. Martin (Dordrecht: Kluwer, 1994), pp. 17–18.

46. John Gunther, author of a popular book on Western Europe, pointed out that Euratom is pronounced "You're at 'em." John Gunther, *Inside Europe Today* (New York: Harper and Brothers, 1961), p. 263.

47. Messina Declaration, available at http://www.let.leidenuniv.nl/history/rtg/res1/messina.htm.

48. See Walter Yondorf, "Monnet and the Action Committee: The Formative Years of the European Communities," *International Organization* 19 (1965), pp. 885–912; Duchêne, *Monnet*, pp. 285–308; and Pascal Fontaine, *Le Comité d'Action pour les États Unis d'Europe de Jean Monnet* (Lausanne: Centre de Recherches Européennes, 1974).

49. See Moravcsik, *Choice for Europe*, pp. 142–144.

50. Ibid., p. 122. On Britain's decision not to join the European Community, see Milward, *UK and the European Community*, Vol. 1, pp. 177–264.

51. Moravcsik, *Choice for Europe*, p. 129.

52. On the Spaak committee and the subsequent intergovernmental conference, see Pierre-Henri Laurent, "Paul-Henri Spaak and the Diplomatic Origins of the Common Market, 1955–1956," *Political Science Quarterly* 85, no. 3 (September 1970), pp. 373–396; Moravcsik, *Choice for Europe*, pp. 86–158; Jeffrey Glen Giauque, *Grand Designs and Visions of Unity: The Atlantic Powers and the Reorganization of Western Europe, 1955–1963* (Chapel Hill: University of North Carolina Press, 2002), pp. 23–33; Enrico Serra, ed., *Il Rilancio dell'Europa e i Trattati di Roma* (Brussels: Bruylant, 1989); Anne Deighton, ed., *Building Postwar Europe: National Decision-Makers and European Institutions, 1948–1963* (New York: St. Martin's Press, 1995); H. J. Eversen and Hans Sperl, *Répertoire de la jurisprudence relative aux traités instituants les Communautés européennes, 1953–1962* (Cologne: C. Heymanns Verlag, 1965); Frances M.B. Lynch, *France and the International Economy: From Vichy to the Treaty of Rome* (London: Routledge, 1997); H. J. Küsters, *Die Gründung der europäischen Wirtschaftsgemeinschaft* (Baden-Baden: Nomos, 1982).

53. See, for instance, Hans Jurgen Küsters, "The Treaties of Rome," in *The Dynamics of European Integration,* ed. Roy Pryce (London: Croom Helm, 1987), pp. 90–91.

54. On Mollet's pivotal role, see Craig Parsons, "Showing Ideas as Causes: The Origins of the European Union," *International Organization* 56, no. 1 (2002), pp. 47–84.

55. Uwe Kitzinger, "Europe: The Six and the Seven," *International Organization* 14, no. 1 (Winter, 1960), p. 28.

56. Marjolin, *Memoirs,* pp. 284–297.

57. Rome Treaty, text available at http://www.europa.eu.int/abc/obj/treaties/en/entoc05.htm.

58. Ibid.

59. Ibid.

60. See, for instance, Yondorf, "Action Committee," pp. 900–905.

3

Constructing the European Community

The year 1958 was noteworthy in Europe not for the birth of the European Community but for two major political crises. One centered on Berlin, the other on Paris. Soviet president Nikita Khrushchev provoked the Berlin crisis by issuing an ultimatum to the three Western occupying powers demanding a change in the city's status. Khrushchev's efforts to oust the Western allies from Berlin, an anomalous enclave of Four Power control deep inside East Germany, culminated in the Cuban missile crisis in 1962, which resulted almost in nuclear war. The Berlin and Cuban crises, as well as crises in the Middle East and the Straits of Taiwan, caused a sharp drop in the temperature of the Cold War and dominated international affairs in the EC's early years.

The French crisis was less far reaching in its international implications but had more impact on the EC. Only five months after the launch of the Community, the French army mutinied in Algiers and threatened to overthrow the government in Paris. That brought the unloved Fourth Republic to an ignominious end. Reluctantly the French parliament granted Charles de Gaulle, who had resigned as leader of the first postwar government in 1946 and lived in self-imposed political exile ever since, extraordinary power to rule unopposed for six months while drafting a new constitution. A large majority of the French electorate endorsed the constitution, with its presidential system of government, in September 1958. De Gaulle duly became president. He resigned in 1969 following widespread student and worker protests the previous year against the conservatism that he personified.

De Gaulle could have wrecked the EC at the outset. Instead he saved it not only by rescuing France in the late 1950s but also by fending off a British proposal for a rival free trade area and by sticking to the schedule for implementation of the customs union in the 1960s. The EC offered a means to achieve key French economic objectives: industrial modernization and agricultural subsidization. De Gaulle also saw the EC as a possible foundation for a Europe independent of the United States, stretching, in his famous phrase, from the Atlantic to the Urals (in western Russia). Britain's attachment to the United States and opposition to the emerging agricultural regime disqualified the country, in de Gaulle's mind, from joining the EC. Hence his celebrated vetoes of Britain's membership applications in 1963 and 1967.

The 1960s was a good time to establish the EC. Gorging on cheap oil imports and engaging in greater international trade, Western Europe enjoyed high employment, low inflation, and unprecedented economic growth. In such a benign economic climate, member states completed the customs union in 1968, eighteen months ahead of schedule. Storm clouds gathered as the inflationary impact of the Vietnam War hastened the end of the Bretton Woods international financial system and Arab oil-producing countries began to flex their political muscles. Détente broke out in East-West relations in the mid-1960s and survived the shock of the Soviet intervention in Czechoslovakia in 1968. Yet de Gaulle's efforts to alter the Atlantic alliance and end the Cold War ultimately came to naught.

De Gaulle had a more profound political impact on the EC than on the wider international system. An avowed intergovernmentalist, in 1965 he challenged the EC's supranationalist ethos by withdrawing French representation in the Council of Ministers, hoping to force other member states to curb the use of qualified majority voting. The ensuing constitutional crisis ended with an agreement not to call a vote in the Council when a member state claimed that important national interests were at stake, thereby enshrining the right to veto. The outcome of the crisis, including the weakening of the Commission's political authority, tilted decisionmaking in the Community firmly toward intergovernmentalism.

This chapter examines the EC's early development, in the shadow of de Gaulle. The record was mixed. By the end of the 1960s the customs union and the common agricultural policy (CAP) were in place, although member states had not yet negotiated a permanent funding mechanism to cover agricultural expenditure. Despite de Gaulle's successful assault against qualified majority voting, supranationalism survived in other areas. In one of the most striking developments of the decade, the European Court issued a number of key rulings that buttressed the supranational character of the Community.

▓ Setting Up Shop

The European Commission set up shop in Brussels in January 1958, in nondescript offices in the appropriately named Avenue de la Joyeuse Entrée. Walter Hallstein presided over a college of nine commissioners, two each from France, Germany, and Italy and one each from the Benelux countries. The number of commissioners matched the Community's range of responsibilities, so that each member had a weighty portfolio to manage. Most of the commissioners were either "political officials" (like Hallstein) or senior politicians. All had participated in various European initiatives and knew each other reasonably well.

© CE/Jamar, Marcelle, Audiovisual Library European Commission

A meeting of the Hallstein Commission in 1964.

The Hallstein Commission is generally seen in a glowing light. Its stature, compatibility, and competence are rarely questioned. Even before the Commission imploded during the constitutional crisis of 1965–1966, however, stresses and strains were evident in the college. A workaholic, Hallstein was austere and aloof. Nobody doubted his commitment to the Community, knowledge of the treaty, or experience of European integration. Nobody doubted either that he was cold and lacked charisma. He was a good chairman but a poor chief. Hoping to cultivate a presidential style of leadership, he kept a greater distance from his colleagues and staff than would otherwise have been the case. Unmarried, he lived alone and rarely entertained. A minority of fellow commissioners shared Hallstein's fervent Eurofederalism. The rest knew that economic integration was a political endeavor but were not ideologically motivated.

As with any group of ambitious individuals, there were resentments and bureaucratic rivalries among the commissioners. Member states allocated portfolios on the basis of perceived national interests rather than the commissioners' abilities and experience. Some commissioners were unhappy with their lot; others were well suited to their portfolios. All fought for resources, which Hallstein allocated on the basis not of immediate needs but of the Community's anticipated activities. As a result, some busy departments were short of staff while others, not yet fully operational, were overstaffed.

Commissioners formed *cabinets* (private offices) and adopted other French administrative practices. Sensitive about being German, Hallstein tried hard to be French. The Commission's location in Brussels reinforced the use of the French language (it would have been politically incorrect to use German so soon after the war), and the appointment as secretary general of Emile Nöel, a senior French official, reinforced the use of French administrative norms. Commissioners met as a college once a week for an all-day session, prepared by their *chefs de cabinet*. The Commission established directorates-general (departments) corresponding to its main tasks and activities; directorates-general in turn spawned directorates and divisions.[1]

Hallstein took responsibility for administrative affairs in the first Commission. Remembering the mess that Monnet had made of setting up the High Authority, Hallstein put his managerial experience in the German foreign office to good use. Unlike the High Authority, which had its own funds and immediate objectives to achieve, initially the Commission depended on the Council for money and had a more relaxed timetable for implementing the EC's main objectives.

Hallstein had a hand in the appointment of most of the Commission's early recruits, at least at the professional (administrative) level. He wanted a meritocracy but appreciated the political constraints on recruitment and promotion in an international organization. With commissioners appointed on the basis of national affiliation, it would have been impossible to keep the Commission staff entirely free of national quotas, however informal. Fortunately the high quality of applicants meant that proportional representation did not impair job performance. Hallstein failed to prevent the establishment of national fiefdoms within the Commission, an almost inevitable by-product of national quotas and often encouraged by national governments. The most striking example was the lock that France established on the agriculture directorate general.

Many of the Commission's staff (the Eurocrats) came from national civil services; others came from the High Authority or straight from university (or from the College of Europe in Bruges). Idealism, adventure, and high remuneration attracted them. Initially there was little job security. The EC was a risky career choice. It looked in 1958 as if the Community might not last long, first because of the constitutional crisis in France and then because of de Gaulle's hostility to supranationalism. Those who joined the Commission from national bureaucracies kept a right of return to their old jobs.

Despite initial uncertainty about the Commission's future, most of the pioneering Eurocrats looked back nostalgically on their first years of service. They lived a privileged life in Brussels, with high salaries, generous allowances, and distinctive license plates. They enjoyed working and socializing in an international milieu. As an early observer later recalled, "The Commission staff didn't just speak several languages; they joked in them, fought in them, made love in them. Speaking of making love, there were lots of European marriages in the early years. Germans married Italians and their children's first language was French. In the backyards of the suburbs surrounding Brussels lived a polyglot of people who were literally married to the European idea."[2]

The Commission introduced legislative proposals, took various policy initiatives, and became a lobbyist for further integration. The Commission came under attack in its early years from Wilhelm Röpke and other leading members of the conservative Mont Pèlerin Society (organized by Friedrich Hayek, the famous German liberal economist). Röpke characterized the Commission as evil incarnate: namely, the institutionalization of state intervention at the European level. The EC, he claimed, was inherently protectionist. It would reverse the trend toward global liberalization and impose a planned economy on Europe.[3] By its nature the Commission was indeed more interventionist than liberal, but interventionist in the cause of the social-market economy. As the Commission remarked in its first action plan, "an economic order based on freedom can only exist in the world of today at the price of constant state intervention in economic life."[4] The liberal economists' fears of the common market were unfounded, except in the case of the CAP, although their onslaught may have helped to counteract a tendency in the Commission toward undue involvement in other policy areas.[5]

The Council and the Committee of Permanent Representatives

The Council came into existence in the form of the Interim Committee even before the formal launch of the Community. The Interim Committee met in late 1957 to consider the Community's approach to the General Agreement on Tariffs and Trade (GATT) and to negotiations then in progress for a wider European free trade area. The Council proper held its first meeting in early January 1958, in Brussels, under the presidency of Belgium (the presidency rotated every six months in alphabetical order of the member states' official names, in their own language). The presidency's role was ill defined; at first it consisted mostly of chairing meetings. A small Council secretariat, recruited from national civil services but independent of national governments, served the presidency. Initially there were few Council formations (such as the foreign ministers or agriculture ministers), reflecting the Community's relatively limited competence. Foreign ministers (forming the General Affairs Council) met most frequently (only once a month). Originally the Council met in the new Palais de Congres before moving in the late 1960s to the Charlemagne building at Schuman Circle, a traffic roundabout at the heart of the new Community district.

Because of the need for continuity in relations between the Council and the Commission, national governments availed themselves of a provision in the treaty to establish a Committee of Permanent Representatives, made up of their most senior officials (at ambassador level). The committee, known by its French acronym Coreper, met weekly to exchange national positions on Commission proposals and prepare Council meetings. The permanent representatives became key intermediaries between the Council and the Commission as well as between national governments and the Community. They spent the working week in Brussels promoting national positions and weekends in national capitals explaining Community developments. Each permanent representative headed an office, the Permanent Representation, staffed by officials from relevant national ministries. By the early 1960s large member states had staffs of forty or fifty officials in their Permanent Representations.

At first the Commission resented Coreper's existence. Commissioners wanted to deal with national ministers, not ambassadors. They feared, correctly, that Coreper would usurp some of the Council's decisionmaking authority. Because Coreper quickly became "one of the most important cogs in the Community machinery" and in effect an unofficial Council configuration, the Commission had little choice but to come to terms with it.[6] Commissioners soon swallowed their pride and attended Coreper meetings in order to explain and defend the Commission's positions.

The history of the EC is really a history of meetings: meetings of the Commission, the Council, and Coreper; meetings of Council working groups, composed of national and Commission officials; meetings within the Commission of heads of divisions, directors, directors-general, *cabinet* members, and *chefs de cabinet*; meetings of national experts and Commission officials to discuss Commission ideas in the preproposal stage; meetings of officials and ministers in national capitals to consider Community developments; meetings among lobbyists and national and Community officials; and bilateral or multilateral meetings of ministers and national officials, often on the margins of other international meetings, to discuss Community affairs. As the Community consolidated its position in the early 1960s, the number and importance of these meetings grew proportionately.

The European Parliament

The history of the EC also included meetings of the European Parliament, ranging from plenary sessions, to committee meetings, to meetings of Parliament officials, as well as the participation of Europarliamentarians and parliamentary officials in meetings with representatives of other Community institutions, national governments, and interest groups. Initially the Parliament was relatively unimportant. It had little legislative authority, and its ability to dismiss the Commission, by a two-thirds majority, was as unusable as a nuclear weapon. Officially called the European Parliamentary Assembly, it was a combined institution of the Coal and Steel Community, Euratom, and the EC and had 142 members appointed by national governments from national parliaments (holders of the so-called dual mandate). The Rome Treaty obliged the Parliament to meet only once a year, in October, to hear a report on the Commission's activities. Like the ECSC Assembly before it, the Parliament met in Strasbourg but held committee meetings in Brussels.

The Parliament attempted from the outset to assert itself and enhance its authority. It could, and did, meet more often than once a year. The Parliament held its first plenary session in March 1958, when members elected Robert Schuman president. In doing so they honored one of the EC's founding fathers and asserted their independence of the Council, which wanted to have an Italian elected president because France, Germany, and the Benelux countries held the presidencies of the executive bodies of the three communities.

Besides their willingness to confront national governments, parliamentarians sent a number of important signals during their first plenary session. One was a determination to press for direct elections, which the treaty provided for subject to a unanimous decision of the Council. Another was an interest in the Community's everyday affairs. Despite its limited legislative role (the Council had to consult the Parliament in a small number of areas), the Parliament established committees along functional lines to report on Commission proposals and Council decisions. The Commission indicated at the Parliament's first plenary session that it viewed the Parliament as an institutional ally and a potential source of legitimacy.[7]

■ Implementing the Customs Union and Fending Off the Free Trade Area

Taking the first step toward implementing the customs union—reducing intra-Community tariffs by 10 percent and increasing quotas by 20 percent in January 1959—assumed greater political than technical importance as the deadline approached. Would the new French government stick to the treaty timetable or, by letting the deadline slip, signal its lack of interest in the Community? Other national leaders, as well as the Commission, presumed that because de Gaulle disdained supranationalism he also disdained the EC. Yet de Gaulle's economic and financial reforms since coming to office in June 1958 put France in a position materially to meet the January 1959 deadline. Indeed, domestic reform and external liberalization were inextricably linked in de Gaulle's approach toward economic modernization. Much to the relief of its EC partners, France announced in late October 1958 that it would honor the treaty timetable.[8]

That approach was fully in accord with de Gaulle's long-time goal of revitalizing the French economy. Just as he had promoted Monnet, a supranationalist, to head the office for economic modernization in 1945, de Gaulle embraced the EC, a supranational organization, as the best means of pulling the French economy into the late twentieth century. Despite their supranationalist trappings, both Monnet and the EC offered something that France needed at the time and could not get elsewhere.

The other member states remained leery of France. The legalistic nature of the French announcement that it would honor the treaty suggested that de Gaulle was merely meeting an obligation, not fully embracing trade liberalization. The true test of de Gaulle's attitude would be his approach to the negotiations then taking place between the EC and the other members of the Organization for European Economic Cooperation (OEEC) to establish a free trade area. By pursuing a larger free trade area, de Gaulle could kill the EC without breaking any treaty obligations; by killing the free trade proposal, de Gaulle could demonstrate his commitment to the EC on more than legal grounds.

Britain launched the idea of a free trade area in the mid-1950s. Fearing that the EC would cause a drop in exports to the Continent, British industry wanted a free trade area at almost any cost. Britain hoped that the idea would lure Germany and the Netherlands, with their lower tariffs and higher volumes of trade, away from the prospective EC.[9] But Britain underestimated the economic and political appeal to the Six of a common market as opposed to a free trade area. With the imminent conclusion of the Rome Treaty, Britain proposed that the free trade area include the EC as a bloc. The least charitable view of Britain's intention, prevalent among the Six, was that having failed to thwart agreement on the Rome Treaty with its initial proposal, Britain now wanted to subsume the EC into a wider free trade area. Led by Britain, the non-EC members of the OEEC pressed for a free trade agreement by December 1958, the eve of the EC's first tariff cuts and quota increases. Otherwise, they argued, the EC's action would discriminate against them.

Regardless of the proposal's merits, each side distrusted the other. Reginald Maudling, the British minister responsible for achieving the free trade area, stoked further suspicion by trying to undermine solidarity among the Six. On a visit to EC capitals, Maudling got a warm welcome in Bonn from economics minister Erhard, a long-time proponent of a free trade area, and in The Hague from a government instinctively sympathetic toward Britain.

Maudling got a frosty reception in Paris. France had already implicitly rejected a free trade area in favor of a common market among the Six with safeguards for sensitive French interests. Why should France now accept a wider free trade area at the risk of jeopardizing the EC? An agreement acceptable to France would require broad policy coordination, strong institutions, and common rules. It would also have to include a special regime for agriculture, which Britain opposed.

To Britain's dismay, the Six maintained a united front in late 1957 and early 1958 within the ministerial committee of the OEEC charged with bringing the free trade area about. Everything came to a halt in April when the French Fourth Republic effectively ceased to function. The ministerial committee did not meet again until July, after de Gaulle's return to power. The British then put their hopes in de Gaulle's well-known aversion to European integration. Instead, de Gaulle chose to implement the common market and end the free trade area negotiations. His decision made domestic political sense. As Miriam Camps observed at the time, "the opposition of French industry to a free trade area was fierce and articulate. . . . Virtually no one in France saw any appreciable economic advantage in the arrangement."[10]

Adenauer resisted pressure from Erhard to keep negotiating with Britain and sided with de Gaulle at their crucial first meeting, in September 1958. Two months later the French government announced its intention of ending the negotiations. The Council of Ministers endorsed what became a Franco-German position at a meeting in Brussels in early December. Here was an early example in EC history of the Franco-German axis at work.[11] Paradoxically it was Erhard, the advocate of a free trade agreement, who informed the British officially of the EC's decision (Germany was then in the Council presidency). The British were furious and refused to let the matter drop. A meeting of the OEEC Council in December 1958 ended in acrimonious exchanges between the British and French ministers.

British prime minister Harold Macmillan told the U.S. administration in October that, rather than accept defeat of the free trade area, "the UK would organize a counter movement of their own and would have to reevaluate her position in NATO."[12] The British followed through on the diplomatic and economic front in early 1959 by inviting six other non-EC Western European countries (Austria, Denmark, Norway, Portugal, Sweden, and Switzerland) to open negotiations to establish a rival trade bloc, the European Free Trade Association (EFTA). The proposed association would not benefit Britain greatly, as Britain's economy dwarfed those of the other prospective EFTA members and Scandinavian tariffs were already low. The main purpose of EFTA was to increase pressure on the EC to reopen negotiations for a free trade area. Britain hoped that the United States, concerned about a Europe "at Sixes and Sevens" (six EC members and seven prospective EFTA members) would twist the EC's arm.

The United States disliked the idea of EFTA, which was much less advantageous economically than the EC. A common market had the potential for greater trade not only among EC member states but also between them and the United States. EU trade creation, the Americans thought, would far outweigh trade diversion. The United States also strongly supported the EC for political reasons: it might help to anchor West Germany in Western Europe, strengthen Western Europe's ability to withstand Communist subversion and Soviet pressure, and stand shoulder to shoulder with the United States in a strong transatlantic community.[13]

The Six Member States and the EFTA Seven

Yet the United States was reluctant publicly to oppose EFTA. Only when negotiations to establish the new organization intensified did Washington lose patience with London. The United States held that a liberal Community trade policy and a successful round of GATT negotiations were the best solutions for all concerned. France, Germany, and the United States were in complete agreement. Even Erhard, impressed by the EC's liberal orientation in trade policy and by U.S. support for the EC, abandoned his initial support for a free trade area.

The United States finally took a stand at the end of 1959. Domestic pressure from business interests concerned about EFTA's emergence and about a possible proliferation of regional free trade areas around the world forced the administration to act. The State Department hatched a plan to transform the OEEC into a broader economic organization that would include the United States, Canada, and possibly Japan. As Secretary of State Christian Herter informed President Dwight Eisenhower in November 1959, this "would constitute an act of creative United States leadership in a recently deteriorating situation. It would greatly increase the opportunity of the United States to influence the makers of European economic policy in two directions—greater European development efforts and actions to compose European trade quarrels on a basis consistent with sound trade relations."[14] That was the genesis of the Organization for Economic Cooperation and Development (OECD), in which the proposal for a Western European–wide free trade area was finally buried.[15]

France and Germany readily accepted the U.S. proposal; Britain did so grudgingly. London held fast to the idea that the EC was a protectionist bloc that would liberalize only under pressure from EFTA. U.S. dealings with Britain on the EFTA issue remained strained well into 1960 (the OECD was established in December of that year). In the meantime, Macmillan warned again about the possible consequences of an EFTA-EC split for Western European security and threatened to withdraw British troops from Germany. A telegram to the State Department from the usually sympathetic U.S. Embassy in London lamented the increasing number of "exaggerated and emotional statements" by the prime minister on the EC, EFTA, and NATO.[16] Under the circumstances, Macmillan's about-face the following year, when Britain applied for EC membership, was truly remarkable.

The launch of the EC brought France, Germany, and the United States closer together on a range of economic issues and further alienated Britain. Fears about the impact of de Gaulle's return to power on the EC were so far unfounded. Despite France's reputation for economic protectionism and de Gaulle's hostility to supranationalism, the government of the new Fifth Republic had endorsed the EC's first tariff cuts and quota increases in 1959, opposed the free trade area, and supported a reasonably liberal EC commercial policy. As a result, the EC's prospects looked far brighter in 1960 than they had at the end of 1958.

Erhard remarked to the Americans in June 1959 that "the development of the [EC] had been more problematical under previous French governments, which had been under the influence of protectionist elements. Now, however, France was stronger politically and economically, as a result of which the Common Market had developed faster and more effectively than had been expected."[17] The development of the EC along lines congenial to Erhard, his U.S. interlocutors, and the traditionally protectionist French was due to a number of factors. Political stability allowed France to undertake economic and financial reforms but, as the U.S. Embassy noted in January 1959, "some lever was required to gear internal corrective measures to world conditions and competition. That lever was supplied by the Common Market and its convenient deadline of January 1, 1959 for action on quotas and tariffs." Implementing the common market, seeing off the free trade area, and supporting a liberal EC commercial policy, the Embassy observed, were clearly in the French national interest and were "*Gaulliste* in [the] fullest sense of the word."[18]

■ The Common Agricultural Policy

At French insistence, the Six agreed in principle in the Rome Treaty to establish a common agricultural policy. Thanks to generous national subsidies, by the late 1950s France produced more food than the country could consume. Governments could not afford to antagonize the powerful farm lobby by reducing subsidies that the national exchequer could ill afford to pay. De Gaulle's government was no exception.[19] France sought to export its agricultural surplus (a cheaper alternative to warehousing or destroying it), but subsidized French products were not competitive internationally. France therefore needed either export markets with guaranteed high prices or generous export subsidies to bridge the gap between higher French prices and lower international prices. France could get both through the CAP: an EC-wide market with guaranteed high prices *and* subsidies for exports outside the EC.

That set France on a collision course with two countries: Germany and the United States. Germany had fewer farmers than France (about 15 percent as opposed to 23 percent of the total population). Germany subsidized its farmers too, but German farmers could never produce enough to feed the entire German population. Consequently, Germany imported a lot of food. France longed to penetrate the German market, but French exports could not compete with cheaper exports from other countries, including the United States, which did not want to be excluded from Germany and other EC markets by a French-inspired CAP.

France also clashed with the Commission over agricultural policy. Vice President Sicco Mansholt, a former Dutch agriculture minister, headed the Commission's large and potentially powerful agriculture directorate-general.

Despite its commitment to a *common* agricultural policy, implying shared sovereignty and Commission supremacy, France and other member states were reluctant to relinquish responsibility for agriculture entirely to the Commission. At the instigation of France, member states set up a standing committee of national representatives in Brussels, the Special Committee on Agriculture, to deal with the Commission on the CAP. Unlike the permanent representatives, who reported to the foreign ministers and therefore had an ecumenical outlook on EC affairs, members of the agricultural committee reported to the agriculture ministers, a notoriously parochial group firmly under the thumb of national agricultural lobbies.

De Gaulle had to work with the Commission in order to realize the CAP (under the terms of the treaty the Commission proposed and implemented policy). But de Gaulle rejected supranationalism and distrusted Mansholt, an ardent Eurofederalist and an economic liberal (by prevailing European standards). That set the scene for a power struggle between France and the Commission over the CAP. Each side needed but distrusted the other.

De Gaulle made no secret of his paramount interest in the CAP. As he put it in his memoirs:

> I must say that if, on resuming control of affairs, I immediately embraced the Common Market, it was as much because of our position as an agricultural country as for the progress it would impose on our industry. To be sure, I was well aware that in order to include agriculture effectively within the Community, we would have to work vigorously with our partners, whose interests were not the same as ours in this domain. But I believed that this was, for France, a sine qua non of her participation. For, in a Community theoretically free of customs duties . . . where the fruits of the earth alone were denied free access, in a grouping of consumers where domestic agricultural products did not enjoy preferential treatment over those from outside, our agriculture would prove to be a burden that would relegate us, relative to the others, to a position of chronic inferiority. In order to impose on the Common Market, as its framework developed, what we considered necessary in this respect, we were thus obliged to put up a literally desperate fight.[20]

The desperate fight did not begin until 1960, when the Commission submitted a CAP proposal followed by various draft regulations on specific products. The challenge for the Commission was to devise Community-wide organizations of agricultural markets that would guarantee farmers a decent living but not generate excessive surpluses, cost too much, and alienate the Community's trading partners. It proved an impossible task. On the one hand, the Commission wanted to base the CAP as much as possible on free market principles; on the other, the Commission endorsed market intervention, including fixed prices and guaranteed sales for basic products and a system of variable levies on agricultural imports based on the difference between lower world prices and higher Community prices. The cost of the CAP would depend to a great extent on who set the price levels. Being susceptible to pressure from farmers, the Council would likely set high prices; less susceptible to such pressure, the Commission would likely set lower prices. As a compromise, the Commission proposed that the Council set general price guidelines within which the Commission would determine precise prices per product.[21]

France pushed for an interventionist CAP with a greater role for the Council than the Commission wanted. Germany was divided on the issue. Erhard and other economic liberals protested that the proposed CAP was too protectionist; the agriculture ministry and farm lobby protested that it was not protectionist enough and would lower German farm incomes. Prevailing prices in Germany were higher than in France but were too high to be adopted on a Community-wide basis. De Gaulle raised the stakes by announcing in June 1961 that France would block transition to the second stage of the customs union at the end of 1961 unless member states reached agreement on the CAP by that time.[22] De Gaulle also impressed upon Adenauer the importance of the CAP for harmonious Franco-German relations, one of the chancellor's key foreign policy objectives.

A series of legendary Council meetings ensued between mid-December 1961 and mid-January 1962. Technically they ended successfully at midnight on December 31, thereby allowing progress on the common market. The agricultural negotiations were really between France and Germany, whose representatives often met separately on the margins of the Council before presenting their colleagues with a fait accompli. Germany went along with France for the sake of the industrial customs union (a greater economic prize for Germany than an agricultural common market) and good Franco-German relations (an overriding strategic objective). According to an academic assessment,

> The outcome of the conflict represented a considerable victory for France, not only vis-à-vis Germany, which became the principal financial contributor to the CAP, but also vis-à-vis the Commission, whose competences, compared with its original proposals, were reduced to a minimum to the benefit of the Council. Like the German government . . . the Commission accepted the CAP as the price to be paid for further integration.[23]

The United States also acquiesced in the CAP for the sake of further European integration, over the objections of U.S. farmers and their political supporters, who feared being shut out of the lucrative European market. The issue became increasingly acrimonious as the CAP was put in place. Karl Brandt, of the U.S. Council of Economic Advisers, warned in September 1960 that

> the EEC must refrain from agricultural autarky. . . . De Gaulle has given in to the rioting French farm organizations . . . the situation is extremely dangerous because it is politically most difficult to unlodge the agricultural

interests from their new protectionist position in the EEC once they have entrenched themselves in it. . . . The European farm organizations, particularly in France and Germany, are past masters in the riot techniques and all sorts of revolutionary pressure tactics.[24]

Brandt wanted the United States to end its "kid-glove tactfulness" and apply all possible pressure on the Europeans to abandon the CAP. On his return from a trip to Europe in November 1962, Agriculture Secretary Orville Freeman complained bitterly about the CAP to President John Kennedy, lamenting that "the French are intractable."[25]

The situation was especially embarrassing for the U.S. administration as it promoted the Trade Expansion Act in 1962. Although the administration touted the act as a means of dealing with the economic challenge of the EC by enhancing the president's authority to negotiate trade agreements, it accepted the implementation in Europe of a trade-distorting CAP. The United States had little choice but to sacrifice economic goals for political ends. William Diebold, a trade specialist who observed the construction of the CAP, reminisced years later that there was "much sweet reason in what American officials said to their European colleagues [about the discriminatory aspects of the CAP], but the situation was thought to be delicate and there were [limits] to what the Americans were willing to do as they accepted the argument that a common agricultural policy was essential to the integration of the Community."[26]

The "Chicken War" of 1962–1963 set a pattern for transatlantic trade relations in the context of the CAP and allowed the administration to appease some of its domestic critics. The dispute erupted in July 1962 when the EC's import regime for poultry came into effect. Whereas U.S. exporters had previously faced a German tariff equivalent to about 4.5 cents per pound, they now faced an EC import fee of about 13.5 cents per pound. The increase caused an immediate drop in U.S. sales, sending farmers and politicians on the warpath. Although poultry exports to Germany represented a fraction of overall U.S.-EC trade, the dispute generated considerable publicity. Hostilities ended when both sides accepted the opinion of a special GATT panel, delivered in November 1963, that upheld U.S. complaints but recommended less compensation than the United States demanded. The EC tacitly acknowledged that the poultry regime, and the CAP in general, was discriminatory; the United States lost market share but won some compensation; and agricultural disputes became a fact of life in a U.S.-EC relationship driven by broader political and economic interests.[27]

▓ The CAP, British Accession, and Grand Designs

Agriculture, Britain's application for EC membership, and contending designs for Europe's future combined to produce the first crisis in the EC's history when de Gaulle vetoed Britain's application in January 1963. In a remarkable change of policy toward the Community, Britain applied to join in August 1961. Britain needed easy access to Western European markets and could get it only by entering the EC. Neither the Commonwealth nor EFTA was an adequate alternative. Sensitive to domestic concerns about possible loss of sovereignty, Macmillan played down the political implications of accession, treating it as an exclusively economic affair.[28]

Britain's application coincided with the launch by the new Kennedy administration of a Grand Design for transatlantic relations. Under the direction of Undersecretary of State George Ball, an old friend of Jean Monnet's, the United States sought to organize transatlantic relations along more equitable lines in order to mollify Europeans' resentment of its preponderant power and strengthen the alliance's political cohesion. Thus the United States wanted a strong EC to emerge as part of a stronger Western Europe, which in turn would strengthen the Atlantic alliance.[29] In Kennedy's famous words, the transatlantic partnership would bind the United States and Europe "on a basis of full equality in all the great and burdensome tasks of building and defending a community of free nations."[30]

Commission president Hallstein's design for Europe and for transatlantic relations complemented that of the United States. Addressing an academic audience in New York, Hallstein compared the histories of U.S. federalism and European integration. "By its very nature," Hallstein observed, " . . . the Community must be an ever-growing, ever-developing organism. . . . Essentially, [it] may be described as a federation in the making. . . . History is on our side."[31] He subscribed fully to the idea of transatlantic partnership at the core of the Grand Design, an idea that seeks to harness "one giant with a number of comparative dwarfs [in] a new system which joins in partnership . . . twin units [that] today are already comparable and which one day will be equal."[32]

De Gaulle had a radically different understanding of history and a competing vision of European union and transatlantic partnership. He envisioned a Europe based on intergovernmentalism rather than supranationslism; a "Europe of the states" rather than a federal Europe; and a Europe genuinely equal with the United States in NATO rather than militarily subservient to Washington.[33] Britain shared de Gaulle's antipathy toward supranationalism but shared Washington's vision of the transatlantic relationship, a vision that sought to hide U.S. hegemony behind a facade of Euro-American equality.[34]

Britain was an important element in the Grand Design of the United States. But the United States viewed Britain's nonmembership in the EC, the nucleus of a uniting Europe, as politically awkward. The Americans were therefore pleased when Britain signaled in early 1961 its intention to apply for EC membership. The decision would have to be Britain's alone. As Ball noted in May 1961, France would portray U.S. support for British membership in the EC as an *"Anglo-Saxon conspiracy."*[35]

In a triumph of hope over experience, the United States wanted Britain to join the EC without reservation. As Kennedy told Adenauer in April 1961, "It is best for the Atlantic Community if the UK joined [the EC] on an unconditional basis."[36] Thus Britain should embrace supranationalism, accept the CAP, and not try to negotiate concessions for the Commonwealth and EFTA. The United States presumed that EC enlargement would benefit U.S. industrial exporters. British membership would also help orient the EC's common commercial policy in a liberal direction (a direction in which it appeared to be heading in any case). Nevertheless, agricultural exporters would probably lose out because of the emerging CAP. Despite U.S. and British concerns about agricultural policy, there is no indication that Washington pushed London to join the EC in order to wreck the CAP from the inside.

The Americans assumed (as did the British) that de Gaulle would not look favorably for political reasons on Britain's application. Ostensibly the French were amenable to British membership, but the Americans had their doubts. Those were not dispelled when de Gaulle told Kennedy in June 1961 that "his position towards British membership is either/or; either full, or none."[37] In other words, Britain was welcome to join as long as it accepted the provisions of the Rome Treaty unconditionally. Belgian foreign minister Paul-Henri Spaak, who carried more weight in Washington than the size of his country warranted, told Ball in February 1962 that "on balance de Gaulle did not want the British in, as it might threaten France's leading role in the Community."[38]

The Fouchet Plan

The EC was germane to de Gaulle's as well as to Kennedy's geopolitical designs. Between 1959 and 1962, de Gaulle made two proposals to promote European political union. The first was for foreign policy cooperation among the Six, supported by a secretariat in Paris. The other member states did not want a secretariat, and the foreign ministers met only twice to discuss political cooperation before de Gaulle launched a more ambitious initiative at a press conference in September 1960, calling for regular meetings of the six heads of state and government to direct intergovernmental cooperation on political, economic, cultural, and defense matters. De Gaulle linked his proposal with separate calls for NATO reform.[39]

A committee under French ambassador Christian Fouchet worked on the proposal in 1961 and early 1962. A number of delegations were suspicious of de Gaulle's intentions. The Dutch and the Belgians, in particular, were wary of possible French or Franco-German hegemony in the EC. They wanted Britain, as a candidate for EC membership, to participate in the talks. They also fretted about the possible impact of de Gaulle's plans on NATO. The negotiations veered between near-agreement and near-collapse for more than a year, depending on the issue in question. Finally the Dutch refused to carry on until Britain was invited to take part. Because of Britain's attachment to a competing vision of transatlantic relations, de Gaulle refused to oblige. De Gaulle seemed unfazed when the talks finally collapsed in April 1962. Indeed, his excessive demands suggest that he might not have expected the so-called Fouchet Plan to succeed.[40] When the talks failed, he turned his strategic attention to bilateral relations with Germany and unilateral action in NATO.

The United States was sanguine about the Fouchet Plan. Monnet, who remained influential in Washington because of his close friendship with Ball, reassured U.S. officials. He was generally optimistic about the EC's prospects and was confident that Britain would soon join. (We now know that Monnet and de Gaulle drew up a secret memorandum in October 1960 in which Monnet agreed to support the Fouchet Plan and de Gaulle promised to maintain the integrity of the Rome Treaty.[41]) If Monnet, an arch-supranationalist, was not concerned about de Gaulle's motives, then surely Washington need not be concerned either. The French government also reassured the United States about its proposals, claiming that they were consistent with Washington's goal of building European union. But Spaak warned Ball in November 1961 that the United States should not be complacent; that the French proposals were "not a step toward political unification, but [were] actually retrogressive."[42] Ultimately, the United States relied on the ability of the other EC member states to keep de Gaulle in check.

Yet Germany's position on the Fouchet Plan and Britain's EC application caused some disquiet in the United States. Clearly, Adenauer was trying to strike a balance between Paris and Washington. Although Germany depended on the United States for its security, Adenauer doubted the military commitment of the United States. Unlike the United States, France supported Adenauer unreservedly during the Berlin crises of 1958–1962. But France could not substitute militarily for the United States.

De Gaulle knew that Adenauer was more interested in binding Germany into the West through EC membership than in developing federal institutions in Europe. Therefore de Gaulle hoped that Adenauer might go along with his efforts to organize Europe along intergovernmental rather than supranational lines. Adenauer's difficulty lay in reconciling de Gaulle's vision of Europe with the Grand Design of the United States and in allaying domestic concern that he was alienating Washington by embracing de Gaulle too closely. The collapse of the Fouchet Plan got Adenauer off the hook, in Washington and in Bonn, at least until de Gaulle turned his attention to developing the Franco-German axis as the basis for his "European Europe."[43]

The question of Britain's EC application also made it difficult for Adenauer to walk a fine line between Paris and Washington. Adenauer disliked Macmillan (the feeling was mutual) and distrusted the British, especially because of their vacillation during the Berlin crises. Nevertheless, Adenauer was well disposed toward British membership in the EC. He knew that the

United States wanted Britain to join, but also that de Gaulle was equivocal, to say the least. Erhard strongly supported British membership for both economic (market access) and political (pro-American and anti–de Gaulle) reasons. Adenauer's cabinet colleagues feared that the chancellor was veering too much in de Gaulle's direction. During a visit to Washington with Adenauer in November 1962, Germany's foreign minister complained to Ball that the chancellor was wavering on the question of British accession. At the request of the German foreign minister, Kennedy warned Adenauer of the possible consequences of a collapse of the negotiations: Britain's Conservative government might fall and be replaced by Labour, a development that could be detrimental to NATO and the Atlantic community.[44]

De Gaulle Says No

In December 1962, Kennedy and Macmillan struck a deal in Nassau to provide U.S. missiles for Britain's supposedly independent nuclear force. De Gaulle saw this as further evidence of British subservience to the United States. Given Washington's oft-stated objective of building an Atlantic partnership on the foundation of the EC and de Gaulle's opposition to the kind of partnership envisioned by the United States, the Nassau agreement demonstrated to de Gaulle the potential political difficulties that Britain's EC membership could pose for France.

The Nassau agreement could not have come at a worse time for Britain's EC prospects. The negotiations in Brussels were at a critical stage, bogged down in dreary technicalities. Although Ball blamed Adenauer and de Gaulle, British reservations were largely at fault for the oppressive political climate surrounding the talks. The British would not, or could not, drop their long-standing misgivings and accept the Rome Treaty wholeheartedly. They remained skeptical of supranationalism (a skepticism that de Gaulle shared), committed to the Commonwealth, and attached to an agricultural system incompatible with the emerging CAP. Britain made many concessions during the negotiations, but not enough to suit the French or allay the concerns of the other member states. This was true especially for agriculture, the importance of which the Americans appreciated for the EC politically as well as economically. As Ball predicted before the accession negotiations began, agriculture became the most contentious issue between Britain and the Six.[45]

The CAP may well have precipitated de Gaulle's rejection of Britain's application, planned in late 1962 and announced in dramatic fashion at a press conference in Paris in January 1963. Whereas de Gaulle was able to pressure or cajole current member states to accept his agricultural proposals, he would have faced formidable—perhaps insurmountable—opposition if Britain, with its radically different agricultural interests and considerable political clout, acceded to the EC before the CAP was fully in place. That was the gist of de

Gaulle's well-rehearsed answer to a prearranged question at the press conference, which amounted to a veto of Britain's application.[46]

France followed up by formally opposing British membership at a Council meeting at the end of January 1963, prompting the Six to end the accession negotiations. The other member states protested de Gaulle's abruptness and unilateralism. Given de Gaulle's personality and previous behavior, they cannot have been too surprised. Nevertheless de Gaulle's action precipitated a crisis in the EC, with the Benelux countries fuming over French intransigence and sulking in the Council of Ministers. In an indirect dig at de Gaulle, Hallstein wrote that the Community should not allow itself "to be subject to . . . those older methods [in international relations] of hegemony . . . reprisal, and blackmail."[47] Yet even Hallstein appreciated that British membership might not have been in the EC's immediate interest. Arguably, the EC survived the shock of de Gaulle's veto better than it would have survived the shock of British accession, which would have brought into the emerging EC a large member state strongly opposed to core Community principles and policies.

Britain took de Gaulle's rebuff as a national affront. The political consequences of the veto were indeed profound. Personally slighted by de Gaulle, Macmillan soon resigned, ostensibly on grounds of ill health. He was the first of many political casualties of Britain's involvement with the EC.

The Elysée Treaty

De Gaulle and Adenauer signed a treaty on Franco-German cooperation in the Elysée Palace at the end of January 1963, a week after the notorious press conference in which de Gaulle rejected Britain's candidacy.[48] Following the failure of the Fouchet negotiations, de Gaulle envisioned the treaty as an alternative approach to political union. The Commission, the small EC member states, and Italy worried more about the implications of the new treaty than about de Gaulle's veto of British membership. Already suspicious of the emerging Franco-German axis, they feared that the treaty would institutionalize Franco-German hegemony in the EC. Hallstein thought that Adenauer was entirely under de Gaulle's influence. Having once been close colleagues, Hallstein and Adenauer now differed fundamentally on the EC's political prospects.

The United States saw a link between the de Gaulle press conference and the Elysée Treaty. In his press conference, de Gaulle rejected British membership in the EC, an intrinsic element of Washington's Grand Design. In the Elysée Treaty, he tried to tie Germany to a rival French design for Europe. Adenauer attempted to assuage the Americans, arguing that the Elysée Treaty would not undermine German support for European integration and Atlantic partnership. After all, a treaty of Franco-German friendship was fully in accord with both Germany's and America's postwar European policies.

French premier Charles de Gaulle (left) and West Germany's Konrad Adenauer, Bad Kreuznach, West Germany, December 11, 1958. Over the years, the two leaders would forge closer ties between France and Germany, historically the "engine" of postwar European unity.

Those reassurances were not enough for the Americans or for Adenauer's domestic critics. The United States took comfort in the resolution passed by the German parliament and attached to the treaty, affirming Germany's commitments to the EC, NATO, and the GATT. The resolution humiliated Adenauer (leading members of his own party supported it). In practical terms, it emasculated the treaty from the French point of view and infuriated de Gaulle. Adenauer's resignation later in 1963 and Erhard's appointment as chancellor ended the ascendancy of the German Gaullists in Bonn and brought German-American relations back to an even keel.

The events of January 1963 left a bitter taste in the Americans' mouths. De Gaulle became a bogeyman in Washington. Mention of his name was enough to incite invective in the White House and State Department (not to mention the Pentagon). Ball, an avid Eurofederalist, could barely contain himself. He revealed his hatred of de Gaulle and concern about the future in a memorandum for President Kennedy in June 1963. "Never at any time since the war," Ball wrote, "has Europe been in graver danger of back-sliding into the old destructive habits—the old fragmentation and national rivalries that have twice brought the world to disaster in the past." What was to blame? "[T]he halting, and at least momentary reversal, of the drive toward unity in Europe. This has come about, as the whole world knows, from [de Gaulle's] abrupt reassertion of old-style competitive nationalism . . . [and] assault on the structure of European unity." Ball warned the president that "each week de Gaulle's France grows perceptibly more absolutist. . . . As a result, the French Communists . . . have been given a new lease on life."[49]

Ball's fears were unfounded. The Fifth Republic was more stable than any regime in modern French history and remained so after de Gaulle's departure. The process of European integration was not thrown irrevocably off track in 1963. Even without de Gaulle it is doubtful that the EC would have moved at the time in an avowedly federal direction. De Gaulle's quest for *grandeur* continued to pit Paris and Washington against each other, notably on NATO and nuclear issues.[50] But the EC was no longer a battleground for competing French and U.S. visions of Europe. Nor, despite these political problems, did the EC falter economically. The customs union remained on track, and other policies were gradually put in place.

◼ The Empty Chair Crisis and the Luxembourg Compromise

No sooner did the dust settle in 1963 than another, more serious crisis appeared on the horizon. It began over Commission proposals for a new financial arrangement for the CAP for the period after July 1965, when the current system of national contributions would expire. In 1970, following completion of the third stage of the transition to the customs union, the EC was supposed to acquire its "own resources," consisting of duties from agricultural and industrial imports, from which the CAP would be permanently funded. Hallstein avidly awaited the advent of own resources because it would probably result in a transfer of budgetary power from national parliaments to the European Parliament in order to counterbalance the transfer of moneys from national budgets to the EC's budget. In the process, the Commission might also acquire budgetary authority. Rather than waiting for the introduction of own resources in 1970, as stipulated in the treaty, Hallstein wanted to bring it forward to 1965, in place of another interim financing measure. Hallstein knew that de Gaulle opposed giving more power to the Parliament and the Commission, but he also knew that de Gaulle looked forward to the introduction of own resources, which would greatly reduce the financial burden on France.

Presuming that de Gaulle would trade a desirable financial outcome for an undesirable political one, Hallstein introduced the controversial budgetary proposals in April 1965. According to Hallstein, the Commission's proposals were consistent with the spirit of integration and the Community's development so far. Hans von der Groeben, a fellow commissioner, claimed that the Commission supported Hallstein unanimously. Robert Marjolin, another commissioner, disagreed, saying that he and a few others opposed Hallstein's ambitious proposals and, given de Gaulle's well-known aversion to supranationalism, predicted a ruinous outcome for the Commission. Given his pragmatism and political contacts in France, Marjolin's assessment sounds more plausible than von der Groeben's.[51]

At first the crisis took on the character of a personal battle between Hallstein and de Gaulle. In a celebrated passage in his memoirs, de Gaulle dismissed Hallstein as "first of all a German who is ambitious for his Fatherland."[52] Yet de Gaulle was an unapologetic nationalist, whereas Hallstein considered himself the personification of European postnationalism. Hallstein relished the trappings of power (the title "President," the diplomatic niceties, the red carpet) not for personal aggrandizement (or so he said), but because he wanted to establish the Commission's political preeminence. De Gaulle scorned Hallstein's political posturing. The president of the French Republic dismissed the president of the European Commission as an upstart and the Commission itself as a collection of stateless technocrats. Hallstein's greatest weakness, de Gaulle knew, was that the Commission president was appointed, not elected.

Politically isolated, Hallstein had few friends in the national capitals, least of all in Bonn, where Erhard was now the chancellor. Erhard could not come out publicly against Hallstein, a fellow German, but he made his position crystal clear. Hallstein backed down even before the fateful Council meeting of June 1965. Other member states, equally unhappy with the Commission's original proposal, wanted instead to negotiate another temporary financial arrangement for the CAP. Such a negotiation would be difficult and time consuming and might not finish by the stipulated deadline of midnight on June 30, 1965. But there was ample precedent for continuing to negotiate after the deadline while technically reaching agreement on time by "stopping the clock." The Five presumed that this is what would happen during the Council meeting that began on June 28.

France Walks Out

De Gaulle had other ideas. Claiming that his partners had violated their commitment to conclude a new financial arrangement by the agreed deadline, Maurice Couve de Murville, de Gaulle's foreign minister and president-in-office of the Council, abruptly ended the meeting in the early hours of July 1.

France then withdrew its representation from the Council but pointedly continued to participate in routine Community business.[53]

De Gaulle did not spell out the magnitude of the crisis until September 1965, when he held a typically imperious press conference. Following a diatribe against the Commission, de Gaulle declared his unwillingness to accept provisions permitting the use of qualified majority voting in a range of new policy areas that were due to come into force in January 1966. De Gaulle had two objections: on principle he refused to countenance qualified majority voting, which smacked of supranationalism; in practice he feared the impact of qualified majority voting on French agricultural and trade interests (under qualified majority voting, a coalition of liberal member states could alter the CAP and thwart French efforts to protect agriculture in the GATT). De Gaulle threatened to continue the boycott until member states agreed upon a new financial regulation for the CAP, the Commission curbed its political ambition, and provisions for qualified majority voting were dropped from the Rome Treaty.

It is difficult to disentangle principle and pragmatism in de Gaulle's conduct of the crisis. As in other case studies of de Gaulle's policy toward the Community, Moravcsik argued that pragmatism triumphed over principle; that de Gaulle was much more concerned with protecting the CAP than scuttling supranationalism.[54] Undoubtedly de Gaulle was preoccupied with the CAP, but the extension of qualified majority voting in 1966 would not necessarily have been detrimental to French interests. Provisions existed before 1966 to use qualified majority voting in certain policy areas. Even so, member states were reluctant to outvote each other on issues that were politically sensitive. An unwritten rule emerged in the EC whereby decisions were generally taken by consensus. Presumably this would have continued after 1966, regardless of a member state's right to call for a vote in a greater number of policy areas. Yet the fact that de Gaulle objected to the extension of qualified majority voting in 1965, when it would cover agricultural and trade policy, rather than in 1961, when it was first introduced, shows the extent of his concern about the CAP.

The other member states had no intention of renegotiating the Rome Treaty, however much de Gaulle disliked it. Although also sensitive about the use of qualified majority voting, they would not succumb to de Gaulle's political blackmail. As with his veto of Britain's membership application, the Five strongly resented de Gaulle's intemperate oratory and unilateral action. They resolved to stand together, but not with the Commission. Spaak, a supranationalist and no friend of de Gaulle's, called for an extraordinary meeting of the Council to resolve the standoff. The meeting was extraordinary in that it was out of sequence and the Commission was not invited to participate.

Both Erhard and de Gaulle faced elections in late 1965. The crisis hardly affected the German election but dominated the French one—the first European election in which the EC was a central issue. German business and agricultural interests strongly supported Erhard's handling of the crisis. Erhard's relatively easy victory allowed the new chancellor finally to move out of Adenauer's shadow and stand up to de Gaulle. French business and agricultural interests, by contrast, opposed de Gaulle's handling of the crisis. Farmers especially feared that de Gaulle's antics would destroy the CAP, although de Gaulle was arguably trying to protect the CAP against the possible vagaries of qualified majority voting. De Gaulle suffered a sharp rebuff in the election, failing to win the first round outright and winning the second round by a relatively small margin.

Ending the Crisis

The electorate sent de Gaulle a clear message. Would he listen and bring the crisis to an end? De Gaulle liked to think that he was above populist politics; that he was a leader, not a follower. Having won the election, he was not beholden to the electorate, at least until the run-up to the next election. Yet the result shocked de Gaulle, as did the continuing hostility of farming and business interests to his handling of the crisis. The result also emboldened the Five, who remained united in opposition to de Gaulle's assault on the Community system.

Despite their annoyance with de Gaulle, the Five tried to get him off his high horse as gracefully as possible. They made little headway at the Council meeting in Luxembourg in mid-January (de Gaulle objected to holding the meeting in Brussels, the Commission's home town). Couve reiterated French objections to qualified majority voting and requested a written agreement among member states to use unanimity in the Council when vital French interests were at risk. He also presented a ten-point document on the Commission's behavior and future relations with the Council. A series of bilateral discussions followed, leading to a second extraordinary Council meeting at the end of January. It was there that the Six hammered out the Luxembourg Compromise, according to which, when "very important interests are at stake," the Council would refrain from taking a decision by qualified majority vote.[55] In effect, the Luxembourg Compromise acknowledged a member state's right to veto legislative proposals. With that, France agreed to take its seat again in the Council.

Member states also approved a code of conduct for the Commission that went some way toward meeting French demands. The Five successfully defended the Commission's exclusive right of legislative initiative but agreed with France on reducing the Commission's political profile. Hallstein faced an uncertain future. De Gaulle detested him, and the German government offered only lukewarm support. Wisely, Hallstein announced in May 1967 that he would step down two months later, when the merger of the EEC Commission, the Euratom Commission, and the ECSC High Authority came into effect.

Resolution of the crisis cleared the way for negotiation of a new financial arrangement for the CAP. Member states finally reached agreement at two marathon (but otherwise orthodox) meetings of the Council, in May and July 1966. As part of the deal France agreed to a German request that all remaining intra-EC tariffs on industrial goods be abolished by July 1968, when the common external tariff would take effect. Thus the customs union would come into being eighteen months ahead of the schedule. The agreement on the CAP and the customs union allowed the EC to relaunch the Kennedy Round of the GATT, which had run aground during the crisis.

The outcome of the crisis looked like a victory for the EC: the treaty was intact; the Five stood as one; France took its seat again in the Council; and the Six soon reached agreement on completing the CAP and the customs union. The hollowness of the EC's position soon became apparent, however. Jean Rey, the new Commission president, was much more attuned than Hallstein to national sensitivities and interests. Under his leadership the Commission became less assertive and ambitious. At the same time, the Council increasingly resembled a forum for traditional intergovernmental negotiation rather than a Community-minded institution. Taking a lead from France, other governments grew less reticent about articulating and defending national interests.

Qualified majority voting was used in the Council after 1966, perhaps even more so than before, but not on politically sensitive issues. Governments rarely invoked the Luxembourg Compromise: it was enough for them to hint that an important national interest was at stake in order to prevent a vote from being taken. Because there was no objective measure of what constituted an important national interest, governments used the term loosely, often under domestic political pressure. The Luxembourg Compromise therefore cast a long shadow over legislative decisionmaking and elevated the national veto to a sacrosanct principle.

■ A Decade of European Community Integration

The tenth anniversary of the Rome Treaty in March 1967 was a somber affair. Member states marked the occasion two months later with a meeting of heads of state and government in the Eternal City. As the only head of state present (the other leaders were prime ministers), de Gaulle was ceremonially supreme. More than six feet tall, he dominated the affair, both literally and figuratively. By then the world's most senior and best-known statesman, he was the center of political and media attention.

De Gaulle came to Rome not to bury the treaty but not to praise it either. There were perfunctory discussions about political union and enlargement, but it was clear that the other member states were treading water until de Gaulle left office. The only concrete agreement reached was to implement the treaty merging the three communities' executive bodies in July 1967. Hallstein, who had just announced his intention to retire, stayed in the background. In a classic display of personal pique, de Gaulle insisted on relegating the Commission president to second-class citizenship at the anniversary event.[56]

Despite the heavy atmosphere at the Rome meeting and throughout the Community in the aftermath of the empty chair crisis, the EC continued to conduct an impressive amount of business. Indeed, in its first ten years of existence the EC achieved a number of goals in the internal and external policy arenas. The most notable setback at the end of the EC's first decade was de Gaulle's second veto of Britain's renewed attempt to join the EC.

Britain's Second Application

This time it was a Labour government, led by Harold Wilson, that spearheaded Britain's accession effort.[57] Wilson was no more committed to European integration than Macmillan had been. Like Macmillan, Wilson knew that Britain needed to join for economic reasons. Britain's situation had worsened since de Gaulle's first veto. By 1967, the "battle for sterling" was at its height. Determined to defend the exchange rate of $2.80 and maintain sterling's reserve currency status, Wilson refused to devalue or take harsh fiscal measures. Instead, the government tightened capital controls and asked the International Monetary Fund (IMF) for help. As a means of redressing Britain's balance-of-payments deficit and restoring the country to economic health, membership in the EC seemed more necessary than ever.

Nevertheless, the issue continued to divide domestic opinion. The Labour government, like the Conservative government before it, included a number of die-hard Euroskeptics. Most Labour Euroskeptics opposed the EC for doctrinaire reasons: they saw it as a capitalist endeavor hostile to workers' rights and as an economic arm of NATO. Some Conservative Euroskeptics opposed the EC for economic reasons—in their view it was socialistic and hostile to business interests—but most disliked the EC because it threatened national sovereignty. Aware of deep divisions in the party and the country, Wilson argued the case for membership on solid economic grounds. He built parliamentary support through a series of lengthy debates, culminating in a successful vote in May 1967 in favor of a second application, which the government duly lodged in Brussels.

De Gaulle seemed well disposed toward Wilson, who carried none of Macmillan's emotional baggage from having dealt with de Gaulle during the war. De Gaulle liked Wilson's advocacy of intra-European technological collaboration and criticism of U.S. policy in Vietnam. But Wilson could not convince de Gaulle that British accession to the EC was compatible with French economic and strategic interests. De Gaulle outlined his misgivings at a press conference in May 1967, only four days after Wilson submitted Britain's second application. Rather than risk "destructive upheavals" by admitting Britain into the EC, especially because of sterling's vulnerability, might it not be better "to preserve what has been built until such time as it would appear conceivable to welcome an England which . . . [will] have undergone a profound transformation?"[58]

The British media immediately dubbed this "the velvet veto," although de Gaulle specifically stated that he was not blocking Britain's entry. Wilson sought clarification at a meeting with de Gaulle in Paris the following month. De Gaulle got straight to the point. Would Britain accept the CAP and distance itself from the United States? Wilson agreed to abide by the CAP, which by then was largely in place, but was more guarded on the question of Anglo-American relations, a sensitive domestic and international issue.

Wilson was still optimistic about Britain's chances because he seemed to have the support of France's partners. Wilson put great store in the advent in Bonn of the Grand Coalition of Christian Democrats and Social Democrats, under Chancellor Kurt Kiesinger and Foreign Minister Willy Brandt. Although Germany had always supported British accession, at the time of the first application Adenauer had deferred to de Gaulle on the issue. Wilson hoped that Bonn's growing irritation with Paris and Kiesinger's apparent willingness to stand up to de Gaulle would strengthen Britain's prospects. Wilson also had a good relationship with Brandt, a fellow Social Democrat. Wilson used Brandt's support for Britain's EC membership to undermine opposition to the EC in his own Labour Party.

The Commission issued an obligatory opinion on Britain's application in September 1967. The Commission developed the theme of widening versus weakening, stressing the need to maintain "indispensable cohesion and dynamism" in an enlarged Community. The Commission did not assess the possible impact on the EC of British accession but urged that negotiations be opened "in order to dispel the uncertainty that still attaches in particular to certain fundamental points," a reference to the CAP and Commonwealth preferences.[59]

The Council discussed Britain's application and the Commission's opinion on a number of occasions in October and November 1967, but another statement by de Gaulle, in a press conference at the end of November, brought the matter to a close. Referring to the Commission's opinion, de Gaulle declared that Britain's economic and political situation precluded EC membership. Earlier in the month, Britain had devalued sterling by 17 percent, partly in response to publicly expressed French doubts about sterling's stability. De Gaulle now twisted the knife, saying that the sterling crisis, as well as Britain's commercial and agricultural policies, made it impossible to open accession negotiations. "To enter at present into any negotiations with Britain and its associate countries," de Gaulle declared, " . . . would lead to the destruction of the European Community."[60]

The irony of this statement was not lost on the British and the Five, considering that de Gaulle risked destroying the EC during the empty chair crisis in order to safeguard French interests. De Gaulle continued to fret about the possible impact of British accession on the CAP. Although the big battles on agricultural policy were over, a permanent financial arrangement (the final piece of the CAP puzzle) was not due to be put in place until 1970. Clearly, de Gaulle did not want Britain to become a member before then.

Strategic considerations also played a part in de Gaulle's decision to veto Britain's second application. In 1966 de Gaulle launched various efforts to undermine U.S. hegemony in NATO and loosen Soviet control in Eastern Europe. The most dramatic of these were his withdrawal from NATO's integrated military command, expulsion of NATO's headquarters from France, much-publicized visit to Moscow, and support for Romania's quasi-autonomous foreign policy. De Gaulle still saw the EC as a potential platform for a pan-European economic and security organization independent of the superpowers. Letting Britain into the EC might have given the appearance that the EC was moving closer strategically to the United States.

For Wilson, the most disappointing aspect of de Gaulle's veto was that Germany went along with it. Whatever Kiesinger and Brandt said privately to Wilson, publicly they were unwilling to confront de Gaulle. Undoubtedly de Gaulle's behavior exasperated Kiesinger and Brandt, but neither would risk alienating France for the sake of an eventuality that looked increasingly inevitable once de Gaulle was out of office. Germany saw economic and strategic advantages in British accession to the EC, but not enough to risk a crisis in Franco-German relations and Community affairs by antagonizing de Gaulle. Faced with French intransigence and Germany's diffidence, Britain put its application on hold in December 1967.

The Kennedy Round and U.S.-EC Relations

In contrast to the ongoing saga of British accession, the conclusion of the Kennedy Round of GATT negotiations, also in 1967, was a concrete manifestation of the advantages of European integration. The fifty-three members of the GATT agreed to reduce tariffs over a five-year period by an average of nearly 40 percent. Acting as a bloc, the Six played a decisive part. The satisfactory outcome of the round demonstrated the value of a common EC negotiating position.

Yet the conduct of the Kennedy Round generated considerable friction within the EC and between the EC and the United States. Within the EC, France and the Five, unofficially led by Germany, clashed over the possible inclusion of agriculture and the extent of the industrial tariff cuts. France did not want the CAP, negotiated and defended at considerable cost, undercut by a global agreement to liberalize trade in agricultural products. Nor did France want to expose its industrial producers, already coping with intra-EC liberalization, to greater global competition. As global industrial liberalization was a lesser evil for France than global agricultural liberalization, de Gaulle struck a deal with Germany to defend the CAP in return for French support for industrial tariff cuts in the GATT.

The Kennedy Round was also a source of friction between the EC and the United States. The United States hoped that the round would yield greater economic and political benefits than turned out to be the case. For instance, the United States drafted its landmark Trade Expansion Act, the legislative basis for participation in the round, partly in anticipation of early British accession to the EC. Among other provisions, the act authorized the president to eliminate duty on articles in categories of goods in which the United States and the EC together accounted for 80 percent or more of world trade. Once Britain had joined the EC, the United States and the EC together would account for at least that amount of world trade in a large number of categories. De Gaulle's veto of Britain's membership negated the provision of the Trade Expansion Act that anticipated EC enlargement and reduced the possible benefit of the Kennedy Round for the United States.[61]

While advocating the Trade Expansion Act in public speeches and testimony before Congress, members of the administration harped on the political as well as the economic importance of the proposed legislation for U.S.-EC relations. In their view, the act and the ensuing Kennedy Round would help cement relations with Brussels and build the Atlantic partnership. Instead, de Gaulle's assault against the Grand Design of the United States eroded U.S. optimism about the transatlantic relationship. More than anything else, de Gaulle's veto of British membership "struck a heavy blow at the idea of partnership which seemed . . . [to have] had such a bright future only several months before. That action alone, seen in retrospect, went a long way towards changing the basic objective of the Kennedy Round from a political to an economic one."[62]

Association Agreements

Apart from the Kennedy Round, the most significant development in the field of external relations during the EC's first decade was the conclusion of association agreements with Greece, Turkey, and a group of African countries, all former colonies of EC member states. The association agreements with Greece and Turkey were qualitatively different from the agreement with the African states, as both Greece and Turkey aspired to EC membership, albeit in the long term. The agreement with Greece, signed in July 1961, called for a customs union within twelve years, although the EC granted Greece numerous extensions for sensitive products. The agreement with Turkey, signed in September 1963, aimed for a customs union after a transition period of unspecified duration. This reflected Turkey's lower level of economic development. The EC acknowledged Greece's aspiration for membership but was more circumspect in its dealings with Turkey. While lauding Greece's contribution to European culture and civilization, the EC questioned Turkey's European credentials.

The EC suspended the association agreement with Greece in response to the right-wing coup in Athens in 1967, which ushered in a military dictatorship. At the same time, political instability and economic turmoil in Turkey caused Ankara's association agreement to languish. By the end of the 1960s the EC had little to show for its association with two strategically important countries whose hostility toward each other would complicate the Community's involvement in the eastern Mediterranean for many years to come.

The association agreement with seventeen African states and Madagascar, signed in Yaoundé, in the Cameroon Republic, in July 1963, superseded the association between the EC and its member states' overseas territories (most of them French colonies), negotiated as part of the Rome Treaty and implemented in January 1958, when the treaty came into operation. In effect, the original association created a free trade area for the EC and the overseas territories. It also channeled aid to the associated territories through a development fund. The nature of the association and the size of the fund, which was separate from the EU budget, divided France and Germany. As with the CAP, France saw Community support for overseas territories as an opportunity to spread the cost of development assistance while continuing to reap the economic rewards. By contrast, Germany resented both the size of its financial contribution to the fund and the Community's close association with a part of the world in which it had little interest.

Although the treaty stipulated that the Council could extend the original association agreement, the granting of independence in the late 1950s and early 1960s to most of the overseas territories meant that a new agreement was necessary. The newly independent states wanted to retain the benefits of the original agreement, whereas the former colonial powers wanted to support their ex-colonies. Once again Germany was in an anomalous position, on the one hand wanting to support Third World development while on the other hand not wanting to perpetuate postcolonial dependency. Negotiation of what became the Yaoundé Convention therefore took place on two fronts: externally between the EC and the African states and internally among the EC's member states.

In the negotiations with the African states, the EC was in the driver's seat politically, economically, and administratively. The African states had little choice but to take what the EC offered them. Within the EC, France prevailed over Germany because of an implicit link between the GATT and the Yaoundé negotiations: in return for French support in the Kennedy Round, Germany acquiesced in the new convention. The United States doubted the Yaoundé agreement's compatibility with the GATT and fretted about its possible discriminatory impact on Latin American exports to the EC. Like Germany, however, the United States overcame its misgivings for the sake of a GATT agreement and for the cause of European integration.[63]

Internal Policy Developments

The EC made considerable progress in the 1960s in policy areas subject to precise provisions and time schedules, such as the customs union, or to intense pressure from a powerful member state, such as the CAP, but little progress in areas covered generally by the treaty or of interest only to less influential member states. Nontariff barriers (such as different national rules on product standards) remained a major obstacle to the free movement of goods, a cornerstone of the customs union. The Commission began the laborious process of harmonization, but soon ran into national resistance. A combination of bureaucratic inertia and member state recalcitrance stymied progress, with many proposals languishing in working groups and never reaching the Council for a decision.

Workers had the right to move freely around the Community, on paper at least. Similarly, citizens of one member state could set up businesses and provide services in another member state, although national governments dragged their feet on the harmonization of relevant national laws, such as mutual recognition of qualifications. Capital liberalization also proved elusive, as governments sought to protect national capital markets despite the growing interdependence of European and global capital markets.

Big business generally welcomed the emergence of the common market, despite its imperfections. According to von der Groeben, "Entrepreneurs were convinced of the project's potential: they procured the necessary equipment and labor ready for the enlarged market, invested appropriately and established trade connections with the other Member States."[64] U.S. multinationals eagerly exploited new opportunities in the European marketplace. Indeed, European businesses complained that U.S. multinationals were better placed and prepared than European companies to operate in a larger economic space.

The Union of Industrial Federations, one of the earliest and most powerful interest groups in Brussels, also complained that the Commission's ethos and activities were not friendly to European business.[65] Private enterprises were wary of competition policy rules that prevented restrictive agreements or abuse of dominant position. National governments complained about another branch of competition policy, which sought to control "state aids" (public subsidies) and liberalize "regulated industries" (companies either owned by or having a special relationship with national governments). Backed by the European Court, the Commission took a number of tough competition policy decisions, although increasing intergovernmentalism in the late 1960s inevitably curbed the Commission's willingness to confront flagrant violations by national governments and national champions (big businesses closely associated with national governments). Nevertheless the Commission and the Court succeeded in the 1960s in establishing the principle, if not yet the practice, of a full-fledged Community-wide competition policy.

Transport was an example of a policy area in which the EC made little progress. The treaty called for a common transport policy, without specifying a schedule. Only the Netherlands, having the most competitive road haulers in the EC, Europe's largest seaport, and lower fuel prices and vehicle taxes than other member states, pushed for implementation of the policy. Germany, a target of intense Dutch competition, resisted. France was indifferent. Far from cooperating more closely, by 1968 the Dutch and the Germans were on the verge of a trade war over draft German legislation to reduce further the number of permits for Dutch trucks on German roads.

Alongside the customs union and common commercial policy, the CAP was the most striking policy innovation in the EC's first decade. It was also the best known, thanks to media coverage of farmers' riots. By the late 1960s the CAP encouraged overproduction and environmental degradation, rewarded large-scale producers unduly, and failed to keep many small farmers on the land. The first sizable food surpluses—butter mountains and milk lakes—appeared in 1968. As with other policy areas, people directed their criticism of the CAP not at member states, where it belonged, but at the Commission, which epitomized the Community system.

The EC made little progress in the 1960s on regional policy. The preamble of the Rome Treaty mentioned the need to reduce regional disparities, but the treaty itself included few redistributive measures. On the contrary, the prevailing ethos, as stated in the treaty, was that the common market should, of its own accord, "promote throughout the Community a harmonious development of economic activities" and thereby achieve cohesion. As an exception to that general rule, the treaty permitted government subsidization of industry in those parts of the EC where "the standard of living is abnormally low or where there is serious unemployment."[66]

The Commission did not believe in the positive impact of market integration on regional development. Nor did Italy, the only member state in the 1960s with major regional disparities (the south of Italy was desperately poor). Italy and the Commission therefore wanted the EC to develop a strong regional policy, including a beefed-up guidance section of the agricultural budget (the part of the CAP devoted to infrastructural development). The Commission organized a major conference on regional disparities in 1961 and established a directorate-general for regional policy in 1967. Nevertheless, the other member states resisted extending Community competence into an area not explicitly covered by the Rome Treaty.

Member states were even more protective of their tax policies, although the Commission scored a big success in the 1960s in the area of harmonization of indirect taxes. The large number of different tax systems and rates in the Community militated against the successful operation of the common market. The Commission's response focused initially on turnover taxes. Specifically, the Commission proposed that member states introduce a common value-added tax (VAT) system. Although France already had such a system and Germany was moving toward it, years of hard bargaining ensued before member states reached agreement. Finance ministers met informally to discuss the Commission's proposal (the Council of Finance Ministers, later one of the Council of Ministers' most powerful formations, did not exist at the time). At their behest, the General Affairs Council adopted directives in 1967 requiring member states to introduce the VAT system, albeit allowing for different rates of application. The Commission got nowhere with a follow-up initiative to harmonize direct taxes, an area not covered in the Rome Treaty. Pending closer economic and monetary integration, member states were unwilling to harmonize other areas of tax policy.

Commission calls for close economic and monetary cooperation among member states, and ultimately for economic and monetary union (EMU) also fell on deaf ears. The treaty called for some economic policy coordination, but not for anything as far-reaching as EMU. The Commission made a strong case for a common economic policy in its action program for the second stage of the common market, published in 1962. Member states agreed only to establish a Monetary Committee to discuss possible monetary policy coordination and a Short-Term Economic Policy Committee to discuss current economic trends and assist the Commission should the Council, acting unanimously under the terms of the treaty, decide to "take special measures to cope with undesirable economic developments."[67] In May 1964 member states established a Budgetary Policy Committee to examine the impact of national budgets on the EC's overall economic development. The three committees consisted of national experts and Commission officials.

The Commission toned down its agitation for EMU in the aftermath of the empty chair crisis. Von der Groeben criticized Marjolin, his colleague in the Commission with responsibility for economic policy, for being too timid.[68] Marjolin was more realistic than reticent: he understood the political situation in France and did not want to risk further conflict with de Gaulle. Nevertheless, Marjolin supported "Community programming": regular economic forecasts and blueprints for policy coordination. Some of the more liberal member states, as well as business interests, resisted this approach, fearing excessive government interference in economic affairs. National attitudes changed later in the 1960s when Germany began to experience rising unemployment and inflation (a German nightmare). Germany's situation strengthened the case for economic policy cooperation among the Six, who adopted the Community's first medium-term economic policy program in March 1966, covering employment policy, budgetary policy, regional policy, and research policy. Far from presaging close economic coordination, however, the program amounted mostly to an exchange of information.[69]

Monetary union seemed unnecessary in any case during the heyday of the Bretton Woods System. Nor could the EC reach a joint position as the system began to unravel in the late 1960s. De Gaulle saw the balance-of-payments deficit of the United States, and the swing from what had been a postwar dollar gap toward a potential dollar glut, as an opportunity to attack the United States on the financial front. Instead of holding onto its excess dollars, France began to convert them into gold in 1967 to protest U.S. expansionary macroeconomic policies and its dominance of the international monetary system.[70] Although critical of U.S. economic and monetary policies, the other member states were more forgiving of an ally who had bailed them out immediately after the war and on whom they depended for military security. De Gaulle's position precluded the adoption of a common EC position on the international monetary situation, although frequent contacts among national central bankers, government officials, and Commission officials presaged the emergence in the early 1970s, when the Bretton Woods System finally collapsed, of a plan for monetary union.[71]

Institutional Accomplishments

The confrontation with de Gaulle in 1965 weakened the Commission considerably. Few of its officials were sad to see Hallstein go—he was a remote and autocratic figure—but most regretted the manner of his departure. The empty chair crisis shook the Commission's confidence and curbed its political activism. The *Economist* magazine, as opinionated then as now, described the Commission in April 1968 as "meek-and-mild . . . over-anxious not to offend any of the governments."[72] The Commission was certainly less prominent in the late 1960s than at the beginning of the decade.

Morale sagged not only in the college but also in the Commission's services. Yet the wide scope of Community activity kept Commission officials busy. The Commission established new directorates-general throughout the 1960s to reflect real or anticipated increases in Community competence. Although some Commission officials fervently believed in Eurofederalism, by the late 1960s enthusiasm for "building Europe" gave way to widespread careerism and cynicism. National interference in staff recruitment and promotion did nothing to instill a sense of Europeanness within the Commission. By the late 1960s the Commission was a singular international bureaucracy, but not a truly supranational one.[73]

The Commission faced a particular administrative challenge in the late 1960s: implementation of the Merger Treaty (fusing the executive bodies of the three communities). Some advocates of European integration hoped that this event, envisioned in the Rome Treaty, would boost the Commission's fortunes. France thought otherwise, and few of its partners advocated strengthening the Commission's powers against de Gaulle's wishes. Instead of discussing the Commission's role, the short intergovernmental conference that presaged the Merger Treaty dealt almost exclusively with administrative details. It took the newly merged Commission some time to overcome the organizational and cultural challenges of fusing three distinct bureaucracies. For an interim period between 1967, when the treaty came into effect, and 1970, when its provisions were fully implemented, the college of the Commission had fourteen instead of the usual nine members.[74]

The Parliament, which also suffered a setback at de Gaulle's hands, displayed a resilience and ingenuity characteristic of its development throughout the EC's history. Europarliamentarians continually agitated in the 1960s for direct elections, despite de Gaulle's firm opposition. Most Europarliamentarians were strongly pro-integration (few Euroskeptical members of national parliaments put themselves forward for appointment to the European Parliament). Europarliamentarians resented their limited legislative role (their institution could only give nonbinding opinions on draft legislation) and pushed for greater power. Thus the Parliament passed numerous resolutions in the 1960s on a wide range of policy and procedural issues and even managed to insinuate itself into policy areas from which it was originally excluded. For instance, the Parliament convinced the Council to establish joint parliamentary committees as part of the institutional infrastructure of the EC's association agreements.

The European Court of Justice, the EC's third "supranational" institution, developed slowly but strikingly in the 1960s. The evolution of EC law was one of the least obvious but most important advances in European integration at the time. In two landmark cases, in 1963 and 1964, the Court promulgated the key principles on which Community law rests: direct effect and supremacy. In *Van Gend en Loos* (1963), a Dutch trucking firm brought a case against Dutch customs for raising the duty on a product imported from Germany, in breach of the treaty's common market provisions. Declaring that the EC "constitutes a new legal order of international law for the benefit of which the states have limited their sovereign rights," the Court ruled that the Dutch firm was indeed protected by the direct effect of Community law. The following year, in *Costa v. ENEL*, a case involving Italy's national electricity supplier, the Court upheld the supremacy of EC law over national law. As member states had definitively transferred sovereign rights to the Community, EC law could not be overruled by national law without the legal basis of the Community itself being called into question.[75]

These were audacious rulings by a new international court, especially in the prevailing climate of Gaullist intergovernmentalism. National governments knew what the rulings portended. Even the most Community-minded of them submitted statements to the Court arguing against direct effect and supremacy, rightly fearing that the Court's rulings would undermine national control of the integration process.[76] National governments may have thought that the two principles were unenforceable without the support of national courts, which would surely be more responsive to national opinion and more attached to national legal prerogatives. If so, member states misjudged the situation. Far from trying to fend off the encroachment of Community law, lower national courts worked closely with the Court of Justice in subsequent decades to implement the principles of direct effect and supremacy.[77]

Overall Impact

The Court of Justice and the EC generally remained remote and largely unknown outside relatively small business, legal, and political circles in the 1960s. EC policies and institutions did not impinge much on the lives of most Europeans. Avid readers of the quality press could have followed the story of the empty chair crisis or of Britain's membership applications. Otherwise, ordinary people knew little and cared less about Brussels.

The EC's existence directly affected the lives of relatively few Europeans. Farmers depended on the CAP for their livelihoods, and some businesspeople enjoyed the benefits of market integration, however limited. Transnational interest groups representing farmers, workers, and employers sprang up in Brussels. Many national politicians and bureaucrats developed a European dimension to their work, perhaps coordinating positions on Community issues at home or participating in working groups and Council meetings in Brussels. A vibrant Brussels apparatus, involving interaction among the EC's institutions, policy coordination at the national and European levels, and lobbying in Brussels and the national capitals, came into being. Although still largely out of the limelight, EC politics and policymaking therefore gradually enveloped Europe's political, bureaucratic, and business elites.

▧ Notes

1. See Anne Stevens (with Handley Stevens), *Brussels Bureaucrats? The Administration of the European Union* (London: Palgrave, 2001), pp. 26–42.

2. George M. Taber, "Remembrance of Things Past: A Former Eurocrat Recalls the Dreams and Ideals of the Early Commission," *Time International*, March 29, 1999, p. 23.

3. See Hans von der Groeben, *The European Community: The Formative Years* (Brussels: Commission of the European Communities, 1985), p. 48.

4. Commission, "Introduction to the Action Program for the Period 1964–1968," Bulletin EC 12-1962, p.1.

5. On the struggle between the state and the market in the EC's early years, see John Gillingham, *European Integration, 1950–2002: Superstate or New Market Economy?* (Cambridge: Cambridge University Press, 2003), pp. 6–16.

6. Altiero Spinelli, *The Eurocrats: Conflict and Crisis in the European Community* (Baltimore: Johns Hopkins University Press, 1967), p. 75.

7. For an account of the Parliament's inaugural session and early institutional developments in the EC, see Miriam Camps, "The First Year of the European Economic Community," Policy Memorandum no. 17, Center for International Studies, Princeton University, November 10, 1958.

8. See Andrew Moravcsik, *The Choice for Europe: Social Purpose and State Power from Messina to Maastricht* (Ithaca, NY: Cornell University Press, 1998), pp. 179–182.

9. On the origin and outcome of the free trade area proposal, see Alan Milward, *The UK and the European Community*, Vol. 1: *The Rise and Fall of a National Strategy, 1945–1963* (London: Whitehall History Publishing in association with Frank Cass, 2002), pp. 231–309; Miriam Camps, "The Free Trade Area Negotiations," Policy Memorandum no. 18, Center for International Studies, Woodrow Wilson School of Public and International Affairs, Princeton University, February 10, 1959; James Ellison, *Threatening Europe: Britain and the Creation of the European Community, 1955–1958* (London: Macmillan, 2000); Frances Lynch, "De Gaulle's First Veto: France, the Rueff Plan and the Free Trade Area," *Contemporary European History* 19, no. 1 (March 2000), pp. 111–136; Jeffrey Glen Giauque, *Grand Designs and Visions of Unity: The Atlantic Powers and the Reorganization of Western Europe, 1955–1963* (Chapel Hill: University of North Carolina Press, 2002), pp. 47–76; Emile Benoit, *Europe at Sixes and Sevens: The Common Market, the Free Trade Association and the United States* (New York: Columbia University Press, 1961).

10. Camps, "Free Trade Area," p. 36.

11. See ibid., pp.15–16.

12. U.S. Department of State, *Foreign Relations of the United States [FRUS], 1958–1960*, Vol. 7, Pt. 1: *Western European Integration and Security; Canada* (Washington, DC: U.S. Government Printing Office, 1993), pp. 67–68.

13. See ibid., p. 121.

14. Ibid., p. 173.

15. See Richard T. Griffiths, "The End of the OEEC and the Birth of the OECD," in *Explorations in OEEC History*, ed. Richard T. Griffiths (Paris: OECD, 1997).

16. *FRUS, 1958–1960*, Vol. 7, Pt. 1, p. 281.

17. Ibid., p. 122.

18. Ibid., p. 98.

19. On France and the CAP, see Andrew Moravcsik, "De Gaulle Between Grain and Grandeur: The Political Economy of French EC Policy, 1958–1970," Pt. 1, *Journal of Cold War Studies* 2, no. 2 (Spring 2000), pp. 3–43.

20. Charles de Gaulle, *Mémoires d'Espoir, suivi d'un choix d'allocutions et messages sur la IVe et la Ve Républiques* (Paris: Plon, 1994), p. 167.

21. On the Commission's role in the development of the CAP, see von der Groeben, *Formative Years*, pp. 70–78, 101–108.

22. Ibid., p. 102.

23. Douglas Webber, "Franco-German Bilateralism and Agricultural Politics in the European Union: The Neglected Level," *West European Politics* 22, no. 1 (January 1999), pp. 45–63.

24. *FRUS, 1961–1963*, Vol. 13: *West Europe and Canada* (Washington, DC: U.S. Government Printing Office, 1994), pp. 275–277.

25. Ibid., p. 279.

26. William Diebold Jr., "A Watershed with Some Dry Sides: The Trade Expansion Act of 1962," in *John F. Kennedy and Europe*, ed. Douglas Brinkley and Richard T. Griffiths (Baton Rouge: Louisiana State University Press, 1999), p. 252.

27. See Herman Walker, "Dispute Settlement: The Chicken War," *American Journal of International Law* 58, no. 3 (July 1964), pp. 671–685; and Ynze Alkema, "European-American Trade Policies, 1961–1963," in *John F. Kennedy and Europe*, ed. Douglas Brinkley and Richard T. Griffiths (Baton Rouge: Louisiana State University Press, 1999), pp. 226–234.

28. On Britain's early relationship with the EC and application for membership, see Milward, *The UK and the European Community*, Vol. 1, pp. 310–441; Wolfram Kaiser, *Using Europe, Abusing the Europeans: Britain and European Integration, 1945–1963* (London: Macmillan, 1996); George Wilkes, ed., *Britain's Failure to Enter the European Community, 1961–1963: The Enlargement Negotiations and Crises in European, Atlantic, and Commonwealth Relations* (London: Frank Cass, 1997).

29. On the Grand Design, see Pascaline Winand, *Eisenhower, Kennedy, and the United States of Europe* (New York: St. Martin's Press, 1993), pp. 245–264; and Giauque, *Grand Designs*, pp. 98–125.

30. John F. Kennedy, "Address at Independence Hall, Philadelphia," July 4, 1962, in U.S. Government, *Public Papers of the Presidents of the United States: John F. Kennedy, January 1 to December 31, 1962* (Washington, DC: U.S. Government Printing Office, 1963), p. 538.

31. Walter Hallstein, "The European Economic Community," *Political Science Quarterly* 78, no. 2 (June 1963), pp. 167, 168, 174. The article was based on a speech that Hallstein gave at Columbia University. See also Walter Hallstein, *United Europe: Challenge and Opportunity* (Cambridge: Harvard University Press, 1962).

32. Hallstein, "The European Economic Community," p. 176.

33. On de Gaulle's strategic vision and European policies, see Frederic Bozo, *Two Strategies for Europe: De Gaulle, the United States, and the Atlantic Alliance* (Lanham, MD: Rowman and Littlefield, 2001); Alain Peyrefitte, *C'était de Gaulle*, Vol. 1: *La France redevient la France* (Paris: de Fallois/Fayard, 1994), and Vol. 2: *La France reprend sa place dans le monde* (Paris: de Fallois/Fayard, 1997); Eric Roussel, *Charles de Gaulle* (Paris: Broché, 2002); and Maurice Vaïsse, *La grandeur. Politique étrangère du général de Gaulle, 1958–1969* (Paris: Fayard, 1997).

34. On Anglo-American relations and the Grand Design, see Stuart Ward, "Kennedy, Britain, and the European Community," in *John F. Kennedy and Europe*, ed. Douglas Brinkley and Richard T. Griffiths (Baton Rouge: Louisiana State University Press, 1999), pp. 317–332.

35. *FRUS, 1961–1963*, Vol. 13, p. 11. Emphasis in the original.

36. Ibid., p. 6.

37. Ibid.

38. Ibid., p. 66.

39. On this proposal, which came to be known as the Fouchet Plan, see Robert Bloes, *Le "Plan Fouchet" et le Problème de l'Europe Politique* (Bruges: College of Europe, 1970); Susanne J. Bodenheimer, "The 'Political Union' Debate in Europe: A Case Study of Intergovernmental Diplomacy," *International Organization*. 21, no. 1 (Winter 1967), pp. 24–54; Pierre Gerbet, "In Search of Political Union: The Fouchet Plan Negotiations (1960–1962)," in *The Dynamics of European Union*, ed. Roy Pryce (London: Croom Helm, 1987), pp. 105–129; and Giauque, *Grand Designs*, pp. 126–157.

40. Andrew Moravcsik argued that this was indeed the case. See Moravcsik, "De Gaulle Between Grain and Grandeur: The Political Economy of French EC Policy, 1958–1970," Pt. 1, *Journal of Cold War Studies* 2, no. 2 (Spring 2000), pp. 34–42.

41. See Moravcsik, "Between Grain and Grandeur," Pt. 1, p. 39; and Oliver Bange, *The EEC Crisis of 1963: Kennedy, Macmillan, de Gaulle and Adenauer in Conflict* (London: Macmillan, 2000), pp. 27–28.

42. *FRUS, 1961–1963*, Vol. 13, p. 52.

43. On Adenauer's relations with the Western allies, see Hans-Peter Schwarz, *Konrad Adenauer: German Politician and Statesman in a Period of War, Revolution, and Reconstruction*, Vol. 2: *The Statesman, 1952–1967* (Oxford: Berghahn Books, 1995), pp. 513–627. On his relations specifically with de Gaulle, see Hermann Kusterer, *Der Kanzler und der General* (Stuttgart: Neske, 1995). On de Gaulle's policy toward Germany and relations with Adenauer, see Pierre Maillard, *De Gaulle et l'Allemagne. Le rêve inachevé* (Paris: Plon, 1990).

44. *FRUS, 1961–1963*, Vol. 13, pp. 122–123, 125–126.

45. See ibid., p. 8.

46. Andrew Moravcsik argued that de Gaulle vetoed Britain's application because "British membership would kill the CAP." Moravcsik, "De Gaulle Between Grain and Grandeur: The Political Economy of French EC Policy, 1958–1970," Pt. 2, *Journal of Cold War Studies* 2, no. 3 (Fall 2000), pp. 4–68. See also Moravcsik, "Beyond Grain and Grandeur: An Answer to Critics and an Agenda for Future Research," *Journal of Cold War Studies* 2, no. 3 (Fall 2000), pp. 117–142; Moravcsik, *Choice for Europe*, pp. 159–237; and Bange, *EEC Crisis*, pp. 108–116. The text of the press conference is in de Gaulle, *Mémoires d'Espoir*, pp. 832–848.

47. Hallstein, "European Economic Community," p. 175.

48. On the Elysée Treaty, see Giauque, *Grand Designs*, pp. 96–113.

49. *FRUS, 1961–1963*, Vol. 13, pp. 204–209. Ball's reverence for Monnet and loathing for de Gaulle are evident in his memoirs. See George Ball, *The Past Has Another Pattern* (New York: Norton, 1982), pp. 96–98.

50. See Thomas Alan Schwartz, *Lyndon Johnson and Europe: In the Shadow of Vietnam* (Cambridge: Harvard University Press, 2003).

51. Von der Groeben, *Formative Years*, pp. 182–186; Robert Marjolin, *Memoirs, 1911–1986: Architect of European Unity* (London: Weidenfeld and Nicholson, 1986), pp. 345–358.

52. De Gaulle, *Mémoires d'Espoir*, pp. 195–196.

53. On the empty chair crisis, see Miriam Camps, *European Unification in the 1960s: From the Veto to the Crisis* (New York: McGraw-Hill, 1966); Maurice Couve de Murville, *Une Politique étrangère, 1958–1969* (Paris: Plon, 1971); John Lambert, "The Constitutional Crisis, 1965–1966," *Journal of Common Market Studies* 7, no. 3 (May 1966), pp. 195–228; John Newhouse, *Collision in Brussels: The Common Market Crisis of 30 June 1965* (New York: Norton, 1967); Françoise de la Serre, "The European Economic Community and the 1965 Crisis," in *European Integration*, ed. F. Roy Willis (New York: New Viewpoints, 1975), pp. 130–153; Moravcsik, *Choice for Europe*, pp. 159–237.

54. See Moravcsik, "Between Grain and Grandeur," Pt. 2; Moravcsik, *Choice for Europe*, pp. 159–237.

55. For the text of the Luxembourg Compromise, see http://europa.eu.int/scadplus/leg/en/cig/g4000l.htm.

56. See F. Roy Willis, *France, Germany and the New Europe, 1945–1967*, rev. and expanded ed. (Stanford, CA: Stanford University Press, 1968), p. 362.

57. On Britain's second application, see Oliver J. Daddow, ed., *Harold Wilson and European Integration: Britain's Second Application to Join the EEC* (London: Frank Cass Publishers, 2002).

58. The text of the press conference is in de Gaulle, *Allocutions et messages*, pp. 1033–1050.

59. Commission, *First Report on the General Activities of the European Communities* (Luxembourg: European Communities, 1968), pp. 346–347.

60. The text of the press conference is in de Gaulle, *Allocutions et messages*, pp. 1057–1075.

61. On the Trade Expansion Act, see Alkema, "European-American Trade Policies," pp. 226–231; and Diebold, "Watershed," pp. 235–260.

62. John B. Rehm, "Developments in the Law and Institutions of International Economic Relations: The Kennedy Round of Trade Negotiations," *American Journal of International Law* 62, no. 2 (April 1968), pp. 406–407.

63. See von der Groeben, *Formative Years*, pp. 83–84, 205; Werner Feld, "The Association Agreements of the European Community: A Comparative Analysis," *International Organization* 19, no. 2 (Spring 1965), pp. 223–249; Isebill V. Gruhn, "The Lomé Convention: Inching Towards Interdependence," *International Organization* 30, no. 2 (Spring 1976), pp. 241–262.

64. Von der Groeben, *Formative Years*, p. 87.

65. Ellen Frey-Wouters, "The Progress of European Integration," *World Politics* 17, no. 3 (April 1965), pp. 460–477.

66. Rome Treaty, text available at http://www.europa.eu.int/abc/obj/treaties/en/entoc05.htm.

67. Ibid.

68. Von der Groeben, *Formative Years*, p. 209, n53.

69. On economic policy cooperation generally, see Von der Groeben, *Formative Years*, pp. 64–66, 141–144, 206–213.

70. See Jacques Rueff, *The Monetary Sin of the West* (London: Macmillan, 1972).

71. See Barry Eichengreen, *Globalizing Capital: A History of the International Monetary System* (Princeton, NJ: Princeton University Press, 1996), pp. 113–135.

72. The *Economist*, April 27, 1968, p. 70.

73. See David Coombes, *Towards a European Civil Service* (London: Chatham House, 1968).

74. See Gordon L. Weil, "The Merger of the Institutions of the European Communities," *American Journal of International Law* 61, no. 1 (January 1967), pp. 57–65.

75. Case 26/62, *Van Gend en Loos v. Nederlandse Administratie der Belastingen*, 1963, ECR 1; Case 6/64, *Costa v. ENEL*, 1964, ECR 585.

76. See Youri Devuyst, "The European Union's Constitutional Order? Between Community Method and Ad Hoc Compromise," *Berkeley Journal of International Law* 18, no. 1 (1999), pp. 1–52.

77. See Karen Alter, "The European Court's Political Power," *West European Politics* 91, no. 3 (July 1996), pp. 458–486.

4

Reversal

The end of the 1960s seemed to herald a new beginning in international relations and a new departure for the European Community. The United States and the Soviet Union settled into a period of détente or reduced tension in their adversarial relationship. This culminated in the Helsinki Accords in 1975, which instituted the Conference on Security and Cooperation in Europe, a vehicle for East-West dialogue and human rights monitoring that helped gradually to undermine Soviet control in Central and Eastern Europe. Ostpolitik, West Germany's new policy of rapprochement toward the Soviet bloc, was a regional manifestation of global détente. Enthusiastically espoused by Willy Brandt, who became chancellor of Germany in 1969 as head of the first Social Democratic government since the war, Ostpolitik stirred domestic as well as international controversy and dominated German politics in the early 1970s.

Charles de Gaulle unexpectedly resigned as president of France at about the same time that Brandt came to office. The sighs of relief in Washington and Western European capitals were audible. De Gaulle's resignation facilitated an improvement in U.S.-European relations and a revival of interest in European integration. Georges Pompidou, de Gaulle's successor, was open minded on the hitherto vexed question of British accession and on new policy initiatives in the Community. At Pompidou's request, national leaders convened in The Hague, the Dutch capital, in December 1969 for what promised to be an epochal event in the history of the EC.

Developments nevertheless proved disappointing. International economics and finance were on the verge of a major upheaval. The Bretton Woods System, synonymous with economic stability since World War II, teetered on the brink of collapse in the late 1960s. A ballooning U.S. trade deficit and inflationary pressure generated by the Vietnam War prompted the United States to float the dollar in August 1971. EC member states responded by launching a plan for economic and monetary union (EMU) with a target date of 1980 for irrevocably fixing intra-EC rates and launching a single monetary policy.

Plans for EMU collapsed under the weight of the oil crisis that followed the October 1973 Arab-Israeli war. The ensuing recession in Western Europe saw rising unemployment, spiraling inflation, and plummeting rates of growth. Far from converging on the path to EMU, member states' economic policies and performances diverged drastically. The EC failed to meet the challenge of widespread economic and financial uncertainty. Despite protestations to the contrary, member states went their own ways. Although the customs union remained intact, efforts to remove nontariff barriers ground to a halt and new obstacles to intra-EC trade came into being. Narrowly defined national interests predominated. The circumstances were hardly favorable for Britain's entry into the EC in 1973.

The greatest political change in Europe at the time took place outside the Community and outside the Soviet orbit as well. In 1974 the Greek military junta collapsed following Turkey's invasion of northern Cyprus, an event regarded in Greece as a national disaster. Two other authoritarian regimes, in Portugal and Spain, ended as well in the mid-1970s. Greece, Portugal, and Spain promptly applied to join the EC. While celebrating the image of the EC as a source of stability for emerging democracies, member states fretted about the financial, institutional, and policy implications of enlargement.

This chapter examines the vicissitudes of European integration during a distinctly unpropitious period. Preoccupied by domestic problems—the resurgence of communism in Italy; violent left-wing protests and terrorism in Germany; strikes and financial collapse in Britain—member states mostly looked inward. For those who bothered to think about it, European integration in the mid-1970s meant excessive harmonization, agricultural overproduction, and a sullen bureaucracy in Brussels. Nevertheless, developments in the European Community were not unremittingly gloomy. There was notable progress on regional policy, social policy, and environmental policy. The European Court continued to produce a body of law that helped to tie the member states together at a time of threatened disintegration. On the institutional front, national leaders decided in 1975 to establish a new body, the European Council, as a means of convening regular summit meetings. The Parliament acquired limited budgetary authority in 1970 and prepared to hold its first direct elections before the end of the decade. The conclusion of a new aid and trade accord between the EC and a group of African, Caribbean, and Pacific countries in Lomé in 1975 enhanced the Community's international profile, as did the launch of European Political Cooperation, a mechanism to coordinate member states' foreign policies.

▧ The Spirit of The Hague

The EC's fortunes looked distinctly unpromising at the beginning of 1969. The Luxembourg compromise continued to cast a long shadow over legislative decisionmaking. De Gaulle's second veto of Britain's application still rankled with the other member states. Following the student riots and worker strikes of May 1968, de Gaulle regained control in France and looked set to stay in power until at least the next presidential election, scheduled for December 1972. The Franco-German engine of European integration stalled. Despite widespread growth in the 1960s, economic trends diverged rather than converged within the Community as a whole. The Commission spoke openly "of crisis, paralysis and even the possible disintegration of the Communities," with advocates of deeper integration "discouraged and pessimistic."[1]

Britain's accession seemed destined to wait until de Gaulle's departure. Yet a curious event in early 1969 hinted that de Gaulle might have changed his mind about letting Britain into the EC. In mid-February, de Gaulle raised with the new British ambassador, Sir Christopher Soames, the idea of closer cooperation among Britain, France, Germany, and Italy on security and defense policy within an enlarged EC. The British never allowed de Gaulle to elaborate. So distrustful were they of France that, fearing a trap, they leaked the gist of de Gaulle's thoughts to the media. De Gaulle was furious: here was further evidence of British perfidy.

De Gaulle may indeed have warmed to the prospect of British accession, especially after the fallout from the events of May 1968 glaringly demonstrated French economic weakness and German economic strength. Germany was also beginning to make diplomatic overtures toward Eastern Europe and the Soviet Union, thereby stoking French fears that the Federal Republic might loosen its moorings in the West. De Gaulle may have seen British accession as a way to counterbalance Germany's economic weight in the EC and tie Germany more firmly into Western Europe. Nevertheless, the EC had not yet agreed on a permanent financial arrangement for the common agricultural policy (CAP). Until it did so, de Gaulle's opposition to British accession probably remained entrenched.

In any event the so-called Soames Affair, a diplomatic tempest in a teapot, firmly closed the door on British accession as long as de Gaulle remained in office. De Gaulle's resignation in April 1969, after losing a referendum on minor constitutional matters that became a personal vote of confidence, suddenly brought the question of British accession to the fore. So closely was de Gaulle associated with the Community's malaise that his unexpected departure raised hopes of a rapid revival of European integration. Deep-rooted frustration with de Gaulle and relief at his departure accounted in large part for the wave of optimism about the EC's future that swept Western Europe at the end of 1969.

Brandt and Pompidou

Georges Pompidou, "solid, dependable, avuncular," won the French presidential election in April 1969.[2] As de Gaulle's prime minister for much of the

1960s, Pompidou was a well-known quantity. In some respects his approach to the EC was typically Gaullist: he defended the Luxembourg Compromise, advocated intergovernmentalism, and strongly supported the CAP. Like de Gaulle, Pompidou embraced the EC primarily for economic reasons. Although keenly interested in the CAP, Pompidou's main goal was to modernize French industry. The Community provided the means to achieve that end. Indeed, the EC's economic importance for France seemed greater than ever in the aftermath of the disastrous May 1968 events.

Unlike de Gaulle, Pompidou appeared open minded on the question of British accession. In view of Germany's growing economic power and diplomatic assertiveness, Pompidou appreciated the strategic importance of enlargement. But he was adamant about safeguarding the CAP. Distancing himself from de Gaulle, Pompidou championed the EC in the presidential election campaign and forged a link between approving enlargement and securing a permanent financial regulation for the CAP. The Soames Affair protected Pompidou from criticism from die-hard Gaullists, for whom Britain's exclusion from the EC had become an article of faith. De Gaulle himself kept quiet during the campaign.

Pompidou's election heralded a major breakthrough on enlargement. It coincided with Brandt's replacement of Kurt Kiesinger as chancellor of Germany. The advent of a new chancellor with an impeccable anti-Fascist past (Kiesinger was a former Nazi) and a desire to reinvigorate Franco-German relations augured well for the EC's revival. Nevertheless, Brandt and Pompidou were not on the same wavelength. Brandt was a Socialist, Pompidou a conservative. Brandt was a moderate supranationalist, Pompidou an avid intergovernmentalist. Pompidou was primarily a technocrat (he had served as prime minister for five years before being elected to parliament for the first time in 1967), Brandt a natural politician. Despite his humble origins, Pompidou was highly educated and detached; because of his humble origins, Brandt was streetwise and down-to-earth.

Those differences need not have divided the two men. What really set them apart was Pompidou's unease about Germany's growing economic and political power. Pompidou fretted incessantly about Ostpolitik, Brandt's foreign policy priority. Pompidou resented Germany's behavior during the exchange rate crises in late 1969. Far from deferring to France, Germany acted unilaterally, first by floating the mark and then by revaluing it. Loud German criticism of the CAP, with its runaway budget and rising food surpluses, also irritated the French.

The Hague Summit

The idea of a post–de Gaulle summit of the Six floated around Community capitals in mid-1969 before France presented it formally at a Council meeting in July. The main agenda items would be enlargement, the CAP, and EMU. Concerned about unilateral German monetary measures and the impact of exchange rate fluctuations on the all-important CAP, and keen to project a European "monetary personality" in transatlantic relations, Pompidou championed closer monetary policy cooperation among EC member states. Having linked enlargement and CAP funding, Pompidou added EMU to the mix. "Completion, deepening, enlargement"—meaning the budget (completion), EMU (deepening), and British accession (enlargement)—became a mantra in the run-up to the summit, scheduled for December in The Hague (the Dutch were then in the Council presidency).

The Hague summit generated considerable public interest. Support for European integration reemerged with a revival of the European Movement, a host of pro-European demonstrations, and a profusion of newspaper articles and letters to the editor. Eager to seize the moment, the Commission and the European Parliament made pre-summit calls for a new commitment by national leaders to greater European integration. Hoping that the summit would give "a new political impetus to the creation of Europe," the Commission stressed the need for enlargement, a financial regulation for the CAP, EMU, greater use of qualified majority voting, and direct elections to the Parliament.[3]

Brandt stole the show at the summit, from which the Commission president was mostly excluded. His opening speech and overall performance were more forceful than Pompidou's. Never prone to understatement, the *Economist* called Brandt's performance "the moment when postwar Germany came politically of age."[4] The summit communiqué did not personalize the proceedings but generally exaggerated the importance of the event, claiming that with Europe at "a turning point in its history," member states "reaffirmed their belief in the political objectives which gave the Community its meaning and purport." The bulk of the communiqué spelled out the significance of completion, deepening, and enlargement. National leaders stressed their determination to pass to the final stage of the common market by the end of the year and make a definitive financial arrangement for the CAP, subject to agreement to fund the Community by its "own resources" rather than contributions from national budgets. National leaders agreed in principle to open accession negotiations but did not stipulate a date. As for deepening, the summiteers approved a range of initiatives, including "a plan in stages" to be worked out in 1970 to achieve EMU; Community support for industrial research and development; and reform of the European Social Fund "within the framework of a closely concerted social policy." Community leaders also asked their foreign ministers to explore options for foreign policy cooperation.[5]

The summit gave rise to "the spirit of The Hague" or, as the Commission put it, "a rediscovered political will [among] the Six Member States" to get the Community going again.[6] Most participants and observers hailed the summit as a landmark in the history of European integration, comparing it to the Messina meeting of foreign ministers in 1955 that led to the Rome Treaty. Their exuberance was understandable, given widespread support for enlargement and closer integration immediately after de Gaulle's departure. Subsequent setbacks in the 1970s served only to strengthen the summit's claim to fame.[7]

Completion

Completion meant bringing the transitional period of the common market formally to an end and switching to a system of "own resources" to fund the EC. There were two sources of such resources: tariffs on industrial imports and levies on agricultural imports, whose rates were determined by common EC policies (the common commercial policy and the CAP, respectively). As those would not be sufficient to cover all the EC's expenditures, member states would have to supplement them with a portion of their value-added taxes.

France had long wanted a budgetary agreement in order to reduce the cost to the national exchequer of agricultural subsidies. Commission proposals for a switch to own resources in 1965 had triggered the empty chair crisis. Now the Commission was more circumspect and France less defensive. At the end of a marathon session in mid-December 1969, the Council agreed to the phased introduction of own resources, including a national contribution of up to 1 percent of value-added tax, between January 1971 and January 1975, when the system would become fully operational. The Commission hailed the "friendly and constructive atmosphere" in the Council as evidence of "the spirit of The Hague."[8]

Related negotiations in the Council on the role of the Parliament amounted to a mini intergovernmental conference. Member states signed the Treaty of Luxembourg in April 1970, amending a number of budgetary and institutional provisions in the Rome Treaty. Thus the Parliament and the Council became the EC's two budgetary authorities, although the distribution of power tilted toward the Council. The agreement also called for the Commission to introduce new proposals within a couple of years for further budgetary reform, thereby implying that member states would grant the Parliament additional authority. Indeed, national leaders agreed in principle at the Copenhagen summit in October 1973 to strengthen further the Parliament's budgetary authority and at the same time set up an independent Community audit board. Further negotiations culminated in the Brussels Treaty of 1975, which included provisions to establish the Court of Auditors.[9]

Deepening

Of the three goals declared at the Hague summit, deepening was less precise than completion or enlargement. It referred primarily to EMU, but included also foreign policy cooperation and regional policy. Foreign policy cooperation added a new dimension to the EC, albeit of an intergovernmental kind. The development of regional policy, an area with considerable integrative potential, became bound up with EMU.

Deepening was supposed to complement enlargement, lest the accession of new member states weaken the cohesiveness of the EC. Yet enlargement had little bearing on French and German motives for EMU. The French saw EMU primarily as a vehicle for constraining German monetary independence and projecting a European monetary identity onto the world stage at a time of increasing financial turbulence. After May 1968, as the franc came under growing pressure, the French also saw EMU as a means of garnering support for their beleaguered currency.

Germany's interest in EMU was more strategic than economic. Brandt weighed every foreign policy option against Ostpolitik, his overriding international interest. Thus Brandt saw EMU as a way to assuage French concerns about Germany's new foreign policy initiative. By the same token, Brandt played down the latent anti-Americanism inherent in Pompidou's conception of EMU and played up the evidence that EMU provided of Germany's continuing commitment to the West, a commitment that pleased the United States as much as it did France.

The Commission's interest in EMU stretched back to Britain's first application for EC membership. In its 1962 action program, the Commission had claimed that EMU would help to deepen integration in an enlarging EC. As it happened, an enlarged EC would have been unable to manage EMU in the 1960s because of Britain's chronic monetary problems. The deteriorating international monetary situation in the late 1960s offered the Commission another opportunity to advocate EMU even before de Gaulle resigned and Britain reactivated its membership application. The Commission therefore submitted the so-called Barre memorandum on EMU in February 1969 (named after Raymond Barre, Commission vice president with responsibility for economic policy).[10]

The Commission's circumstances in the late 1960s were far different from what they had been at the beginning of the decade when it first contemplated an initiative on EMU. At that time the Commission was on the crest of the integration wave, implementing the first stage of the customs union and negotiating a landmark agreement on agricultural policy. In 1969, by contrast, the Commission was caught in an intergovernmental undertow and cowed in the aftermath of the empty chair crisis. Accordingly, the Barre memorandum on EMU was less a bold initiative for further integration than a cautious call for what the French government now wanted: monetary policy coordination and short-term support for balance-of-payments difficulties. Barre was a pillar of the French establishment; he would not have taken such an important step without the French government's knowledge.

With Germany showing more independence on international monetary policy, France wanted to tie its powerful neighbor into a common European position. Moreover, the development of the CAP in the late 1960s gave France a strong incentive to coordinate monetary policy lest exchange rate fluctuations distort common prices and impair farmers' incomes. That is exactly what happened in 1969 when the French devalued in August and the Germans revalued in October, having floated for the previous two months. Pending the possible achievement of EMU, member states agreed to establish a complicated system of additional subsidies and border taxes—so-called Monetary Compensatory Amounts—to compensate farmers for exchange rate fluctuations.

France and Germany changed their exchange rates in 1969 without consulting the other member states, despite an earlier undertaking to do so. Apart from their impact on the CAP, the French and German realignments shook prevailing confidence in the stability of exchange rates, something taken for granted in the 1960s. Because fixed rates were presumed to have contributed decisively to the decade's unprecedented economic growth and prosperity, policymakers were generally averse to exchange rate flexibility and floating regimes.

At the Hague summit, national leaders therefore instructed the Council, together with the Commission, to draw up a plan in 1970 for the establishment in stages of EMU. The Council entrusted the task to Pierre Werner, prime minister and finance minister of Luxembourg and a long-time advocate of deeper integration.[11] The Werner committee comprised the chairmen of the EC's relevant monetary and economic policy committees as well as a representative of the Commission. In effect, an official of each national government sat on the committee. Although the committee's members did not represent national interests, the committee's deliberations reflected national positions on the issues under discussion.

The goal of EMU seemed simple enough—fixed exchange rates, a common monetary policy, and a single monetary authority—but member states differed about how best to achieve it. Governments disagreed among themselves about the necessity for economic convergence, the design and role of common institutions, and the desirability of a common currency. A major split emerged among finance ministers and within the Werner committee between the "economists," reflecting German and Dutch preferences, and the "monetarists," reflecting French and Belgian preferences. The economists insisted that a high degree of economic policy convergence had to precede monetary union; the monetarists held that monetary union would bring economic convergence in its wake. The issue was far from academic. Countries such as Germany and the Netherlands (and initially Italy), with balance-of-payments surpluses, did not want constantly to bail out countries such as France and Belgium, with chronic balance-of-payments deficits. By contrast, the French and Belgians wanted to enjoy the benefits of monetary stability at the expense of the more stringent EC member states without having to pay the domestic political price of undertaking macroeconomic policy reforms.

Contending economist and monetarist perspectives were apparent at the Hague summit. Although the Werner committee's initial report of May 1970 veered toward the monetarist position, its final report of October 1970 endorsed what Brandt later called the "iron rule" of parallel progress on economic convergence and monetary policy coordination.[12] Thus, in the first stage of the road to EMU, member states would narrow their exchange rate margins and launch medium-term monetary support measures. In the final stage member states would revise the Rome Treaty in order to establish new institutions at the European level and transfer power to the Parliament to counteract the loss of national authority over economic and monetary affairs. The Werner Plan was hazy about what would happen in the second stage. According to one of the earliest academic assessments of EMU, the gap between the first and the third stages "was simply enormous."[13]

The Werner Plan's endorsement of parallelism and call for institutional change outraged Pompidou. So did the plan's call for treaty reform. Although un-Gaullist in his willingness to contemplate EMU, Pompidou was neo-Gaullist in his opposition to supranationalism, especially when it involved the power of the Parliament. Thus, on institutional as well as substantive grounds, France and Germany stood on opposite sides of the EMU divide.

The differences between them became fully apparent at a rancorous meeting of the Council in December 1970. Brandt and Pompidou patched things up at a Franco-German summit in January 1971. Brandt faced conflicting domestic pressures. On the one hand, the Christian Democratic opposition castigated him for unnerving France by his pursuit of Ostpolitik. Brandt could assuage France and undermine domestic criticism by making concessions to Pompidou on EMU. On the other hand, the German central bank, a hallowed institution, preferred flexible to fixed exchange rates as a means of promoting price stability. Brandt attempted to square the circle by endorsing EMU in principle while playing down its institutional implications.[14] The outcome of the bilateral summit allowed the Council soon afterward to endorse the general goal of EMU, adopt various measures originally proposed in the Barre plan, and approve the Commission's third medium-term economic program. Ever inclined to grasp at straws, the Commission hailed the "far-reaching political implications" of these "historic" developments.[15]

The Council's decisiveness on relatively minor aspects of EMU disguised major differences between France and Germany, which would have become more apparent had EMU gone according to the Werner Plan. In the event, the international monetary crises of 1971 blew it off course. The first crisis struck in May, when a massive flow of funds from the United States into Germany put pressure on Bonn to revalue. Germany pressed for a joint EC float, threatening otherwise to float the mark unilaterally. France opposed floating, fearing that a rise in the value of the franc would render French exports uncompetitive (German exporters had similar concerns about the mark). France instead advocated a de facto devaluation of the dollar through a rise in the price of gold. This was something that Germany, more sensitive than France to U.S. interests, was unwilling to countenance. Having failed to reach agreement in the Council on a joint EC strategy, Germany and the Netherlands floated their currencies while other member states imposed capital controls. Thus member states found it impossible to narrow the range of intra-EC rate fluctuations in June 1971, as called for in the Werner Plan.

The second monetary crisis struck in August 1971 when the United States officially ended the convertibility of the dollar to gold, introduced a hefty import surcharge, and launched various measures to promote the sale of U.S. goods at home and abroad. Once again, EC member states failed to act together. A meeting between President Richard Nixon and Pompidou in the Azores in December 1971 set the stage for the Smithsonian agreement later in the month to realign exchange rates and finally devalue the dollar. The Smithsonian agreement established a margin of fluctuation of 2.25 percent on either side of the new dollar parity. That meant a possible fluctuation of 4.5 percent between any two EC currencies. Concerned about the consequences for the CAP and the customs union of such a wide spread, Pompidou pressed Brandt to limit intra-EC margins to 2.25 percent within the permissible 4.5 percent range. The Council agreed to do so in February 1972 through a system of intra-EC intervention and debt settlement. That was the origin of the wonderfully evocative "snake in the tunnel," an arrangement that allowed the currencies of EC member states to wiggle up and down within a narrower band than the one prescribed in the Smithsonian agreement.

The exchange rate crises of 1971 undermined the EC's confidence and sowed additional discord between Brandt and Pompidou. Although the snake in the tunnel seemed to put EMU back on track, monetary developments in 1972 were almost as rocky as before. The snake gyrated widely, shedding participating currencies like old skins.[16] As a concession to Pompidou, national leaders agreed at the Paris summit in October 1972 to establish within the next few months a European Monetary Cooperation Fund for the second stage of EMU. In what many of them knew to be a leap of faith, they also reaffirmed their commitment "irreversibly to achieve [EMU] . . . with a view to its completion not later than December 31, 1980."[17]

Enlargement

British hopes of joining the EC revived in 1969 after de Gaulle's resignation and Pompidou's election victory. Once the British reactivated their application, the Council asked the Commission to submit a new opinion. The Commission advocated the reopening of negotiations as soon as possible. Britain interpreted the Hague communiqué at the end of the year as an endorsement of the Commission's position.[18]

Although a Labour government revived Britain's application in 1969, a Conservative government conducted the accession negotiations that brought Britain into the EC. In June 1970, only two weeks before the opening of negotiations, the Conservatives defeated Labour in the general election, and Edward Heath replaced Harold Wilson as prime minister. It was testimony to the continuity in official British policy, despite deep fissures in Conservative as well as Labour ranks, that the new government endorsed the old government's position and began the negotiations on schedule at the end of June.

Unlike Wilson, who was equivocal about EC membership, Heath was enthusiastic. Heath's conservatism, paternalism, and moderate intergovernmentalism appealed more to Pompidou than Wilson's socialism, egalitarianism, and indifference to the EC. Heath's personal interest in European integration heightened the government's determination finally to join. As Sir Con O'Neill, Britain's chief negotiator in 1970–1971, put it, "What mattered was to get into the Community and thereby restore our position at the center of European affairs which, since 1958, we had lost. The negotiations were concerned only with the means of achieving this objective at an acceptable price."[19]

■ From Six to Nine

Accession involved two sets of negotiations: one between Britain and the Six, represented by the Council presidency; the other among the members states themselves. Formal negotiations took place in Brussels at ministerial and deputies levels. Ministerial meetings were ceremonial and stilted; deputies meetings were more productive. As in any set of negotiations, most of the important work took place in bilateral and multilateral meetings in the margins of official sessions. As the talks progressed, the feeling grew that the decisive negotiations were not between Britain and the Six or even among the Six themselves, but between Britain and France. Thus, diplomatic contacts between the two governments, primarily via the British embassy in Paris, where Sir Christopher Soames was still ambassador, were crucial to the success of the negotiations.

Despite the air of inevitability about eventual enlargement, there was no guarantee that the negotiations would succeed. Pompidou could hardly veto Britain's application outright, even if he wanted to. The other Five would not defer to Pompidou as they had deferred to de Gaulle. Brandt made it clear that another French veto was unacceptable. But Pompidou could drag out the negotiations or insist on terms unacceptable to Britain.

Nothing much happened during the exploratory stage of the negotiations from May until December 1970. The negotiations could only begin in earnest when member states ratified the Luxembourg Treaty (on Community funding) at the end of the year. Much to Britain's dismay, there was little progress either in the new year. As O'Neill recalled, "the first four months of 1971 were months of stagnation, exasperation, virtual deadlock and increasing apprehension about the outcome."[20] Despite general agreement on the desirability of British accession, deep differences separated both sides on specific issues. The most contentious of these were fish, food, and finance.

Much to Britain's surprise and annoyance, the Council adopted a common fisheries policy, which had long been on the EC's agenda, on the same day that the accession negotiations began. This looked like a blatant effort to reach an agreement among the Six on an issue of great interest to Britain and the other applicants before enlargement took place. Because it gave member states unlimited access to each other's waters, the fisheries policy incensed Britain's fishing community. Under pressure from the applicants (the issue infuriated the other candidates as well), the Six relented and agreed to modify the fisheries policy.[21]

The common fisheries policy was the only Community policy that the Six agreed to change as a result of enlargement. By contrast, the CAP was sacrosanct. That did not prevent Britain and the Six from fighting over specific commodities that enjoyed privileged access to Britain: Commonwealth sugar and New Zealand butter. Britain wanted to honor and extend the terms of the Commonwealth Sugar Agreement that permitted large-scale importation into Britain of sugar from developing Commonwealth countries. The sugar lobby, led by wealthy British importers rather than poor Commonwealth producers, "was perhaps the best organized and most active of all the British interest groups seeking to influence the negotiations."[22] On the other side, France defended the interests of domestic sugar beet producers as well as producers in countries associated with the EC under the Yaoundé Convention. As the Yaoundé Convention and the Commonwealth Sugar Agreement were up for renegotiation in 1974, both sides agreed to accept the status quo until then.

New Zealand butter was a stickier point. Implausible though it seems, it was an issue dear to the hearts of many British voters. Britons were less enamored of the product than of the people of New Zealand, thanks to family connections and the country's steadfastness during World War II. (New Zealand lamb, another British favorite, did not pose a problem because the Community did not yet have a market organization for sheep meat.) New Zealand butter was of more than sentimental importance: New Zealand supplied about 40 percent of Britain's butter needs, a market share that French and Dutch producers wanted to acquire.

The question of New Zealand butter was so sensitive politically that, as Sir David Hannay, a senior British official, observed, "without the acquiescence of the New Zealand government [in a butter deal] it was rather doubtful that the terms of Britain's accession would have been approved by the

House of Commons."[23] France drew the obvious conclusion and leveraged New Zealand butter to win concessions from Britain on another issue in the accession negotiations: the EC budget. Britain's initial offer in the budget negotiations—a contribution of 3 percent in 1973 going up to 15 percent in 1977—was ludicrously low. Britain soon realized that France would agree to allow New Zealand butter into the EC only if Britain agreed to make a much higher contribution to the budget. In the end, Britain agreed to pay 8.64 percent in 1973, rising to 18.92 percent in 1977. That was a great deal for New Zealand farmers, at British taxpayers' expense.[24]

The success of the negotiations ultimately hinged on agreement at the highest political level. With summitry increasingly prevalent, the negotiators presumed the breakthrough would happen at either a Franco-German or an EC summit. Instead, the breakthrough came at a summit between Britain and France in May 1971. The contrast with previous summits between de Gaulle and supplicant British prime ministers could not have been greater. Heath and Pompidou got on extremely well together. They wanted to send a positive signal about the negotiations and about the EC's future. With the CAP financially secure and Germany increasingly assertive, Pompidou wanted enlargement finally to proceed. Heath and Pompidou held a glowing postsummit press conference in the same room in which de Gaulle had launched his famous diatribes against British accession.

The foreign ministers fleshed out the political agreement reached by Heath and Pompidou on the linked problems of New Zealand butter and Britain's budgetary contribution. "When, after two all-night sessions, the meeting ended a little before 5:00am on 23 June, all were convinced that the negotiations would succeed." Thus, to use the phrase current at the time, "the back of the negotiations was broken."[25] The negotiators mopped things up, formally concluding the talks in January 1972.

There was intense media speculation as the British negotiations came to an end about the demise of the Franco-German axis and the rise of an Anglo-French axis. Undoubtedly, Pompidou was increasingly impatient with Brandt's approach to monetary policy and Ostpolitik and embraced Heath partly to snub the German chancellor. But Brandt was unperturbed. He knew that common Franco-German interests were deeper than either Anglo-French or Anglo-German interests. British and French antipathy toward supranationalism bothered Brandt more. Heath and Pompidou were equally Gaullist when it came to the defense of national interests in Community decisionmaking. Back in London after the Paris summit, Heath gave a ringing defense of the Luxembourg Compromise (a member state's right to veto legislation). Member states, he told the House of Commons, "should not attempt to override a single country in something which it considers to be of vital national interest."[26]

Developments in Britain during the accession process also cast a pall over the successful outcome of the negotiations. British public opinion, never at

British prime minister Edward Heath (center) signs Britain into the common market, in Brussels, Belgium, 1972. Ireland, Norway, and Denmark also signed accession treaties at this meeting.

ease with European integration, turned more and more against accession. By playing down the political costs and exaggerating the economic advantages of membership, the government gave ample ammunition to British Euroskeptics. In a harbinger of things to come, Wilson, the Labour Party leader, complained openly about the terms of accession.[27]

Although later known for their vitriolic hostility to the EU, most British newspapers applauded the outcome of the negotiations. The *Times* and the *Telegraph*, rabidly Euroskeptical by the early 1990s, swam against the tide of opinion in the early 1970s by championing British entry. In an October 1971 editorial, the *Telegraph* made "no apology for the fact that the balance is in favor of entry. We have supported entry in principle from the start, and consider the present terms acceptable." The tabloids were almost evenly split on the issue, with the mass-circulation *Express* then, as later, venting its spleen against Brussels bureaucrats, lost sovereignty, and the inevitable end of British greatness. The *Mirror* illustrated its support for British accession by featuring scantily clad "Euro-Dollies" (photos of women from the six member states).[28]

The key debate in the House of Commons took place in October 1971, shortly before the negotiations ended but when the contours of the accession treaty were generally known. The government won by a large majority, with most members of the two main parties voting in favor. Nevertheless, a sizable minority of Conservatives and almost half the Labour parliamentary membership voted against. Positions hardened in 1972, when Britain ratified the accession treaty through parliamentary enactment of the European Communities Bill. Wilson denounced Heath's accession terms in uncompromising language, Labour antimarketeers were in full cry, and Heath had difficulty reining in his own anti-EC dissidents. The depth of division on the European question, and Wilson's determination to exploit it politically, raised a red flag across the Channel.

The Other Applicants

Britain was not the only candidate for EC membership in the early 1970s. The others were Denmark, Ireland, and Norway, countries with close economic ties to Britain (although Denmark's and Ireland's were much closer than Norway's). The four applicants negotiated separately but contemporaneously with the Six. Like Britain, each of the three smaller countries had strong Euroskeptical elements.

There was some concern in Ireland about the impact of EC membership on neutrality, a legacy of the independence movement earlier in the century. The Irish government declined Washington's invitation to join NATO in 1949 because of Britain's "occupation" of Northern Ireland. Although the EC was not a military organization, the Rome Treaty's commitment to "ever closer union" suggested that the EC would develop a defense policy some time down the road. In the meantime, most Irish people accepted that, for economic reasons, Ireland could not stay out of the EC if Britain went in. For political reasons too, Ireland was better off inside a larger association of states than living permanently in Britain's shadow. Far from wanting to remain outside even if it was feasible to do so, a majority of Irish people saw EC membership as an opportunity to modernize society and transform the economy. Simply put, the Irish wanted to be more worldly and wealthy. The prospect of "Brussels money" flowing into the pockets of Irish farmers made the EC even more attractive. Ireland's negotiations were relatively easy, although Ireland complained about the common fisheries policy and successfully pressed for derogations in certain policy areas.

Euroskepticism was more entrenched in Norway. As Norwegians liked to point out, having become independent of Sweden in relatively recent times, Norway was leery of joining another union of states, albeit voluntarily. Yet Ireland, which had also emerged from an unhappy union with a larger neighbor, avidly pursued EC entry in order to enhance its de facto independence. Moreover, joining a Community of which Sweden was not a part would surely have enhanced Norway's position vis-à-vis the old imperial power. But Norway's antipathy toward the EC ran deeper than national identity. Farmers were concerned that subsidies would fall if they participated in the CAP, conservatives fretted about the social impact of accession, and fishermen resented the common fisheries policy.

Opinion in Denmark was equally divided over EC membership, although the economic arguments weighed heavily in favor of joining. Denmark could not afford to reduce its market access to Britain and looked forward to gaining unrestricted access to German markets. Yet Nordic solidarity, a cultural rather than an economic concept, pulled many Danes in the opposite direction, away from the EC. Remembering the war years, many Danes opposed the idea of closer association with Germany. A change of government in October 1971 brought the Euroskeptical Social Democrats to power. The new government took a harder line on a number of issues, including fisheries, important in Denmark because of the country's control over Greenland and the Faeroes.

The 1972 Referenda

Four countries held referenda on enlargement in 1972: three of the applicant states and one member state. The applicants were Ireland, Denmark, and Norway; the member state was France. The French referendum of 1972 is now largely forgotten, but it had an interesting impact on Britain, the sole applicant state not to hold a referendum on EC accession. The French referendum on whether to approve enlargement preceded the others. Pompidou's announcement of it took everyone by surprise. Legally France could ratify the accession agreements only by a vote in parliament. Therefore the referendum was purely advisory. Pompidou had personal and political motives for calling it. Personally, he must have known by early 1972 that he was seriously ill (he died two years later). He wanted to be remembered as a European as well as a French statesman. Already he envisioned the Paris summit later in the year as making a major contribution to the construction of Europe, albeit along intergovernmental lines. A successful referendum would emphasize France's commitment to the Community and enhance Pompidou's European credentials.

Politically, Pompidou wanted to split the opposition and strengthen his position within the Gaullist camp. The Communists opposed the existence of the Community, whereas the Socialists supported British accession. A referendum on enlargement was a sure way to accentuate the division between Pompidou's left-wing rivals. As for the Gaullists, what better way to cut the feet from under critics of enlargement within his own party than by using a classic Gaullist device—a referendum—to buttress his own position? Yet Pompidou was careful not to follow de Gaulle's precedent by threatening (or promising) to resign if the result was negative. As it happened, the result was favorable, but not overwhelmingly so. Only 60 percent of the electorate turned out to vote, of which 61 percent voted "yes." Many voters stayed away from the polls or voted against for domestic rather than European reasons. Pompidou was bitterly disappointed.[29]

The referendum was soon forgotten in France (so much so that President François Mitterrand called a referendum on the Maastricht Treaty for similar reasons in 1992 and nearly lost). Its legacy was more enduring across the Channel not because of the result, but because of the ammunition it gave to antimarketeers in the British Labour Party. During the 1970 general election campaign, neither Heath nor Wilson endorsed the idea of a referendum on EC membership. Referenda were repugnant to Britain's cherished principle of parliamentary sovereignty (a nationwide referendum had never been held in Britain). Left-wing opponents of EC membership seized on the French example as one to be emulated in Britain; right-wing opponents championed the principle of parliamentary sovereignty and were unlikely to be inspired by French political ideas or developments. Wilson promised that, if elected next time round, he would renegotiate the terms of membership and hold a referendum on the outcome. Wilson might have adopted that position anyway, but the impact of the French referendum was obvious.

The outcome of the Irish referendum, held in May, was never in doubt. The two biggest political parties vigorously advocated a "yes" vote; the small Labour Party campaigned against. The Irish people knew on which side their bread was buttered. A whopping 83 percent voted in favor of membership (the turnout was 77 percent). Next came the Norwegian referendum at the end of September. Those opposed to membership, drawn from all walks of life but representing especially agricultural and fishing interests, polled 54 percent (the turnout was 78 percent). The prime minister, who had turned the referendum into a vote of confidence, duly resigned (he was the first politician to lose office directly as a result of the EC). The final referendum took place in Denmark, one week later. Danish and other supporters of membership feared that the Norwegian result might have had a domino effect. If it did, the consequence was not enough to tip the balance against membership. The result was a respectable 63 percent in favor (the turnout was 90 percent).

These were the first in a number of referenda on the EU held mostly in the same countries in the years ahead. From the perspective of 1972 they seemed like one-time events. The referenda showed that opinion in Norway and Denmark, Scandinavian countries that eschewed participation in earlier stages of integration, was finely poised between supporters and opponents of EC membership; that Irish support for the EC was solid; and that the situation in France was less certain than the government thought. It seemed at the time as if the sizable minority of Danes who voted "no" would soon be reconciled to their fate. In the event, unease about EC membership grew in Denmark and elsewhere throughout the Community, including Ireland.

The EC on the Eve of Enlargement

EC leaders convened in Paris in October 1972 for their first meeting since the Hague summit in 1969. Concerned about the timorous spirit of The Hague, Pompidou wanted another summit to symbolize the EC's continued revival. Indeed, it seemed as if the Community was on the move again. The Luxembourg Treaty of 1970, which established the system of own resources and granted budgetary authority to the Parliament, was in effect. The first stage of EMU was underway, with member states frequently reaffirming their determination to launch the second stage on time, in January 1974. Most impressive of all, the accession negotiations had ended successfully. Despite the disappointing results of the French and Norwegian referenda, the Community was about to encompass Britain, Denmark, and Ireland. Member states billed the summit as a celebration of enlargement as much as anything else and invited the leaders of the three candidate countries to attend. In the aftermath of the French referendum and in the run-up to the German general election, both Pompidou and Brandt had reason to accentuate positive aspects of European integration.

Superficially also, the summit was a success. Pompidou made a strong speech in favor of deeper integration. He claimed that EMU was necessary in order to counter currency speculation, fight inflation, create "a distinctive European monetary zone," and contribute to reform of the international monetary system. Brandt kept a low profile at the summit, thereby allowing Pompidou and Heath to share the limelight. The summit communiqué contained an impressive list of immediate objectives, ranging from the establishment of the European Monetary Cooperation Fund and the launch of the second stage of EMU, to the creation of a regional development fund, to the strengthening of social, industrial, and science and technology policies. The communiqué contained a short final paragraph proclaiming that EC leaders had "set themselves the major objective of transforming, before the end of the present decade . . . the whole complex of the relations of [the] member states into a European union." It called on the EC's institutions to draw up a report on the subject before the end of 1975.[30]

Taken out of context, the communiqué's endorsement of European union became a caricature of the wildly optimistic state of integration in the early 1970s. In fact, national leaders tacked the statement onto the communiqué almost as an afterthought. It was Pompidou's idea. Far from connoting a commitment to supranationalism, the communiqué's final paragraph merely indicated Pompidou's general support for integration and concern about his legacy. None of the summiteers took literally the idea that there would be a European Union by 1980.

Despite the conviviality and apparent success of the Paris summit, the EC was in some disarray in the early 1970s. Like most spectral beings, the spirit of The Hague proved more apparent than real. There were major institutional and policy differences among member states, a growing chasm in Franco-German relations, and a marked decline in the Commission's fortunes. Smaller member states resented the drift toward intergovernmentalism that was evident not only in the Commission's continuing decline but also in the persistence of the Luxembourg Compromise, the rise of summitry, and the big member states' dominance of European Political Cooperation (foreign policy cooperation).

Launched in 1970 in response to Germany's preoccupation with Ostpolitik, European Political Cooperation sought to improve the flow of information among member states on major foreign policy issues and help them to formulate joint positions. At French insistence, foreign policy cooperation was rigidly intergovernmental. In order to emphasize the difference between member states meeting "in European Political Cooperation" and in the Council, on one infamous occasion foreign ministers met in the morning in Copenhagen to discuss foreign policy (Denmark was then in the Council presidency) before flying to Brussels in the afternoon to discuss Community business. Needless to say the Commission and the Parliament were originally excluded from foreign policy cooperation.

The supranationalist Dutch pressed in the early 1970s for an end to the rigid distinction between foreign policy cooperation and Community business, for greater use of qualified majority voting in the Council, and for reform of the Rome Treaty to counter growing intergovernmentalism in the EC. They were rebuffed not only by the French but also by the Germans who, despite supporting supranationalism, were unwilling to confront France on the matter. The Dutch campaign petered out in 1972, when Britain's impending accession put the final nail in the coffin of treaty reform along supranational lines.

The Germans had other battles to fight with the French. Germany grew increasingly resentful in the early 1970s of the runaway costs of the CAP. Helmut Schmidt, Germany's finance minister, made no secret of his opposition to excessive agricultural subsidies.[31] That put Schmidt at loggerheads with France and with the agriculture minister in his own government, who wanted the highest prices possible for Germany's farmers. France's agriculture minister at the time was none other than Jacques Chirac, later president of France. Chirac's combative style exacerbated Franco-German tension over agricultural prices.[32] Schmidt especially resented the widespread perception that Germany, on account of its recent past, should be the paymaster of Europe. As one observer remarked, there was a tendency to view Germany's large contribution to the EC budget as "a form of delayed war reparations."[33]

French concern about the conduct and direction of Ostpolitik overshadowed Franco-German relations at the time. Pompidou was pathologically suspicious of Brandt's motives. Ostpolitik's growing momentum and Brandt's increasing international stature alarmed Pompidou and his influential foreign minister, Michel Jobert. Although Brandt was at pains to inform the French, bilaterally and in European Political Cooperation, about developments in the East, he could never put their minds at rest.

On one thing, at least, Brandt and Pompidou saw eye-to-eye. They both disliked the Commission: Pompidou for ideological reasons, Brandt because he never warmed to it. The Commission still drafted reports, communications, and legislation on a wide range of issues, but its influence languished without support from Paris or Bonn. For instance, in March 1970 the Commission released a memorandum on industrial policy in the EC calling for completion of the internal market and encouragement of transnational mergers. The so-called Colonna Report (named after the commissioner responsible for industrial strategy) withered on the vine.[34]

By common consent it was Italy's turn to nominate a candidate for president in 1970 when Jean Rey stepped down. No prominent Italian wanted to go to Brussels. Eventually the government nominated Franco Malfatti, the minister for post and telegraphs. A good speaker, Malfatti liked to orate about the lamentable state of European integration. Beyond that he had little impact on the Community. He resigned as Commission president in 1972 to return to Italian politics, leaving Sicco Mansholt, the father of the CAP, to finish his term of office. François-Xavier Ortoli, a senior French official with close connections to the French government, became the next Commission president.

Member states' determination to keep control over the two main items on the EC's agenda in the early 1970s, EMU and enlargement, further undermined the Commission. The process of enlargement strengthened the role of the presidency and the member states' permanent representatives in Brussels at the expense of the Commission. Con O'Neill, the chief British negotiator, noted how the member states "made it very clear that the Commission must operate as the servant of the Six."[35] Indeed, member states did not allow the Commission to sign the accession treaties. This triggered a typical outburst from Malfatti: "There are times," he told the Parliament in February 1972, "when prejudice replaces judgement, when an academic, legalistic approach replaces considerations of what is politically desirable."[36]

■ Surviving the Storm

The year 1973 should have been a banner one for the EC. Instead enlargement seemed anticlimactic, despite lofty statements by politicians from the acceding and existing member states. Their words had a hollow ring not only because of prevailing political and economic circumstances but also because Britain and Denmark were reluctant new entrants. At a time when the European ideal appeared to be faltering, it was highly unlikely that British accession would spark a renaissance in the EC.

A change of government in Britain in early 1974 brought Wilson back to power, partly on the strength of a promise to renegotiate Britain's entry terms and put the result to a referendum. The ensuing renegotiation and referendum overshadowed Britain's membership in 1974 and early 1975, to the intense irritation of the other member states. By that time the EC was battling gale force winds. In late 1973, following the war in the Middle East, Arab producers quadrupled the price of oil and embargoed the port of Rotterdam to protest the Dutch government's support for Israel. The sudden, astronomical oil price rise threw Europe's economies into a tailspin while the embargo tested the member states' solidarity and nascent procedures for foreign policy cooperation.

The response of the Community and its member states was far from flattering. Efforts to negotiate an energy policy failed dismally. Member states initially went their own ways on policy toward the Middle East. Recession and spiraling inflation hastened economic divergence among member states, put an end to EMU, and threatened to roll back existing levels of market integration, notably through the proliferation of nontariff barriers to trade. The Commission remained weak, and member states haggled over the size and composition of the soon-to-be directly elected Parliament.

Under the circumstances, the EC showed remarkable resilience. Although EMU stalled and an energy policy never emerged, there were noteworthy developments in other areas, notably regional policy, social policy, environmental policy, and overseas assistance. The EC also acquired a higher political profile, thanks largely to the coordination of the member states' positions at the Conference on Security and Cooperation in Europe through the mechanism of European Political Cooperation. National governments appreciated

The Nine Member States

the benefits of the customs union and the CAP, despite obvious faults. Habits of transnational cooperation in the EC were deeply ingrained.

Harmonization

The Rome Treaty empowered the Community to harmonize member states' laws in order to promote and maintain the common market. This could be done under either Article 100 (subject to unanimity in the Council) or other, sector-specific articles (generally subject to qualified majority voting). In exceptional cases, such as intellectual property rights, the treaty provided for harmonization by international convention (treatylike agreements). The Commission, with a monopoly on legislative initiative, took an aggressive approach to harmonization in the early 1960s until the onset of the empty chair crisis and adoption of the Luxembourg Compromise. Apart from a spurt of harmonization of customs legislation in late 1968 and 1969 following completion of the customs union, and in other areas in the warm afterglow of the Hague summit, the rate of harmonization slowed down in the early 1970s.[37]

Faced with rampant intergovernmentalism and the disruptive impact of enlargement, the Commission adopted a more pragmatic, politically sensitive approach to harmonization. The Commission proposed fewer and better measures. In 1973 the Council approved a program on harmonization and an Action Program for Industrial Policy. These contained a legislative agenda for harmonizing measures with a deadline of December 1977 for the enactment of many of them. But progress was slow. The Council adopted only eleven directives in 1973, thirteen in 1974, and twelve in 1975. By the mid-1970s, numerous draft directives were stuck in the EC's decisionmaking pipeline.

Under adverse economic circumstances, national governments were more susceptible than ever to pressure from businesses resisting harmonization in order to protect domestic market share. The absence of unanimity gave governments an excuse to prevent the Council from enacting harmonization measures. Enlargement made matters worse because "political attitudes to harmonization in Denmark and the United Kingdom . . . [varied] from the politely skeptical to the stridently hostile."[38] National governments and publics alike pilloried the Commission for its alleged obsession with uniformity. The Commission admitted that "technical obstacles and quantitative restrictions . . . are both utterly depressing terms," but argued that the persistence and proliferation of nontariff barriers to trade gravely impaired the common market's potential and eroded public confidence in the Community.[39]

Economic and Monetary Union

In early 1973 another large influx of dollars into Germany triggered a crisis every bit as serious as the monetary crises of 1971 and 1972. Soaring inflation, rising unemployment, widening trade deficits, and oil price shocks made a mockery of the Community's commitment to EMU, a commitment reiterated at the Copenhagen summit in October 1973. Taking a pragmatic approach, Commission vice president Carlo Scarascia Mugnozza told the Parliament in January 1974 that "until our economic structures have been truly harmonized, and until we really begin removing disparities between the Member States, EMU will remain at the stage of abstract ideas and pious wishes. This is one of the main lessons, perhaps even the most important lesson, to be learnt from the events of 1973."[40]

Discussions about transitioning to the second stage of EMU became increasingly unreal. As if to emphasize the point, the franc floated free of the snake in January 1974, just as the second stage of EMU was due to begin. Far from becoming an instrument of exchange rate stability for all EC currencies, the snake shrank to accommodate only a handful of currencies centered on the mark. EC leaders had little choice but to note, at the Paris summit in December 1974, "that internal and international difficulties have prevented . . . the accomplishment of expected progress on the road to EMU" while affirming for the record that "in this field their will has not weakened."[41]

By the mid-1970s EMU, was a "non-issue," relegated to "the second division of Community interests."[42] Instead of deepening integration, EMU had driven France and Germany farther apart while becoming a symbol of the Community's impotence in the face of international monetary turmoil and economic recession. Commission president Ortoli lamented in February 1976 "the absence of any decisive progress towards EMU." Although circumstances were largely to blame, Ortoli identified "a lack of conviction too."[43]

This was the gist also of a report on European integration by a group headed by Robert Marjolin, the influential former commissioner. Convened by the Commission, the Marjolin committee concluded that EMU owed its demise to a lack of understanding of what was involved as well as a lack of political will: "It was as if the governments had undertaken the enterprise in the naïve belief that it was sufficient to decree the formation of an EMU for this to come about at the end of a few years, without great effort or difficult and painful economic and political transformations." The hard-hitting report, a fitting sequel to the optimistic Werner Plan, closed a troubled chapter in EMU history.[44]

Regional Policy

Like a rising tide lifting all boats, the impact of market integration was supposed to close the gap between the Community's rich and poor regions. The Six were relatively homogeneous economically, apart from a big gap between the rich north and poor south of Italy. The Italian government had little faith in the ability of market integration to help the impoverished south unless accompanied by generous financial instruments for regional development. Lacking political leverage, the Italians failed in the 1960s to convince other member states to establish and endow a meaningful regional policy. Only the Commission strongly supported Italy, but the Commission's influence was weak in the aftermath of the empty chair crisis.

The political situation changed in the early 1970s, first with the onset of EMU, then with the prospect of enlargement. The Commission and Italy argued that EMU would widen regional disparities within and among member states. French and German interest in EMU gave the Commission and Italy some leverage to press for a regional policy with teeth.[45]

The impending accession to the EC of Britain and Ireland, two countries with pressing regional problems—there were large disparities among Britain's regions and between Ireland as a whole and the other member states—drew more attention to regional policy. Even before enlargement formally took place, Britain, Italy, and Ireland formed an unofficial bloc of countries agitating for a European Regional Development Fund, with Britain taking the lead. Apart from the presumed merits of financial assistance for poorer regions, the British government had a strong political incentive to establish the fund. Because it imported more agricultural products than other Community countries and had a small farm sector, Britain would contribute relatively more in agricultural levies to the Community's budget and get back relatively less in agricultural subsidies. That was a sensitive point domestically and a political gift for the increasingly anti-EC Labour opposition. The government desperately needed to establish the fund, not only to help Britain's disadvantaged regions but also to strengthen the case at home for EC membership.

Every member state thought regional development a good thing, worthy at least of rhetorical support. There was little opposition to regional policy on neoliberal ideological grounds, as surfaced in the 1980s under British prime minister Margaret Thatcher. While sympathizing with the goal of equitable regional development, however, the rich member states did not want to pay for a financial instrument to achieve it. Already opposed to greater EC expenditure on agriculture, Germany, the perceived paymaster of Europe, strongly resisted the establishment of the fund. Yet Brandt understood Heath's domestic political predicament (although Brandt was a Socialist and Heath a Conservative, they shared the goal of keeping Britain in the Community).

Member states struck a deal at the Paris summit in October 1972, giving "a high priority . . . to the aim of correcting, in the Community, the structural and regional imbalances which might affect the realization of economic and monetary union." National leaders undertook to coordinate their regional policies and instructed the EC's institutions to establish a regional development fund before the end of 1973, to be financed from the beginning of the second stage of EMU from the Community's own resources.[46] That was a considerable coup for Heath because it guaranteed a new source of Community expenditure in Britain.

Agreeing to establish the fund was one thing; coming up with the money was another. The summit communiqué did not mention a sum, leaving the Commission and the Council to work out the details. George Thomson, one of Britain's first two commissioners, received the regional policy portfolio. In March 1973 he produced the so-called Thomson Report on regional disparities in the EC, a report mandated by the Paris summit of October 1972. Thomson toiled throughout the year to build member state support for the fund, but faced stiff German resistance. The Commission's proposals, submitted to the Council in October 1973, called for an endowment of 2.25 billion units of account from 1974 to 1976 and included provisions for eligibility and disbursement. Germany balked at the high price, which nonetheless represented less than 1 percent of the EC's budget.

The Middle East war and its aftermath destroyed whatever chance there was of reaching agreement on the fund at the Copenhagen summit in October 1973. Preoccupied with the oil crisis, national leaders floundered about for a common energy policy. Heath failed to link an agreement on energy policy to an agreement on regional policy. Even if he had, there was little prospect of an energy policy agreement. Little of substance emerged from the Copenhagen summit. The EC reiterated its commitment to establish the fund by January 1974 but merely recommended that the Council decide at its next meeting on the fund's size and the criteria for disbursement.

The outcome of the Copenhagen summit did nothing to help Heath in the ensuing election campaign. He was defeated largely on domestic economic grounds (Britain was riven by strikes), although growing popular discontent with developments in the Community undoubtedly helped his opponents. Wilson came back to office in February 1974, demanding a renegotiation of Britain's accession terms and an agreement on the fund. A change of leadership in Germany three months later, when Schmidt replaced Brandt, hardly boosted the fund's prospects. Like Wilson, Schmidt was a Socialist. But Schmidt had a reputation for holding the line on Community spending. Schmidt's position was popular at home, except among farmers when it came to the CAP.

The issue receded for much of 1974 until, in the run-up to the Paris summit in December, the Commission proposed a compromise on the fund's size (1.4 billion units) and disbursement (each country should get something). By that time a change of leadership in France as well as in Germany proved fortuitous. With France in the Council presidency, Valéry Giscard d'Estaing, who saw himself as the Community's savior, wanted the Paris summit to succeed. Ireland and Italy threatened to stay away unless there was a good prospect of a deal on the fund. Giscard also proposed changes in the fund's disbursement that would benefit France. Thus Giscard was more interested than Pompidou in regional policy and Schmidt was more willing than Brandt to pay for it. Having revived the Franco-German axis, Schmidt the statesman was unwilling to jeopardize the success of the Paris summit for the sake of several million units of account.

The deal struck in Paris in December 1974 established a fund of 1.3 billion units of account for the years 1975–1977. Italy (40 percent), Britain (28 percent), and France (15 percent) got the lion's share. According to the summit communiqué, the fund was to become operational in January 1975, but member states wrapped up the details only in March of that year.[47] Thus a fund smaller than originally envisioned, spread out among more countries than originally contemplated, eventually came into being.

Repeated delays in establishing the fund, bitter disputes among member states about its size and operation, and open association of the issue with Britain's budgetary contribution diminished the fund's immediate importance for the EC. The size of the fund was a pittance compared to the amount of money necessary to improve the poorer regions' prospects, particularly at a time of economic recession. Nevertheless the launch and subsequent implementation of the fund were noteworthy developments. Member states learned to collaborate with each other and with the Commission to develop regional policy at the European level. The story of the regional fund could be interpreted as an egregious example of horse-trading among national governments, but it also showed that further integration was possible even at the worst of times.

Social Policy

Developments in social policy also belie the impression that the mid-1970s was a time of unremitting setbacks for the EC. The 1969 Hague summit communiqué acknowledged the importance of social policy and the desirability of reforming the European Social Fund, an item of EC expenditure provided for in the Rome Treaty. Brandt, a Social Democrat, had a particular interest in these issues. Not wanting to be seen as a callous conservative and aware of France's original insistence on including social policy provisions in the Rome Treaty, Pompidou also advocated an active social policy in the early 1970s. Thus the 1972 Paris summit communiqué contained the disingenuous statement that national leaders attached "as much importance to vigorous action in the social field as to the achievement of the economic and monetary union."[48] To prove the point, national leaders invited the EC's institutions, in consultation with labor and employers, to draw up an action program by January 1974, including reform of the social fund.

The Commission had a strong bureaucratic incentive to push social policy. It drafted the social action program, which the Council adopted in January 1974. The program included measures to promote employment, better living and working conditions, worker participation in industrial decisionmaking, and equal treatment of men and women in the workplace. With the onset of the oil crisis and ensuing recession, however, the program seemed a luxury rather than a necessity, despite its supposed employment-enhancing measures. In the 1974 Paris summit communiqué, EC leaders merely reaffirmed the importance of the social program and, in a sure sign of inaction, emphasized the role of the Economic and Social Committee, a purely consultative body. As for the European Social Fund, the communiqué declared that the Council would decide, "when the time is ripe . . . whether and to what extent it will be necessary to increase the resources of the social fund."[49]

The Council enacted some social policy legislation in the early and mid-1970s, including directives on workers' information and consultation rights and on equal pay and equal treatment for men and women. A number of landmark rulings of the European Court further strengthened equal rights for women in the workplace. In addition, the EC established two agencies—the European Foundation for the Improvement of Living and Working Conditions and the European Center for the Development of Vocational Training—to conduct research on social policy issues. By contrast, company law measures that included provisions for worker participation became bogged down in disputes among member states and between trade unions and employers' organizations over which model of industrial democracy to use. Although disappointing by the rhetorical standards of summit communiqués, the EC's record on social policy was nevertheless significant at a time of serious political and economic uncertainty.

Environmental Policy

Environmental policy was not specifically mentioned in the Rome Treaty. Environmental legislation in the 1960s was therefore narrow and technical, justified either as an internal market measure or on the basis of a vague commitment in the preamble of the treaty to improve "the living and working conditions" of the people of Europe. As the environmental movement gathered momentum throughout Western Europe, member states and the Commission developed a keen interest in broader aspects of environmental policy. Hence the short statement in the 1972 Paris summit communiqué inviting the EC's institutions "to establish, before July 31, 1973, a program of action [on the environment] accompanied by a precise timetable."[50] That was the genesis of the EC's first Environmental Action Program, which, like the second one in 1977, listed various measures that were essentially corrective in nature. The action plans and attendant legislation were a humble beginning for a policy area that would later assume great importance for the EU.

Energy Policy

Unlike most other policy areas, energy policy was an unmitigated disaster for the EC in the mid-1970s, a time of obvious need for common action in the aftermath of the oil crisis.[51] The Rome Treaty did not mention a common energy policy, largely because the other founding treaties dealt explicitly with coal and atomic power. It was only in 1968 that the Commission submitted to the Council the First Guidelines for a Common Energy Policy, which languished for years. The Council's inaction can be explained by member state inertia as well as by wide variations within the Community in national energy use and industry ownership. As the international energy situation worsened in the early 1970s, Heath pressed successfully for a paragraph in the 1972 Paris summit communiqué calling for "the Community institutions to formulate as soon as possible an energy policy guaranteeing certain and lasting supplies under satisfactory economic conditions."[52]

That seemed prescient, but when the oil crisis broke a year later, Britain drew back from a common energy policy, preferring to make sweetheart deals with the oil-producing countries and develop its own North Sea reserves. More ominously, the oil crisis split France and Germany when France, like Britain, chose to strike out alone and Germany advocated a common approach. Franco-German relations, under strain over Ostpolitik and EMU, now faced an "extraordinary mood of suspicion and recrimination generated by the energy issue."[53] Inevitably, the oil crisis dominated the Copenhagen summit of October 1973. Equally inevitably, despite issuing a ringing declaration on the "European Identity," which dealt mostly with the Community's external relations, national leaders failed to agree on a common position on energy. A separate, nonbinding declaration attached to the communiqué merely reiterated the need for the "orderly functioning of a common market for energy" and "concerted and equitable measures to limit energy consumption."[54]

Relations with the United States complicated matters. Henry Kissinger, Nixon's hard-charging national security adviser, declared 1973 the "Year of Europe." Although intended to mend fences with Europe following recent transatlantic financial turmoil, its effect was to antagonize the Europeans further. Sensitive to Kissinger's overbearing manner and especially to U.S. concerns about the EC's emerging mechanism for foreign policy cooperation, Europeans reacted skeptically to the U.S. initiative. When the oil crisis broke, some Europeans, notably the French, saw Kissinger's call for a concerted Western response as additional evidence of U.S. determination to dominate transatlantic relations.

Preferring to respond unilaterally to the oil crisis, at first France refused to participate in an energy conference convened by the United States in Washington in February 1974. France eventually relented, consenting to Community as well as member state representation there. But France criticized Germany, then in the Council presidency, for its handling of the Community's position at the conference and declined to join the International Energy Agency, a U.S.-sponsored oil consumers' group. Community disarray over energy policy continued in the mid-1970s. At the Paris summit in December 1974, national leaders called on the Community's institutions "to work out and implement a common energy policy in the shortest possible time." That was wishful thinking, as was a plea by Ortoli that 1975 become "the year of the common energy policy."[55]

The Lomé Convention

The year 1975, a year generally devoid of progress in European integration, was notable for the conclusion of the Lomé Convention between the EC and forty-six developing countries. Lomé was more than a successor agreement to the second Yaoundé Convention of 1969, which expired in January 1975. As well as including British ex-colonies in Africa, the Caribbean, and the Pacific (as a result of Britain's recent accession to the Community), Lomé sought to put relations between the EC and the developing countries on a new footing, in keeping with prevailing global concerns about the yawning North-South divide. Instead of renegotiating a traditional donor-recipient relationship, the EC sought to establish a new partnership with its member states' ex-colonies. Negotiations with the African, Caribbean, and Pacific countries began in July 1973 and ended in February 1975 when both sides signed the new convention in Lomé, the capital of Togo.[56]

Unlike the prelude to the earlier conventions, the Lomé negotiations involved a genuine give-and-take between both sides. The disparate grouping of African, Caribbean, and Pacific countries was surprisingly united. Growing sympathy in the developed world for the plight of poor countries, especially in the aftermath of the global oil crisis, buoyed the African, Caribbean, and Pacific negotiators. The complex negotiations, due to end in December 1974 at the close of the French presidency of the Council, ran into the next presidency. That gave Ireland, a new EC member state presiding over the Council for the first time, an opportunity to bask in the international limelight. Garret FitzGerald, Ireland's foreign minister, claimed that "Ireland had a clear advantage in presiding over this negotiation. The [African, Caribbean, and Pacific countries] knew that we were sympathetic to them and that . . . we had no national interests to defend"[57]

The resolution of last-minute disputes over sugar and EC financial assistance paved the way for the final agreement, which included a development assistance package; a system of generalized preferences in trade; an export stabilization mechanism to guarantee commodity export prices regardless of global market fluctuations; a host of innovative aid and technical assistance programs; a special agreement on sugar favorable to exporters from the African, Caribbean, and Pacific countries; and a revised institutional framework. Both sides hailed the agreement as marking a new departure in North-South relations.

Although the Lomé Convention drew welcome attention to the EC's international role at a time of internal economic difficulties, its impact on European integration was mixed. The Commission played an important supporting role in the negotiations, especially because of the prominence of Claude Cheysson, a former French diplomat with extensive experience in Africa, who held the development portfolio. But the Council presidency predominated. The Parliament acquired useful experience in development policy and a role in the EC's external relations through its participation in the Lomé Convention's joint parliamentary body.

Britain's Renegotiation and Referendum

Development in the EC in the mid-1970s played out against the backdrop of Britain's renegotiation and referendum.[58] Under pressure from a strong Euroskeptical faction within the governing Labour Party, Wilson called for a renegotiation of Britain's entry terms after narrowly winning the February 1974 general election. Wilson increased Labour's lead in the general election that he unexpectedly called in October 1974, but not enough to lessen his dependence on the anti-EC faction.

James Callaghan, Britain's foreign secretary, kicked off the renegotiation at a Council meeting in April 1974. Britain's demands were mostly financial: Britain wanted to contribute less to the budget and get more from it, mainly through the proposed regional development fund. The other foreign ministers acknowledged the justice of Britain's demands but resented the way that Callaghan made his case. It looked to them as if Callaghan was presenting a diktat rather than a reasonable set of requests.

As with the original accession negotiations, France was pivotal to the success of the renegotiations. Because the stakes were so high, a final settlement could only be reached at an EC summit. Giscard's evident disdain for Wilson did not help matters. Schmidt, a fellow Social Democrat who sympathized with Wilson's difficult domestic situation, acted as honest broker. Schmidt made a highly influential speech in favor of Britain's continued EC membership at the Labour Party conference in November 1974. Wilson, in turn, publicly signaled a commitment to continued EC membership if the renegotiation ended successfully. Schmidt then organized a dinner for Giscard and Wilson on the eve of the Paris summit in December 1974, giving the French and British leaders an opportunity to explain their positions to each other.

The breakthrough in Paris on the size and distribution of the regional development fund satisfied one of Wilson's main demands. As for Britain's budgetary contribution, EC leaders asked the Commission and the Council "to set up as soon as possible a correcting mechanism . . . in the framework of the system of 'own resources' . . . [to] prevent . . . the possible development of situations unacceptable for a member state and incompatible with the smooth working of the Community."[59] The phrase *correcting mechanism* became code for a British rebate. Community leaders agreed in Paris to wrap up the renegotiations at their next meeting, in Dublin in March 1975 (the first meeting of the newly constituted European Council).

The Commission duly published a set of proposals on the budgetary question in January 1975. The Council of Ministers started to work out an agreement on the size of Britain's rebate that Community leaders could endorse at the summit. Inevitably, the leaders themselves became involved in last-minute bargaining. Eventually they struck a deal in Dublin on a "correcting mechanism" to provide a rebate large enough to help Wilson win the referendum in June 1975.

Based on the Dublin agreement, Wilson advocated a "yes" vote.[60] Yet the Labour Party remained deeply divided on the question of EC membership. The opposition Conservative Party was also divided, but less so. Thatcher, the new Conservative leader, personified the approach of many in her party: she liked the EC economically but not politically. That is, she supported economic integration and intergovernmentalism but opposed political integration and supranationalism. For constitutional reasons, Thatcher wanted the British people to decide the issue through their elected representatives in parliament, not directly in a referendum. Once parliament approved the referendum, however, she campaigned wholeheartedly for a "yes" vote.

With leaders of the two main parties, as well as the business establishment, advocating a positive result, the outcome of the referendum was hardly in doubt. Roy Jenkins, a leading Labour Party moderate, and Edward Heath, the former Conservative prime minister, led the bipartisan "Britain in Europe" campaign. The result of the referendum was a healthy 67 percent in favor of staying in the EC and 33 percent against, with a turnout of 64 percent. That should have put the matter to rest, but Britain's EC's membership remained a bitterly divisive issue in the Labour Party. According to Jenkins, "the handling of the European question by the leadership throughout the 1970s did more to cause the [Labour] Party's disasters of the 1980s than did any other issue."[61]

The process of EC enlargement was inherently disruptive, bringing with it a need to absorb new languages, administrative cultures, officials, and national perspectives. The process of British accession was especially disruptive because it brought into the EC a large member state with a strong strain of Euroskepticism. The negative impact of British accession was immediately apparent in the Council, where leading Euroskeptics such as Tony Benn and Peter Shore represented Britain until Labour lost the 1979 general election. It was also evident in the parliament, where Labour members initially refused to take their seats. By contrast, British officials in the Commission, Council sec-

retariat, and Parliament generally favored European integration and contributed to the institutions' smooth operation.

Shortly after the referendum, Wilson announced that "the debate is now
over . . . the historic decision has been made . . . we look forward to continuing to work with [our partners] in promoting the Community's wider interests
and in fostering a greater sense of purpose among the member states."[62] Those
were hollow words. There was no prospect of an Anglo-French entente driv-
ing the Community forward or of a trilateral Anglo-French-German axis
replacing the bilateral Franco-German axis as a motor of European integration. According to one academic assessment,

> all that British diplomacy appeared to have accomplished [after four years of
> membership] was to persuade the French that partnership with an over-
> powerful Germany was more conducive to their interests than a special rela-
> tionship with the UK, and the [other member states] that the French, though
> still in many respects unregenerate nationalists, were tolerable compared
> with the British. Community politics was still too often a case of one against
> the rest.[63]

Now the "one" was Britain, not France.

Franco-German Friendship

Close Franco-German accord in the mid-1970s, personified by the friendship
between Giscard and Schmidt, contrasted not only with the sorry state of
Anglo-French and Anglo-German relations but also with strained Franco-German relations earlier in the decade. Giscard won the presidential election following Pompidou's death in May 1974; Schmidt became chancellor following Brandt's unexpected resignation at the same time. The change of
leadership brought a breath of fresh air to relations at the highest level
between France and Germany. Giscard and Schmidt had worked together as
finance ministers in the early 1970s. They understood economics and, as
Jobert, France's former foreign minister, noted acerbically, "*ils se tutoient en
anglais*" (they chatted familiarly to each other in English).[64] Notoriously
haughty, Giscard regarded Schmidt as an intellectual equal. Yet Giscard was a
head of state and not merely a head of government. On ceremonial occasions
Giscard always took precedence over Schmidt and other Community leaders.

Giscard was a moderate conservative, not a Gaullist (although the
Gaullists had a majority in the French parliament). In his view the EC was
interesting intellectually, important economically, and congenial politically.
Giscard was neither a rigid intergovernmentalist nor an enthusiastic supranationalist. He was willing to allow majority voting in the Council and direct
elections to the Parliament, but only to balance the overt intergovernmentalism of the European Council, his institutional baby. The narrowness of his

election victory (Giscard won the second round by only 51 percent to 49 percent) and the vigilance of the Gaullists in parliament kept Giscard's propensity toward more integration firmly in check.

Schmidt faced no such domestic political constraints. By the mid-1970s Ostpolitik had run its course, and the Christian Democrats could no longer make political capital out of the risk it supposedly posed to European stability and German security. Brooding by nature, Schmidt became preoccupied later in the decade with a deadly terrorist campaign by Far Left extremists and what he saw as the irresponsible global leadership of the United States. Schmidt viewed European integration as inherently beneficial for Germany but was far from enthusiastic about the process. He liked dealing with Giscard and generally shared his partner's perspective on the EC.

Close personal relations between Giscard and Schmidt complemented a convergence of French and German interests in the EC. Germany had the strongest economy in the Community; the Federal Republic weathered better than the other member states the international economic turmoil of the mid-1970s. Giscard wanted to emulate German economic policy in order to replicate Germany's economic performance. As a result, French preferences moved closer to Germany's on a range of hitherto divisive issues. Thus Giscard accepted the primacy of price stability, agreed to cooperate on international energy issues, and echoed Schmidt's criticism of the U.S. global economic role (in that regard Schmidt moved more in the direction of traditional French thinking).

Institutional Adaptation

One of the most striking institutional developments in the 1970s, closely associated with Giscard and Schmidt, was the emergence of a new body, the European Council, to provide general strategic direction for the EC.[65] A trend toward summitry already existed before Giscard and Schmidt came to power. As the range of issues covered by the Community increased and the domestic stakes rose, national leaders, rather than ordinary government ministers, needed to reach political agreement on a host of important issues (EMU and enlargement were obvious examples). As member states sought to coordinate their foreign policies more closely, notably through the mechanism of European Political Cooperation, regular meetings of national leaders seemed essential rather than discretionary. Accordingly, EC leaders decided in Copenhagen in October 1973 to meet more frequently "whenever justified by the circumstances and when it appears necessary to provide a stimulus or to lay down further guidelines for the construction of a united Europe . . . [or] whenever the international situation so requires."[66]

According to the Copenhagen communiqué, "it will be for the country providing the President [of the Council] to convene these meetings and to make detailed proposals concerning their preparation and organization." France, in the Council presidency, convened a summit in Paris in December 1974. It was there that the national leaders agreed "to meet, accompanied by the ministers of foreign affairs, three times a year," in a format called the European Council. They also instructed their foreign ministers to end the rigid distinction between the conduct of Community business and European Political Cooperation. Henceforth, foreign ministers meeting in the General Affairs Council could hold foreign policy discussions. In a related measure, the leaders declared that "greater latitude will be given to the permanent representatives so that only the most important political problems need be discussed in the Council."[67]

Giscard's advocacy of European summitry initially raised the hackles of the small member states. Garret FitzGerald, Ireland's foreign minister, saw in the proposed European Council "an initiative preconcerted between the 'Big Three,' a move towards the 'Directoire' or Directorate that some of us [in the Council of Ministers] had begun to fear."[68] It reminded the Dutch of de Gaulle's proposals for closer intergovernmental cooperation, which they blocked after a bitter political battle in 1962. The small member states were mollified only when Giscard agreed that the European Council would not be a formal decisionmaking body and would respect the Commission's role in the Community system.

The decisions taken in Paris to launch the European Council, legitimize European Political Cooperation as a Community activity, strengthen the role of the member states' permanent representatives, and boost the position of the Council presidency suggested a strong tilt toward intergovernmentalism. Eager to provide at least the appearance of a counterbalancing tilt toward supranationalism, Community leaders agreed in Paris on a number of other potentially important procedural and institutional changes. Foremost among these was an accord that direct elections to the Parliament "should be achieved as soon as possible," which meant in practice "at any time in or after 1978." EC leaders also agreed, despite Danish and British reservations, to strengthen the Parliament's role, "in particular by granting it certain powers in the Communities' legislative process." Together with a call for the Parliament to "be more closely associated with the work of the Presidency" in the conduct of European Political Cooperation, the outcome of the Paris summit was a success for supranationalism as well as for intergovernmentalism.[69]

Yet measures to strengthen intergovernmentalism went into operation immediately, whereas those intended to strengthen supranationalism languished for some time. Member states squabbled for years over the composition of the directly elected Parliament and over the date of the first direct elections. Small member states were overrepresented in the existing Parliament. Giscard wanted to increase the size of the directly elected Parliament and redress the balance in favor of the large member states. The small member states resisted, seeing the issue as further evidence of French insensitivity to their interests. Giscard seemed personally committed to holding direct elections, although he faced stiff domestic opposition from his Gaullist allies.

Another row then erupted over when exactly to hold the elections. Most member states wanted to hold the elections on the same day, in May or June 1978. But there was no consensus on what that day should be. Some member states favored a Sunday, others a Thursday. All agreed eventually to spread the elections over Thursday through Sunday and to start the count only after the last ballots were cast throughout the Community. Agreement on the number and allocation of seats proved more difficult, with the British pressing for more seats so that Scotland would not be underrepresented in relation to Ireland and Denmark (Scottish nationalism was then on the rise). The dispute over apportionment began at the Luxembourg summit in April 1976, where the small member states stood their ground and Giscard left in a huff. Cooler heads prevailed at the next summit, in July 1976, when member states finally hammered out an agreement. By that time it was too late to schedule the first elections in 1978, hence the decision to hold them in June 1979. In the meantime the idea of increasing the Parliament's legislative powers fell by the wayside.

Member states failed to deliver another reform implicitly promised in the Paris summit communiqué: making greater use of qualified majority voting in the Council when important national interests were at stake and reining in the national veto. As the Luxembourg Compromise (the right to veto) was originally a French device, Giscard's openness to qualified majority voting seemed revolutionary. It was equally surprising that Britain, the new guardians of intergovernmental orthodoxy, appeared willing to abandon unanimity.

In fact, the Luxembourg Compromise remained firmly in place. Garret FitzGerald, president-in-office of the Council in early 1975, tried to wean member states away from unanimity. When he first suggested using qualified majority voting, James Callaghan, Britain's foreign secretary, refused to budge. FitzGerald scored a minor coup at the end of Ireland's presidency when he managed to get a decision taken by qualified majority voting (an exemption for Botswana beef from the EC's import levy, something that Britain wanted). FitzGerald was delighted with his one-upmanship of Callaghan. But it meant little in the great scheme of things. As FitzGerald admitted, "the Council soon reverted to the practice of deciding all issues, however trivial, on the basis of unanimity."[70] And so it remained until the early 1980s.

Apart from British recalcitrance, economic and political circumstances in the mid-1970s were not conducive to moving away from unanimity. Reeling from the impact of recession and rising unemployment, member states were unwilling to be outvoted in Brussels on legislation that could, in the short term at least, exacerbate the situation at home. Under intense pressure from businesses clamoring for protection, national governments were on the defensive in the Council. In what appeared to be a zero-sum game, member states would not abandon the right, as they saw it, to block legislation in Brussels by invoking or threatening to invoke the Luxembourg Compromise.

Giscard's and Schmidt's attitudes toward the Commission also undermined supranationalism. Schmidt's "disapproval of the Brussels bureaucracy was notorious."[71] Like many chancellors before and since (Konrad Adenauer and Helmut Kohl were major exceptions), Schmidt looked down on the Commission and never nominated top-flight Germans to join it. Only in 1976, when EC leaders mulled over the selection of the next Commission president, did Schmidt show an interest in having a political heavyweight fill the position. The French were even more dismissive of the Commission, although they fought hard to mold the institution in their own image and to insinuate French officials into its upper echelons. Obsessed with status, Giscard tried to deny the Commission president membership in the European Council.

Perhaps because he was French and therefore appreciated Giscard's preoccupation with protocol, Commission president Ortoli meekly acquiesced in Giscard's treatment of him. Yet Ortoli was aware of the threat posed by the European Council to the Commission's weak position and to supranationalism in general. The European Council, Ortoli told the Parliament in February 1975, "represents a major change in spirit and may, if we are not careful, shake the institutional structure set up by the Treaties to their foundations."[72] A year later Ortoli seemed assuaged. "The risk is still there," he told the Parliament, "but I am in no doubt that something has been gained: the European Council has provided us with a new organ capable of taking major decisions under the Treaties which set the future course of the Community and its member states. . . . On the whole, the European Council can be said to be an asset."[73] Undoubtedly the European Council was an asset, but as long as the Commission president was merely tolerated at its meetings, neither the Commission nor the Community could reach their full potential.

The Commission was hamstrung in the mid-1970s not only by poor leadership but also by the disruptive impact of enlargement. The addition of four new commissioners (two British, one Irish, and one Dane) increased the college to thirteen members, not an unreasonable number given the scope of the Commission's responsibilities. The influx of new officials into the Commission's services (departments) was more difficult to digest. There was a major reshuffle in the senior ranks in order to accommodate officials from the acceding member states and maintain the informal system of national quotas. The arrival of British, Irish, and Danish officials in the Commission gradually undermined the ascendancy of the French language and administrative culture, just as Pompidou had feared that it would. Cultural, organizational, and personnel changes preoccupied the Commission for some time after enlargement. Nevertheless, the new officials were generally communitarian in their outlook. Only in the Council Secretariat did the British and Danes insert officials with primarily national perspectives.

■ Prospects for European Union

At the Paris summit in December 1972, national leaders requested the EC's institutions to draw up in 1975 a report on how best to transform, by the end of the decade, "the whole complex of the relations of member states into a European union."[74] The wheels began to turn in February 1974 when the Council instructed Coreper to prepare a draft report on European union. Coreper first compiled a questionnaire on the subject, which the Council approved and sent to member state capitals and to the other institutions in June 1974. Referring to discussions among foreign ministers on the subject, FitzGerald confessed that *"no one knew what European union meant."*[75] Meeting in Paris in December 1974, EU leaders stressed the importance of institutional input in order to help them understand the "overall concept of European union." They asked Leo Tindemans, Belgium's prime minister and an earnest Eurofederalist, to submit a comprehensive report by the end of 1975, based on reports from the EC institutions, consultations with national governments, and input from "a wide range of public opinion in the Community."[76]

The Commission, Parliament, and Court duly presented reports in mid-1975. Both the Commission and Parliament called for more supranationalism in the Community but refrained from promoting an ambitious agenda or timetable for European union. The Court, a highly supranational but supposedly apolitical body, restricted itself to calling for judicial reform. During visits to national capitals, Tindemans heard a variety of opinions, ranging from the Europhoric Italians to the Europhobic Danes. The British government received Tindemans warmly after the successful outcome of the referendum in June 1975 but impressed upon him London's lack of enthusiasm for further integration.

Tindemans presented his report to the European Council in December 1975.[77] It described European union as a stage of integration located between the existing EC and a full-fledged federation. In keeping with its author's predilection, the report urged member states to move in a federal direction, however slowly, and contained a set of policy and institutional prescriptions. Tindemans stressed the importance of EMU and a common foreign and security policy. In deference to Atlanticist sentiment in Denmark and neutralist sentiment in Ireland, he ruled out the development of a common defense policy (although he proposed a common armaments procurement program). Tindemans recommended deeper integration in other areas as well, notably social and regional policy, and urged the EC to become more citizen-friendly by launching new policies and programs intended to appeal to a public increasingly apathetic about integration.

Institutionally, Tindemans recommended a stronger Commission and Parliament while endorsing the emergence of the European Council. He suggested that the Commission president be appointed by the European Council and approved by Parliament and have the freedom in turn to appoint his own commissioners (it would have been revolutionary at the time to suggest that the Commission president might be a woman). Tindemans recommended increasing the soon-to-be directly elected Parliament's legislative and oversight authority. More controversially, he proposed giving the Parliament a shared right of legislative initiative. Tindemans suggested reforming the Council by curtailing the use of unanimity in favor of qualified majority voting, extending the presidency's time in office to one year, and coordinating the work of the various sectoral councils. One of his most contentious recommendations was that the more integration-minded member states be allowed to cooperate more closely in a number of policy areas. This was an obvious reaction to British and Danish recalcitrance and to Ireland's reticence about defense policy cooperation.

The Tindemans Report went too far for most member states and ran afoul of the Commission, which did not like the idea of a two-tier EC or of sharing its right of initiative with the Parliament. Each member state rejected one or more of Tindemans's key proposals. France and Britain were the most reactionary. France disliked almost everything in the report; Britain resented particularly the proposals for differentiated integration and more qualified majority voting (Britain seemed open to the idea of a stronger Commission president, perhaps because by common consent it was Britain's turn to nominate the next incumbent). Germany reacted positively to the report but insisted that member states undertake major economic reforms before joining (or rejoining) the currency snake.

Not surprisingly, the Tindemans Report had a short shelf life. The European Council discussed it fleetingly before asking the foreign ministers to report on it. The foreign ministers duly sent it to Coreper. Coreper finally drafted a report on the report for the foreign ministers, who then reported to the European Council. By that time Tindemans knew the score. His fellow EC leaders thanked him effusively for his efforts on their behalf and asked the Commission to draft an annual report on progress toward European union.[78]

It seems surprising that the European Council even bothered to ask Tindemans, an avowed Eurofederalist, to write the report on European union. Yet the request fit a pattern in the post–de Gaulle period of ratcheting up the rhetoric of European integration without providing much follow-through. Clearly, most politicians were attached to the idea of European union but were unwilling to do much about it during such difficult political and economic times.

Despite its lamentable fate, however, the Tindemans Report proved prescient for a later stage of European integration. The European Union that emerged in the 1990s contained many elements mentioned in the report: EMU, foreign and security policy cooperation, an emerging defense policy, stronger regional and social policies, greater parliamentary power, more use of majority voting, and differentiated integration. Although far from being a blueprint for the Community's development, the Tindemans Report provided a reference point for the EC's revival and transformation into the EU. For that reason alone it was a worthwhile political exercise, and a reminder that the 1970s was not such a disastrous decade for the EC after all.

▨ Notes

1. Commission, *Third Report on the General Activities of the European Communities* (Luxembourg: European Communities, 1970), p. 12.

2. Philip Thody, *The Fifth French Republic: Presidents, Politics and Personalities* (London: Routledge, 1998), p. 56.

3. Commission, *Third Report*, pp. 484–486.

4. The *Economist*, "Survey of Germany," January 10, 1970, p. xxvii.

5. Commission, *Third Report*, pp. 486–489.

6. Commission, *Fourth Report on the General Activities of the European Communities* (Luxembourg: European Communities, 1971), p. x.

7. See Michel Jobert, *L'Autre regard* (Paris: Grasset, 1976), pp. 185–186; Haig Simonian, *Privileged Partnership: Franco-German Relations in the European Community, 1969–1984* (Oxford: Clarendon Press, 1985), pp. 83–84; Willy Brandt, *My Life in Politics* (New York: Viking, 1992), pp. 245–246.

8. Commission, *Third Report*, p. 18.

9. See Richard Corbett, *The European Parliament's Role in Closer EU Integration* (Basingstoke: Palgrave, 1998), pp. 93–97.

10. For an account of monetary integration before 1972, see A. I. Bloomfield, "The Historical Setting," in *European Monetary Unification and Its Meaning for the United States,* ed. L. B. Krause and W. S. Salant (Washington, DC: Brookings Institution, 1973); John Gillingham, "Jean Monnet and the Origins of European Monetary Union," in *The European Union: From Monnet to the Euro,* ed. Dean J. Kotlowski (Athens: Ohio University Press, 2000); Hans von der Groeben, *The European Community: The Formative Years* (Brussels: Commission of the European Communities, 1985), pp. 206–216.

11. On the Werner committee and report, see Loukas Tsoukalis, *The Politics and Economics of European Monetary Integration* (London: Allen and Unwin, 1977); Alfred Steinherr, ed., *Thirty Years of European Monetary Integration from the Werner Plan to EMU* (London: Longmann, 1994); Niels Thygesen, "The Emerging European Monetary System: Precursors, First Steps and Policy Options," in *EMS: The Emerging European Monetary System,* ed. Robert Triffin (Brussels: National Bank of Belgium, 1979); and D. C. Kruse, *Monetary Integration in Western Europe: EMU, EMS and Beyond* (London: Butterworths, 1980).

12. Brandt, *My Life in Politics*, pp. 266–267.

13. Tsoukalis, *Monetary Integration*, p. 102.

14. See Simonian, *Privileged Partnership*, pp. 91, 127.

15. Commission, *Fifth Report on the General Activities of the European Communities* (Luxembourg: European Communities, 1972), p. ix.

16. See Tsoukalis, *Monetary Integration*, pp. 126–129.

17. Commission, *Sixth Report on the General Activities of the European Communities* (Luxembourg: European Communities, 1973), pp. 6–9.

18. See Sir Con O'Neill, *Britain's Entry into the European Community: Report by Sir Con O'Neill on the Negotiations, 1970–1972* (London: Whitehall History Publishing in association with Frank Cass, 2000) p. 13.

19. O'Neill, *Britain's Entry*, p. 60.

20. Ibid., p. 65.

21. See ibid., pp. 252–253.

22. Uwe Kitzinger, *Diplomacy and Persuasion* (London: Thames and Hudson, 1973), p. 129.

23. See O'Neill, *Britain's Entry*, pp. xii–xiii.

24. Ibid., pp. 143–148, 174–175.

25. Ibid., pp. 5, 74.

26. Quoted in Kitzinger, *Diplomacy and Persuasion*, p. 124.

27. White Paper, The United Kingdom and the European Communities, July 1971.

28. See Kitzinger, *Diplomacy and Persuasion*, pp. 338–346.

29. See Simonian, *Privileged Partnership*, pp. 128–130.

30. Commission, *Sixth Report*, pp. 6–9.

31. See Simonian, *Privileged Partnership*, pp. 221–223.

32. See ibid., pp. 178–179.

33. Kitzinger, *Diplomacy and Persuasion*, p. 98.

34. Commission, "Industrial Policy in the European Community," COM(70)100, March 1970. See Michelle Egan, *Constructing a European Market: Standards, Regulation, and Governance* (Oxford: Oxford University Press, 2001), pp. 72–73.

35. O'Neill, *Britain's Entry*, p. 71.

36. Quoted in Commission, *Fifth Report*, p. x.

37. On harmonization, see Alan Dashwood, "Hastening Slowly: The Community's Path Towards Harmonization," in *Policy-Making in the European Communities,* ed. Helen Wallace, William Wallace, and Carole Webb (London: John Wiley and Sons, 1977), pp. 278–279; Egan, *European Market*, pp. 67–81; and Carol Cosgrove Twitchett, ed., *Harmonization in the EEC* (New York: St. Martin's Press, 1981).

38. Dashwood, "Hastening Slowly," p. 291.

39. Commission, *Seventh Report on the General Activities of the European Communities* (Luxembourg: European Communities, 1974), p. ix.

40. Commission, *Fifth Report*, p. xxi.

41. Commission, *Eighth Report on the General Activities of the European Communities* (Luxembourg: European Communities, 1975), pp. 297–304.

42. Tsoukalis, *Monetary Integration*, p. 154.

43. Commission, *Eleventh Report on the General Activities of the European Communities* (Luxembourg: European Communities, 1978), p. ix.

44. See Robert Marjolin, *Memoirs, 1911–1986: Architect of European Unity* (London: Weidenfeld and Nicolson, 1986), p. 363.

45. On the relationship between EMU and regional policy, see Tsoukalis, *Monetary Integration*, pp. 121–122, 148.

46. Commission, *Sixth Report*, pp. 6–9.

47. Commission, *Eighth Report*, pp. 297–304.

48. Commission, *Sixth Report*, pp. 6–9.

49. Commission, *Eighth Report*, pp. 297–304.

50. Ibid.

51. See Robert A. Black, "Plus ça Change, Plus C'est la Même Chose: Nine Governments in Search of a Common Energy Policy," in *Policy-Making in the European Communities,* ed. Helen Wallace, William Wallace, and Carole Webb (London: John Wiley and Sons, 1977), pp. 165–196

52. Commission, *Sixth Report*, pp. 6–9.

53. Simonian, *Privileged Partnership*, p. 213.

54. Commission, *Seventh Report*, pp. 489–491.

55. Ibid., p. xiii.

56. See Frans A.M. Alting von Geusau, ed., *The Lomé Convention and the New International Economic Order* (Leiden: A. W. Sijthoff, 1977); Isebill V. Gruhn, "The Lomé Convention: Inching Towards Interdependence," *International Organization* 30, no. 2 (Spring 1976), pp. 241–262.

57. Garret FitzGerald, *All in a Life: An Autobiography* (Dublin: Gill and Macmillan, 1991), p, 151; see pp. 152–153 for an amusing account of the signing ceremony in Lomé.

58. See David Butler and Uwe Kitzinger, *The 1975 Referendum* (London: Macmillan, 1976).

59. Commission, *Eighth Report*, pp. 297–304.

60. The question was "Do you think that the United Kingdom should stay in the European Community (the Common Market)?" See Butler and Kitzinger, *Referendum*, p. 1.

61. Roy Jenkins, *Life at the Center: Memoirs of a Radical Reformer* (New York: Random House, 1991), p. 342.

62. Speech to the House of Commons, June 9, 1975. Quoted in Butler and Kitzinger, *Referendum*, p. 145.

63. Peter Ludlow, *The Making of the European Monetary System* (London: Butterworths, 1982), p. 27.

64. Quoted in the *Economist*, July 26, 1975, p. 6.

65. On the origins and development of the European Council, see Annette Morgan, *From Summit to Council: Evolution of the EEC* (London: Chatham House, 1976); Jan Werts, *The European Council* (Amsterdam: North-Holland, 1992); Simon Bulmer and Wolfgang Wessels, *The European Council: Decision-Making in European Politics* (Basingstoke: Macmillan, 1987).

66. Commission, *Seventh Report*, pp. 487–491.

67. Ibid.

68. FitzGerald, *All in a Life*, p. 134.

69. Commission, *Eighth Report*, pp. 297–304.

70. FitzGerald, *All in a Life*, p. 148.

71. Ludlow, *Making of the European Monetary System*, p. 27.

72. Commission, *Eighth Report*, p. xi.

73. Commission, *Ninth Report on the General Activities of the European Communities* (Luxembourg: European Communities, 1975), p. viii.

74. Commission, *Sixth Report*, pp. 6–9.

75. FitzGerald, *All in a Life*, p. 132. Emphasis in the original.

76. Commission, *Eighth Report*, pp. 297–304.

77. Leo Tindemans, *Report on European Union*, Bulletin EC S/1-1976.

78. The fate of the report can be traced in the Commission, *Eleventh General Report*.

5

Recovery

The early 1980s was one of the most difficult periods in the history of European integration. The fall of the shah of Iran in 1978 triggered a second oil crisis in less than a decade, reversing Europe's fragile economic recovery. A sharp rise in the value of the dollar and economic downturn in the United States compounded the problem. Western Europe's economy slipped back into recession as growth ground to a halt, inflation soared, the balance of payments worsened, and unemployment crept stubbornly upward. There were wide variations in economic performance among member states, with Germany faring best and Britain and Italy faring worst.

The international situation was tense. East-West relations were on a renewed collision course in the late 1970s following the Soviet Union's deployment in Eastern Europe of new, mobile, intermediate-range missiles capable of hitting targets in Western Europe. After much hand-wringing within NATO, the allies agreed to pursue a "dual track" approach to counter the Soviet threat: deploying intermediate-range missiles in Western Europe while negotiating an arms control agreement with the Soviet Union. East-West relations deteriorated further when the Soviets invaded Afghanistan in December 1979 and helped impose martial law in Poland in December 1981. The impending deployment of NATO missiles in November 1983 increased tension not only with the Soviet Union but also within the alliance. Thousands of antinuclear demonstrators took to the streets in Western Europe, while some NATO governments accused Washington of wanting only to deploy new missiles, not negotiate an arms control agreement.

Christopher Tugendhat, a commissioner at the time, predicted that "future historians will probably record that the way in which the achievements of the early years [of the EC] were maintained and markets kept open during the successive oil shocks and the deep economic recession of the 1970s and early 1980s in itself constitutes a considerable success."[1] Yet appearances were deceptive. As this chapter shows, the real success of the EC in the early 1980s was to lay the foundation for the acceleration of integration that followed later in the decade. Responding to the challenges of renewed recession, declining global competitiveness (especially in the high-technology sector), and rising East-West tension, national leaders looked increasingly to the EC for solutions to their problems. Behind a facade of weak leadership, the Commission pursued an aggressive strategy to restructure European industry and complete the internal market. At the same time, the Parliament exploited the opportunity of direct elections to strengthen its institutional position and advocate greater economic and political integration. Big business in Western Europe, reeling from recession and eager to exploit an integrated market, supported the Commission's industrial strategy and urged member states to remove nontariff barriers to trade.

Member state, Commission, parliamentary, and business interest in deepening integration resulted in a series of initiatives that, despite their hortatory nature, presaged the launch of the European Union in the early 1990s. Yet, bitter battles over Britain's demand for a larger budget rebate and the costs of the common agricultural policy (CAP) overshadowed the EC's impending revival. Only when member states finally resolved their differences in June 1984 did the extent of the EC's renaissance become apparent. The budgetary agreement paved the way for Portuguese and Spanish accession, an event of great symbolic importance for the EC. Even more important, by establishing a committee on institutional reform, which recommended an intergovernmental conference to revise the treaties, member states triggered a series of developments that culminated in the launch of the European Union.

■ Fair Winds

The setbacks in the early 1980s were all the more striking because the EC's situation appeared to be improving in the late 1970s. The EC's economic performance was mixed. On the one hand, there was progress in the fight against inflation and in efforts to restore balance-of-payments equilibrium; on the other hand, growth rates fell and unemployment rose. Despite continuing pressure on governments to protect home industries, the Commission detected in 1977 "a growing political interest in seeking Community solutions to common problems."[2] The Commission reported at the end of 1978 that "on the whole the economic outlook . . . [is] more promising, and the gradual recovery now underway gives reason to hope that the Community is beginning to emerge from the crisis."[3]

Before the second oil crisis triggered renewed recession in 1980, prospects for closer political integration also looked good. Roy Jenkins, a senior British politician, brought a breath of fresh air to Brussels when he became Commission president in January 1977. French president Valéry Giscard d'Estaing and his prime minister, Raymond Barre, a former Commission vice president, unabashedly espoused further integration. Despite (or perhaps because of) growing concerns about the international situation and an upsurge in domestic terrorism, German chancellor Helmut Schmidt collaborated closely with Giscard on Community affairs. Both seemed eager to shake the EC out of its lethargy and get Western Europe moving again.

Two issues on the EC's agenda symbolized the endurance of European integration. One was Greek accession, the other direct elections to the Parliament. Progress on both was sporadic in the mid-1970s. Negotiations on Greek accession, begun in July 1976, slowed to a crawl in 1977, and the European Council decided to postpone direct elections until June 1979. Giscard and Schmidt rescued the enlargement negotiations, portraying them and direct elections as evidence of the EC's revival. Their advocacy of a European monetary system in 1978, to meet national and international monetary policy objectives, added to the impression that the EC was sailing satisfactorily ahead.

Greek Accession

Greece returned to democracy in July 1974 when Constantine Karamanlis, a former prime minister and widely respected politician, formed a new center-right government after the collapse of the dictatorial colonels' regime. Bowing to deep-seated Greek resentment of the United States for its support of the colonels and backing of Turkey in the Cypriot conflict, Karamanlis pulled Greece out of NATO's military command. Yet he also pressed for quick accession to the EC. Due in no small part to his handling of foreign affairs, Karamanlis won the general election in November 1974.

Greece was then desperately poor, with a per capita income less than 25 percent of the EC average. Karamanlis saw EC entry as the key to his country's international rehabilitation, political stabilization, and economic modernization. He hoped that joining the EC would bolster Greek security vis-à-vis Turkey, with whom Greece endured a long-standing enmity and against whom Greece had nearly gone to war in 1974. But the prospect of EC accession was not universally popular in Greece. The Panhellenic Socialist Movement, a new political party founded by Andreas Papandreou, strongly opposed membership. Papandreou was an unreconstructed Socialist who saw the EC as a political arm of NATO and an instrument of capitalist exploitation.

Papandreou tapped latent Greek hostility toward the EC. The 1961 association agreement yielded few practical benefits for Greece before the EC "froze" it in 1967 in response to the military coup. Despite the EC's seemingly tough response to the coup, many Greeks resented what one academic called "the fundamentally pusillanimous attitude of the Community towards the Colonels' dictatorship."[4] Lingering Greek suspicion of the EC emboldened the Socialists' opposition to membership and gradually strengthened Papandreou's position.

Greece applied to join the EC in June 1975. Member states responded positively. With European integration seemingly moribund, the prospect of

Greek accession provided a welcome morale boost. The Commission took a more cautious approach in its opinion on Greece's application, published in January 1976. Although also welcoming the prospect of eventual Greek accession, the Commission pointed out problems with the existing association agreement, especially in the areas of agriculture, competition policy, and state aids. Given Greece's relative impoverishment and the likely impact of Greek accession on the EC's relations with Turkey, the Commission urged a lengthy "pre-accession period." That was a polite way of saying that Greece was not yet ready to join the EC.[5]

The Greek government reacted badly to the Commission's opinion. So did the Council, which endorsed Greece's application in February 1976. A statement by German foreign minister Hans-Dietrich Genscher typified the member states' attitude. Speaking from the heart rather than the head, Genscher declared that "Greece, only recently returned to the democratic fold, would march in future with the Community of European nations."[6] Exploiting such sentiments to the full, Greece began accession negotiations in July 1976. Despite the slow pace of the negotiations, Karamanlis received a strong mandate to press ahead when he won the November 1977 election. At the same time the Socialists emerged as the largest opposition party.

The accession negotiations proceeded slowly because of inadequate information about economic conditions in Greece, due perhaps to administrative incapacity in Athens. Undoubtedly attitudes in the Council changed during the negotiations, especially after Portugal and Spain applied to join the EC. Having paid little attention to the economic implications of Greek accession, the Council realized the potentially negative impact of large-scale Mediterranean enlargement. Member states feared that giving generous entry terms to Greece would set a bad precedent for the negotiations with Portugal and Spain. Without doubt, "the unexpectedly rapid approach of first Portugal and then Spain towards the Community transformed the context of Greece's application."[7]

Karamanlis's greatest concern was that the EC would "globalize" the negotiations by lumping together the Greek, Portuguese, and Spanish applications. The prime minister cited the 1961 accession agreement, which envisioned Greek entry in 1984, as proof that Greece was entitled to special treatment. He embarked on a tour of national capitals in early 1978 to press his case, warning member states of the likely impact on Greek public opinion of protracted, joint accession negotiations. Because France was more concerned than other member states about the potential impact of Spanish accession, Giscard's attitude was crucial. Karamanlis, who had lived in exile in Paris during the colonels' regime, pulled out all the stops. Giscard received him warmly, urging the Council in February 1978 that Greece be allowed to join by 1980.

The risk of having their accession negotiations merged with those of Portugal and Spain concentrated Greek minds. Although some hard bargaining

lay ahead, the second stage of the negotiations, beginning in mid-1978, proceeded rapidly. The accession treaty, signed in Athens in May 1979, was a
tribute to Karamanlis's acumen and skill. Ratification went smoothly, despite
the Socialists' opposition to membership. Greece joined the EC, to great fanfare, in January 1981. The EC reveled in Greece's accession, especially in
light of the budgetary dispute with Britain and the Community's slide once
again into a political and economic quagmire.

Direct Elections to the European Parliament

Direct elections were another development in the late 1970s that signaled an
improvement in the EC's fortunes. Fervent Eurofederalists, an endangered
species by that time, hoped that direct elections would accelerate moves
toward European union. Some member states, notably Britain, Denmark, and
France, strongly opposed any increase in the Parliament's powers; others,
such as Germany, Italy, and the Netherlands, favored a more influential Parliament but did not push the point. The Commission supported direct elections, hoping to enhance its own legitimacy and strengthen the supranational
side of the Community system. The Parliament itself did not demand new
powers at the time lest it raise the hackles of hostile member states.[8]

Yet the first direct elections, held in June 1979, failed to generate much
interest or excitement throughout the EC. National political parties controlled
the selection of candidates and ran the campaign. Many voters saw the elections as a referendum on the performance of their national governments. The
turnout (63 percent) was low by the standard of national elections, although it
varied from country to country. The results confirmed the dominance in the
Parliament of the rival Social Democrats and Christian Democrats: the Socialist Group won 113 seats (27.5 percent); the European Peoples' Party (the EC-
wide political party established by the Christian Democrats in 1978 in anticipation of direct elections) won 110 seats (26.8 percent).[9]

Given the much larger size of the directly elected Parliament and the
retirement of many sitting members, most members elected in 1979 were new
to the job. Some, especially from Britain and Denmark, were Euroskeptical,
but the vast majority favored deeper European integration and wanted to
enhance the Parliament's importance in the EC as a whole. A core group of
Euroenthusiasts filled leadership positions, ranging from the presidency and
vice presidencies to the heads of the committees and party groups.

About 10 percent of the new members held the dual mandate (they had
seats in both a national parliament and the European Parliament). Because the
dual mandate formed a bridge between national parliaments and the European
Parliament, the Danish government wanted all Europarliamentarians to continue to hold the dual mandate after direct elections. Yet holders of the dual
mandate inevitably gave priority to their national obligations, often neglecting

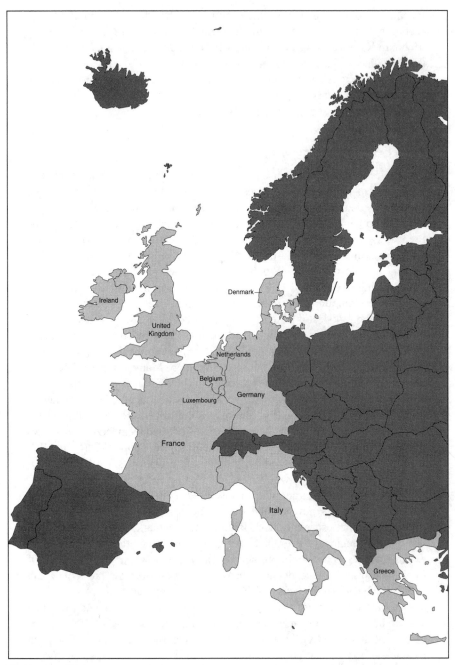

The Ten Member States

EC affairs and further undermining public confidence in the Parliament. Although it was better institutionally for the Parliament not to have members who also held seats in national parliaments, the rapid demise after 1979 of the dual mandate weakened the link between the European and national levels of governance.[10]

The European Monetary System

The European Monetary System (EMS) also symbolized the EC's apparent renaissance in the late 1970s.[11] The EMS was the second major monetary policy initiative undertaken in the EC, the first being the Werner Plan for economic and monetary union (EMU). The abandonment of the Werner Plan in the mid-1970s and the demise of the currency snake, to which it gave rise, hardly instilled confidence in another monetary policy initiative within a relatively short time. Indeed, embarrassing memories of the EC's failure to achieve EMU by 1980 led member states to tone down their rhetoric about the EMS. Far from proclaiming the EMS a step toward EMU, member states saw it for what it was: an effort to reduce exchange rate fluctuations among participating currencies in order to fight inflation, increase investment, and improve economic performance throughout the EC. Only the Commission claimed that the EMS aimed to promote deeper integration, although the relative success of the system, which nobody predicted at the time, undoubtedly contributed to the EC's revival later in the 1980s.

The birth of the EMS is generally associated with Giscard and Schmidt, but Commission president Roy Jenkins conceived the idea. He had a number of motives: to revitalize European integration, put himself and the Commission at the center of Community affairs, revive interest in EMU, and help the Community cope with international exchange rate instability. Jenkins raised the idea in a lecture at the EC-sponsored European University Institute in Florence in October 1977. He tried to interest Schmidt in the idea during a visit to Bonn in November 1977 but found the chancellor in a characteristically gloomy mood, preoccupied with an extreme-left-wing terrorist campaign and unwilling to take a lead in the EC.[12] The Commission issued a communication on EMU in November 1977, but the European Council paid little attention to it at a summit in Brussels the following month.[13] Only Belgium, in the Council presidency and staunchly Eurofederal, supported the Commission's position.

Schmidt had a sudden change of heart in early 1978, perhaps because of another drop in the dollar's value. Persistent depreciation of the dollar and a corresponding appreciation of the mark reduced the competitiveness of German exports and threatened German jobs. The United States appeared to be recovering economically at the expense of Germany's prudence and prosperity. Schmidt accused U.S. president Jimmy Carter of taking a cavalier approach to international monetary matters. Schmidt wanted to cushion Germany from the impact of U.S. action (or inaction) by establishing a European-wide monetary system and also demonstrate to the United States that Europeans were willing and able to respond to poor U.S. leadership in international economic affairs.

With the zeal of the convert, Schmidt championed a monetary policy initiative in the EC, relegating Jenkins and the Commission to the sidelines.[14] Instead, Schmidt chose Giscard as his main partner. The idea of the EMS appealed to Giscard intellectually and had far more weight coming from Schmidt than Jenkins. Giscard and his prime minister, Raymond Barre, author of the Commission's influential memorandum on EMU in 1969, embraced the proposal enthusiastically. The advantage to France of linking the weak franc to the strong mark was obvious, especially if Germany would bear the cost of maintaining parity between them.

From that time onward the EMS became a Franco-German initiative.[15] Giscard and Schmidt unveiled an early version of it at the European Council in Copenhagen in April 1978. The others resented somewhat this classic example of Franco-German high-handedness but wanted their currencies to participate in the proposed system. Only James Callaghan, Britain's prime minister, demurred, partly to protest Franco-German behavior but largely because of the negative reaction of Euroskeptics in the Labour Party and concerns about national sovereignty.

French and German officials had a free hand to work out the details of the EMS before presenting them at the next European Council in Bremen, at the beginning of Germany's presidency in July 1978. Jenkins vividly described the British delegation's late arrival at the summit and studied indifference to the subject under discussion: "They marched [into the European Council] in single file like a jungle expedition into hostile territory, first Callaghan, then [foreign minister] Owen, then six or seven senior officials, then about fifteen bearers carrying about twice that amount of red despatch boxes, which must . . . have been more for show than use during a twenty-four hour period."[16] Although understandable for domestic political reasons, Callaghan's attitude once again demonstrated Britain's aversion to deeper European integration.

The Franco-German proposal called for an exchange rate mechanism using a parity grid and a divergence indicator based on the European currency unit (ECU), an artificial unit of account made up of a basket of participating currencies, weighted according to their values. Currencies could fluctuate against each other within a band of plus or minus 2.5 percent of their value. Finance ministers and central bankers would have to agree to parity changes. Germany insisted that weak currency countries (like France and Italy) take fiscal and monetary policy measures and not rely solely on intervention by strong currency countries (notably Germany) to stay within the agreed-upon band (this was reminiscent of the debate between the "economists" and the "monetarists" during the EMU negotiations of the early 1970s).

National and Commission officials worked throughout 1978 in a number of specialized committees to finalize details of the scheme. Prime Minister Giulio Andreotti wanted Italy to participate from the outset, although experts doubted if the weak lire could stay in the exchange rate mechanism. Ireland wanted to join as well, despite the Irish currency's parity with sterling, which would stay outside the mechanism. Both Ireland and Italy requested financial assistance from the EC in the form of larger allocations from the Regional Development Fund in order to cushion the impact of EMS participation. To complicate matters further, France and Britain insisted that their shares of the Regional Development Fund not diminish in relations to those of Ireland and Italy, and Germany balked at paying the extra cost.

Community leaders thrashed out a final agreement at their summit in Brussels in December 1979. Schmidt saved the day with an offer of extra financial assistance, thus ensuring that all member states except Britain would participate in the exchange rate mechanism. The EMS was to have started operating in January 1979 but a demand by Giscard for the abolition of monetary compensatory amounts, a device used since the early 1970s to cushion the common agricultural policy from exchange rate fluctuations, caused a delay. Because of the mark's tendency to rise against other currencies, the compensatory system helped prop up agricultural prices in Germany and were a source of resentment in France. Yet it was odd for Giscard to delay implementation of the EMS, a showpiece of Franco-German cooperation and leadership in the EC, for the sake of the compensatory system. He may have wanted to ingratiate himself with French farmers, always a worthwhile endeavor for French politicians. Giscard got his way when agriculture ministers agreed in March 1979 to abolish the compensatory system without specifying a timetable. The EMS then went into operation.

The EMS was highly unusual in the EC. Only member states could participate in it, although none was obliged to do so (Britain's opt-out proved the point). It was not based on the EC treaties, although closer monetary policy cooperation, culminating in EMU, was a cherished Community objective. It did not emerge from a formal Commission proposal, although two Community bodies, the Council of Economic and Finance Ministers and the Committee of Central Bank Governors, ran it. Ultimately, the EMS demonstrated the utility of European integration during a generally unpropitious period: it could not have come into being had the EC not already existed.

▥ In the Doldrums

Despite those promising developments in the late 1970s, the EC sank into the doldrums in the early 1980s. The second oil shock of 1979 choked off the tentative economic recovery of the preceding two years. The slowdown began in earnest in the second quarter of 1980. Growth stagnated, unemployment rose, and the balance of trade deteriorated. Only inflation began to drop, thanks in part to the success of the EMS. The Commission feared for the future of the common market, lamenting member states' tendencies "to resort to unilateral, national action which not only makes it harder to impose a common discipline but can also be the gradual undoing of what the Community has so far achieved."[17] The Commission warned in 1980 that "overt or covert protectionism" on the part of member states was fragmenting the internal market, damaging the EC's international credibility, and giving the EC's main trading partners an additional competitive advantage.[18]

The political situation was equally unpropitious. Unpopular and undermined by Jacques Chirac, his erstwhile prime minister, Giscard lost the French presidential election in May 1981. François Mitterrand, his successor, pursued a dash for economic growth that strained the country's public finances, put the franc under intense pressure, and called the future of the EMS into question. Schmidt lost office in 1982, when the Free Democrats, the minority party in the coalition government, jilted him in favor of Helmut Kohl and the Christian Democrats. During his first years in office Kohl devoted little time to the EC.

British prime minister Margaret Thatcher, by contrast, had a large majority in parliament and a definite domestic and international agenda. The EC did not loom large in her thinking, except as a source of resentment against Britain's excessive budgetary contribution. Her demand for a massive rebate both characterized and contributed to the EC's malaise in the early 1980s. Greek accession turned into a major political liability when Papandreou won the general election in 1981 and adopted a policy of obstruction toward the EC. To add insult to injury, Greenland voted in a referendum in February 1982 to leave "the geographical scope of the Treaties" (the remote country was a dependency of Denmark).

The twenty-fifth anniversary of the signing of the Rome Treaty was therefore a somber affair. Tugendhat, who attended the commemoration ceremony in Brussels on behalf of the Commission, painted an amusing portrait of it. Thatcher "wore black and looked forbidding"; Mitterrand, though still relatively new in office, "had already acquired that aura of unapproachability so characteristic of French presidents"; and Schmidt "was obviously impatient with all the fuss." After the lackluster speeches, "as we all trooped across the road to the Royal Palace for lunch, I could not help reflecting upon the uninspiring nature of the whole affair. The drizzle, which had replaced the fog, seemed to provide a fitting finale." The next day, news reached EC leaders at a dreary meeting of the European Council of the death of Walter Hallstein, the Commission's first president. "The symbolism inherent in the timing of Hallstein's death seemed unmistakable and attracted widespread comment. It was as if an ideal as well as a man was being declared dead."[19]

By the 1980s, many questioned the European Economic Community's viability, including the venerable *Economist* magazine. The March 1982 issue featured this somber cartoon, happily for Europe an erroneous read on union's future. © 1982 The Economist Newspaper Ltd. All rights reserved. Reprinted with permission. Further reproduction prohibited.

Institutional Inertia

Institutional inertia underlay the sense of drift. At the end of the 1970s the EC settled institutionally into a state best described by the French word *lourdeur* (heaviness or dullness). The Commission was a leaden bureaucracy; the Council lacked direction; and the Luxembourg Compromise (a member state's right to veto legislation) was an article of faith. The EC still suffered institutionally from the impact of the first enlargement. The Commission acquired four new commissioners without acquiring a greater range of responsibilities. Two of the new member states, Britain and Denmark, were avowedly intergovernmentalist and hostile to the Commission and the Parliament.

The prospect of renewed enlargement (Greece, Portugal, and Spain were then hoping to join) drew attention to the EC's institutional inadequacies. Some of the other member states suspected Britain of wanting enlargement in order to weaken the EC. A remark by Prime Minister James Callaghan in October 1977 summed up Britain's position: "the dangers . . . of an over-centralized, over-bureaucratized and over-harmonized Community will be far less with twelve member states than with nine."[20] There was no question of radically redesigning the EC's institutional architecture in response to enlargement, only of streamlining the existing institutional structure.

Ireland linked the use of qualified majority voting and enlargement in 1975, when Greece applied to join. The Benelux countries, Italy, and the Commission also questioned the institutional implications of enlargement, especially after Portugal and Spain submitted applications. France and Britain, and to a lesser extent Germany, seemed happy with the status quo. Nevertheless the EC's manifest inefficiency in the late 1970s, when enlargement returned to the forefront of Community affairs, made it impossible for even the most sanguine of member states to ignore institutional reform.[21]

Giscard therefore suggested in 1978 that the European Council appoint a small committee "to consider adjustments to the machinery and procedures of the Community institutions" that would not necessitate formal treaty change.[22] Chosen after the usual haggling over nationality and political orientation, the committee's members—the "three wise men"—were Robert Marjolin (France), a former vice president of the Commission; Barend Biesheuvel (the Netherlands), a former prime minister; and Edmund Dell (Britain), a former government minister. Marjolin, the committee's chairman, had no illusions about the job, remarking that "the wisdom with which the [wise men] are credited vanishes the moment they hand in their conclusions."[23]

The wise men's report, presented to the Council presidency in October 1979, painted an unflattering picture of the EC. Before addressing specific institutional issues, the wise men lamented the EC's poor progress in the 1970s, due to "substantive problems stemming from economic and political constraints." The wise men saw the member states' failure to sustain the EC's "integrative momentum" as "a sign of something fundamentally wrong," noting that "the role of the machinery and institutional procedures is a strictly secondary one."[24] Nevertheless it was on that secondary role, and especially on the functioning of the Council and Commission, that the wise men duly concentrated.

The Commission. Roy Jenkins was president of the Commission when the wise men wrote their report. Jenkins's arrival in Brussels in January 1977 injected some life into the institution. Having spent his entire career in British politics, Jenkins was a Brussels outsider. Yet his political stature as a senior British politician and enthusiasm for European integration excited hopes in Brussels and among the more integration-minded member states that he would reinvigorate the Commission.

The horse-trading among member states over the allocation of Commission portfolios opened Jenkins's eyes to the reality of Brussels life. Tugendhat, who received one of the portfolios, recalled the "heated arguments round the Commission table and behind closed doors in the President's office, lasting in all for about twelve hours . . . as colleagues fought bitterly for position. This was despite the extensive preparatory talks conducted beforehand by Jenkins . . . with the individuals concerned and their governments."[25] Perceived national interest, even more than personal pride, accounted for what Jenkins called "the night of the long knives."[26]

Jolted by the experience, Jenkins got off to a slow start in Brussels. His first six months as Commission president coincided with Britain's lackluster presidency of the Council. Jenkins fought a bitter battle with Giscard for the right to represent the Commission at the summit of major industrialized countries (the G7) in London in May 1977. Nothing would have come of Jenkins's idea for a monetary policy initiative in November 1977 had Schmidt not hijacked it. The prevailing political climate was simply not conducive to Commission activism. By 1978 it looked as if Jenkins's presidency would be as forgettable as any since Walter Hallstein's.

As the wise men pointed out in their report, the office of the president was politically and institutionally weak. There were too many commissioners and too few weighty portfolios. The commission's directorates-general (departments) resented the size and influence of commissioners' *cabinets*, or private offices. Promotion at the higher levels of the civil service depended on nationality and networking, not merit. Morale was low throughout the institution.

The relationship between Jenkins and Giscard, president of what was still the EC's most influential member state, epitomized the relationship between the Commission and the Council. So suspicious of Giscard was Jenkins that he detected in Giscard's proposal for a committee of wise men "a desire . . . to cut down the power of the Commission, to reduce or eliminate our political role, our connection with Parliament, and half to amalgamate us with the Council secretariat and with Coreper [the member states' permanent representatives], and thus to make us all servants of the European Council."[27]

Even if that were Giscard's intention, the wise men would never have condoned it. After all, Marjolin was a former Commission vice president who appreciated the Commission's importance and decried its current weakness.

Thus the wise men recommended strengthening the powers of the president, notably in the allocation and reshuffling of portfolios. Nevertheless, the committee deplored what it saw as "a lack of coherence, and increasing bureaucracy, in [the Commission's] own internal operations" and recommended reducing the number of commissioners to one per member state.[28]

The wise men's recommendations for Commission reform dovetailed with those of another report on the subject. That was by Dirk Spierenburg, a former member of the Coal and Steel Community's High Authority. At Jenkins's request Spierenburg studied the Commission and submitted a series of proposed reforms in September 1979. They ranged from the role of the *cabinets* to recruitment, promotion, and other personnel problems. Spierenburg proposed the depoliticization and modernization of the institution through a radical program of internal reform.[29]

The Council and European Council. The Luxembourg Compromise (a member state's right to veto) continued to stymie decisionmaking in the Council of Ministers in the late 1970s. According to the wise men's report, "an atmosphere has developed [in the Council] in which—even on minor issues and in quite humble forums [such as in working groups]—States can obstruct agreement for reasons which they know full well to be insufficient, but which are never brought into the open let alone seriously challenged by their colleagues." The wise men recommended greater use of qualified majority voting, as stipulated in the treaties, "after an appropriate but limited effort for consensus has been made." That would not necessarily mean a vote always being taken, as the mere prospect of voting would encourage member states to compromise. A member state that nonetheless insisted on invoking the Luxembourg Compromise should say "clearly and explicitly . . . that very important interests are at stake, and . . . take responsibility for the consequences in the name of its whole Government."[30] The wise men recognized the importance of the European Council but did not see it as a panacea for the EC's problems, especially as decisions that should have been taken in the Council were being pushed up to the European Council. At the other end of the Council hierarchy, the wise men recommended strengthening the decisionmaking capacity of the member states' permanent representatives in Coreper.

Lack of action. Neither the wise men's report on general institutional reform nor the Spierenburg report on Commission reform was ever implemented. Jenkins lacked the political support in national capitals to act on them. The Spierenburg report achieved cult status among scholars of the Commission because of its prescience and farsightedness. It was only in 2000, when the commission undertook major internal reform in the wake of a corruption scandal, that some of the report's recommendations finally saw the light of day.

Giscard, who proposed the wise men's report, damned it with faint praise at the European Council in Dublin in November 1979. He noted with pleasure the report's criticism of the Commission and endorsement, however tepid, of the European Council. Then he let the matter drop. After all, the report also criticized successive Council presidencies for lack of direction. The French presidency, in the first half of 1979, was particularly poor, with Giscard engaged in a procedural dispute with the Parliament and preoccupied with domestic political problems. After a perfunctory discussion of it at the Dublin summit, the wise men's report sank into obscurity.

The British Budgetary Question

Whereas the EC's institutional problems percolated under the surface, the debilitating British Budgetary Question (BBQ) dominated meetings of the European Council between 1979 and 1984. No wonder that for Roy Jenkins the BBQ came to mean the Bloody British Question. At issue was not only the size of Britain's contribution but also the composition of the budget itself. The EC spent most of its money on agricultural subsidies and supports (the CAP devoured about 70 percent of the budget in 1980). Given the relentless increase in agricultural spending, the EC was bound to hit the limit of "own resources" in the early to mid-1980s. Member states would then have to agree either to increase the size of their value-added tax contribution or to decrease spending on agriculture. Both were unpopular choices. On the one hand, national governments wanted to keep as much of their value-added tax receipts as possible in order to fund domestic programs; on the other hand, farmers kept a wary eye on agricultural prices and fiercely defended the CAP.

Because it imported relatively more from outside the EC than most other member states and had a smaller agricultural sector, Britain paid disproportionately more into the EC budget and got disproportionately less out of it. The Labour government wanted a better budget deal for Britain as part of the renegotiation of accession terms in 1974–1975, but settled for relatively little. Only when Thatcher came to power in 1979 did Britain seriously address its budgetary imbalance in the EC. Thatcher knew instinctively that the British public would back her in a fight against Brussels to right such an obvious wrong.

Thatcher could not abide the CAP. Whereas French and German leaders saw it as part of the original bargain to bind their countries together after the war, she saw the CAP solely as a market-distorting mechanism. Thatcher viewed the EC as a collection of sovereign states cooperating closely for mutual economic gain. Other EC leaders, she suspected, aspired to an EC that was "interventionist, protectionist, and ultimately federalist." At the root of the CAP and the Community lay the Franco-German axis, which, Thatcher believed, "diminished Britain's capacity to influence events" and was "a factor to be reckoned with."[31]

Thatcher's approach to the CAP meshed with her domestic priorities. Being obsessed at home with cutting public spending in order to cure Britain's chronic fiscal problems, it would have been contrary to her nature and political instincts to allow the EC to spend public money profligately. Most other EC leaders saw things differently. They cared little about fiscal rectitude when it came to "Brussels money." Thatcher disliked the phrase "own resources" not only because of its inelegance but also because it disguised what for her was a fundamental truth: that money handed over to the EC was "ours," not "theirs," and that Britain contributed too much and was entitled to a generous rebate.

Thatcher set out "to limit the damage and distortions caused by the CAP and to bring financial realities to bear on Community spending."[32] A visit by Schmidt to London in May 1979 gave her an early opportunity to make a case against the CAP and for a British rebate. Schmidt was one of the few foreigners, excluding Americans, whom Thatcher liked (although he was a Social Democrat, she admired his domestic economic policies and advocacy of EC financial reform). Thatcher told Schmidt "straight away that although Britain wanted to play a vigorous and influential role in the European Community, we could not do so until the problem of our grossly unfair budgetary contribution had been resolved."[33]

Schmidt's visit set the scene for the Strasbourg summit in June 1979, intended to celebrate the first direct elections to the Parliament. Giscard and Schmidt were used to dominating the European Council; Thatcher decided to shake things up. Tugendhat, a commissioner at the time, faulted Giscard and Schmidt for condescending to Thatcher. He was certain "that Mrs. Thatcher's sex was a complicating factor." The first female member of the EC's most exclusive club, Thatcher was neither demure nor submissive. From then on, Tugendhat observed, the budgetary question "became inexorably caught up with the pride, prejudice and personalities of the heads of state and governments involved."[34] Giscard wanted to postpone discussion of the budget at the Strasbourg summit. "And so," as Thatcher recalled, "at my very first European Council I had to say no."[35] It was a word the other summiteers would hear repeatedly in the years ahead.

The Dublin summit in November 1979 ended in acrimony when Thatcher rejected a Commission analysis of the budgetary problem. A game of brinkmanship ensued. Thatcher implicitly threatened to withhold Britain's budgetary contribution (an illegal act), and Giscard and Schmidt speculated about relegating Britain to second-class EC membership (a legal impossibility). Foreign ministers searched for a solution in early 1980 while their agricultural counterparts agreed to yet another increase in CAP spending. Although the atmosphere at the next summit was "a good deal better than in

Dublin," it was not good enough to facilitate a breakthrough.[36] That came only after a marathon, eighteen-hour-long meeting of the General Affairs Council in May 1980 when Britain was offered a two-thirds rebate covering a three-year period.

Thatcher reluctantly accepted the offer. The European Council endorsed the agreement at the Venice summit in June 1980, at which Schmidt urged wider budgetary reform, especially in view of imminent Greek accession. That was easier said than done, not least because Germany's agricultural minister was among the most aggressive supporters of higher farm prices. Nevertheless, Thatcher succeeded in getting budget reform on the EC's agenda and in temporarily resolving the contentious question of Britain's contribution. As everybody knew, however, Thatcher would return to the charge in 1983 when the terms of the Venice agreement were due to expire.

The first round of the BBQ ended in victory for Thatcher, but Britain paid a high political price. Other EC leaders had hoped that after the shilly-shally-ing of Wilson and the barely concealed hostility of Callaghan, British policy toward the EC would improve under Thatcher. Many recalled Thatcher's first political battle on becoming Conservative Party leader: campaigning for Britain's continued EC membership in the run-up to the 1975 referendum. They had hoped that Thatcher would contribute to the EC's development, as eventually she did by advocating completion of the internal market. In the meantime, Thatcher's dogged pursuit of a budgetary rebate on terms acceptable only to Britain alienated her fellow heads of state and government. Even Tugendhat, a sympathizer, observed that "the longer [the budgetary question] lasted the more isolated Britain became and the more this single issue came to dominate British European policy."[37]

Obdurate though she was, other EC leaders preferred to deal with Thatcher than with her Labour Party opponents. At the time the Labour Party was officially committed to pulling Britain out of the EC and repealing "those sections of Community law which have been imposed on the UK and which we do not find acceptable."[38] The prospect of the Labour Party's coming to power appalled Britain's EC partners. Despite their frustration with the current British government, few of them welcomed the prospect of conducting arduous withdrawal negotiations with a new British government. The contemporaneous negotiations on Greenland's withdrawal from the EC were difficult enough.

The Mediterranean Morass

The EC's involvement with Greece, Portugal, and Spain in the early 1980s was a source of considerable friction and mutual frustration. No sooner had Greece joined the EC in January 1981 than the Socialists won the general election and Papandreou became prime minister. Despite having opposed EC membership, Papandreou decided not to take Greece out of the EC but to strike a better bargain for his country within it. No doubt impressed by Thatcher's antics, Papandreou demanded special concessions for Greece, ostensibly to help the country's economy adapt to membership. The Greek government sent Brussels a formal memorandum outlining its position on the economic impact of membership in March 1981.

Negotiations on the Greek memorandum continued sporadically for the next four years. In a communication to the Council in March 1983, the Commission proposed that the EC assist the Greek economy through regional policy and other redistributive measures, rather than through derogations to the treaties.[39] Most of the proposed special measures would be encapsulated in the so-called Integrated Mediterranean Programs. The European Council approved the Commission's approach in Stuttgart in June 1983, but bad blood between Papandreou and other EC leaders delayed a final agreement and contributed to the collapse of the Athens summit in December 1983, which ended even without a communiqué being issued.

The state of negotiations on the Greek memorandum mirrored the state of negotiations on Portuguese and Spanish accession, at least until a political breakthrough in 1982. Both Portugal and Spain embarked on the road to EC membership in the mid-1970s. Following a period of turmoil in the aftermath of the revolution that ousted the authoritarian regime in April 1974, Portugal stabilized politically and applied to join the EC in March 1977. Public opinion and most political parties in Portugal strongly supported EC accession as a sure way to consolidate democracy and promote prosperity. Like Greece, Portugal wanted the EC to consider its application separately from Spain's. That proved impossible for the EC to do. In view of the two countries' propinquity and the timing of their applications (Spain applied four months after Portugal), the EC conducted parallel accession negotiations, starting with Portugal in October 1978 and Spain in February 1979. Strong reservations in France and Italy about the economic implications of Spanish accession undoubtedly slowed down the negotiations with Portugal.

In its opinion of May 1978 the Commission identified a number of impediments to early Portuguese accession. The Commission predicted difficult negotiations on agriculture, free movement of people, and textiles, which accounted for over 40 percent of Portugal's industrial output and 33 percent of its exports. Initially Portugal had hoped to join as early as January 1983. The delay in beginning substantive negotiations until 1980 convinced the Portuguese government of the unlikelihood of accession until at least the middle of the decade.

Like Portugal, Spain wanted to join the EC for political and economic reasons. Politically, Spain wanted to regain international respectability after decades of authoritarian rule under Gen. Francisco Franco. Economically, Spain wanted to continue the process of industrial and agricultural modernization begun in the later years of the Franco regime but stunted by Spain's exclusion from the EC. A center-right government began the post-Franco transition and set Spain on the road to EC accession. Under the influence of former German chancellor Willy Brandt in the international socialist movement, the opposition Spanish Socialist Party transformed itself into a modern Social Democratic party. Unlike the Greek Socialists, the Spanish Socialists strongly supported EC membership.

France and Italy looked forward to the EC's postaccession center of gravity's tilting more toward southern Europe but had serious reservations about the impact of Spanish accession on the CAP. By increasing the EC's agricultural area by 30 percent and its farm work force by 25 percent, Spain's entry would have major budgetary implications. In addition, France, Italy, and Spain would compete directly in the production of fruit, vegetables, and olive oil. The ever-vigilant French agricultural lobby swung into action during the parliamentary elections in March 1978 and in the run-up to the presidential elections in May 1981. Giscard declared in a speech to French farmers' leaders in Paris in June 1980 that "the Community should give priority to completing the first enlargement" before undertaking another one. The president's office later clarified his remarks to mean that they applied to Portugal and Spain, not to Greece, which was set to join in January 1981.[40]

The member states (and the rest of the world) were reminded of the political imperative of bringing Spain into the EC when a group of military officers attempted a coup in the Spanish parliament in January 1981. Despite the European Council's expression of support soon afterward for the accession to the EC of "a democratic Spain," the accession negotiations merely plodded along in 1981 and 1982.[41]

Mitterrand was as susceptible as his predecessor to the French farmers' lobby. Fisheries and textiles remained major stumbling blocks in the negotiations with both countries. Apart from economic concerns, Mitterrand was not yet sufficiently interested in the EC's revival to see Mediterranean enlargement in a positive light. Nevertheless, the EC and its member states were not entirely to blame for the slow pace of the negotiations. The Spanish government seemed reluctant to accept all the obligations of membership, such as introducing a value-added tax and curtailing state subsidies. The European Council urged Spain in November 1981 to "make good use of the period until accession for careful preparations . . . by introducing the necessary reforms so that the potential benefits for both sides can be realized."[42]

■ Picking Up Speed

Notwithstanding the apparent impasse on enlargement and other contentious issues, reports of the EC's demise in the early 1980s were greatly exaggerated. The institutions continued to function and lay the groundwork for the EC's resurgence later in the decade. Despite poor presidential leadership, the Commission took important initiatives to restructure the steel industry, promote collaboration in the high-technology sector, and complete the internal market. Energized by the first direct elections, the Parliament reorganized itself internally and pushed for greater integration in a host of policy areas. The EMS was a surprising success and helped restore confidence in the utility of economic integration.

Perhaps the most striking change in the early 1980s was in the outlook of the member states. Reeling from renewed economic recession and frustrated with the EC's apparent stagnation during the preceding ten years, governments chafed at the constraint imposed by unanimity in the Council, swung toward support for deeper integration, and sought a stronger EC presence on the international stage. Nowhere was this more consequential than in France, where Mitterrand changed direction in 1982 and 1983 and became an advocate of deeper political and economic integration. The ongoing British budgetary question nevertheless obscured the EC's brightening prospects.

Ending the Budgetary Battles

Thatcher was resoundingly reelected in June 1983. She owed her success partly to the unelectability of the Labour Party, due in no small measure to its pledge to withdraw from the EC, and largely to the "Falklands factor," the victory dividend from the war against Argentina in the south Atlantic for control of the disputed Falklands/Malvinas Islands. Flushed with success on the battlefield and in the ballot box, Thatcher returned to the fray in Europe. She demanded a permanent solution to the budgetary dispute at the Stuttgart summit in June 1983.

At her inaugural summit in Strasbourg in June 1979, Thatcher was new to the European Council and faced the formidable alliance of Giscard and Schmidt. By 1983 she was a veteran of the European Council and faced Mitterrand and Kohl, the relatively new leaders of France and Germany, who had not yet revived the Franco-German axis. Weak domestically and uninterested in the minutiae of the EC budget, Mitterrand and Kohl were no match for Thatcher. Kohl would have liked to resolve the issue during his first Council presidency, in early 1983, but the necessary groundwork had not been done. EC leaders decided to postpone the matter until their meeting in Athens in December 1983.

The Athens summit was a disaster. The other EC leaders heartily disliked Papandreou, who made no secret of his determination to get as much as possible out of the EC while contributing as little as possible to its political or economic development. Usually EC leaders wanted the president-in-office to be able to proclaim a successful summit, regardless of the main agenda items or the actual outcome. In this case the others harbored such ill will toward

Papandreou that they would not agree even on a concluding communiqué and made no secret of the summit's failure. But poor preparation and Papandreou's presidency were not entirely to blame for lack of progress on the BBQ. Thatcher suspected that Mitterrand wanted to delay a settlement until France took over the presidency from Greece, so that he could then claim a diplomatic victory.[43]

Thatcher wanted a permanent British refund as part of a long-term reform of the EC's finances. By the end of 1983 the EC was approaching bankruptcy. The EC's inability to get agricultural spending under control compounded the problem. In 1979 the Council introduced a modest change in the system of price guarantees and imposed a so-called coresponsibility levy on dairy farmers to help meet the costs of storing or subsidizing exports of surplus produce. When the coresponsibility levy failed to curb excess output, the Commission proposed a production quota. Usually Ignaz Kiechle, Germany's powerful agriculture minister and a staunch defender of Bavarian dairy farmers, would have quashed the idea. This time, however, Kiechle saw milk quotas as the only alternative to price cuts.

Negotiations on the proposed milk quotas and other CAP reforms, on the terms of Britain's rebate, and on reconfiguring the size of the value-added tax contribution to the EC's own resources were part and parcel of the budgetary question. A global agreement seemed likely at the Brussels summit in March 1984, under the French presidency. A decision by agriculture ministers shortly before the European Council to curtail CAP spending by introducing milk quotas augured well for the success of the summit. But at the summit itself, Garret FitzGerald, Ireland's prime minister, rejected the draft agreement that, because of the structure of Irish agriculture, would have badly hurt the Irish economy (the dairy sector accounted for nearly 10 percent of Ireland's GDP).

As Thatcher mischievously remarked, "we never seemed to get by [at a European Council] without a tear-jerking homily on the predicament of Ireland from . . . Garret FitzGerald, who was determined if he could to exempt his country from the disciplines on agricultural spending."[44] In FitzGerald's opinion, the proposed milk quota threatened a vital national interest. He left the summit, thereby implicitly invoking the Luxembourg Compromise (national veto). In his memoirs, FitzGerald denies that he walked out, saying that he merely left the room temporarily.[45] Whatever the case, the other EC leaders got the message and gave Ireland a special dispensation.

The Brussels summit failed not because of FitzGerald's implicit veto antics but because the participants were again unable to solve the BBQ. Disagreement centered on the basis as well as the size of Britain's rebate. France seemed to be steering the meeting to a successful conclusion when Kohl changed the dynamic of the negotiation by proposing an annual rebate for the next three years. Thatcher flatly rejected this, not only because she considered it insufficient (although by any measure it was a generous offer) but also because it was not a permanent solution. France and Italy's refusal after the summit to lift a veto on the payment of Britain's 1983 rebate further infuriated Thatcher.[46]

EC leaders finally resolved the long-standing BBQ at the Fontainebleau summit in June 1984. Eager for a settlement, Mitterrand and Kohl coordinated their positions before the summit began. Perhaps equally eager to put the issue behind her, Thatcher was surprisingly conciliatory. The earlier agreement on milk quotas undoubtedly helped as well. All agreed at Fontainebleau on a permanent rebate in the form of a fixed percentage each year of the difference between Britain's value-added tax contribution to the EC and Britain's receipts from the EC. Thatcher worked down from an initial demand of 70 percent and the others worked up from an initial offer of 60 percent. Thatcher held out for 66 percent and Kohl for 65 percent. Mitterrand, the summit host, convinced Kohl to give Thatcher the extra 1 percent. Together with an agreement to raise the ceiling on value-added tax contributions to 1.4 percent (pending a further increase after Portugal and Spain joined the EC) and a vague commitment to curb CAP expenditure, this brought the budget saga to a close. Nevertheless, the unrelated question of a supplementary budget for 1984, pitting Britain against the rest, still had to be resolved.

"In every negotiation," Thatcher wrote, "there comes the best possible time to settle: this was it."[47] Thatcher was as tired of the budgetary question as the others were. She was inclined to settle in mid-1984 also because of rising impatience at home with her obstructionism in Brussels. Her stridency in the European Council, often caricatured in the media, embarrassed many Britons. More important politically was her declining support within the Conservative Party.[48]

Mitterrand's renewed calls in mid-1984 for a renegotiation of Britain's relationship with the EC may also have persuaded Thatcher to bring the dispute to an end. In a famous speech at the Parliament in May 1984, Mitterrand raised the prospect of a two-speed EC, with Britain relegated to the slow lane. It seems unlikely, however, that Thatcher would have taken such threats seriously. She had her own understanding of what a two-speed EC meant: "Those who pay more are in the top group and those who pay less are not."[49] The most important factor in ending the dispute may have been simply that, like her EC partners, Thatcher wanted to move on and breathe new life into the Community. Resolution of the BBQ cleared the way not only for Portuguese and Spanish accession but also for a constructive debate about the EU's future.

Tugendhat, who sympathized with Thatcher, claimed that "no other European leader could have held out for so long nor secured so much against the opposition of all the rest."[50] Yet the dispute could have been resolved sooner, arguably to Britain's advantage. In monetary terms, Thatcher might have won greater or equal concessions at an earlier stage in the negotiations.

Politically, by protracting the dispute she forfeited whatever residual goodwill existed toward Britain in the EC.

Poor personal chemistry exacerbated the situation. Kohl detested Thatcher; Mitterrand found her oddly fascinating. Thatcher disliked both Kohl and Mitterrand. Such intense feelings mattered in the European Council, a highly intimate decisionmaking forum. By 1984, when the dispute finally ended, Thatcher was the second-least popular member of the European Council (Papandreou was ahead of her by a long shot).

Resolution of the BBQ finally removed a persistent irritant in relations between Britain and the other member states. Resentment at the unfairness of its budgetary contribution was never far beneath the surface of British attitudes toward the EC. With the issue resolved, Britain could assess EC membership on its merits rather than on the basis of a budgetary quirk. Euroskeptics must have regretted the removal of an injustice that automatically engendered hostility in Britain toward Brussels.

The long-running dispute at least instilled in other member states concern about excessive EC expenditure. As more of the original member states became net contributors to the budget, especially after the accession of Portugal and Spain, Thatcher's preoccupation with the EC's public finances became less peculiar. Yet the lure of a bountiful CAP was undiminished. The milk quota failed to curb overproduction and hardly slowed down the rate of growth of CAP expenditure. Although the European Council agreed in Fontainebleau to cut spending on the CAP, it also agreed to increase the size of the EC's budget. As the *Economist* observed, "by agreeing to raise the EC's income, the Ten [member states] have removed the most direct pressure for reforming a runaway farm policy, namely the threat of running out of money."[51]

Portuguese and Spanish Accession

It was only when Mitterrand changed economic tack in 1982 and 1983, due largely to international constraints and domestic opportunism, that the end of the Portuguese and Spanish negotiations finally hove into sight. Yet it was another year before Mitterrand issued a declaration unequivocally advocating enlargement. Mitterrand's epiphany coincided with important political changes in the candidate countries. In Portugal, the able and energetic Mario Soares formed a government in June 1983. Soares endeared himself to the EC when his government reached an agreement with the International Monetary Fund that included measures to reduce the country's substantial foreign debt and further restructure the economy. Soares cultivated close relations with Mitterrand, a fellow Socialist. During a tour of EC capitals later in 1983, Soares impressed his interlocutors with Portugal's determination to become a model member state. Rapid agreement on a number of outstanding issues quickly followed in the accession negotiations. Much to Soares's annoyance, however, the fate of Portugal's application hinged on the outcome of Spain's negotiations.

Following the Socialist Party's landslide victory in the 1982 general election, Felipe González reinvigorated Spain's effort to join the EC. Young, personable, and passionately pro-European, González emulated Soares by visiting EC capitals and wooing national leaders. In anticipation of EC membership, González introduced badly needed but politically painful domestic economic reforms. The accession negotiations proceeded well, although a number of tricky areas, notably agriculture and fisheries, became increasingly contentious. An informal summit of the prime ministers—all Socialists—of the EC's Mediterranean member states and applicant countries (France, Italy, Greece, Portugal, and Spain) in October 1983 paved the way for a breakthrough. At a meeting in Luxembourg only two days later, farm ministers approved rules to organize the EC's fruit, vegetable, and olive oil markets with a view to enlargement. Unencumbered by looming parliamentary or presidential elections, Mitterrand could afford to make concessions, although it was not until the Dublin summit in December 1984 that the EU resolved some last-minute agricultural issues.[52]

Fisheries remained the final item on the agenda of the accession negotiations. The EC was reluctant to give Spain unrestricted access to its territorial waters: the Spanish fleet was larger than the combined Community fleet and had a notoriously insatiable appetite. Repeated clashes between Spanish trawlers and French and Irish naval vessels in 1984 emphasized the sensitivity of the issue. So did attacks by Spanish fishermen against trucks from EC member states to protest the seizure of Spanish trawlers and retaliatory action by French truckers at the Spanish border. The two sides eventually concluded a fisheries agreement in early 1985.

Resolution of the BBQ cleared the way for Portuguese and Spanish accession. Having reached a budgetary agreement, the Fontainebleau European Council set January 1986 as the date for Portugal and Spain to join the EC.[53] In a move calculated to reassure González of French goodwill, Mitterrand flew to Madrid immediately after the summit to report personally on the outcome.

The negotiations with Portugal and Spain took six years to complete. Ratification of the accession agreements took another twelve months. Altogether, more than eight years elapsed between the two countries' applications to join and their entry into the EC. Portuguese and Spanish accession reinforced a lesson of the first enlargement: the road to EC membership was long and arduous for all concerned. Digesting Portuguese and Spanish accession would be equally challenging. Although enthusiastic about European integration, Portugal and Spain were much poorer than the existing member states, apart from Greece and Ireland. Yet they brought to the EC a new Mediterranean dimension and foreign policy orientation, which led to the strengthening of

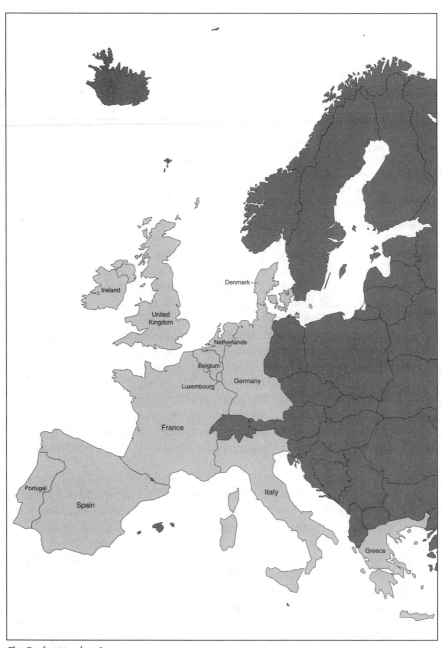

The Twelve Member States

economic and political relations with Latin America, a part of the world hitherto of little interest to the Community.

Commission Activism

The state of the Commission in the early 1980s mirrored that of the EC itself.
Superficially, at least, the Commission was weak and demoralized. Worn out
after battling Thatcher on the budget and Giscard on the Commission's role
and responsibilities, Jenkins gladly returned to domestic politics in Britain at
the end of his term in office, where he confronted Thatcher on surer ground.
The European Council selected Gaston Thorn, a former prime minister of
Luxembourg, to succeed Jenkins. Although thoroughly familiar with the EC,
Thorn seemed detached and ill at ease in Brussels. Regardless of his personal
shortcomings, Thorn was unfortunate to be Commission president at such a
difficult time. The Commission president could only be as effective as the
most influential national leaders wanted him to be. In Thorn's case, Giscard
openly disdained the Commission, Schmidt was indifferent toward it, and
Thatcher heartily disliked it. Although Mitterrand replaced Giscard early in
Thorn's tenure and Kohl replaced Schmidt a year later, initially the new leaders of France and Germany showed little enthusiasm for European integration.

The Commission persevered—in the face of widespread public and political skepticism—in advocating deeper integration. Whereas Thorn soon faded
into the background, some of the other commissioners relished the challenge
of promoting integration at such an unpropitious time. Foremost among them
was Vice President Etienne Davignon, a former Belgian diplomat who had
also served in the Jenkins Commission. As the commissioner with responsibility for industrial affairs, Davignon sought to restructure old industries and
encourage new ones while also pushing for completion of the internal market.

Steel. In October 1980, the Commission declared a "manifest crisis" in the
EC's steel industry, under the terms of a hitherto-unused article of the Coal
and Steel Community treaty. At Davignon's direction, the Commission imposed production quotas and other measures to give firms time to adjust to a
massive slump in the steel market that brought the industry almost to its
knees. The Commission's action required the unanimous approval of the
Council, something notoriously difficult to get. The Commission's task was
made more difficult by opposition from workers and employers, fearful for
their livelihoods. In the end, even the fiercely anti-interventionist British government supported the Commission because a Commission-imposed regime
was preferable to a beggar-thy-neighbor policy of protectionist measures by
individual member states. As it was, the Commission acted only after the collapse of the steel industry's voluntary crisis management plan. The Commission's action forced the European steel industry to restructure, albeit at a cost

of lost jobs and closed plants. While blaming the Commission for imposing tough measures, national governments took credit for the industry's rescue.

High technology. In the early 1980s, industry, national governments, and the Commission grew increasingly concerned about Western Europe's inadequacies in the high-technology sector, especially in view of intense competition from Asia and the United States. Davignon resolved to put the Commission at the forefront of efforts to improve European competitiveness by promoting collaboration among industries and universities. Davignon contacted the heads of major European manufacturers in the high-technology sector, urging them to consider the virtues of working together, something that the persistent economic recession in any case predisposed them to do. Not wanting to scare off European industrialists by raising the specter of Commission intrusiveness, Davignon kept discreetly in the background.

Davignon pushed through a reorganization of the Commission to bring under a single directorate-general all the departments responsible for research programs. The Commission then sent the Council a communication on the EC's research and development strategy for the 1980s, emphasizing the need to adopt a comprehensive approach by incorporating all EC research projects into a general framework program. The Council responded positively, noting that a broad consensus existed on the desirability of developing scientific research at the European level and improving the efficiency of the EC's research and development activities. The council of research ministers, which had met only sporadically in the 1970s, sprang back to life in the early 1980s. The Council adopted the EC's first framework program for research and development in 1983, covering the period 1984–1987. The European Council encouraged greater EC involvement in research and development, especially during the French presidency in the first half of 1984. Resolution of the budgetary dispute at the Fontainebleau summit in June 1984 facilitated funding of the new framework program, although not as generously as the Commission wanted.

The EC's renewed interest in research and development covered a range of issues but focused mostly on "industries of strategic importance." In 1982 the Council agreed on a pilot phase for the European Strategic Program for Research and Development in Information Technology (ESPRIT). This provided limited funding for collaborative research projects involving major manufacturers, small firms, and universities in the EC. ESPRIT proved extremely popular, although its impact was more symbolic than real. The research may not have produced scientific breakthroughs, but it bolstered confidence in the Commission's ability to advance the interests of European business.[54]

The internal market. As well as pursuing a bold industrial strategy, the Commission aggressively championed completion of the internal market. As early as 1979, the Commission signaled its determination to remove nontariff barriers and technical barriers to trade by following up on the landmark ruling by the Court of Justice in the *Cassis de Dijon* case, which arose out of a prohibition against the importation into Germany of Cassis, a French liqueur, on the grounds that it failed to meet Germany's alcohol-content standards. The Court ruled in February 1979 that because Cassis met French standards and did not pose a health risk, it could not be kept out of the German market.[55]

The Commission used the ruling to develop the principle of mutual recognition of national regulations and standards. Despite a general treaty prohibition on technical barriers to trade, governments frequently invoked an escape clause in the treaty allowing them to impose their own product standards for reasons of health and safety. In the event of differences among member states, the treaty provided for "approximation" (harmonization) of standards, an arduous and politically sensitive process that caused a huge backlog of proposals in the Council. Building on the Cassis case, the Commission proposed that instead of trying to harmonize a potentially limitless number of product standards throughout the EC, member states should recognize and accept each other's standards as long as they satisfied certain health and safety concerns.[56]

On a broader front, the Commission continued in the early 1980s to outline the advantages to be gained from a fully functioning internal market. In June 1981 the Commission drafted a communication for the European Council on the importance of market integration. At its summit in Luxembourg later that month, the European Council agreed that "a concerted effort must be made to strengthen and develop the free internal market, which lies at the very basis of the European Community."[57] Later in the year the Commission pressed the Council to pass a number of measures intended to simplify formalities at internal borders in the areas of customs, taxation, and statistics.[58]

The Commission pressured national governments to act, focusing on the politically powerful European Council. Indeed, the European Council devoted more attention in 1983 and 1984 to internal market issues, despite the distraction of the ongoing budgetary dispute. Sensing the imminent end of the protracted BBQ, the Commission prepared a detailed paper for the Fontainebleau summit on a variety of internal market issues, ranging from the abolition of customs barriers to the free movement of people, capital, and services. In its postsummit communiqué, the European Council duly called for completion of the internal market.[59]

The Commission's industrial strategy and agitation for completion of the internal market appealed to big business in Europe, which needed little prompting on the virtues of market integration. On the initiative of Guy Gyllenhammer, the head of Volvo, the leaders of some of Europe's biggest industries formed the European Round Table to lobby at the highest level for a single market. Although his own firm was located in Sweden, a nonmember state, Gyllenhammer appreciated the advantages for Volvo of a borderless EC, which he hoped that Sweden would join. Wisse Dekker, the head of Philips, the large Dutch electronics company, and a leading member of the European Round Table, published a pamphlet in 1984 calling for completion of the internal market by 1990.[60] Gyllenhammer and Dekker were in the vanguard of "an important and vocal constituency . . . impatient for an end to such things as customs delays at borders, conflicting national standards in data processing or arcane rules on property ownership . . . and pressing for the completion of the internal market."[61] Private sector support for deeper economic integration quickly got the attention of European politicians.

European Parliament Activism

Less influential than the Commission and therefore of less interest to European business, the directly elected Parliament also pressed in the early 1980s for completion of the internal market. A number of members formed a cross-party "intergroup," known as the Kangaroo Group, to lobby for the removal of internal borders in the EC. Members of the group were strategically placed in the Parliament to advance various reports and resolutions calling for action on the internal market. Thus the Parliament asked two economists to write a report on the cost for European business of having to operate in an incomplete internal market. The ensuing report foreshadowed the Commission's more extensive and better-known study on "the cost of non-Europe" later in the decade.[62]

The Parliament suffered a political setback in 1980 when the Council refused to accept its amendments to the budget, obliging the EC to limp along on a system of "provisional twelfths" (monthly expenditure based on the previous year's budget) and forcing the directly elected Parliament to make do with the operational budget of the smaller, indirectly elected Parliament. The Parliament wisely compromised in July 1980.[63] At the other end of the budgetary procedure, the Parliament refused to grant discharge in November 1984 of the 1982 budget (in other words, the Parliament rejected the accuracy of the Commission's accounting for Community expenditure). The Parliament claimed that this amounted to censure of the Commission, which should have resulted in the Commission's resignation. Its credibility impaired, the Commission hung on until January 1985, when a new Commission was due in any case to take over.[64] The incident showed that the Parliament and the Commission, although institutional allies, were not destined always to get along. It also validated an observation by Roy Jenkins that direct elections produced "a potentially formidable new Parliament . . . which [the Commission] approached with a mixture of respect and apprehension."[65]

The Parliament aggressively exercised oversight of the Commission and, where possible, the Council in other areas as well. Parliamentary committees held more hearings, and members tabled more questions on a variety of policy issues. For its part, the Commission introduced new procedures for dealing with the demands of parliamentary plenary sessions and committee meetings. In 1981 the Parliament began the practice of voting on the incoming Commission, setting a precedent for the acquisition of formal investiture powers many years after.

It was in the legislative area above all that the Parliament sought to expand its limited role. At the time the treaties provided for parliamentary involvement in legislative decisionmaking only through the consultation procedure. Thus the Parliament could submit an opinion on a legislative proposal, which the Council generally ignored. In an effort to assert its authority, the directly elected Parliament challenged the validity of a Council directive on the grounds that the Council had acted before receiving the Parliament's opinion. In its so-called Isoglucose ruling of 1980, the Court supported the Parliament and struck down the directive, proclaiming that the consultation procedure "reflects at Community level the fundamental principle that the peoples should take part in the exercise of power through the intermediary of an elected assembly."[66]

The Isoglucose ruling strengthened the Parliament's political position. By threatening to delay its opinion and thereby delay the enactment of legislation, the Parliament leveraged its position in the legislative process.[67] Moreover, the Isoglucose ruling enhanced the Parliament's claim to be the institution best placed to close the so-called democratic deficit, a term first used in the 1970s to describe the apparent gap between the governed and the governing in the EC. The Parliament used the Court's defense of "the fundamental principle" of public participation in government at the EU level "through the intermediary of an elected assembly" like a battering ram over the years to extend its legislative decisionmaking role, first through the cooperation procedure and later through the co-decision procedure.

The Parliament was particularly active in promoting European union. The wise men remarked in their report in 1979 that the term *European Union* "has been the subject of much empty talk during the last few years." Their most encouraging prognosis was that "everything [that] strengthens the Community's internal unity, and its unity and that of the Nine in dealings with the rest of the world, constitutes progress towards European Union."[68] The Commission's annual reports on the subject held out little hope in the early 1980s for a political breakthrough. Nevertheless some members in the first directly elected Parliament saw themselves as the vanguard of a movement to recast the EC in a federal direction and achieve European union. A group of them, led by Altiero Spinelli, the irrepressible Italian former commissioner and Eurofederalist, decided to use the Parliament as a constitutional convention and draft a treaty on European union.

In July 1980, Spinelli invited like-minded members, from all political parties, to the Crocodile restaurant in Strasbourg. By the end of the year the "Crocodile club" had grown from ten to seventy members. Dedicated to reviving and reforming the EC, the club's proposals ranged from completion of the single market to replacing the EC with a federal European Union. Thanks to the work of the Crocodile club, between 1980 and 1982 the Parliament passed no less than eight resolutions advocating institutional reform and deeper political and economic integration.

Too large to meet and eat in its favorite Strasbourg restaurant, the Crocodile club moved to a committee room in Brussels, thereby inaugurating the Parliament's influential Committee on Institutional Affairs. With Spinelli in the pivotal role of *rapporteur* (report writer), the committee set out to draft a new treaty. Knowing that most national governments were likely to dismiss Spinelli as naive and excessively ambitious, the committee proceeded cautiously, deliberately, and responsibly. With the help of some academic experts, subcommittees worked on issues such as the legal personality of the proposed union and its institutional structure, competence, and relationship with the member states. The Draft Treaty Establishing the European Union finally emerged. In one of the most famous votes ever taken in the Parliament, a majority of members of all political persuasions voted for the draft treaty in February 1984.[69]

Far from being an unrealistic call for a United States of Europe, the draft treaty was a blueprint for a more efficient, democratic, and far-reaching organization of European states along federal lines. Its preamble stated that the EU would be responsible only for tasks that could be undertaken better in common at the European level than by member states acting alone at the national level. This was an early articulation of the principle of "subsidiarity" (member states' rights) that came to the fore in the late 1980s.

Despite its moderation and the political support of some sympathetic member states, the draft treaty had little chance of ever being implemented. Nevertheless, its existence, and the attention lavished on it by Mitterrand during France's Council presidency in early 1984, contributed to the momentum developing in the mid-1980s in favor of treaty reform. The Parliament naturally looked back on the draft treaty as a precursor of the 1992 Maastricht Treaty on European Union. The draft treaty certainly was prescient, with many of its features finding their way, in some form or other, into subsequent treaty reforms. But it would be an exaggeration to say that the draft treaty triggered the revival of the EC later in the 1980s.

The Parliament scheduled its vote on the draft treaty to generate publicity in the run-up to the second direct elections, in June 1984. Yet the draft treaty got little serious media coverage, and the second direct elections were even more disappointing than the first ones (the turnout was two percentage points lower than in June 1979). Once again, the European elections seemed to consist of little more than separate national elections (Luxembourg even held a general election on the same day).

Member State Activism

Although the Parliament's draft treaty was too far-reaching for most member states, many national governments in the early 1980s wanted the EC to regain momentum. European integration seemed more necessary than ever in the context of rapid globalization and heightened East-West tension. The Luxembourg Compromise (a member state's right to veto) continued to impede decisionmaking in the EC, prompting Belgium to insist on the use of qualified majority voting during its Council presidency in the first half of 1982. But that was a small step on the road to EC reform, on which governments devoted increasing time and attention.

Genscher-Colombo and the Stuttgart Declaration. Eager to reassert German leadership in the EC and eager also to assert the leadership of his Free Democratic Party within the coalition government, Foreign Minister Genscher prepared an initiative to revive the EC. Because Franco-German relations were slightly unsettled after Mitterrand's election victory, Genscher chose Emilio Colombo, his Italian counterpart, rather than the French foreign minister, to cosponsor the initiative. Perennially pro-EC, Italy was delighted to share the limelight with Germany, hoping both to raise its international profile and intrude upon the traditional Franco-German axis.

Genscher and Colombo called for a nonbinding European Act in November 1981, in a speech to the Parliament. They proposed institutional improvements, such as greater use of qualified majority voting and more power for the Parliament, to enhance the EC's effectiveness and legitimacy. Their main policy focus was on external relations. European Political Cooperation, the existing mechanism for foreign policy coordination, was patently inadequate, as shown by the member states' response to the Soviet invasion of Afghanistan in 1979 and the imposition of martial law in Poland in 1981, despite subsequent procedural improvements.

Genscher and Colombo urged member states to bring security and defense issues into European Political Cooperation. The imposition of sanctions by the EC against Argentina before and during the Falklands/Malvinas war in early 1982 demonstrated a willingness to act collectively in the event of clear-cut external aggression, although not without domestic difficulties for Ireland and Italy. Nevertheless, governments were far apart on the possibility of developing a security and defense dimension in the EC. Wanting to restrict discussions on security and defense to NATO, Thatcher opposed the idea. A number of small member states agreed. Papandreou resisted deeper European integration in general and closer security cooperation in particular. As a matter of principle Denmark did not want European integration to move into the security realm. Sensitivity to a vague but popular notion of neutrality caused the otherwise indifferent Irish government to object to any initiative that touched on security and defense in the EC.

Member states finally endorsed a watered-down version of the Genscher-Colombo proposals in the form of the Solemn Declaration on European Unity, at the Stuttgart summit in June 1983. The declaration called for closer cooperation on foreign policy and security and deeper European integration. Taking the view that "I could not quarrel with everything, and the document had no legal force," Thatcher reluctantly went along with it, later regretting that the Stuttgart declaration turned out to be "the linguistic skeleton on which so much institutional flesh would grow."[70]

A British proposal. While dismissing the wooliness and idealism of the Stuttgart declaration, Thatcher supported the idea of deeper integration. Her main interests were economics and international relations. She saw the EC as potentially useful in both respects. Completion of the internal market would benefit Britain economically, and foreign policy cooperation could help to promote British interests internationally. Accordingly, Thatcher brought to the Fontainebleau summit in June 1984 a paper proposing deeper market integration and better foreign policy cooperation. She preferred informal institutional arrangements to formal treaty changes. Because unanimity hindered completion of the internal market, member states should agree among themselves to vote in the Council on internal market measures.[71] Apart from its intrinsic merits, Thatcher wanted her proposal to signal a commitment to the EC and end Britain's isolation after the long-running budgetary dispute.

Mitterrand leads the way. Of all the national leaders, it was Mitterrand who led the way in revitalizing the EC. Mitterrand had long supported European integration but had little experience of the EC before becoming president in May 1981. He fought the campaign on domestic issues, promising, if elected, to reform the economy radically along Socialist lines. Mitterrand seemed either unaware of or uninterested in the fact that his policy prescription differed widely from the prevailing neoliberal orthodoxy not only in Britain and the United States but also in most European countries run by Social Democratic governments.

True to his word, on being elected president Mitterrand instituted extensive social and economic reform. Banks and industries were nationalized, new labor laws enacted, and welfare benefits increased. Mitterrand tried to jump-start growth and cut unemployment through old-fashioned Keynesian reflationary policies. The economic consequences were disastrous. Popular consumption increased, but not enough to make a dent on unemployment. Inflation rose, the trade balance worsened, and the budget deficit grew. "By mid-1982, it had become clear that Socialist economic policies had failed: the old taunts that the Left was synonymous with economic profligacy reappeared."[72]

Jacques Delors, Mitterrand's finance minister, urged an immediate retreat. Mitterrand hesitated, hoping to hold the line at temporary austerity measures introduced in June 1982. The definitive turning point came in March 1983 on the question of continued participation in the exchange rate mechanism of the EMS. Keeping the franc in the mechanism required an economic policy U-turn; removing it would have meant risking a free-fall in the franc's value and turning France's back on Germany and the EC. Staying in the mechanism was politically unpalatable because it necessitated a devaluation of the franc (however small) and acceptance of a rigorous austerity plan involving large tax increases and major public spending cuts. Although generally more susceptible to political than economic arguments, Mitterrand uncharacteristically but wisely heeded the advice of financial experts rather than party hacks.[73]

Far from resenting the EMS for having forced a painful decision on him, Mitterrand embraced it as an instrument of French economic salvation. As the French economy improved (although unemployment remained stubbornly high), he switched his attention from the domestic to the European arena, where he appeared to have more room to maneuver. Mitterrand became an avid champion of deeper integration and wide-ranging institutional reform. His newfound European vocation "combined a mixture of idealism, realism, and self-interest; regardless of his motives, for Mitterrand the EC became an intensely *personal* affair."[74] The president's pet projects ranged from closer collaboration in high technology to strengthening the Parliament's role in the Community system. Having greeted the Genscher-Colombo proposals with indifference in 1981, Mitterrand welcomed the Parliament's draft treaty enthusiastically in 1984.

Mitterrand's zest for European integration reached its zenith in the first half of 1984 during France's presidency of the Council. He wanted to resolve the debilitating budgetary dispute in order to clear the decks for bold new initiatives. Mitterrand outlined his vision for the EC in a famous speech to the Parliament in May 1984, calling for wide-ranging institutional reform and intensive Community involvement in a range of internal and external policies. His support for greater supranationalism was at variance with the usual French position. For instance, Mitterrand advocated more use of qualified majority voting despite the fact that the Luxembourg Compromise reflected traditional French preferences for decisionmaking in the Council. On external relations, Mitterrand called for a permanent secretariat for the conduct of foreign policy cooperation (an old Gaullist objective) and urged member states to make a common defense effort.[75]

The final summit of the French presidency, held in the spectacular setting of the palace of Fontainebleau, was the crowning moment of Mitterrand's European reawakening. Thatcher was the fly in the ointment. The EC could hardly get going again as long as the budgetary question remained unresolved. Hence Mitterrand's determination to put the issue behind them. Mitterrand reveled in a success of the summit for France and for Europe, although both Kohl and Thatcher also claimed credit for the budget breakthrough.

Mitterrand sought to assert French leadership of a revived EC and to reinvigorate the Franco-German axis. His relations with Kohl, who became chancellor a year after Mitterrand became president, were cordial but not close. Like Mitterrand, Kohl was immersed in domestic politics, attempting to consolidate his grip on government. Also like Mitterrand, Kohl did not have much experience of the EC before coming to power, although he had a keen sense of the EC's political importance for Germany and historical significance for Europe.

Thatcher detected what she called "a gush of Euro-idealism" at the European Council in March 1984, with Mitterrand and Kohl becoming "quite lyrical on the subject of getting rid of frontier controls, which they seemed to invest with a high symbolic significance."[76] The prime minister's dismissiveness of such talk and thoughts demonstrated the vast difference between her, on the one hand, and Mitterrand and Kohl, on the other. Shared idealism, rooted in an appreciation of the practical benefits for their countries of closer European integration, drew Mitterrand and Kohl together. Nothing symbolized the extent of their personal rapprochement more than the poignancy of Mitterrand and Kohl holding hands during a visit in September 1984 to the World War I battlefield of Verdun, as they listened to each other's national anthems. It was unimaginable that Thatcher and Kohl would have behaved similarly in such a setting.

▧ Notes

1. Christopher Tugendhat, *Making Sense of Europe* (New York: Columbia University Press, 1988), pp. 43–44.

2. Commission, *Eleventh Report on the Activities of the European Communities* (Luxembourg: European Communities, 1978), p. 17.

3. Commission, *Twelfth Report on the Activities of the European Communities* (Luxembourg: European Communities, 1979), p. 18.

4. Richard Clogg, "The Greek Political Context," in *Greece and the European Community,* ed. Loukas Tsoukalis (Farnborough: Saxon House, 1979), p. 119.

5. Commission, "Opinion on the Greek Application for Membership," Bulletin EC S-2/76.

6. Quoted in Werner Feld, *West Germany and the European Community: Changing Interests and Competing Policy Objectives* (New York: Praeger, 1981), p. 55.

7. William Wallace, "Grand Gestures and Second Thoughts: The Response of Member Countries to Greece's Application," in *Greece and the European Community*, ed. Loukas Tsoukalis (Farnborough: Saxon House, 1979), pp. 21–38.

8. See Richard Corbett, *The European Parliament's Role in Closer EU Integration* (Basingstoke: Palgrave, 2001), pp. 48–50.

9. Commission, *Thirteenth Report on the Activities of the European Communities* (Luxembourg: European Communities, 1980), p. 27.

10. See Corbett, *European Parliament's Role,* pp. 52, 67–69, 78.

11. For an account of the EMS, see Daniel Gros and Niels Thygesen, *European Monetary Integration: From the European Monetary System Towards Monetary Union* (London: Longman, 1992); David J. Howarth, *The French Road to European Union* (Basingstoke: Palgrave, 2001), pp. 21–54; Peter Ludlow, *The Making of the European Monetary System* (London: Butterworths, 1982); Andrew Moravcsik, *The Choice for Europe: Social Purpose and State Power from Messina to Maastricht* (Ithaca, NY: Cornell University Press, 1998), pp. 238–313; Horst Ungerer, *From EPU to EMU: A Concise History of European Monetary Integration* (Westport, CT: Quorum Books, 1997); Robert Triffin, ed., *EMS: The Emerging European Monetary System* (Brussels: National Bank of Belgium, 1979).

12. Roy Jenkins, *European Diary, 1977–1981* (London: Collins, 1989), pp. 168–169.

13. COM(77)620 final, November 1977.

14. Roy Jenkins, *Life at the Center: Memoirs of a Radical Reformer* (New York: Random House, 1991), pp. 470–471.

15. See Haig Simonian, *Privileged Partnership: Franco-German Relations in the European Community, 1969–1984* (Oxford: Clarendon Press, 1985), p. 277.

16. Jenkins, *Life at the Center*, p. 479.

17. Commission, *Fifteenth Report on the Activities of the European Communities* (Luxembourg: European Communities, 1982), p. 18.

18. Commission, *Sixteenth Report on the Activities of the European Communities* (Luxembourg: European Communities, 1983), p. 18.

19. Tugendhat, *Making Sense*, pp. 69–71.

20. Quoted in Wallace, "Grand Gestures," p. 38, n15.

21. See Loukas Tsoukalis, "Second Round of Enlargement and the Mediterranean," in *Greece and the European Community*, ed. Loukas Tsoukalis (Farnborough: Saxon House, 1979), p. 162; Wallace, "Grand Gestures," p. 34; Garret FitzGerald, *All in a Life: An Autobiography* (Dublin: Gill and Macmillan, 1991), pp. 144–145; Commission, "General Considerations on the Problems of Enlargement," COM(78)120 final, April 20, 1978.

22. Bulletin EC 12-1978.

23. Bulletin EC 11-1979.

24. Ibid.

25. Tugendhat, *Making Sense*, pp. 140–141.

26. Jenkins, *Diary*, pp. 25–26.

27. Ibid., p. 311.

28. Bulletin EC 11-1979.

29. Dirk Spierenburg, "Proposals for Reform of the Commission of the European Communities and Its Services," Brussels, Commission, September 1979.

30. Commission, *Thirteenth Report*, pp. 211–224.

31. Margaret Thatcher, *Downing Street Years* (New York: HarperCollins, 1993), pp. 61, 62.

32. Ibid., p. 63.

33. Ibid., pp. 34–35.

34. Tugendhat, *Making Sense*, pp. 121–122.

35. Thatcher, *Downing Street Years*, p. 65.

36. Ibid., p. 84.

37. Tugendhat, *Making Sense*, p. 123.

38. Quoted in John Palmer, "Britain and the EEC: The Withdrawal Option," *International Affairs* 58, no. 4 (Autumn 1982), p. 640.

39. Commission, "Greece in the Community: Assessment and Proposals," Bulletin EC-3, 1983.

40. See *Le Monde*, June 7, 1980, p. 1.

41. Bulletin EC 2-1981.

42. Bulletin EC 11-1981.

43. Thatcher, *Downing Street Years*, pp. 541–544.

44. Ibid., p. 337.

45. FitzGerald, *All in a Life*, pp. 485–486.

46. See Thatcher, *Downing Street Years*, pp. 539–540; Stephen George, *An Awkward Partner: Britain in the European Community* (Oxford: Oxford University Press, 1998), p. 155.

47. Thatcher, *Downing Street Years*, p. 545.

48. See George, *Awkward Partner*, pp. 157–158.

49. Quoted in the *Daily Express*, June 4, 1984, p. 4.

50. Tugendhat, *Making Sense*, p. 124.

51. The *Economist*, June 3, 1984, p. 38.

52. Bulletin EC 12-1984.

53. Bulletin EC 6-1984.

54. On technology policy in the EC in the early 1980s, see Margaret Sharp, "Technology and the Dynamics of Integration," in *Economic Development of the EEC*, ed. Richard T. Griffiths (Cheltenham: E. Elgar, 1997), pp. 518–533; Wayne Sandholtz, *High-Tech Europe: The Politics of International Cooperation* (Berkeley: University of California Press, 1992).

55. Case 120/78, *Rewe-Zentral AG* v. *Bundesmonopolverwaltung für Branntwein* (1979), ECR, pp. 649–675. For an assessment of the Cassis case, see Karen J. Alter and Sophie Meunier-Aitsahalia, "Judicial Politics in the European Community: European Integration and the Pathbreaking Cassis de Dijon Case," *Comparative Political Studies* 26, no. 4 (January 1994), pp. 535–560; Michelle Egan, *Constructing a European Market: Standards, Regulation, and Governance* (Oxford: Oxford University Press, 2001), pp. 94–104; G. Garrett and B. Weingast, "Ideas, Interests, and Institutions: Constructing the EC's Internal Market," in *Ideas and Foreign Policy: Beliefs, Institutions and Political Change,* ed. J. Goldstein and R. Keohane. (Ithaca, NY: Cornell University Press, 1993).

56. Commission, *Fourteenth Report on the Activities of the European Communities* (Luxembourg: European Communities, 1981), pp. 85–86.

57. Bulletin EC 6-1981.

58. Commission, *Fifteenth Report*, pp. 78–79.

59. Bulletin EC 6-1984.

60. Wisse Dekker, *Europe 1990: An Agenda for Action* (Eindhoven: Philips, 1984).

61. Margaret Sharp, Christopher Freeman, and William Walker, *Technology and the Future of Europe: Global Competition and the Environment in the 1990s* (New York: Pinter, 1991), p. 73.

62. Michel Albert and Robert James Ball, *Toward European Economic Recovery in the 1980s: Report to the European Parliament* (New York: Praeger, 1984).

63. See Corbett, *European Parliament's Role*, pp. 98–99.

64. See ibid., p. 125.

65. Jenkins, *Diary*, p. 375.

66. Isoglucose Cases 138/79 and 139/79 ECR (1980), pp. 333 and 339.

67. See Corbett, *European Parliament's Role,* pp. 119–120.

68. Bulletin EC 11-1979.

69. For an account of the draft treaty, see Roland Bieber, Jean-Paul Jacqué, and Joseph Weiler, eds., *An Ever Closer Union: A Critical Analysis of the Draft Treaty Establishing the European Union*, European Perspectives Series (Luxembourg: Office of Official Publications of the European Community, 1985), and Corbett, *European Parliament's Role,* pp. 142–172.

70. Thatcher, *Downing Street Years*, p. 314.

71. The British paper, "Europe: The Future," is reproduced in *Journal of Common Market Studies* 23 (1984), pp. 74–81. See also George, *Awkward Partner*, pp. 158–159.

72. Alistair Cole, *François Mitterrand: A Study in Political Leadership* (London: Routledge, 1994), p. 35.

73. See ibid.; David J. Howarth, *The French Road to European Union* (Basingstoke: Palgrave, 2001), pp. 55–82.

74. Cole, *Mitterrand*, p. 122. Emphasis in the original.

75. François Mitterrand, "Speech to the European Parliament," May 24, 1984, reprinted in *Vital Speeches of the Day*, August 1, 1984, pp. 613–623.

76. Thatcher, *Downing Street Years*, p. 538.

6

Transformation

The transformation of the European Community in the late 1980s occurred in response to a new era of globalization. Rapid technological change and fierce international competition forced Western European countries to deepen economic integration. The single market program, intended to prepare the EC for the challenge of globalization, meant going back to the future: back to the untapped potential of the Rome Treaty in order to give the EC a competitive edge in the emerging global marketplace. The main innovation of the Single European Act (SEA), the treaty change that triggered the EC's resurgence, was to break the logjam in Council decisionmaking, thereby facilitating the enactment of single market legislation. Monetary union was a logical sequel to market integration, but one that raised serious political questions and concerns.

The late 1980s was a period of major political as well as economic and technological change. Mikhail Gorbachev, who came to power in the Soviet Union in 1985, launched a program of openness and economic reform that fueled independence movements in Central and Eastern Europe. The accession in 1986 of Portugal and Spain, two former dictatorships, emphasized the EC's political as well as economic importance for countries in transition. French and German leaders saw these developments in Central and Eastern Europe, which raised the specter of German unification, as an additional reason to deepen integration and, in the process, cement Germany's ties to its western neighbors. British prime minister Margaret Thatcher saw the developments as a victory for democracy and neoliberalism and a sign that centralization and political integration in Western Europe were bound to fail. Events moved more rapidly than anyone expected at the end of the decade, with the sudden fall of the Berlin Wall and imminent unification of Germany.

Jacques Delors became president of the Commission just as the EC was about to take off. But coincidence is not the same as causation. Delors was fortunate to have assumed office at such an auspicious time. After more than a decade of poor performance, Europe's economy was on the upswing. National governments had already decided in principle to complete the internal market, exploit economies of scale, and confront together the challenge of

Jacques Delors served as president of the European Commission from 1985 to 1995, and personified the transformation of the European Community.

globalization. By seizing the moment, crafting a program to establish a single market by the end of 1992, and promoting integration in other policy areas, Delors personified the EC's extraordinary revitalization in the late 1980s.

Without a benign economic and political climate and strong support from powerful national leaders, Delors might well have gone down in history as a competent but commonplace head of the Brussels bureaucracy. Instead, Delors basked in the glow of the successful Mediterranean enlargement and single market program and spearheaded the drive for economic and monetary union (EMU). Europeans liked the slogan "1992," the target date for completion of the single market and shorthand for the entire undertaking. For a brief, shining moment, the EC was popular, even fashionable, before the new European Union overreached itself in the early 1990s.

■ The Single European Act

There was near unanimity among the EC's member states in the mid-1980s on the desirability of deeper market integration. Jacques Delors, who undertook a tour of national capitals in late 1984 as Commission president-designate, got the message loud and clear. Delors was primarily interested in more glamorous and ambitious objectives, such as EMU and defense policy cooperation. Reactions in national capitals convinced him to scale back and push instead for completion of the internal market. Given the presumed link between market integration and monetary union, Delors envisioned the internal market project not as an end in itself but as a means toward the greater goal of EMU.

The key question was not whether but how to complete the internal market. Member states generally agreed that the legislative steps necessary for further market integration could not be taken without recourse in the Council to qualified majority voting. They could either agree informally to use qualified majority voting without changing the treaty or negotiate a legally binding commitment to use qualified majority voting and, possibly, introduce other institutional reforms, such as extending the legislative role of the Parliament. Changing the treaty would require an intergovernmental conference of member state representatives.

Initially Delors doubted whether an intergovernmental conference was either necessary or feasible. He appreciated the link between qualified majority voting and the internal market program but thought that member states could agree informally among themselves to become more efficient decision-makers in the Council. Simply put, they needed to wean themselves off the national veto. Impatient to achieve results as soon as possible, Delors also feared that a conference would prove too contentious and time consuming to have much impact on the EC before the end of the decade. Thus, at the outset of his presidency, Delors did not advocate the negotiations on treaty reform on which he later built his formidable reputation.[1]

Removing the Mediterranean Roadblock

An important piece of unfinished business in early 1985 blocked enlargement and other important initiatives. That was the Greek demand for financial assistance to meet the costs of the country's adjustment to EC membership and to compensate for the anticipated diversion of funds from Greece as a result of impending Portuguese and Spanish accession. The other member states made some concessions in 1984 by providing assistance for various agricultural, social, and transport projects.[2] But an overall solution needed to be found within the framework of the Integrated Mediterranean Programs, an assistance package for the existing and prospective Mediterranean member states.

Andreas Papandreou, the Greek prime minister, threw the December 1984 Dublin summit into disarray by demanding a generous agreement on the Mediterranean programs in return for allowing enlargement to go ahead. Although relieved for once not to be the odd person out, Thatcher was outraged by Papandreou's behavior. As a staunch opponent of additional EC expenditure, Thatcher did not want to allocate more money to regional development. What irked her was "not just the fact that Greece was holding [the EC] to ransom, nor even the particular tactics used, but still more the fact that, though Greece had been accepted into the Community precisely to entrench its restored democracy, the Greeks would not now allow the Community to do exactly the same for the former dictatorships of Spain and Portugal."[3] Apart from holding up Portuguese and Spanish accession, Papandreou's antics threatened to hold up progress on the single market program.

Realizing that the Greek problem had to be resolved before the EC could advance on other fronts, Delors, who became Commission president in January 1985, threw himself into the fray with characteristic energy and resolve. A month later, the Commission proposed a solution involving a seven-year program of grants and loans to help the EC's Mediterranean regions "adjust under the best conditions possible to the new situation created by enlargement."[4] Italy, in the Council presidency, desperately wanted a settlement not only because it would benefit directly from the Mediterranean programs but also because, as a staunchly Eurofederal member state, it could then devote its remaining time in the presidency to promoting deeper integration. On the eve of a summit in March 1985, foreign ministers agreed on the final points in the Portuguese and Spanish accession negotiations during forty hours of talks without a break for sleep (a Community record). When praised for his stamina, Italian foreign minister Giulio Andreotti commented wryly that "after twenty-five years in Italian government, it's really not so difficult."[5]

Yet enlargement still depended on a resolution of the Mediterranean programs, which necessitated intense negotiations among EC leaders at the Brussels summit. Despite Thatcher's legendary intransigence and Papandreou's legendary obstructionism, the sum finally agreed upon, 6.6 billion ECU, of which Greece would receive approximately 30 percent, was higher than what Thatcher had wanted and lower than what Papandreou had wanted. The outcome was a success for the Italian presidency and for Delors, who had staked his political reputation on ending the dispute. Having taken responsibility for the issue, failure to reach a settlement would have undermined Delors's credibility at the outset of his Commission presidency. After the Brussels summit, a relieved Delors declared in typical melodramatic fashion that "all the family quarrels have been sorted out. The family is now going to grow and we can think of the future."[6]

The Dooge Report

A combination of Commission, parliamentary, and member state agitation in favor of deeper European integration culminated in a decision at the Fontainebleau summit in June 1984 to convene a committee of national leaders' (and the Commission president's) personal representatives to ponder the EC's future. The Ad Hoc Committee on Institutional Affairs started work in the fall of 1984, under the chairmanship of Jim Dooge, an Irish senator and former foreign minister.[7] Distrustful of the committee, Thatcher appointed to it Malcolm Rifkind, a junior foreign minister, vigorous advocate of deregulation and market integration, and staunch defender of national sovereignty. French president François Mitterrand's appointee could not have been more different. He was Maurice Faure, a close associate of the president, signatory of the Rome Treaty, and lifelong champion of European union.

Opinion within the committee spanned the spectrum of member state preferences. At one end the Italian representative favored radical treaty reform along the lines of the Parliament's Draft Treaty Establishing the European Union; at the other end Britain's representative wanted an informal agreement among member states to complete the internal market and coordinate their foreign policies more closely. Committee members generally favored using qualified majority voting in the Council on most internal market issues, without necessarily renouncing a member state's right to veto legislation by invoking the Luxembourg Compromise.

The committee's final report, presented to the European Council in March 1985, identified a number of priorities for the EC. These included "a homogeneous internal economic area" (that is, a single market), greater use of voting in the Council, some more power for the Parliament and the Commission, and new initiatives in selected areas, including foreign policy. Reflecting the diversity of opinion among the committee's members, inevitably the report included numerous reservations and minority opinions. For instance, the committee's chairman dissociated himself from the report's recommendation that member states coordinate their security as well as their foreign policies. Although Dooge and the Irish prime minister, Garret FitzGerald, would happily have abandoned Irish neutrality, they were constrained by the public's sentimental attachment to it. More important than Ireland's position on neutrality was the reservation expressed by three committee members—British, Danish, and Greek—on the report's key conclusion, that the European Council convene an intergovernmental conference to negotiate treaty reform.

The European Council decided to discuss the Dooge Report at its next meeting, in Milan in June 1985. The breakthrough on the Mediterranean programs, the prospect of imminent enlargement, the Dooge Report, and the Commission's white paper on the internal market buoyed hopes of an imminent revival of European integration. Indeed, the Italian government wanted to crown its presidency of the Council with a decision in Milan to launch a conference on treaty reform. Sensing the change of wind, Delors fully supported Italy's effort to win a commitment by the European Council to hold an intergovernmental conference. Once more on the defensive, Thatcher opposed treaty reform, advocating instead an informal agreement (a Milan Accord) to improve decisionmaking in the Council and to coordinate member states' foreign policies more closely.

The Milan Summit

The outcome of the Milan summit depended not on the ambition of the Italian presidency, the opportunism of Delors, or the recalcitrance of Thatcher but on the positions of Mitterrand and German chancellor Helmut Kohl. They surprised the others by pushing strongly at the summit for a decision to convene an intergovernmental conference, despite rumors of a strain in Franco-German relations.[8] Thatcher was incensed. Here was another example of the power and perfidy of the Franco-German axis. Italy's prime minister, Bettino Craxi, then set a precedent in the European Council by calling for a vote on the question. During a brief adjournment, FitzGerald saw "Margaret Thatcher, coming from the far end of the room . . . pushing her way through the crowd" standing around Craxi.[9] Thatcher left the unfortunate Craxi in no doubt about her opinion of him and of his proposal for an intergovernmental conference. Undaunted and assured of Franco-German support, Craxi reconvened the meeting and asked the national leaders to vote yea or nay. The result was predictable: seven in favor; three (Britain, Denmark, and Greece) against.

The Milan summit may have looked like a major breakthrough for European integration, but the unwillingness of three member states to hold an intergovernmental conference was worrisome. As member states could approve treaty changes only by unanimity, Britain, Denmark, and Greece would have every opportunity to block progress. Not that they needed to apply the brakes all the time: the other member states had so many competing preferences that unanimity would surely prove elusive. As long as Britain could keep its partners focused on market integration and as long as the result of the conference did not threaten their perceived vital interests, the three minority member states were willing to participate in it, however reluctantly.

The Intergovernmental Conference

A major intergovernmental conference was a novel event in 1985. Previous conferences had focused on narrow objectives, such as budgetary reform in 1970 and 1975. The door was now open for broader reform on a range of policy and institutional issues. As Delors remarked at the opening session, "conferences like this one are not convened every five or ten years. There may not be another between now and [the year] 2000."[10] Another conference indeed took place in 2000, but Delors could not have foreseen that, thanks largely to the success of the Single European Act, the 2000 conference would be the fifth in fifteen years (there were two in 1990–1991 and one in 1996–1997).

The conference began in September 1985, after the sacrosanct August summer holiday. Portugal and Spain, on the verge of joining the EC, observed the proceedings. Negotiations among the member states took place at a number of levels. Senior officials (mostly the permanent representatives to the EC, most of whom had sat on the Dooge Committee) met regularly to negotiate changes to the existing treaty. Member states' political directors—senior foreign ministry officials based in the national capitals—met less often to negotiate changes to European Political Cooperation (the mechanism for foreign policy coordination). Both sets of negotiations took place in Brussels. The foreign ministers reviewed progress and tried to move the negotiations along at their monthly Council meetings. Defending their turf, the economic and finance ministers discussed a possible treaty change on monetary policy cooperation at their own Council meetings. Finally, the European Council reached political agreement on the most contentious issues in the conference at its regularly scheduled summit, in Luxembourg in December 1985. As well as the formal negotiating sessions, negotiators at all levels participated in numerous informal bilateral and multilateral meetings where much of the real work was done.[11]

Like the Parliament, the Commission was not formally a party to the negotiations; unlike the Parliament, however, the Commission had a seat at the table. Delors took charge of the Commission's input into the negotiations, working with a small team of trusted officials and bypassing the commissioner with responsibility for institutional affairs, a political lightweight. Delors's strategy in the conference was to link the goal of the internal market to progress on institutional reform and in selected policy areas, such as cohesion and social affairs. Without a commitment to EC-wide economic cohesion, Delors argued, the gap between rich and poor member states would become unacceptably wide, both morally and politically. Similarly, without stronger labor legislation at the European level, workers would be disadvantaged by greater market integration and become alienated from the EC. Delors also kept his eye on the prize of monetary union. How could the market be fully integrated without common monetary and macroeconomic policies? The political and economic logic of a large, vibrant internal market, Delors thought, pointed inexorably toward EMU.

Under Delors's direction the Commission submitted proposals in a variety of policy areas and got the negotiations going. So much so that, according to one observer, "the [conference] in its initial stages took the form of a dialogue between the Commission and member state governments."[12] Delors calibrated the Commission proposals not only to extend the frontier of European integration but also to appeal to member states' interests and allay their concerns. Sensitive to the positions of the three recalcitrant member states, Delors emphasized the advantages of market integration for the British, environmental policy for the Danes, and cohesion policy for the Greeks.[13]

Despite Delors's energy and enthusiasm, the conference got off to a sluggish start. Britain's annoyance after the Milan summit gave way to complacency as France and Germany took a back seat in the negotiations. The French government's position seemed far more restrained than Mitterrand's rhetoric suggested that it would be, especially on institutional issues such as qualified majority voting and the role of the Parliament.[14] Nor was Germany willing to take the lead. Italy's initial optimism soon evaporated. Indeed, the Italian government's high hopes for the conference "appeared dashed after Milan."[15] Luxembourg, in the Council presidency, cooperated closely with the Commission but was careful not to antagonize the more reluctant member states.

The Commission lost ground in the conference as the negotiations finally gathered momentum in November 1985. With agreement expected at the summit in December, member states began to assert their positions. There was little difficulty defining the internal market ("an area without internal frontiers in which the free movement of goods, persons, services and capital is ensured") or approving the target date of 1992, but member states disagreed on the institutional steps necessary to bring it about.[16] Following intensive negotiations, member states agreed to allow voting on harmonization, but only for approximately two-thirds of the measures identified in the Commission's white paper. The remainder, on sensitive issues such as indirect taxation, remained subject to unanimity.

The possibility of enhancing the EC's democratic credentials by increasing the power of the Parliament was one of the most contentious issues in the conference. Most member states balked at giving the Parliament the power of legislative co-decision with the Council. National representatives agreed instead to increase the Parliament's authority through the so-called cooperation procedure (the right to a second reading) for certain single market measures and through a new power of assent for accession and association agreements. By contrast, there was general agreement among member states on strengthening the Commission's executive powers, at least in principle.

On other policy issues, Greece and Ireland, supported by the Commission and conference observers Portugal and Spain, advocated a major increase in Community spending on poorer regions through a revitalized cohesion policy. They could not have succeeded in the face of British opposition without strong German support. Germany also favored the inclusion of environmental policy in the treaty, as did Denmark and other environmentally conscious member states. Most member states supported adding provisions to the treaty for cooperation in research and technology development, without agreeing on how much money should be allocated to it. Social policy, anathema to Thatcher's conservative government, was one of the most difficult items to resolve at the conference.

The conference gave member states an opportunity to reform the mechanism for foreign policy coordination (European Political Cooperation) and bring it under the umbrella of the Rome Treaty. The political directors considered various submissions from national governments, notably Britain and, jointly, France and Germany. Member states generally agreed on the need to make the EC's external economic policy and the member states' foreign policies more consistent with each other. Neutral Ireland, pacifist (though NATO member) Denmark, and idiosyncratic (though also NATO member) Greece succeeded in excluding any reference to defense policy from the agreement eventually reached on European Political Cooperation, which continued to limit foreign policy discussions to "the political aspects of security" but included a number of useful procedural changes.

Notwithstanding their joint submission on European Political Cooperation, France and Germany were not particularly pushy in the conference. They intervened mostly to ensure that the conference would propose greater use of qualified majority voting in decisionmaking on the single market and a greater legislative role for the Parliament. Despite differences between them on most institutional and policy issues, the two countries were eager to achieve meaningful treaty reform. Roland Dumas and Hans-Dietrich Genscher, the foreign ministers of France and Germany, were exceedingly close; much closer than Mitterrand and Kohl. A joint intervention by them at a foreign ministers' meeting at the end of November neutralized the opposition of some of their colleagues to parts of the proposed agreement.

Mitterrand and Kohl became directly involved in the discussion about EMU. Delors, with the support of the Belgian government, pushed for a commitment to greater economic and monetary policy cooperation. Britain adamantly opposed; France was in favor; and Germany equivocal. Kohl agreed to support Mitterrand in return for a French commitment to liberalize capital movements.[17] Thatcher was again outraged but, in order to secure the bigger prize of deeper market integration, accepted a reference in the treaty to the importance of economic and monetary policy cooperation "for the further development of the Community." A stipulation that further steps toward monetary union involving institutional change could be taken only in another conference, which Britain would surely veto, reassured Thatcher.[18]

Although EC leaders engaged in lengthy, detailed negotiations at the Luxembourg summit in December 1985, their exchanges were free of the rancor that had marred meetings of the European Council in the early 1980s. The difference this time was the convergence of interest among the main players in promoting market integration through treaty reform. Thatcher, Mitterrand, and Kohl now had a common goal. In order to achieve a positive result at the summit, Thatcher said that she "would have to seek alliances with other governments, accept compromises and use language which I did not find attractive."[19]

Thatcher's reasonableness surprised some members of her own government, notably the Chancellor of the Exchequer (finance minister) Nigel Lawson. Having urged her before going to Luxembourg not to mention EMU in the treaty, Lawson "was skeptical of the wisdom of the deal she had struck. I felt that we had embarked upon a dangerous slippery slope towards EMU; whereas the move to majority voting, which had been strongly urged by Delors as essential if Europe was to regain the momentum it had latterly lost, would have been agreed even without EMU."[20] Lawson's comments revealed growing discord within the British government on the EC, with ardent Euroskeptics doubting Thatcher's willingness or ability to hold the line against deeper European integration.

It was at the summit also that the European Council approved a Commission proposal to conclude a single agreement incorporating all treaty changes, rather than separate agreements on EC and foreign policy cooperation reform: hence the name Single European Act (it was called an act because the word treaty was too controversial). Foreign ministers continued working on a few outstanding issues, including social policy, until the end of January 1986. Nine of the twelve member states then signed the act in Brussels in mid-February. Denmark delayed doing so until the (successful) outcome of a referendum on the act later in the month; Italy delayed in order to protest the agreement's seemingly limited extension of the Parliament's powers; and the Greek government delayed until certain that Denmark and Italy would sign. The three holdouts—Euro-enthusiastic Italy, Euroskeptical Denmark, and Euro-ambivalent Greece—finally signed the act at a special ceremony in The Hague at the end of February 1986.

Outcome

The SEA was a relatively short and seemingly innocuous document. It did not challenge head-on the Luxembourg Compromise (a member state's right to veto legislation), but its extension of qualified majority voting to most single market measures was a significant chink in the armor of unanimity. Indeed, the link between the single market and qualified majority voting formed the core of the SEA. The extension of the Parliament's legislative authority was an important institutional innovation, although it did not go far enough to satisfy the Parliament and its supporters in the conference.

The SEA also linked completion to the single market with greater economic cohesion, on the one hand, and stronger social policy, on the other. As part of a tidying-up exercise, the SEA brought environmental policy and foreign policy cooperation into the treaty, while keeping the latter strictly on an intergovernmental basis. Mention of monetary policy in the SEA seemed no more than symbolic.

The SEA included various declarations dealing with specific member state concerns. For instance, Ireland won a derogation (or exemption) from the single market for its fragile insurance industry, and Portugal insisted on an undertaking that changes in decisionmaking as a result of the SEA "must not damage sensitive and vital sectors of the country's economy."[21] Such declarations, an inevitable result of intergovernmental bargaining, were mostly for domestic political consumption.

The Commission and the more integration-minded member states were disappointed with the outcome of the conference, especially with the exclusion of key single market measures from qualified majority voting and the relatively limited increase in the Parliament's power. A despondent Delors wondered whether the SEA would suffice to bring about the internal market by 1992. He also regretted that France and Germany had not undertaken bold initiatives and that progress at the conference had been reduced to the level of the lowest common denominator. By contrast, Thatcher was delighted, claiming to have held the line against the use of qualified majority voting on harmonization of taxation and the free movement of people and to have conceded only minimal new powers to the Parliament. The SEA, she declared, was "good for British business."[22] Thatcher was right about the commercial benefits of the SEA but wrong about its broader impact. She and Delors, and everybody else for that matter, underestimated the significance of the treaty changes that emerged from the intergovernmental conference.

Ratification

Most national parliaments ratified the SEA without much difficulty. The Italian parliament was most critical of the SEA, complaining that it was too restrictive. Ratification in Germany fueled an ongoing debate about the role of the state governments in EC decisionmaking. The Danish government failed twice in late January 1986 to win parliamentary support the SEA, being unable to allay parliamentarians' concerns about the presumed loss of Danish sovereignty inherent in the greater use of qualified majority voting in Council decisionmaking. The government then put the issue to a referendum in February 1986 in which 56 percent of voters (in a 74 percent turnout) supported the SEA. Despite the Greek government's complaints about the EC, the Greek parliament easily ratified it.

Failure to ratify the SEA in Ireland before the agreed deadline of December 1986 caused a delay in the act's implementation throughout the EC. The problem was due to a court case brought by a citizen concerned about the impact of the SEA's foreign policy provisions on Irish sovereignty. In a dramatic decision at the end of December 1986, Ireland's highest court agreed with the plaintiff and mandated a referendum in order to ratify the act. The government easily won the referendum (70 percent in favor; but only a 45 percent turnout), clearing the way for implementation of the SEA in July 1987.

Except in Denmark and Ireland, ratification did not attract much public attention. There was little awareness then that European integration was on the verge of a major revitalization. Those who participated in the ratification debates had little inkling that the SEA would presage a remarkable transformation of the EC. Like the heads of state and government who concluded the conference in December 1985, most national parliamentarians saw the SEA as a set of uninspiring treaty amendments rather than a harbinger of unprecedented economic and political change.

■ The Single Market Program

When he was sworn in as Commission president in January 1985, Delors saw that completion of the single market was not only a worthy end in itself but also a means toward the EC's revival and possible transformation. Delors's decision to champion the single market program may have been "a grudging compromise for a man who had greater ambitions for Europe," but it showed a pragmatic streak in an otherwise visionary leader.[23] By going back to basics and emphasizing one of the original objectives of the Rome Treaty, Delors could hardly be accused by jealous national leaders of overweening ambition. Delors made his choice of the internal market clear in his first address to the Parliament as Commission president and mentioned 1992—the end of two consecutive Commission mandates (the Commission's term in office was then four years)—as a possible deadline for its implementation.[24]

The White Paper

At Delors's prompting, the European Council tasked the Commission in March 1985 with drafting a program for completing the internal market. Delors delegated the work of drafting the white paper, or detailed set of proposals, to Lord Arthur Cockfield, the commissioner with responsibility for the internal market. Thatcher had nominated Cockfield, a former trade secretary in her government, to the Commission and insisted that he get the internal market portfolio. She wanted him not only to help remove barriers to trade but also to hold the line in Brussels against spillover into other policy areas. Cockfield met her expectations for the internal market but otherwise disappointed the prime minister. Cockfield was, she later lamented, "the prisoner as well as the master of his subject. It was all too easy for him . . . to go native and to move from deregulating the market to reregulating it under the rubric of harmonization. Alas, it was not long before my old friend and I were at odds."[25]

By contrast, Cockfield and Delors hit it off immediately, even though they could not have been more different. Cockfield was upper class and conservative; Delors lower middle class and moderately left-wing. They had difficulty communicating directly, as Cockfield had no French and Delors had little English. But they understood each other well. Both were committed to drafting and implementing a program to liberalize the European market. They played to different galleries. A former businessman, Cockfield was an ideal ambassador for the Commission to the business community; a former trade unionist, Delors helped to reconcile organized labor to an initiative against which traditional trade unionists instinctively recoiled.

Although relatively few people in the Commission were involved in drafting the white paper, the exercise reverberated throughout the institution. Commission officials, however far removed from the drafting process, sensed that the Commission and the EC were about to turn a corner. Delors wanted to give the Commission new direction and strong leadership. For its part, the Commission looked forward to a fresh start and enhanced importance after nearly two decades of drift. A single market strategy suited both Delors's and the Commission's objectives of reinvigorating the Brussels bureaucracy and returning the Commission to center stage.

Perhaps the most famous policy prescription ever promulgated in the EU's history, the white paper contained a compelling rationale for further economic integration. Cockfield later described it as "one of the best [ever] expositions of Community policy, Community philosophy and Community aspirations."[26] Its final paragraph explained the initiative's broader purpose:

> Just as the Customs Union had to precede Economic Integration, so Economic Integration had to precede European Union. What this White Paper proposes therefore is that the Community should now take a further step along the road so clearly delineated in the treaties. To do less would be to fall short of the ambitions of the founding fathers of the Community; . . . it would be to betray the trust invested in us; it would be to offer the peoples of Europe a narrower, less rewarding, less secure, less prosperous future than they could otherwise enjoy. That is the measure of the challenge that faces us. Let it never be said that we were incapable of rising to it.[27]

The white paper listed approximately three hundred measures necessary to complete the internal market by the target date of December 31, 1992. The Commission finished the white paper, in record time, because many of the measures listed in it were already on the drawing board, a legacy of the Commission's earlier internal market efforts. Cockfield organized the measures under three categories of barriers to integration: physical, technical, and fiscal. Intended to achieve the free movement of goods, people, capital, and services, the white paper constituted a detailed action plan against which Commission officials, politicians, and businesspeople could measure progress toward a single market. The European Council endorsed the white paper without debate at the Milan summit in June 1985.

Implementing the Single Market Program

The Single European Act gave the green light and supplied the institutional machinery necessary to implement the single market program.[28] Although the

SEA came into effect only in July 1987, the Council decided before then to enact single market measures as expeditiously as possible. The Commission fed the Council a steady stream of proposals, most of which went also to the Parliament under the new cooperation procedure. The Dutch presidency, in the first half of 1986, gave the Parliament a list of decisions taken by qualified majority vote to show that the taboo on voting in the Council was now broken.[29] The succeeding British presidency made completion of the single market its top priority.[30] Britain was unusually at ease in the EC at that time: 1986 was an interregnum for Britain between the budgetary battles of the early 1980s and the epic struggle over EMU in the late 1980s.

During negotiation of the SEA, some unsympathetic national officials and members of the Council secretariat complained that giving the Parliament the right to a second reading of draft legislation was a recipe for delay and disaster. Partly to prove them wrong but mostly to enhance its credibility as a legislative body, the Parliament reorganized its rules of procedure in 1986 and was ready to put cooperation into practice when the SEA finally came into effect in July 1987. Fearing the worst, the *Financial Times* wondered in April 1987 whether the SEA "will change anything in the real world, other than introduce complex new negotiations between the member states and the Parliament."[31] Indeed, there were teething troubles with the cooperation procedure, which took the remainder of the year to work out. On the whole, the Parliament made the most of the new procedure to advance the internal market and advance its own position in the EC system.

It was in 1987 that the phrase *single market* became widely used instead of *internal market,* largely because of the program's association with the Single European Act. This reflected the popularization of the program, which by the end of 1987 was a staple item in newspapers as well as radio and television programs throughout the EC. The slogan "1992" unexpectedly caught people's imaginations. For the first time in its history, the EC became a topic of general discussion among Europeans interested in current affairs. Delors (but not Cockfield) became a household name.

Business opinion was ahead of the general public in its enthusiasm for European integration. Even before the SEA came into effect, European businesspeople immersed themselves in the single market program. The Commission, member state governments, and the private sector organized conferences and published newsletters on how to exploit a frontier-free Europe. Large enterprises were best positioned to do so. In 1987 and 1988, merger mania swept the EC as companies attempted to realize economies of scale and improve their cross-border distribution networks. Sixty-eight major mergers and acquisitions took place in the EC in 1987; three hundred the following year.[32]

A report on the benefits of the single market, entitled *The Cost of Non-Europe*, stoked business and public interest in what soon became known as the 1992 program. The report was the result of a huge, Commission-funded research project led by Paolo Cecchini, a former Commission official and noted Italian economist. Cecchini drew on data from the four largest member states and on a comparison with the United States to quantify the cost to the EC of maintaining a fragmented market. The report examined everything from the cost to firms of the administrative procedures and delays associated with customs formalities, to the opportunity cost of lost trade, to the costs to national governments of border controls. In early 1988, Cecchini released his findings in a massive, sixteen-volume publication as well as a condensed single-volume version.[33] Although later criticized for its methodology and shown to be overoptimistic in its conclusions, the Cecchini Report contributed to the hype surrounding the single market program.[34]

Buoyed by the publication of the Cecchini Report, the program came into its own in 1988. Resolution early in the year of the budgetary dispute over funding for cohesion cleared the decks for the German presidency's single-minded effort to implement the single market. By the end of the German presidency, the Commission had submitted most of the proposals outlined in the white paper, and the Council had agreed on a common position (the first stage in the cooperation procedure) for over one hundred of them. Inevitably, the more difficult issues, such as tax harmonization, veterinary and plant health, and the free movement of people, remained on the drawing board. In a move that had major implications for EMU, the European Council agreed in Hanover in June 1988 to liberalize all capital movements as early as July 1990, with exceptions until December 1992 for Greece, Ireland, Portugal, and Spain. This was a major political turning point in the program and prompted the European Council to declare in its communiqué that achievement of the single market was now irreversible. Delors, cautious by nature, was less sanguine about the success of the program, although he conceded some months later that "we are almost on the threshold of the irreversible."[35]

A Hard Slog

Despite the euphoria surrounding the program, the work of enacting and implementing the necessary legislation was arduous, time consuming, and unglamorous. The process involved hundreds of national, Commission, and Parliament officials; national politicians, commissioners, and Europarliamentarians; and lawyers and lobbyists. Draft legislation worked its way through dozens of committee meetings in national capitals, Commission and Parliament offices, and Council chambers before emerging in the pages of the *Official Journal* as full-fledged directives. Implementing the single market program was a Herculean bureaucratic task of which most consumers of EC legislation were mercifully unaware.

The greatest appeal of the program for many ordinary Europeans was the promised abolition of border posts. The white paper included numerous proposals to eliminate customs formalities, paperwork, and inspections. Accompanying measures included miscellaneous provisions such as duty-free admission for the fuel in the tanks of trucks, an end to routine checks on passenger car documentation, and a new statistical system for tracking trade among member states once border posts had disappeared. Other steps to make possible the abolition of borders covered plant and animal health requirements, the livestock trade, and trade in agricultural products. The Council adopted almost all the necessary measures by the end of 1992.

The EC had less success liberalizing the movement of people. In order to pressure other member states to open their inner-EC borders, France, Germany, and the Benelux countries signed an agreement in Schengen, Luxembourg, in 1985 to eliminate all frontier formalities. Greece, Italy, Portugal, and Spain signed up to the agreement by the end of 1992, but Britain, Denmark, and Ireland, citing security and other concerns, remained outside the Schengen framework. Administrative delays in implementing the complex provisions of the agreement meant that border posts remained in existence between signatory states after the stipulated achievement of the single market program.

The removal of fiscal barriers would also have an immediate and obvious impact on many ordinary Europeans. The white paper included an ambitious set of initiatives for harmonizing taxation, a prerequisite for eliminating borders (where many taxes were assessed), and also for reducing distortions and segmentation of the market through disparate tax practices. Thus the white paper called on member states to harmonize value-added tax rates and to develop a system for charging value-added tax on cross-border sales once border posts were eliminated. The Council eventually adopted a general framework for harmonization in October 1992, which set a standard rate of 15 percent or above in each member state as of January 1993. The Council reached only a provisional agreement before 1992 on who should pay value-added tax and where they should pay it. Businesses complained vociferously about the complexity of the reporting system, smaller firms doubted the feasibility of shipping goods across borders, and consumers wondered about the supposed benefits of tax harmonization.

By contrast, consumers benefited immediately from a Council decision in March 1991 to eliminate restrictions on cross-border purchases of items subject to excise taxes—mainly fuels, liquor, and tobacco—for personal use. As a result, citizens were allowed to carry up to 800 cigarettes, 90 liters of wine, 110 liters of beer, and 10 liters of spirits across borders for their own use. Britons, often on cross-channel day trips, were quick to reap this reward of the single market program.

While availing themselves of the removal of restrictions on the cross-border purchase of liquor and tobacco, consumers took advantage also of the pressure successfully exerted on national governments by airport authorities and ferry operators not to end duty-free sales for people traveling within the

EC. Because many airports and ferry operators gathered a large part of their revenues from highly profitable duty-free sales, the Council agreed to delay the demise of duty-free shopping until 1999. Thus shrewd British shoppers could buy duty-free drink and cigarettes on the ferry while going back and forth to buy inexpensive drink and cigarettes in France.

The bulk of the single market program consisted of arcane measures to remove technical barriers to trade, covering product standards, testing, and certification; movement of capital; public procurement; free movement of labor and the professions; free movement of services; transport; new technologies; company law; intellectual property; and company taxation. Of these, standards, testing, and certification had the biggest impact on European business.[36] The white paper sought to maximize mutual recognition of national regulations and standards, not to abolish harmonization. Where harmonization remained essential, the white paper proposed a two-track strategy. First, a new approach would limit legislative harmonization to essential health and safety requirements with which products had to conform. Member states would have to transpose those fundamental requirements into national regulations but could not impose further regulatory requirements on the products in question. Second, where the new approach was not appropriate, the old approach of developing a single, Community-wide, detailed set of technical specifications for a given product would remain in place. As a result, the single market program was not simply deregulatory. According to a contemporary assessment, "although the language [of the program] is borrowed from neoliberalism, the actual proposals often involve a high degree of regulation in terms of harmonization of basic standards. On balance . . . 1992 is less an exercise in deregulation than in regulatory reform."[37]

The new approach required the Commission to contract with the relevant European organizations to develop voluntary European standards. Manufacturers adhering to those standards would be presumed to comply with the essential requirements set in the relevant directive, and their products would therefore be assured free circulation throughout the EC.[38] But the European standards bodies were unable to keep up with the numerous new approach directives, covering a wide range of products. They reacted badly to a Commission report in 1989 suggesting ways to remove bottlenecks, which also raised concerns outside the EC that hasty standards setting could lead to divergences between European and international standards. Because of the serious backlog in the development of standards in the EC by the end of 1992, manufacturers of products covered by the new approach directives faced uncertainty and disruption over the pace at which European standards could be developed and introduced.

Despite these and other imperfections, the single market program was a successful undertaking. In general, the white paper functioned as intended. By tying so many elements to a politically coherent and attractive vision, the

Commission managed to push the Council into adopting proposals that would not otherwise have generated much support. For its part, the SEA gave the Council the means to act. Implementation of the program created a climate in which individuals as well as firms could begin to identify themselves as European and look for opportunities beyond their own borders. It also restored the image of the EC as a vital and modern entity, not least in the eyes of the EU's neighbors and trading partners.

The International Impact

The single market program had an immediate and unexpected impact on the EC's external relations and role in the world. Just as it had attracted the attention of businesspeople and ordinary citizens in the EC, "1992" quickly caught on outside the EC's borders. Foreign governments and business interests took a keen interest in the program's development and implementation. To the Commission's surprise, external reaction to the EC's internal economic reorganization was not altogether favorable. "Fortress Europe" became a catchphrase in the United States to signal concern about the implications of the single market program for nonmember states. The Commission had given little thought to the external perception of the program and responded to international criticism by emphasizing its commitment to free trade and open markets. In an effort to allay growing concern beyond the EC's borders, the European Council declared at the Rhodes summit in December 1988 that "the single market will be of benefit to Community and non-Community countries alike. . . . The internal market will not close in on itself. 1992 Europe will be a partner and not a fortress Europe."[39]

The phrase "Partner Europe" lacked the resonance and appeal of "Fortress Europe." The Community's main trading partners remained unconvinced that the post-1992 European market would be as accessible as the European Council promised. Exporters to the EC of textiles, bananas, and cars had legitimate concerns. In order to eliminate internal borders, the EC abolished many quotas and other restraints imposed by individual member states under the terms of the Rome Treaty and replaced some of them with a set of EC-wide quotas or voluntary restraint agreements. The most egregious of these protected the EC's textile and car industries as well as banana producers in some member states' former colonies. The EC's post-1992 banana regime became a source of bitter contention between the EC and the United States, which championed the interests of so-called dollar bananas from Latin America.

The contemporaneous Uruguay Round of the GATT gave the EC's trading partners a good chance to test the Community's commitment to maintaining a liberal international regime. It also gave the Community an opportunity to leverage concessions from its trading partners based on the single market's purported benefits. At the same time, the EC launched a public relations campaign in the United States to persuade U.S. businesspeople and politicians of the advantages of the program. Large U.S. businesses already represented in Europe appreciated the advantages of an integrated European market. Others decided to locate operations there in order to insure against exclusion. As the single market program progressed, U.S. and other avid 1992-watchers lost their initial skepticism about the single market program. The Uruguay Round of global trade liberalization talks failed to end at its scheduled deadline of December 1990 not because of disputes over market access for manufactured goods and services but because of the EC's refusal to concede larger cuts in agricultural subsidies, a subject beyond the scope of the 1992 program.

The European Economic Area

Concern about possible exclusion from the single market led some members of the European Free Trade Area (EFTA) to contemplate EC membership, especially after the commissioner for external relations asserted, in May 1987, the EC's sole decisionmaking authority and the primacy of integration among the existing member states over EC-EFTA cooperation.[40] The economic impetus for EC accession became so strong that neutral Austria applied to join in July 1989, despite the Soviet Union's disapproval. Neutral Sweden, where Volvo and other economic interests pressed for EC entry, decided not to apply for membership, despite rapid changes in the international system in the late 1980s.[41]

Until it digested the accession of Portugal and Spain and implemented the single market program, the EC was not interested in acquiring new members. Hoping to fend off applications from the EFTA countries, in January 1989 Delors proposed "a new form of association [between the EC and EFTA], with common decision making and administrative institutions."[42] Austria's application spurred Delors to press ahead with this initiative, which became known as the European Economic Area. Thus began what one senior Commission official described as "the most complex negotiations [that] we have ever conducted on behalf of the EC."[43] On the internal market alone, the EFTA countries had to adopt approximately fourteen hundred existing Community acts covering over ten thousand pages of legislation. Contentious issues included truck transit through Austria and Switzerland from EC countries and access for Community fishing boats to Icelandic and Norwegian waters. Talks were particularly difficult over institutional arrangements, with the EC eventually offering to consult the EFTA countries on certain draft legislation and to establish a panel of EC and EFTA judges to adjudicate European Economic Area–related disputes. The proposed dispute-resolution mechanism triggered a ruling by the Court of Justice against the draft European Economic Area agreement in December 1991. Renewed EC-EFTA negotiations settled the

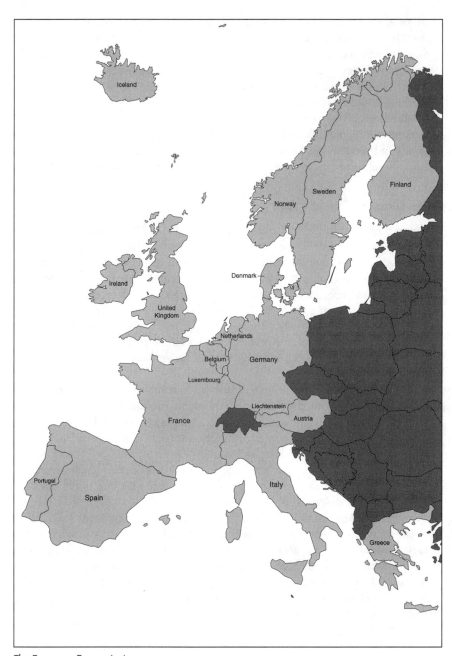

The European Economic Area

dispute-resolution issue and paved the way for an acceptable agreement in May 1992.

Yet the European Economic Area failed in its original aim of allowing the EFTA countries to enjoy the benefits of the single market without having them become members. By the time that the European Economic Area came into operation in January 1993, most of the EFTA countries saw the agreement as a staging post, not an alternative, to EC membership. With the Cold War over, the Soviet Union gone, and Russia agreeable to the EFTA countries' accession, neutrality was no longer a reason for them not to apply to join the EC. The compatibility of neutrality with the EC's efforts to develop a common foreign and security policy was another matter, however. Eager to enjoy the full economic benefits of EC membership as opposed to the limited economic advantage of European Economic Area membership, most of the EFTA countries applied to join the EC in 1991 and 1992.

Solidarity Through Cohesion and Social Policy

The Single European Act included an implicit bargain to share the wealth of the single market program among rich and poor member states and among all classes of society. Given his background in the French labor movement and his strong social conscience, Delors was deeply committed to the idea of solidarity in the EC. He had pushed hard to include a section on cohesion (the reduction of economic disparities between richer and poorer countries) and provisions for a stronger social policy in the SEA. The next step was to flesh them out by reorganizing and allocating more money for the structural funds—the means by which cohesion would be implemented—and developing a social policy program. Any mention of money in the EC was bound to be contentious. It immediately put Thatcher, a foe of additional public expenditure, on the alert. Ideologically, Thatcher opposed cohesion and social policy because she believed that the market, not the state or the EU, should regulate the economy and society. Other EU leaders, even nominally conservative ones, had no problem in principle with cohesion or social policy. Some were reluctant to allocate more money to the structural funds; others, notably from the poor member states, wanted a major increase in structural funds spending. All were ambivalent about social policy, not wanting to offend employers by imposing strict rules in the workplace or workers by seeming to neglect their interests.

Cohesion

The cohesion battle began in February 1987 when Delors, following up on the still-unratified SEA, released a package of budgetary proposals.[44] These included major increases in funding for research and development, transport, environmental policy, and, especially, cohesion. For instance, Delors proposed a doubling of spending on the structural funds, with a particular focus on regions with a per capita income below 75 percent of the EC average. That meant Greece, Ireland, Portugal, and Spain. To cover the increase in Community spending, Delors proposed a new budgetary resource, based on member states' GDP. At the same time, partly to allay Thatcher's concerns, Delors proposed reining in spending on the CAP and imposing better budget discipline. The Delors package was spread over a five-year time frame (1988–1992) in order to avoid debilitating annual budgetary disputes.

Just as Delors used the voluminous Cecchini Report to bolster his arguments in support of the single market, he cited a report by Tommaso Padoa-Schioppa to make a compelling case for reform of the structural funds. Published in April 1987, the report stressed "the serious risks of aggravated regional imbalances in the course of market liberalization." In a memorable rebuke of neoliberal assumptions, it warned that "any easy extrapolation of 'invisible hand' ideas into the real world of regional economics in the process of market opening would be unwarranted in the light of economic history and theory."[45]

The battle lines were now drawn between Thatcher and those who supported a massive increase in the size of the structural funds, notably Delors and Felipe González, the prime minister of Spain and unofficial leader of the four countries that would benefit most from the measure (the cohesion countries, including chilly Ireland, soon became known as "Club Med"). Thatcher dismissed Delors as an unelected Socialist spendthrift. She heaped scorn on González, another Socialist but, as an elected head of government, her peer in the European Council. Surely, she thought, "in the long term a proud, ancient nation like Spain would baulk at continued loss of national self-determination in exchange for German-financed subsidies."[46] Indeed Germany, as the largest contributor to the Community's coffers, would determine the fate of the cohesion policy. Kohl's position was therefore pivotal in the negotiations on the Delors package. In principle Kohl supported cohesion, but in practice he did not want to increase the size of the EC budget. Nor did he want to antagonize German farmers by reducing Community spending on agricultural subsidies.

The dispute over the Delors package rumbled on through 1987, overshadowing implementation of the single market program. The Club Med countries were reluctant to legislate for market liberalization in Brussels as long as their demands for more spending on the structural funds were not met. Given the political sensitivity of the matter, inevitably discussion of the Delors package dominated the European Council. Summit meetings in 1987 resembled summits in the early 1980s, with Thatcher refusing to sanction more Community spending while tenaciously defending Britain's rebate, and most of the other leaders urging acceptance of the Delors proposals.

The Delors package was an unwelcome piece of unfinished business for the German presidency in early 1988. It placed Kohl in a dilemma: as chancellor he wanted to protect German farmers from cuts in subsidies and German taxpayers from a hike in Germany's contribution to the EC's budget; as president-in-office of the Council he wanted to resolve a festering dispute that threatened to delay implementation of the single market program, another German interest. At a special summit in Brussels in February 1988, Kohl compromised on the budget increase and Thatcher relaxed her demand for cuts in guaranteed cereals' prices. Britain's rebate remained intact, and German farmers continued to be subsidized at the high level to which they were accustomed. The cohesion countries got a doubling of the structural funds by 1992, and the German presidency won accolades for resolving the budgetary dispute. But the EC was the real winner: cohesion became a vital instrument of economic and political integration, and agreement on the Delors package removed a major obstacle on the road to 1992.

Following agreement on the Delors package, the Council adopted regulations in June and December 1988 reforming the EC's structural funds (the means by which the EC promotes cohesion). These included concentrating structural funds on five major objectives. Objective 1, covering "regions whose development is lagging behind," was the main source of funding for Club Med and, financially, the largest objective. Another reform introduced the partnership principle, through which the Commission involved regions, not just national governments, in formulating and implementing structural policy. That gave the EU's regions, which varied from relatively powerless entities in centralized nation states (such as France) to powerful states in federal countries (such as Germany), a vested interest in European integration and an incentive to cultivate relations with Brussels. As a result, the Commission and the regions were complicit in a political process that sought to undermine the authority of national governments and devolve power from national capitals upward to the European and downward to the regional levels.

Social Policy

From the beginning of his presidency, Delors expressed a strong personal interest in social policy, focusing on women's rights, workers' rights, and working conditions. One of his first acts as Commission president was to launch a dialogue between the "social partners"—representatives of employers and workers—at the European level. The European Union of Employers' Confederations was already well established in Brussels. Representing employers' organizations throughout the EC, it was a wealthy, influential interest group. By contrast, national trades unions were poorly organized transnationally in Brussels. Delors sought to rectify that by boosting the standing of the European Trade Union Confederation.

Big business in Europe was instinctively wary of the Commission. That was a legacy of the Monnet and Hallstein years and reflected also the private sector's general distrust of government. The Commission and big business had established a rapprochement in the early 1980s when Commissioner Davignon collaborated with the European Round Table, the elite group of leading industrialists, on high-technology projects and on internal market issues. Delors's obvious trade union sympathies and keen interest in social policy once again raised big business's suspicion of the Commission. Big business watched with alarm as the Commission's social affairs directorate-general grew increasingly influential. Although Cockfield and Martin Bange-mann, the commissioner with responsibility for industrial affairs, were unof-ficial emissaries to big business, Delors, like Monnet before him, felt that big business had the resources and the connections to look after itself. By con-trast, Delors was willing to reach out to small business, which risked being left behind in the scramble to gain commercial advantage from the single market program. A scheme to assist small and medium-sized enterprises therefore became an important flanking policy for the single market.

In a victory for Delors and the Left-leaning national governments, the SEA introduced qualified majority voting for the "health and safety of work-ers." As the employers' federation feared that it would, this provision produced the largest and most important body of social policy legislation in the late 1980s, the high point of social policy in the history of the EU. Moreover, the qualified majority voting provision for health and safety legislation opened a loophole through which the Commission tried to enact other social policy measures. It also emboldened Delors to explore the broader "social dimension" of the 1992 project. Most member states were willing to go along with him, the obvious exception being Thatcher's Britain. Despite her objections, the Euro-pean Council noted in Hanover in June 1988 that, as the internal market had to be conceived "in such a manner as to benefit all our people," it was necessary to improve working conditions, living standards, protection of health and safety, access to vocational training, and dialogue between the two sides of industry.[47]

The Commission developed the social dimension of the single market program in a paper in September 1988 that outlined the intellectual and eco-nomic rationale for a vigorous social policy. Delors then proposed a charter of basic social rights and asked the sleepy Economic and Social Committee, an institution that represented vocational interests in the EC, for an opinion. Roused from its slumber, the committee produced a report supporting Delors's initiative, despite the misgivings of its employers' representatives. Delors's main political support came from France, where Mitterrand, a Social-ist, was happy to champion a European initiative that had a particular appeal to voters on the Left. Mitterrand put social policy near the top of his agenda during France's Council presidency in the second half of 1989. Confident of French support, Delors produced a draft Community Charter of the Funda-mental Social Rights of Workers, with an attached "action program" of nearly fifty measures, about half of which required legislation at the European level. Thanks to Mitterrand's advocacy of it, eleven of the twelve national leaders adopted the social charter at the summit in Strasbourg in December 1989. Thatcher was the lone dissenter.

Like cohesion, social policy was a divisive issue between Britain and the other member states. Whereas Britain eventually accepted cohesion policy, it continued to resist social policy. The difference, perhaps, was that Britain's outright rejection of cohesion might have jeopardized implementation of the 1992 program because Club Med and its supporters could have blocked the enactment of single market measures. Also, Britain stood to benefit from the proposed increase in spending on structural funds, as the new Objective 2 included economic conversion and modernization in declining industrial regions. By contrast, social policy would not have benefited Britain directly and was not a make-or-break issue for the single market program.

▓ Notes

1. Jacques Delors, "Speech to the European Parliament," Bulletin EC-S/1 1985, p. 23. See also Ken Endo, *The Presidency of the European Commission Under Jacques Delors: The Politics of Shared Leadership* (New York: St. Martin's Press, 1999), p. 137.

2. See Commission, *Eighteenth Report on the Activities of the European Communities* (Luxembourg: European Communities, 1985), p. 27.

3. Margaret Thatcher, *Downing Street Years* (New York: HarperCollins, 1993), pp. 545–546.

4. Bulletin EC 2-1985.

5. Quoted in the *Financial Times*, April 2, 1985, p. 3.

6. Quoted in *Le Monde*, April 2, 1985, p. 1.

7. The European Council established a second committee to consider ways of boosting popular awareness of and interest in the EC. That was the Ad Hoc Committee on a Peoples' Europe, chaired by Pietro Adonnino, a former Italian member of the European Parliament. The Adonnino Committee discussed issues ranging from taxation, to freedom of movement, to mutual recognition of degrees and diplomas, as well as symbols of further integration, such as an EC flag and anthem and the minting of European coins. Its report was far less consequential than that of the Dooge Committee, but led, among other things, to the adoption of Beethoven's "Ode to Joy" as the EC's anthem.

8. See the *Journal of Common Market Studies, 1985 Annual Review*, p. 335.

9. Garret FitzGerald, *All in a Life: An Autobiography* (Dublin: Gill and Macmillan), p. 596.

10. Quoted in Marina Grazzo, ed., *Towards European Union*, Vol. 2 (Brussels: Agence Europe, 1986), p. 23.

11. On the conference and its outcome, see David Cameron, "The 1992 Initiative: Causes and Consequences," in *Europolitics,* by Albert Sbragia (Washington, DC: Brookings Institution, 1992), pp. 23–74; Andrew Moravcsik, *The Choice for Europe: Social Purpose and State Power from Messina to Maastricht* (Ithaca, NY: Cornell University Press, 1998), pp. 314–378; Wayne Sandholtz and John Zysman, "1992: Recasting the European Bargain," *World Politics* 42 (1989), pp. 95–128; Jean de Ruyt, *L'Acte*

unique européen: Commentaire, 2nd ed. (Brussels: Editions de l'Université de Brux-elles, 1987); and Helen Drake, *Jacques Delors: Perspectives on a European Leader* (London: Routledge, 2000), pp. 78–112.

12. Endo, *Delors*, p. 141.

13. See ibid., pp. 142–143.

14. See Alistair Cole, *François Mitterrand: A Study in Political Leadership* (London: Routledge, 1994), pp. 126–127.

15. *Journal of Common Market Studies, 1985 Annual Review*, p. 338.

16. Text for the Single European Act is available at http://www.europa.eu.int/abc/obj/treaties/en/entoc113.htm.

17. Endo, *Delors*, p. 146.

18. See Kenneth Dyson and Kevin Featherstone, *The Road to Maastricht: Negotiating Economic and Monetary Union* (Oxford: Oxford University Press, 1999), pp. 155–156.

19. Thatcher, *Downing Street Years*, p. 548.

20. Nigel Lawson, *The View from No. 11: Britain's Longest-serving Cabinet Member Recalls the Triumphs and Disappointments of the Thatcher Era* (New York: Doubleday, 1993), pp. 893–894.

21. Text of the Single European Act is available at http://www.europa.eu.int/abc/obj/treaties/en/entoc113.htm.

22. Quoted in the *Journal of Common Market Studies, 1985 Annual Review*, p. 337; see also Stephen George, *An Awkward Partner: Britain in the European Community* (Oxford: Oxford University Press, 1998), pp. 184–185.

23. Drake, *Delors*, p. 80.

24. Bulletin EC S/1-1985.

25. Thatcher, *Downing Street Years*, p. 545; see also Arthur Cockfield, *Creating the Internal Market* (London: Wiley Chancery Law, 1984).

26. Cockfield, *Internal Market*, p. 4.

27. Commission, "Completing the Internal Market," COM(85)310 final, Brussels, March 1985.

28. On the single market program, see Bill Lucarelli, *The Origin and Evolution of the Single Market in Europe* (Aldershot: Ashgate, 1999); R. Bieber et al., *1992: One European Market* (Florence: European University Institute, 1988); Michelle Egan, *Constructing a European Market: Standards, Regulation, and Governance* (Oxford: Oxford University Press, 2001), pp. 109–132; Jacques Pelkmans and Alan Winters, *Europe's Domestic Market* (London: Routledge, 1988); Michael Calingaert, *The 1992 Challenge from Europe: Development of the European Community's Internal Market* (Washington, DC: National Planning Association, 1990).

29. See *Journal of Common Market Studies, 1986 Annual Review*, p. 339.

30. See George, *Awkward Partner*, pp. 187–189; Helen Wallace, "The British Presidency and the EC's Council of Ministers: The Opportunity to Persuade," *International Affairs* 62, no. 4 (Autumn 1986), pp. 583–599.

31. The *Financial Times*, April 11, 1987, p. 2.

32. See the *Economist*, February 13, 1988, pp. 46–47, and July 9, 1988, p. 30. See also D. Mayes, ed., *The European Challenge: Industry's Response to the 1992 Programme* (Hemel Hempstead: Harvester Wheatsheaf, 1991).

33. Commission, *Research on the "Cost of Non-Europe": Basic Findings*, 16 Vols. (Luxembourg: Office of Official Publications of the European Communities, 1988); Paolo Cecchini, *The European Challenge, 1992: The Benefits of the Single Market* (Aldershot: Wildwood House, 1988). See also Michael Emerson et al., *The*

Economics of 1992: The EC's Assessment of the Economic Effects of Completing the Internal Market (Oxford: Oxford University Press, 1988).

34. John Kay, *1992 Myths and Realities* (London: London Business School, 1989).

35. Quoted in *The Times* (London), October 27, 1988, p. 6.

36. Egan, *European Market*, pp. 52–58, 121–131; Desmond Dinan, *Ever Closer Union: An Introduction to European Integration*, 2nd ed. (Boulder, CO: Lynne Rienner Publishers, 1999), pp. 353–359.

37. Renaud Dehousse and Giandomenico Majone, "The Institutional Dynamics of European Integration: From the Single Act to the Maastricht Treaty," in *The Construction of Europe,* ed. S. Martin (Dordrecht: Kluwer, 1994), p. 95.

38. See Egan, *European Market*, pp. 133–165.

39. Bulletin EC 12-1988.

40. Bulletin EC 5-1985.

41. See Dinan, *Ever Closer Union,* pp. 446–450.

42. Bulletin EC S/1-1989.

43. Quoted in the *International Herald Tribune*, February 15–16, 1992, p. 1.

44. Commission, "Making a Success of the Single European Act," COM(87)100, Brussels, January 1987.

45. Tommaso Padoa-Schioppa et al., *Efficiency, Stability and Equity: A Strategy for the Evolution of the Economic System of the European Community* (Oxford: Oxford University Press, 1987), p.10.

46. Thatcher, *Downing Street Years*, p. 746.

47. Bulletin EC 6-1988.

7

Achieving European Union

The Treaty on European Union, concluded in Maastricht in December 1991, was one of the greatest milestones in the history of European integration. Despite its manifest drawbacks, the treaty produced an impressive political entity: an organization of European states with strong federal attributes. Yet the delay in implementing the treaty and therefore in launching the EU, due to protracted and contentious ratification debates, robbed the occasion of much of its luster. Public opinion, which seemed solidly behind the single market program, recoiled at the complexity and incomprehensibility of the treaty and was highly ambivalent about some of its main features, including economic and monetary union (EMU). Concerns about the "democratic deficit" resurfaced with a vengeance in the early 1990s.

Only a few years earlier most European leaders rode a wave of Europhoria. President François Mitterrand in France, Chancellor Helmut Kohl in Germany, and Prime Minister Felipe González in Spain were all reelected in the late 1980s largely on the strength of their Euro-credentials. Jacques Delors became the best-known and most powerful Commission president because of his association with the single market program. British prime minister Margaret Thatcher alone opposed deeper integration. That brought her into conflict not only with Mitterrand and Kohl, but especially with Delors, whom she saw as the root of all evil: a French Socialist determined to establish an undemocratic European superstate.

Within a short time, public and political attitudes toward European integration soured. Economically, the EC fell on hard times. The brisk growth of the late 1980s, and with it support for the single market program, suddenly dissipated. At the same time, the end of the Cold War had a profound impact on the course of European integration and on public perceptions of the EU. Imminent German unification reinforced Mitterrand's and Kohl's determination to achieve EMU. Plans for the free movement of people within the EU and fears of mass migration from Central and Eastern Europe increased member states' interest in cooperating on asylum, immigration, and policing under the rubric of justice and home affairs. The Gulf War and the collapse of

Yugoslavia strengthened the momentum already developing in the EC toward a common foreign and security policy, and possibly a defense policy as well.

Yet public opinion seemed wary of these initiatives. Fear of German domination of the EU reverberated during the Danish and French referenda on ratification of the Maastricht Treaty in 1992. The EU's ineffectualness in Yugoslavia dented public confidence in the putative common foreign and security policy. The inclusion of the principle of subsidiarity in the treaty and efforts by EU leaders to make it meaningful in response to the ratification crisis left most people cold. Accordingly, the launch of the EU in November 1993, nearly two years after the Maastricht Treaty, was both a high point and a low point in the history of European integration.

■ Economic and Monetary Union

The success of the single market program and the existence of the European Monetary System (EMS) brought EMU back onto the EC's agenda in 1987 and 1988. Participation in the exchange rate mechanism of the EMS helped member states to achieve a degree of economic convergence and exchange rate stability. The experience of working together in the exchange rate mechanism also reconciled many government officials and politicians to the prospect of EMU. Ten years earlier, Leo Tindemans had reported regretfully that there was not enough trust between national governments to transfer responsibility for EMU to a central European authority.[1] By the late 1980s, the EMS had spawned a network of officials in the Commission and national capitals committed to close monetary policy cooperation.

Operational problems with the EMS, however, led to calls for its reform and possible replacement by EMU. The German mark was the system's de facto anchor currency, and other central banks followed the German Central Bank's anti-inflationary policies. Germany's partners resented the "asymmetry" of a system that was so obviously dominated by the mark and by German policy preferences. Pressure on the French franc following a large fall in the value of the dollar triggered a revaluation of the stronger currencies in the exchange rate mechanism in January 1987 and sharpened French criticism of the system. France pressed for better coordination of monetary policies and greater flexibility in exchange rate intervention. That resulted in the so-called Basle-Nyborg agreement of September 1987 (negotiated by the Committee of Central Bank Governors in Basle and endorsed by the economic and finance ministers in Nyborg) to strengthen the EMS, notably by monitoring monetary developments and coordinating interest rate policies more closely and by relaxing the rules on intervention.[2] The agreement helped the EMS to respond better to fluctuations in international currency markets, such as the upheaval after the Wall Street crash in October 1987, but did not address the underlying problem of asymmetry.

Chafing at the ascendancy of the German Central Bank while acknowledging the benefits of German-inspired monetary policy preferences, French officials warmed to the idea of a monetary union in which France would be on a par with Germany. At the same time the single market program, which included proposals for the liberalization of capital movements, provided an increasing impetus toward EMU. The maintenance of exchange rates within the EC seemed inconsistent with and contradictory to the objectives of the single market. Already enthusiastic about the single market program, business leaders began to take an interest in monetary union. Valéry Giscard d'Estaing and Helmut Schmidt, authors of the EMS, formed a high-level committee to lobby for EMU.

The relationship between the single market program and the EMS provided an additional argument in favor of EMU. Tommaso Padoa-Schioppa developed the point in an influential report in early 1987 on the implications of the single market for the EC's economic system. "In a quite fundamental way," Padoa-Schioppa pointed out, "capital mobility and exchange rate fixity (in the exchange rate mechanism) together leave no room for independent [national] monetary policies." Because a unified market with a free flow of capital could put the EMS under great strain, Padoa-Schioppa recommended the establishment of a monetary union.[3]

The momentum of market integration, continuing asymmetry in the EMS, and the possible impact of free capital movements on the exchange rate mechanism prompted Edouard Balladur, France's finance minister, to draft a memorandum for the Council of Economic and Finance Ministers (Ecofin) in January 1988 entitled "Europe's Monetary Construction." After reviewing the history of the EMS and the trajectory of the single market, Balladur concluded that the EC should adopt "a single currency . . . [and a] common central bank." The Balladur memorandum signaled France's dissatisfaction with the status quo and willingness to embrace EMU.[4] A similar memorandum the following month by Hans-Dietrich Genscher, Germany's foreign minister and president-in-office of the Council of Ministers, was even more significant. Although writing in a personal capacity, Genscher endorsed the idea of a common currency and a European central bank, modeled of course on the German Central Bank. Genscher's initiative indicated Germany's growing openness to EMU, although the central bank remained opposed to the idea.

Genscher's trial balloon emboldened Delors to advocate EMU more openly. Not wanting to detract attention from the single market program and stir up sentiment against EMU, Delors had so far moderated his public statements on the subject. With the single market well on track and the budget package out of the way, Delors turned his attention squarely to EMU. As it was, Delors had responsibility within the Commission for economic and monetary affairs. Accordingly, he attended the monthly meetings of the Committee of Central Bank Governors, a key monetary policy body that met in Basle, at the headquarters of the Bank for International Settlements. Delors sought to ingratiate himself with the central bankers, a notoriously cliquish group. In particular, he cultivated relations with Karl-Otto Pöhl, president of the German Central Bank, one of the most influential members of the committee and a presumed opponent of EMU.[5]

Having responsibility in the Commission for monetary policy, Delors also attended meetings of Ecofin, which played an important role in the evolution of EMU. The General Affairs Council (of foreign ministers) was also influential and vied with Ecofin for supremacy in monetary policy matters. But the European Council was the most powerful body, not only because of the political sensitivity of EMU but also because, as stipulated in the Single European Act, any effort to establish EMU would require the convening of an intergovernmental conference, in which the European Council would negotiate the final deal.

Delors had the great advantage of being a member of the European Council, although as Commission president he carried less weight than the national leaders, at least of the larger member states. Within the European Council, and on the question of EMU generally, Mitterrand and Kohl were the key players. Since his economic about-face in 1983, Mitterrand openly espoused greater European integration, a subject that had interested him throughout his political career. Indeed, Mitterrand made "the construction of Europe" the leitmotiv of his presidency.[6] He favored EMU and, in the mid-1980s, nudged Kohl to take a stronger stand on the issue. During a visit to Aachen in October 1987, seduced by the charm of the historic town hall and the spirit of Charlemagne, Mitterrand spoke glowingly of a common Franco-German destiny. As the motor of European integration, France and Germany should spearhead closer cooperation in a range of areas, including monetary policy.[7]

Kohl, another lifetime advocate of European integration, was susceptible to arguments in favor of EMU. Yet Kohl faced strong resistance from the German Central Bank, which did not trust the political instincts and policy preferences of the French and Italian monetary authorities and did not want to lose its dominant position in the EMS. Germans deeply respected the views of the central bank, an independent body with an impeccable record of monetary policy management. As a cautious and astute politician, Kohl would not confront the central bank on the question of EMU until and unless circumstances changed and German public opinion became more open to the idea.

Circumstances began to change in the late 1980s not only within the EC, where implementation of the single market program generated interest in EMU, but also in the Soviet Union, where Mikhail Gorbachev's policies of economic and political reform began to have an impact abroad. Developments in the Soviet Union raised the specter of the old German question. A visit to Moscow in July 1986 convinced Mitterrand of the importance of tying Germany more tightly into Europe should Gorbachev's reforms result in significant strategic change. Equally aware of what was happening in the Soviet Union and sensitive to French concerns, Kohl was happy to commit Germany unequivocally to deeper European integration. EMU would be a sure sign of Germany's intentions.[8]

Mitterrand and Kohl had ample opportunity to discuss EMU together. The close relationship between Roland Dumas and Genscher, the French and German foreign ministers, was equally important for the evolution of Franco-German thinking on the subject. Dumas was Mitterrand's most trusted interlocutor. He and Genscher spoke regularly on the telephone and met frequently in the Council and other forums. Genscher, the leader of the junior party in Kohl's coalition government, was not close to Kohl, but his position as foreign minister and coalition partner gave him considerable influence in Bonn.

The Delors Committee and Report

Following up on Genscher's memorandum, Delors and Genscher floated the idea of convening a special committee to chart the road to EMU. Mitterrand, who easily defeated Jacques Chirac in the presidential election of May 1988, partly on the strength of his Europeanism, swung fully behind them. Reveling in the success of the German presidency, especially after reaching agreement on the Delors budgetary package in February 1988, Kohl became increasingly assertive on EMU. He and Delors struck a deal in the run-up to the Hanover summit in June 1988: Kohl would propose to the European Council that the committee should consist mostly of the central bank governors, with Delors in the chair. The European Council's acceptance of Kohl's proposal and establishment of the Delors Committee, consisting of twelve central bank governors, two commissioners (including Delors), and three independent experts, put EMU at the forefront of the EC's agenda.[9]

It was also in Hanover that the European Council reappointed Delors as Commission president. This may have seemed a foregone conclusion, but Thatcher's support was nonetheless surprising. In her memoirs, Thatcher claims that Delors's reappointment was virtually unstoppable and that she was then unaware of the extent of his Eurofederalism.[10] Neither claim rings true. Thatcher had withstood greater pressure in the European Council in the early 1980s and could hardly have had any illusions about Delors's ideas. Nevertheless, it would have taken considerable courage to blackball Delors's reappointment as Commission president, although she could more easily have prevented his appointment as chair of the committee on EMU. Thatcher may have presumed that Pöhl, president of Germany's central bank and a stout defender of national monetary policies, would hold the line in the committee against EMU.

According to the foremost chroniclers of EMU, "the decision to have Delors chairing the . . . committee and the remit given to it unleashed a powerful momentum behind EMU and a single currency."[11] Delors took the challenge of chairing the committee extremely seriously. He worked hard to master complicated economic and monetary policy issues and tried not to dominate meetings, as he usually liked to do. Within the Commission, however, Delors was obsessive and secretive. He relied on a handful of trusted officials, mostly in his own cabinet, and did not consult the other commissioners much. When challenged by them, Delors retorted disingenuously that, as chair of the committee, he was acting in a personal capacity on behalf of the European Council, not as president of the Commission.[12]

The committee's brief was to outline concrete steps for the realization of EMU. The committee met in Basle, at the end of regular meetings of the Committee of Central Bank Governors, on which most of its members served. It began deliberations in September 1988 and presented its report in April 1989. During that time even the most reluctant committee members rose to the intellectual challenge of devising a strategy for EMU. Delors strove to keep everyone on board and produce a unanimous report without sacrificing key elements of a common economic and monetary policy. His success in doing so was a tribute to his negotiating and mediating skills and a good reflection on the committee's composition and operation.[13]

The Delors report identified four basic elements of economic union: the single market, competition policy and other market-strengthening mechanisms, cohesion, and macroeconomic policy coordination. It defined monetary union as "the assurance of full and irreversible convertibility of currencies; the complete liberalization of capital transactions and full integration of banking and other financial markets; and the elimination of margins of fluctuation and the irrevocable locking of exchange rate parities."[14] That would require a single monetary policy, although not necessarily a single currency. The committee proposed a European System of Central Banks, consisting of a central institution and constituent national central banks, to manage the single monetary policy. Participating national central banks would be independent and pursue price stability as their primary objective. Clearly, that was a concession to the German Central Bank and, more broadly, to German political and public opinion.

The report is best known for proposing a three-stage approach to EMU. During the first stage, capital movements would be fully liberalized and there would be closer macroeconomic policy cooperation among member states. The European System of Central Banks would be established in the second stage, and margins of fluctuation within the exchange rate mechanism would be progressively narrowed. Finally, the third stage would see the irrevocable fixing of exchange rate parities, with the transfer of full responsibility for EMU to Community institutions.

Pessimistic by nature, Delors was disappointed with the committee's report. He regretted that it did not call emphatically for a single currency and that there were no deadlines or automatic mechanism for the transition from one stage to another. Nevertheless the report stated that "the creation of [EMU] must be viewed as a single process" and that "the decision to enter upon the first stage should be a decision to embark on the entire process." The report also recommended that Stage One, which did not require treaty change, should start no later than July 1990, when capital movements were due to be liberalized as part of the single market program.[15]

The Delors report elicited a mixed response among national leaders. Thatcher was livid with the governor of the Bank of England for signing the report and felt betrayed by Pöhl as well. Thatcher was in no doubt about Delors's intentions and about the centrality of EMU to the EC's agenda. The British government was then in the midst of a furious debate about possibly joining the exchange rate mechanism. Nigel Lawson, the Chancellor of the Exchequer, urged British participation both for its own sake and in order to strengthen Britain's credibility in the EC. Far from wanting to establish EMU, Lawson wanted Britain to continue to oppose it from within the exchange rate mechanism. Geoffrey Howe, Britain's foreign secretary, also opposed EMU but favored a more positive British policy toward the EC. Thatcher's notorious intransigence on EC issues drove a wedge between her and the finance and foreign ministers, but united the finance and foreign ministers in their resentment of her. Division at home reduced the effectiveness of Britain's opposition abroad to EMU. It also drove Lawson, Howe, and, eventually, Thatcher from office.[16]

Momentum for EMU

The reaction to the Delors report in other national capitals was generally positive, although Ecofin, resentful of its exclusion from the process of drafting the report, responded coolly to the committee's findings. The outcome of the next meeting of the European Council, in Madrid in June 1989, would be decisive for the future of the report and the fate of EMU. Spain, in the Council presidency for the first time, jumped on the EMU bandwagon as a means of establishing its European credentials and, possibly, leveraging more money for cohesion policy. González, the Spanish prime minister, was a close ally of Mitterrand's. With France due to succeed Spain in the Council presidency, Mitterrand and González closely coordinated their positions on EMU. Feeling more confident of his position vis-à-vis the central bank after Pöhl signed on to the Delors report and mindful of the changing strategic situation in Central and Eastern Europe, Kohl was willing in Madrid to endorse EMU fully.

The European Council accordingly agreed in Madrid "progressively to achieve economic and monetary union as provided for in the [Single European Act]" and endorsed the Delors report as a blueprint for action.[17] The European Council decided that Stage One would begin in July 1990 and that an intergovernmental conference would be convened to decide when and how to move to the next stages. Thatcher was completely outflanked. The only concession to Thatcher by the others was not to set a date for the launch of the conference. Moreover, under pressure from her finance and foreign ministers, Thatcher agreed at the Madrid summit that Britain would participate eventually in the exchange rate mechanism.

Mitterrand carried the momentum generated at the Madrid summit into the succeeding French presidency. The strategic dimension of EMU, looming in the background since Gorbachev's ascendancy in the Soviet Union, suddenly jumped to the forefront in the fall of 1989 as anti-Communist protests in East Germany grew increasingly vociferous. Instead of ordering military intervention, as Soviet leaders had done in similar situations in Hungary in 1956 and Prague in 1968, Gorbachev allowed the protesters to breach the Berlin Wall in November 1989.

With the prospect of imminent German unification, the geopolitical situation in Europe changed overnight. Clearly discomfited by the prospect of a united Germany, Mitterrand was more determined than ever to tie Germany tighter into the EC through the rapid achievement of EMU. He conveyed that message to Kohl and other Community leaders at an extraordinary summit in Paris only a week after the Berlin Wall came down. Mitterrand was irritated when Kohl outlined a ten-point program for German and European unification, in a speech to the German parliament at the end of November 1989, without consulting Paris. Despite Kohl's commitment in the speech to deeper European integration, Mitterrand sought proof of Kohl's intentions at the Strasbourg summit in December 1989.

Mitterrand's instinctive evocation of the German question strained relations between Paris and Bonn. Yet Kohl had no intention of changing the course of postwar German foreign policy. He was happy to cement the link between German unification and European integration at the Strasbourg summit. A key passage in the summit's conclusions proclaimed that German unification "should take place peacefully and democratically, in full respect of the relevant agreements and treaties . . . in a context of dialogue and East-West cooperation . . . [and] in the perspective of European integration."[18] More concretely, the connection between German unification and European integration manifested itself in the decision to hold an intergovernmental conference on EMU following the German elections in October 1990.[19] As Mitterrand announced after the summit, this represented "the sole objective link" in the European Council's deliberations between German and European unification.[20]

The Commission maintained the momentum toward EMU throughout 1990 with a series of pronouncements on the subject. Foremost among these was the Commission's much-quoted cost-benefit analysis of EMU. The report's title, *One Market, One Money*, reinforced the link between the single market program and EMU and became a mantra for advocates of a single currency.[21]

EMU was therefore well on track in the run-up to German unification, which merely confirmed the member states' commitment to hold an intergovernmental conference on the subject. The European Council decided in Dublin in June 1990 to begin the conference on EMU, and a separate conference on political union, in Rome in December 1990. Two months before the launch of the conferences, the European Council agreed to begin the second stage of EMU in January 1994. Thatcher alone dissented. Despite having agreed to bring sterling into the exchange rate mechanism in October 1990, she balked at committing herself further to EMU. Thatcher's obstructionism in Rome, and her resistance throughout the year to German unification, weakened her position within the government to the point that her cabinet colleagues ousted her as prime minister the following month.[22] Far from Thatcher's killing EMU, EMU helped to kill Thatcher politically.

■ The Changing Political Context

Peaceful revolution in Central and Eastern Europe, German unification, and, ultimately, the collapse of the Soviet Union were the most obvious manifestations of the changing political context of European integration in the late 1980s and early 1990s. In addition, implementation of the single market program and the momentum behind EMU changed the political situation within the EC. Questions about the accountability and legitimacy of EC institutions that had percolated beneath the surface for a number of years quickly came to the fore. Concern about the democratic deficit, initially expressed in the late 1970s at the time of the first direct elections to the Parliament, became more common. The impact of market liberalization and integration on people's everyday lives, and the likely impact of EMU on national sovereignty, raised troubling governance issues.

In Thatcher's view, democracy itself was at risk. The prime minister recoiled at what she saw as the increasing and excessive centralization of power in Brussels. The single market program was to have facilitated as much deregulation as possible at the national level and as much reregulation as necessary at the European level. Thatcher saw plenty of evidence of European reregulation but little evidence, outside Britain, of national deregulation. She loathed the Commission, with its unelected and barely accountable college and bloated bureaucracy adrift from the member states. In her view, Delors personified all that was wrong with Brussels. She thought him duplicitous, overweening, and unbearable. As in her dealings with most continental leaders, personal antipathy clouded political judgment.

There is no doubt that Delors *was* overbearing at times. He was openly ambitious for himself, the Commission, and the EC. Employing phrases frequently used in France but jarring to British ears, he advocated "the construction of Europe" and the creation of a "European social space." Delors announced as early as January 1985 that the Commission was "the engineer" of European integration.[23] He leveraged the single market program for political commitments to cohesion and social policy and made no secret of his ultimate objective: EMU. He was more influential than national leaders at meetings of the European Council and acted at summits of the seven most-industrialized countries (G7) as if he represented Europe.

Although the Commission's importance and profile rose along with Delors's prominence, Delors's success cost the institution dearly. The college increased in size in January 1986, following the accession of Portugal and Spain. Complaining that the college was already too large, Delors turned his back on the expanded Commission. Although the first Delors Commission (1985–1989) is generally credited with being the most successful in the EU's history, Delors rarely worked with all its members. Pascal Lamy, "the most forceful and feared" *chef de cabinet,* protected Delors from other commissioners as well as from Commission officials, thereby allowing Delors to focus on "public relations, negotiations with governmental leaders, and the conceptualization of new policy initiatives."[24] Other commissioners and senior officials resented the power of Delors's clique. The Commission as a whole became fractious and unmanageable as its responsibilities grew without a commensurate increase in its resources and with poor direction from the top. Delors greatly exacerbated the Commission's management deficit, which became glaringly obvious after his departure.

Despite its internal problems, outsiders viewed the Commission as an institution on the ascendant, firmly at the center of EC decisionmaking. Delors famously declared in July 1988, a month after his reappointment as Commission president, that in ten years' time, "80 percent of our economic legislation, and perhaps even our fiscal and social legislation as well, will be of Community origin."[25] That was too much for Thatcher, who used the opportunity of an invitation to speak at the College of Europe in Bruges, a bastion of Eurofederalism, to deliver a blistering rejoinder. Thatcher articulated an intergovernmentalist view of the EC and defended Britain's role in it. She peppered her address with barbed attacks against Delors and the Commission. The most evocative of these was the best-remembered part of her speech: "We have not successfully rolled back the frontiers of the state in Britain only to see them reimposed at a European level with a European superstate exercising a new dominance from Brussels."[26]

Thatcher's speech was music to the ears of British Euroskeptics, who formed the Bruges group in her honor. The British tabloid press, staunchly conservative and generally Euroskeptical, had a field day. By contrast, Thatcher's antics embarrassed moderates in Britain. The Labour Party, until recently committed to pulling Britain out of the EC, swung back in favor of membership in response to Delors's social policy agenda and in reaction against Thatcher's denunciation of Brussels. The Conservative Party, once a bastion of pro-Europeans, became increasingly divided between rabid Europhobes and traditional Europhiles.

Both Thatcher and Delors believed that history was on their side. Each of them interpreted events in Central and Eastern Europe in that light. For Thatcher, the collapse of communism and the Soviet system demonstrated the bankruptcy of Western European socialism and the futility of trying to centralize power in Brussels. For Delors, they demonstrated the appeal of European integration and the importance of consolidating supranational institutions. In June 1989 the European Council, of which Thatcher and Delors were members, welcomed the "profound changes" sweeping the Soviet bloc. Delors was gratified when the countries of Central and Eastern Europe expressed eagerness for EC membership. Surely countries so conscious of their newfound sovereignty and independence would not want to join the EC if they thought that it resembled the old Soviet Union? Nevertheless, Thatcher increasingly compared the EC to the Soviet Union. Her only comment on the membership aspirations of the Central and Eastern European countries was to express hope that enlargement would weaken the EC politically and derail prospects for EMU.

Thatcher strongly opposed German unification and the de facto enlargement of the EC to incorporate East Germany. An infamous outburst by Nicholas Ridley, a close friend and cabinet member, reflected Thatcher's thinking on Germany and Europe. In an interview published in July 1990, Ridley not only regretted the emergence of an "uppity" Germany but also denounced EMU as "a German racket."[27] By contrast, Delors endorsed German unification early and wholeheartedly. Mitterrand was equivocal but jumped on the bandwagon when he realized that unification was unstoppable. With strong U.S. support, Kohl seized the opportunity presented by Gorbachev's moderation and the breach of the Berlin Wall to unify Germany before a possible coup in the Soviet Union closed the window of opportunity. What to Thatcher (and Mitterrand) looked like unseemly haste was to Kohl an opportunistic response to unexpected developments. Kohl interpreted the Christian Democrats' victory in the first free elections in East Germany, in March 1990, as a mandate for immediate unification. At breakneck speed and with a generous exchange rate for the East German mark, he launched German monetary union in July 1990. Full unification followed three months later.[28]

The fact of a larger, unified Germany on the edge of an independent Central and Eastern Europe promised (or threatened) to change the character of the EC. United Germany accounted for 27 percent of the EC's GDP and, with 77 million people, 25 percent of the EC's population. If traditional European trade patterns, sundered throughout much of the twentieth century, reasserted themselves, Germany would become the hub of a vibrant, pan-European marketplace. Strategically, the center of gravity could shift within the EC from

West to East; from France to Germany. The Franco-German motor would be hard pressed to keep European integration moving in a direction fully congenial to France.

Events in Germany and farther east intensified member states' interest in institutional and policy reforms other than EMU. In a speech at the College of Europe in Bruges in October 1989, where Thatcher had issued her infamous antifederalist manifesto a year earlier, Delors linked the themes of reform in Central and Eastern Europe and reform in the EC. Calling for a huge "leap forward" to meet the economic and strategic challenges confronting the Community, Delors endorsed the idea of political union. Specifically, Delors proposed greater competence for the EC in a range of areas, including foreign policy and security, more efficient decisionmaking, and more subsidiarity (decentralization of power). He also advocated greater power of the Parliament as a means of increasing the EC's legitimacy.

Delors and other EC leaders pushed hard in early 1990 for reform of the EC's institutions and policies. Belgium was the first member state to submit a formal proposal for political union in March 1990. It called for greater democracy and increased efficiency in the EC and for a common foreign and security policy instead of the existing system of foreign policy cooperation.[29] The Parliament, which stood to gain from any effort to increase the EC's legitimacy, eagerly endorsed political union in a series of resolutions in 1990. The Italian government, traditionally a strong supporter of the Parliament and deeper European integration, threw itself behind the idea. Only Britain and Denmark remained unconvinced of the need for an intergovernmental conference on political union.

As with EMU, the essential impetus for political union came from France and Germany. Following the East German elections of March 1990, it was obvious to Mitterrand that German unification was inevitable. Hoping to anchor Germany further in the EC and patch up his differences with Kohl, Mitterrand suggested a Franco-German initiative on political union. Accordingly, Mitterrand and Kohl requested an extraordinary meeting of the European Council to discuss the possibility of convening an intergovernmental conference on political union alongside the conference on EMU. Kohl and Mitterrand did not define political union but identified four elements of it: greater democratic legitimacy, more efficient decisionmaking, coherent socioeconomic policies, and the development of a common foreign and security policy.[30]

Meeting in Dublin in April 1990, the European Council endorsed the idea of a second intergovernmental conference but, in deference to Thatcher, did not set a date for it. The European Council again took up the issue in June 1990, at the regularly scheduled Dublin summit. This time the other EC leaders agreed without dissent to open two conferences, on EMU and political union, in Rome in December 1990. Realizing the futility of objecting to it, Thatcher reluctantly went along with the European Council's declared aim of transforming the EC "from an entity mainly based on economic integration and political cooperation into a union of a political nature, including a common foreign and security policy."[31] Thatcher wanted EC member states to have a stronger international presence and impact but opposed further political integration.

While Italy, in the Council presidency in the second half of 1990, laid the groundwork for the launch of the two intergovernmental conferences, the EC confronted the administrative and economic challenges of incorporating East Germany into the fold. A special group of commissioners, led by Martin Bangemann, Germany's senior commissioner, met weekly to provide overall direction. The achievement of German unity, in October 1990, raised a host of legal, financial, institutional, and policy issues for the EC. Contrary to Mitterrand's expectation only one year previously, German unification preceded EMU. Nevertheless, Kohl, secure in office after winning the first all-German general election in October 1990, seemed more committed than ever to achieving not only EMU but political union as well.

Thatcher's ouster in November 1990, on the eve of the intergovernmental conferences, seemed a fitting prelude to a further acceleration of European integration. Delors was gleeful, although as the *Economist* noted, Thatcher's removal robbed the EC of "the grit around which the other eleven formed their Euro-pearl."[32] Delors need not have worried. John Major was every bit as intransigent as his illustrious predecessor, except that he obstructed Community business with a smile.

Thatcher's departure coincided with the high point of Delors's power. Far from growing more influential during the intergovernmental conferences, Delors began to fall from grace in 1990. Other national leaders, not only Thatcher, grew resentful of his political ascendancy and high public profile. Even sympathetic member states felt that the Commission was exceeding its authority and getting too big for its boots. Although he remained an important player during the rest of his presidency, Delors must have sensed that the short era of unbridled Commission activism was at an end. Paradoxically, the Commission's power peaked just as the EC embarked on the road to European Union.

▓ The Maastricht Treaty

In December 1990, member states launched the intergovernmental conferences on EMU and political union.[33] The conferences concluded a year later, at the Maastricht summit, with agreement not only to revise the existing treaties but also to promulgate a new treaty on European Union. There was consensus at the outset of the conferences on the meaning of EMU, but not on how to organize or achieve it. The subject of political union was more amorphous. Nobody thought that it meant the establishment of a unitary political system, a federal United States of Europe. The most that ardent Eurofederalists hoped for was a further transfer of responsibility for various policy areas from the national to the European level, more supranational authority for the Commission and the Parliament, and the extension of qualified majority voting in the Council of Ministers. In general, they sought to extend the EC's already apparent federal features. There was little doubt that the conferences would transform the EC into the EU, but the form and substance of the union were still up for grabs.

The 1985–1986 intergovernmental conference that resulted in the Single European Act was a precedent for the conduct of the 1990–1991 conferences. At the regular working level, the foreign ministers' personal representatives (mostly the member states' permanent representatives in Brussels) negotiated political union, and senior officials from national central banks and finance ministries negotiated EMU. At the next level, the foreign and finance ministers, meeting on the margins of their respective councils, reviewed progress and negotiated some of the politically more contentious issues. Finally, national leaders tackled the most difficult and sensitive questions at meetings of the European Council. At all levels negotiators met informally, bilaterally or multilaterally, on the margins of conference sessions or on other occasions to move the process along.

EC leaders hoped to wrap up the conferences at their summit in Luxembourg in June 1991. In the event, the conferences continued for another six months, ending in Maastricht in December. Apart from the ceremonial opening of the conferences in Rome in December 1990, conference sessions took place during the presidencies of Luxembourg and the Netherlands, the same countries that had presided over the conference that preceded the Single European Act. Many of the officials and politicians participating in the conferences had participated also in the 1985–1986 conference, thus contributing to a strong esprit de corps among the negotiators. As in the earlier conference, the Commission participated at all levels in the 1990–1991 conferences, although it lacked the authority to block a final agreement.

Procedurally, the 1990–1991 conferences differed from the earlier conference in one important respect. Whereas the Dooge Committee had prepared the ground for the Single European Act and the Delors Committee prepared the ground for EMU, no preparatory committee prepared the ground for political union. That caused some confusion early in the conference about the scope of political union and the precise agenda of the negotiations. It may also have resulted in the conference's lasting longer than the negotiators intended it to.

EMU

As Dyson and Featherstone observed: "The Delors report provided a vital basis of technical legitimacy for EMU and set the key parameters for the subsequent treaty negotiations."[34] Nevertheless, there was much for the conference to decide. Sensitive to pressure from the German Central Bank, German negotiators insisted that responsibility for monetary policy at the European level reside in a single, independent institution with the unambiguous, statutory mandate of maintaining price stability. In other words, the European Central Bank (ECB) should replicate the German Central Bank. The German Central Bank also warned against establishing a European central bank at the beginning of Stage Two, before the launch of the single currency. Finally, German negotiators insisted on the importance of economic convergence between prospective EMU participants, even if it meant that not every member state would be able to participate in Stage Three from the outset. Weary of battling Delors in Brussels and Kohl in Bonn, German Central Bank president Pöhl resigned in 1991, well before the end of his second term.

Hans Tietmeyer, his successor, was an equally aggressive defender of the central bank's interests. Throughout 1991, Pöhl and Tietmeyer pressured the government by alerting the public to the implications of EMU, pointing out that other European countries lacked Germany's historical fear of inflation and warning that the proposed ECB might not be as rigorously independent of political control as the German Central Bank was. The German government got the message and held the line in the conference, although the German public only woke up to the import of EMU on the eve of the Maastricht summit, thanks largely to a banner headline in the mass-circulation *Bild* newspaper that proclaimed "The End of the D-Mark."

France had different institutional and policy preferences for EMU. Lacking a tradition of central bank independence, France wanted to put the ECB under some form of political control but conceded the impossibility of doing so well before the conference began. Indeed, as part of the bargain on EMU, France agreed to make its own central bank independent. France strongly urged the establishment of the ECB at the start of a relatively short Stage Two rather than at the start of Stage Three, as Germany advocated. According to the French, a functioning ECB and a strict timetable for the introduction of the single currency would encourage economic convergence among member states. As the ECB could not perform its main function until the beginning of Stage Three, the Germans feared that establishing it sooner would undermine its purpose and prestige.

Luxembourg, in the Council presidency and therefore chairing the conference, submitted a draft treaty text on EMU in May 1991. It included a relatively insubstantial Stage Two, in which the Committee of Central Bank Governors would try to coordinate national monetary positions. The ECB would be established on the eve of Stage Three, but the European Monetary Institute, a forerunner of the ECB, would be established at the beginning of Stage Two. The purpose of the monetary institute, which would subsume the Committee of Central Bank Governors, was to promote economic and monetary policy cooperation among member states and prepare procedurally for the launch of Stage Three. The Luxembourg draft also addressed the contentious questions of convergence criteria, the possibility of a two-tier system within the EU of EMU participants and nonparticipants, and whether member states could opt out of the single currency.

Negotiators in the conference accepted that a degree of convergence was imperative in order to launch Stage Three. That raised an obvious question: Should Stage Three begin before all member states met the convergence criteria, thereby creating a two-tier EU? Moreover, should countries be allowed to opt out and not participate in Stage Three, even if they met the convergence criteria? Before the conference opened, it was widely accepted that, because all member states could not meet relatively strict convergence criteria in a timely fashion, Stage Three would indeed begin with less than a full complement of EU member states. The unspoken presumption was that Greece, Portugal, and Spain would be in the second tier, and maybe Italy as well. Potential second-tier countries fretted about the political impact of not participating in Stage Three from the outset. Fear of marginalization became a major inducement for Italy and Spain, two large and proud member states, to make the first cut for full EMU membership.

The finance ministers, who discussed the Luxembourg draft in May 1991, agreed that a two-tier system was inevitable. A general consensus emerged that any member state capable of meeting the convergence criteria but preferring not to participate in Stage Three would have the right to opt out. Just as no member state would be allowed to prevent others from moving to Stage Three, no member state would be forced to adopt the single currency. In concrete terms, that meant that Britain and Denmark would not block movement toward Stage Three, in which they would not be obliged to participate. Major described the opt-out provision of the proposed treaty as "a clause that we have secured enabling us to opt-in. If we wish, when we wish, and in the conditions that we judge to be right."[35]

A formula emerged in the conference whereby Stage Three would be launched as early as January 1997 if a majority of member states met the convergence criteria; otherwise it would commence in January 1999 with however many member states met the criteria. There were intense negotiations about the criteria themselves. The negotiators eventually went along with German demands for seemingly strict criteria: an average inflation rate not exceeding by more than 1.5 percent that of the three best-performing member states, a budget deficit of less than 3 percent of GDP and a public debt ratio not exceeding 60 percent of GDP, an annual nominal long-term interest rate not exceeding by more than 2 percent that of the three best-performing member states, and participation of a country's currency within the normal margins of the exchange rate mechanism for at least two years, without devaluations.

As envisioned in the Delors report, member states agreed in the conference that an independent European System of Central Banks, consisting of the ECB and national central banks, would be established on the eve of Stage Three. The ECB's governing council, made up of a six-member executive board (appointed by the European Council) and the governors of the national central banks, would be the highest decisionmaking body, with overall responsibility for monetary policy, foreign exchange operations, management of member states' official foreign reserves, and the smooth operation of the payments system. The main objective of the System of Central Banks, like that of the German Central Bank, was to maintain price stability.

The negotiations on EMU were almost complete before the Maastricht summit, which dealt largely with contentious issues of political union. Nevertheless, a link existed between both sets of negotiations, especially for Germany, which had the most to lose from EMU and the most to gain from political union. By agreeing to EMU, Germany would be giving up its much-loved mark and surrendering control over national monetary policy and de facto control over European monetary policy through the European Monetary System. With political union, Germany stood to gain a familiar federal-like system of European governance in which controversial domestic issues, such as asylum policy and defense, might be resolved and a more powerful Parliament, with a large German contingent, would play a greater role. Frustrated by the recalcitrance not only of Britain but also of France and other supposedly integrationist member states, Kohl threatened before the Maastricht summit to veto EMU without a far-reaching agreement on political union. Although it lacked credibility, Kohl's threat indicated the seriousness with which he took the negotiations on political union.

Political Union

Unlike EMU, political union covered a large number of disparate institutional and policy issues. They ranged from the extension of qualified majority voting in the Council, to the role of the Parliament, to social policy, to the transformation of European Political Cooperation into the common foreign and security policy. Member state positions varied widely. Britain was in a minority of one in a number of cases, but was by no means the only member state that doggedly argued its case. Whereas the April 1991 Luxembourg draft text on EMU contained about 80 percent of the agreement eventually approved at the Maastricht summit in December, much of the agreement on political union was still undecided as the conference came to an end.

What kind of entity would the EU be? One of the most contentious questions was whether to describe it as a federation. The Luxembourg presidency included the phrase "federal goal" in its draft treaty, but Britain would have none of it. Douglas Hurd, the foreign secretary, rejected "the implications which, in the English language, the phrase 'federal goal' carries."[36] The English word *federal* was perfectly acceptable to Americans, but not to British conservatives, despite their close affinity with the United States. A British Europarliamentarian explained the problem: "On the continent [federalism] is a harmless label, neither exciting nor controversial. In Britain, it carries connotations of unspeakable disloyalty and unmentionable perversity."[37]

At the Luxembourg summit in June 1991, Major denounced the draft treaty's reference to a "federal goal." To his intense irritation, the incoming Dutch presidency changed the phrase only to "federal vocation." As the conference intensified, Major escalated his campaign to excise the "F-word." The other Community leaders finally agreed shortly before the Maastricht summit to drop "federal" from the treaty in return for some British concessions in key policy areas. "What does the word matter, as long as we have the actual thing?" Delors wondered.[38] It mattered a lot to Major because conservative Euroskeptics were watching his every move. Prominent among them was Thatcher, now a backbencher in the House of Commons and a bitter opponent of any concessions to Brussels.

The row over the structure of the EU seemed equally arcane, yet it dominated the conference in mid-1991. Sensitive to British and Danish determination to restrict the proposed common foreign and security policy and cooperation on justice and home affairs to intergovernmental decisionmaking, the Luxembourg presidency proposed that the EU consist of three pillars: the Rome Treaty (pillar one), the common foreign and security policy (pillar two), and justice and home affairs (pillar three). Member states were divided on the issue. Most wanted the common foreign and security policy and justice and home affairs to operate on an intergovernmental basis, but felt that the EU should have a unitary structure, what the Belgian foreign minister later called a "tree with branches" rather than a "temple with pillars."[39] The Rome Treaty, which already included a variety of decisionmaking mechanisms, could incorporate the common foreign and security policy and justice and home affairs as well. Delors invested heavily in the discussion about the EU's architecture, fearing that the proposed pillar system would cut the Commission and the Parliament off from the common foreign and security policy and justice and home affairs, which is exactly what some member states wanted.

Despite an agreement at the Luxembourg summit in June 1991 to establish the three pillars, the new Dutch presidency attempted to restore the EU's unitary structure. Major traveled to The Hague in September 1991 to caution the Dutch to stick to the Luxembourg formula. Other member states sympathized with the Dutch position but were unwilling to engage in a pitched battle with Britain over the EU's architecture. The Dutch went ahead anyway and produced a new draft treaty with a unitary structure. At a foreign ministers' meeting at the end of September, only Belgium and the Commission supported the text that the Dutch prime minister had earlier proclaimed "acceptable to all our partners."[40] The near-unanimous rejection of the new draft treaty on "Black Monday" was a serious setback for the Dutch presidency and its supporters. It put an end to debate at the conference about the EU's structure and ensured that the treaty agreed to in Maastricht included the three pillars.

The first pillar. In addition to its provisions on EMU, the Maastricht Treaty included a number of important revisions of the Rome Treaty that fell under the EU's first pillar. The treaty's main institutional reforms involved a modest extension of qualified majority voting in the Council and a major extension of the Parliament's legislative authority. The aim was to increase decisionmaking efficiency while enhancing the EC's democratic legitimacy. Member states were well aware that the Single European Act had deepened the so-called democratic deficit, despite its extension of the Parliament's legislative role under the cooperation procedure. In a measure of public dissatisfaction with the EC and lack of enthusiasm for the Parliament, the turnout in the elections of June 1989 was smaller than in the previous elections, in 1984 and 1979. Nevertheless, the Parliament and its supporters, notably Belgium, Germany, and Italy, lobbied during the intergovernmental conference to increase the legislative power of the Parliament.

Concern about a widening democratic deficit undermined the resistance of member states unsympathetic to the Parliament. These ranged from Britain, which opposed extending the Parliament's power for reasons of national sovereignty, to Ireland, which disliked the Parliament because of the country's small representation there. Following protracted negotiations, member states agreed to extend the Parliament's power considerably but not as much as the Parliament wanted. Thus the Maastricht Treaty switched the decisionmaking basis of a number of policy areas from the original consultation procedure to cooperation (right to a second reading) and switched some others, notably relating to the internal market, from cooperation to the new co-decision procedure (shared legislative authority with the Council). As a result, cooperation became the most important procedure used in EU legislative decisionmaking, although the co-decision procedure was the most far-reaching in terms of the Parliament's powers.

The co-decision procedure elevated the Parliament almost to the legislative equal of the Council. Through an extremely complicated mechanism, it gave the Parliament the right to a third reading of draft legislation and established a conciliation committee in which representatives of the Council and the Parliament could attempt to agree on a compromise text at the final stage. Many Europarliamentarians complained that co-decision gave the Parliament only a limited right of rejection rather than a positive right of approval, whereas many members of the Council and its secretariat complained that the procedure was too complicated for the Parliament to master. Just as it amended its rules of procedure in 1986 to make the most of the cooperation procedure, however, the Parliament soon introduced procedural changes to exploit the potential of codecision without further impairing the efficiency of the EU's notoriously cumbersome decisionmaking apparatus.

The outcome of the conference was satisfactory for the Parliament in other respects as well. For instance, the Maastricht Treaty extended the assent procedure to all international agreements that set up institutions or had major financial implications. Although excluded from the treaty's intergovernmental pillars, the Parliament exploited its enhanced power of assent to play a limited role in the conduct of the common foreign and security policy. The treaty also introduced the assent procedure into a number of internal EU affairs, such as the creation of a uniform procedure for elections to the Parliament, adoption of provisions for EU citizenship, residency rights, and use of the structural funds. The treaty extended significantly the Parliament's oversight role by giving Parliament a right of inquiry, a more formal right of petition, and the right to appoint an ombudsman to field complaints about maladministration in the EU's institutions. Finally, the treaty obliged member states to consult the Parliament before nominating a new Commission president and obliged a new Commission to win a vote of approval in the Parliament.

Despite complaining about the outcome, the Parliament emerged from the conference a major institutional winner. By contrast, the Commission was lucky not to have had its formal powers seriously curtailed. In a sign of the backlash against the Commission, a number of member states raised the possibility of ending the Commission's exclusive right to initiate legislation and allowing the Council to amend Commission proposals by qualified majority instead of unanimity. As Delors told the Parliament in April 1991, changes of that kind would have gravely undermined supranationalism and turned the Commission into "a sort of general secretariat" for the Council.[41]

Apart from institutional reforms intended to increase accountability and legitimacy, member states added a number of treaty provisions to assuage popular concerns and give the EU wide appeal. Chief among these was a clause enshrining the principle of subsidiarity, which stated that the EU should only involve itself in issues that could best be dealt with at the European rather than the national level. Precisely because it was a statement of principle, subsidiarity was notoriously difficult to define in practice, as the EU would discover in due course. The Commission interpreted subsidiarity as a self-denying ordinance, whereas the less integration-minded member states used it as an opportunity to roll back intrusive or expensive Community policies.

Felipe González wanted to leave his mark on the Maastricht Treaty by including in it the concept of EU citizenship. Other member states agreed on condition that it not conflict in any way with national citizenship.[42] In an effort to make the EU seem more relevant and useful to ordinary people, the treaty redefined or expanded Community competence in a number of policy areas, such as education, culture, the environment, and consumer protection. As in the conference that led to the Single European Act, González championed the cause of cohesion, this time arguing that moves toward EMU justified an additional redistribution of money to the poorer member states. Once again he succeeded. As a result, cohesion became a major objective of the EU, and member states promised to set up a Cohesion Fund by the end of December 1993 to contribute to environmental and transport projects, mostly in countries with a per capita GDP less than 90 percent of the Community average, and a program designed to achieve convergence.

Social policy was the final stumbling block at the Maastricht summit. Delors and eleven national leaders wanted a package of social policy provisions called the "social chapter" included in the treaty. This would have extended qualified majority voting and given a greater role to the "social partners" (employers' and employees' representatives). Major adamantly refused. The issue almost derailed the conference and was resolved only late in the evening of the second day of the Maastricht summit when the eleven agreed to remove the contentious chapter from the treaty. Instead, they attached a protocol to the treaty along the lines of the proposed chapter, allowing them to use EU institutions and decisionmaking procedures to develop social policy without British participation.

The second pillar. The common foreign and security policy was one of the trickiest issues in the conference. Foreign and security policy was at the core of national sovereignty. Whereas member states were willing to pool responsibility for monetary policy, they were not about to establish a truly *common* foreign and security policy, let alone a truly *common* defense policy. There was no impetus to share sovereignty on security and foreign policy as there was on economic and monetary policy. Member states had markedly different foreign policy interests, orientations, and traditions. The most that they could aspire to achieve was a high degree of coordination.

As the EC's international profile rose, thanks to the single market program and moves toward EMU, the gap between external economic and political influence widened. For instance, events in Central and Eastern Europe called for a concerted Community response. At the July 1989 G7 summit in Paris, the United States asked the Commission to orchestrate Western aid to Hungary and Poland and later to all of Central and Eastern Europe. The Commission happily obliged, but the EC did not have a common foreign policy toward the region. Member states coordinated their positions through European Political Cooperation but lacked joint instruments of diplomatic persuasion.

The discrepancy between the EC's external economic policy and traditional foreign policy became even more apparent in the run-up to the conference following the Iraqi invasion of Kuwait in August 1990. The EC reacted promptly and forcefully to the crisis in the Gulf: within two days it embargoed oil from Iraq and Iraqi-occupied Kuwait. Member states used European Political Cooperation to issue a joint condemnation of Iraq's action. Beyond that, they could do little together. France convened a meeting of the Western European Union in Paris on August 1990 to discuss a possible military response, but the Western European Union did not include every EC member state. Italy reached the obvious conclusion and called for a merger of the Western European Union and EC. Meeting in Rome in October 1990, the European Council "noted a consensus to go beyond the present limits in regard to security," but could not agree on the scope, content, and procedure of the common foreign and security policy or the Western European Union's relationship with the putative EU.[43]

Any discussion of defense inevitably led to a discussion of NATO. France wanted to develop an EU defense capability in part to strengthen the European pillar of NATO; Britain was more sensitive to U.S. concerns; and Germany leaned intellectually toward the French position but politically toward the British position. The United States made its disapproval of a European defense identity or capability known early in the conference, thereby nixing discussion of the issue. Denmark, Greece, and Ireland, who opposed the militarization of the EU, breathed a sigh of relief. U.S. concern about the impact of a European defense policy on NATO, or on U.S. hegemony in NATO, got the EU off the hook. Even without U.S. interference, member states would have had difficulty agreeing on such far-reaching changes.[44]

The formula eventually included in the Maastricht Treaty allowed for "the eventual framing of a common defense policy, which might in time lead to a common defense." The treaty also recognized the Western European Union as "an integral part of the development" of the EU, which could ask the Western European Union "to elaborate and implement the [EU's] decisions and actions . . . [that] have defense implications."[45] At the same time the more Atlanticist member states were careful to reassure the United States that nothing in the treaty could be construed as undermining NATO or the role of the United States in it. In a separate development, the Western European Union members that were also in the EC agreed at the end of the Maastricht summit to admit Greece to full Western European Union membership. Although not specifically an EC issue, Greece had made membership in the Western European Union one of its main objectives during the conference in an effort to distinguish itself further from fellow NATO member but non–Western European Union member Turkey.

Just as the Gulf War during the early stages of the conference demonstrated the limits of the EU's foreign and security policy, the disintegration of

Yugoslavia later in the conference demonstrated the difficulty of devising joint EU positions on tricky international issues. Like the United States, EC member states cautioned secessionist states not to break away from the Yugoslav federation at the end of the Cold War. When Slovenia and Croatia did so anyway and the Yugoslav army intervened in Slovenia, the EC immediately sent a mission to mediate between both sides. Hostilities broke out just as the European Council was convening in Luxembourg in June 1991. The troika of EC foreign ministers (from the current, preceding, and succeeding presidencies) left Luxembourg for a dramatic overnight peace mission to Belgrade. Reflecting the EC's self-confidence and naïveté at that stage of the Yugoslav conflict, one member of the troika observed that "when we went on this mission . . . [we] really had the feeling that the Yugoslav authorities thought that they were talking to Europe, not just to a country incidentally coming by but to an entity whose voice counts."[46] Commenting on the EC's apparent coming of age, the foreign minister of Luxembourg, then in the Council presidency, declared that "this is the hour of Europe, not of the Americans."[47]

The foreign ministers soon regretted their rash statements. Fighting in Slovenia ended quickly with the withdrawal of the Yugoslav army. But a savage war broke out in Croatia as the Serb-dominated federal forces attempted to bring the breakaway republic to heel. The new round of hostilities unleashed a level of brutality last seen in Europe during World War II. The EC had a limited array of instruments at its disposal to try to end the fighting, including economic sanctions and inducements, and diplomatic recognition or isolation of the warring parties. The EC was not in a position to take military action, although individual member states could do so either on their own, under United Nations auspices, or as part of a NATO or Western European Union operation. Even if the EC had had the authority to act militarily, member states would have been able to undertake only limited peacekeeping operations.

The EC convened a peace conference in The Hague in September 1991 for leaders of the warring factions. But the EC was unable to exert much pressure on either side. The EC's potential diplomatic leverage came under internal strain when Germany began to press for recognition of Croatia and Slovenia in the fall of 1991. Other member states fretted about Germany's newfound international assertiveness and feared that diplomatic recognition of the breakaway republics would inflame the situation. Matters came to a head at a Council meeting in mid-December. After ten hours of fierce debate, the foreign ministers agreed to draw up criteria for recognition of new states in Yugoslavia and the disintegrating Soviet Union. The other member states succumbed to German pressure and recognized Croatia and Slovenia in January 1992.

The deterioration of the Yugoslav situation and the row within the EC about diplomatic recognition coincided with the Maastricht summit. Despite the obvious need for a robust foreign and security policy, member states approached the subject guardedly in light of events in Yugoslavia. Germany's support for Croatian independence jogged memories of the Nazi regime's support for the Croatian Fascists fifty years earlier and sparked an ugly media frenzy in France. The mood during the closing stages of the negotiations on political union was not conducive to the development of an EC defense identity, let alone a fully functioning foreign and security policy.

The section of the Maastricht Treaty dealing with foreign and security policy was therefore relatively restrained. It outlined the policy's objectives, called for "systematic cooperation" between member states, and provided for "joint action" by the EU in the foreign and security policy realm. In a big departure in an intergovernmental area, the treaty allowed for majority voting to implement joint actions, but only if governments first agreed unanimously on the principle of joint action. That clumsy compromise undermined the effectiveness of joint actions and reflected continuing sensitivity among member states about the common foreign and security policy. Aware of the unsatisfactory nature of the new arrangement, member states agreed in Maastricht to convene another intergovernmental conference in five years' time to review progress on foreign, security, and defense policy cooperation.

The third pillar. Because of the provisions in the single market program for the free movement of people and fears in Western Europe that the end of the Cold War would trigger a huge influx of migrants from Central and Eastern Europe, issues such as immigration, asylum, and control of cross-border crime were high on the agenda of the conference that produced the Maastricht Treaty. Member states were already addressing these issues in a number of ways. As long before as the mid-1970s, for instance, justice ministers and officials had formed the so-called Trevi group to facilitate cooperation on terrorism and cross-border crime.

At the dawn of the single market program, in 1985, the original member states, minus Italy, reached agreement in Schengen, a small town in Luxembourg, on steps to expedite the removal of border checkpoints. The so-called Schengen arrangement became a laboratory for the eventual abolition of barriers to cross-border travel within the EC. It covered everything from police cooperation, to the rights of "guestworkers" (long-term workers in the EC, mostly from Turkey and North Africa), to fiscal fraud. Most of the other member states subsequently signed on to Schengen, but Britain and Ireland remained resolutely aloof (Britain because it wanted to retain complete control of its own borders; Ireland because it formed part of a free travel zone with Britain).

Responding to a massive increase in the numbers of immigrants and asylum seekers in Western Europe in the early 1980s, justice ministers established the Ad Hoc Immigration Group of Senior Officials in 1986. Although confined to EC member states and served by the Council secretariat, the Ad

Hoc Group operated on an informal, intergovernmental basis. Its most notable accomplishment was to draft the 1990 Dublin Convention on the handling of asylum applications submitted in the EC.

The fall of the Berlin Wall and the anticipated arrival in Western Europe of hordes of Central and Eastern Europeans focused member states' minds on the all-encompassing area of justice and home affairs. The intergovernmental conference on political union gave governments an opportunity to bring immigration and asylum, and police and judicial cooperation, into the putative EU. Given national sensitivities on internal security issues, however, they decided to confine justice and home affairs to a separate, intergovernmental pillar, with minimum Commission involvement.[48]

Thus the treaty's third pillar would cover a number of areas of common interest: asylum, immigration, control of external borders, customs cooperation, cooperation in combating drugs and fraud, judicial cooperation in civil and criminal matters, and police cooperation. Realizing the centrality of these issues to economic integration, member states included a provision in the treaty making it possible down the road to move some of these areas into the first (supranational) pillar. The Schengen agreement remained outside, but closely related to, the treaty's provisions on justice and home affairs.

Outcome

Whereas in 1985–1986 there was one intergovernmental conference but talk of two final acts (one on regular treaty reform and the other on foreign policy cooperation), in 1990–1991 there were two conferences but agreement from the outset to have only one treaty. The treaty, worked out in the waning hours of the Maastricht summit, was a notable achievement. Within four years of reemerging on the agenda of European integration, EMU was a primary objective of the new EU. Member states committed themselves to striving for a single monetary policy and a single currency, although not all of them would participate in it.

The treaty's intergovernmental pillar on foreign and security policy was less a radical departure than a continuation of the member states' efforts since the early 1970s to coordinate their foreign policies. The change of name from European Political Cooperation to the common foreign and security policy was more portentous than the likely impact of the new instruments outlined in the second pillar. The third pillar, on justice and home affairs, also reflected continuity rather than change, although member states promised in the treaty to cooperate more closely than hitherto on immigration, asylum, policing, and judicial affairs.

The treaty's extension of Community competence into several new areas, increase in the scope of qualified majority voting, expansion of the cooperation procedure, and introduction of co-decision had major implications for the

EU. The European level of governance became increasingly entrenched, with the Council and the Parliament playing key legislative roles. Despite its political decline, the Commission remained a key actor in the EU. The establishment of a Committee of the Regions symbolized the member states' recognition of another level of governance in the EU system.

The treaty included another important innovation: the institutionalization of differentiated integration. Social policy included an opt-out for Britain. Not every member state would participate in Stage Three of EMU, at least at the outset, and Britain could choose not to participate at all. Differentiated integration had long been mooted as a solution to the recalcitrant member states' unwillingness to go along with new policy initiatives. Now, for the first time, the EU enshrined the principle and endorsed the practice of member states either choosing or not being obliged to participate in core activities.

There were no absolute winners or losers in the intergovernmental conferences. The appeal of the final agreement was that each member state could claim victory even though no member state got everything that it wanted. France was happy to have EMU but disliked many of its characteristics. Germany would have preferred stronger provisions on political union. Denmark favored the EU's emphasis on environmental policy but felt that other provisions encroached too much on national sovereignty. Ireland was happy to dip into the promised Cohesion Fund but worried about the domestic political implications of the common foreign and security policy. Although disliking most of the treaty, Major could claim on returning from the summit that last-minute agreement on the social protocol represented "game, set, and match" for Britain.[49] The other EU leaders thought Major's sporting metaphor amusing. After all, they made similar claims to their home audiences about the significance of the treaty, but with less fanfare.

Ratification

The Maastricht Treaty engendered greater public interest than did the Single European Act, not least because European integration had progressed so far and so fast during the intervening years. Inevitably, EMU was the main thing on people's minds. Europeans were generally uneasy about the prospect of losing their national currencies and adopting a common currency. Nevertheless, national governments were confident that ratification would proceed smoothly. When they signed the treaty at a special ceremony in Maastricht in February 1992, foreign ministers confidently predicted that the treaty would be ratified in time to come into force in January 1993.

Denmark and Ireland were the only two member states constitutionally obliged to hold a referendum on ratification. The Danish vote was scheduled first, in June 1992. Danes were notoriously ambivalent about the EC. Despite rumblings of discontent in the run-up to the referendum, most observers, in

Denmark and abroad, presumed that the result would be positive. To everybody's surprise, Danes voted by a narrow margin—50.7 to 49.3 percent—to reject the treaty. The result sent shock waves throughout the EU.

There were many reasons why so many Danes voted "no." Some were specific to the treaty; others pertained to the EU generally. Some were rational; others not. They ranged from vague concerns about EMU, to fear of united Germany's influence in the EU, to worries about the erosion of Denmark's high environmental standards. Many Danes rightly complained about the incomprehensibility of the treaty, although few of them tried to read it. Despite serious dissatisfaction throughout Denmark with the country's EC membership and with the terms of the treaty, the result could have gone either way. After all, fewer than 30,000 votes separated the two sides.

The fact that the narrow majority was on the "no" side confronted the EU's leadership with a serious problem. Unless ratified in all member states the treaty could not be implemented. National governments were loath to renegotiate the treaty but realized that they would have to offer special concessions to the Danish electorate in order to secure a positive result in a second referendum. More broadly, Community leaders grasped that Denmark's rejection of the treaty was symptomatic of widespread popular dissatisfaction with the institutions and procedures of European integration. Indeed, the Danish referendum result soon became synonymous with the democratic deficit.

Ireland's endorsement of the Maastricht Treaty in a referendum held only two weeks later was cold comfort for EC leaders, who presumed that Ireland's support for European integration was unwavering. The Irish result—69 to 31 percent—seemed a healthy endorsement of the treaty. Yet the turnout in the referendum (57 percent) was low by Irish standards. Having warned the electorate that the country would lose billions of pounds in EC assistance in the event of a "no" vote, the prime minister hailed the result as "a tribute to the maturity of the Irish people."[50] Yet the most striking aspect of the referendum, as other Community leaders surely noted, was that so many Irish voters either abstained or voted against.

Meeting in Lisbon at the end of June 1992, EC leaders sought to appease Danish voters and reassure European citizens by fleshing out the principle of subsidiarity. The Commission immediately dropped a number of proposals that did not warrant legislation at the European level. EC leaders also redoubled their efforts to make the EU's operations more open, accessible, and comprehensible.

A major test of the treaty's survivability came in September 1992, when France held a referendum on the treaty. The French parliament had already ratified the treaty, but Mitterrand called for a popular endorsement of it nonetheless. Mitterrand was certain of a positive result, hoping thereby to turn the tide against Euroskepticism. He also had domestic political motives (he wanted to deepen divisions in the conservative opposition over the treaty).

Mitterrand miscalculated badly. He split his own Socialist Party as much as he did the conservatives and almost caused a rejection of the treaty in France. Taking victory for granted, the government did not begin to campaign in earnest until after the August holidays, whereas the opposition mobilized early against the treaty. Advocates of a "no" vote exploited popular concerns about German unification, monetary union, and the EC's lamentable efforts to halt the fighting in Bosnia, the latest and most violent Balkan battleground. Having staked the reputation of his presidency on achieving deeper European integration, Mitterrand risked a humiliating repudiation by an electorate disgruntled with his domestic policies and unimpressed by his international escapades.

In the final, desperate days of the campaign, both sides used outlandish arguments to try to win over wavering voters. The normally staid *Le Monde* warned on the eve of the referendum that a "no" vote would "be for France and for Europe the greatest catastrophe since Hitler's coming to power."[51] Opponents characterized the treaty as a sellout to Germany, a surrender of French independence and the end of *grandeur*. Both sides invoked the legacy of de Gaulle. It was easier for opponents than proponents of the treaty to do so, but the government's point man in the campaign managed to claim that a "no" vote "would destroy the collective work of Charles de Gaulle, Georges Pompidou, Valéry Giscard d'Estaing, and François Mitterrand."[52]

The result of the referendum was a small majority in favor of ratification: the vote was 51.05 percent for and 48.95 percent against, with a turnout of 70 percent. As a seasoned politician, Mitterrand knew that the fact of a majority mattered more than its size. But his domestic and European strategy backfired. The French referendum brought the treaty into further disrepute. There could be no doubt now about the extent of public dissatisfaction with the treaty in France and in other member states.

The Danish and French results emboldened Euroskeptics in Britain, whose influence in the governing Conservative Party was disproportionate to their numbers. Major won the general election of April 1992 not on the strength of the government's record but because a majority of the electorate still distrusted the Labour Party to form a government. Faced with a virulent Euroskeptical wing in his party and a rabidly anti-EU popular press, Major procrastinated. The currency crisis of September 1992, which lost the Bank of England billions of pounds and prompted the government to pull sterling out of the exchange rate mechanism of the EMS, soured British opinion on the treaty. Instead of bringing it up for ratification in the House of Commons before the stipulated deadline of December 1992, Major decided to wait until after the second Danish referendum, scheduled for May 1993.

Ironically, Britain was in the presidency in the second half of 1992 when the ratification crisis was at its height. A big industrial dispute overshadowed the special summit in Birmingham, in October 1992, to discuss the treaty's prospects. Other leaders despaired of Major's political acumen and ability to steer the EC out of its current crisis. Earlier, the Danish government had produced a lengthy white paper outlining various options for a solution to the ratification crisis. That formed the basis for a number of Danish opt-outs from the terms of the Maastricht Treaty, which the European Council approved in Edinburgh in December 1992. Chief among these were Danish nonparticipation in the third stage of EMU and in foreign policy decisions with defense implications.

Also in Edinburgh, the European Council discussed subsidiarity on the basis of reports from the Council and the Commission. Thus the summit conclusions contained a lengthy section providing guidelines for the application of subsidiarity and giving examples of legislative proposals that met the key criteria of "need for action and intensity (proportionality) of action" at the European level. The European Council called for an interinstitutional agreement (among the Council, Commission, and Parliament) on the concrete application of subsidiarity. In a related move, the European Council adopted a number of specific measures to promote transparency and openness. The most dramatic of these was a decision to televise the opening session of Council meetings and publish the record of formal votes taken in the Council.[53]

The European Council's desperation demonstrated the profound political impact of the ratification crisis. Member states and the Commission had been aware since the mid-1980s of the existence of a democratic deficit but had addressed the problem only in piecemeal fashion. The ratification crisis, and later the accession of Nordic countries with a strong tradition of open government, finally galvanized the EU to tackle the problem, going beyond merely increasing the power of the Parliament. By then it may have been too late, as the democratic deficit had become ingrained in public perceptions of the EU. *Subsidiarity,* a word and a concept that few people understood, seemed to accentuate rather than alleviate the situation.

Buoyed by the Edinburgh agreement, a new Danish government succeeded in convincing a majority of the electorate to ratify the treaty in the referendum in May 1993. The result was a comfortable majority of 56.8 percent in favor. Buoyed in turn by the Danish vote, but dogged by conservative Euroskeptics, Major brought the treaty up for ratification in the British Parliament in August 1993. In the meantime ratification proceeded smoothly in most other member states. The exception was Germany, where, despite large majorities in favor of the treaty in both houses of parliament, a legal challenge to the treaty's constitutionality held up ratification until the outcome of a court case.

Passage of the ratification legislation in the British Parliament and the ruling of the German constitutional court on the compatibility of the treaty with German law removed the last hurdles impeding implementation of the treaty, which finally came into effect in November 1993. EU governments, institutions, and other actors quickly mastered the treaty's provisions. EMU was already on track, the common foreign and security policy was implemented, and member states began to cooperate more closely on justice and home affairs issues. The name "European Union" caught on quickly, in Europe and abroad. Yet the ratification crisis spoiled the occasion and presaged serious political problems for the fledgling EU.

▓ Notes

1. Leo Tindemans, *Report on European Union*, Bulletin EC S/1-1976, p. 20.

2. See Horst Ungerer, *From EPU to EMU: A Concise History of European Monetary Integration* (Westport, CT: Quorum Books, 1997), pp. 338–347.

3. Tommaso Padoa-Schioppa et al., *Efficiency, Stability and Equity: A Strategy for the Evolution of the Economic System of the European Community* (Oxford: Oxford University Press, 1987), pp. 3, 13.

4. Kenneth Dyson and Kevin Featherstone, *The Road to Maastricht: Negotiating Economic and Monetary Union* (Oxford: Oxford University Press, 1999), pp. 162, 164–165.

5. Ibid., p. 708.

6. See Alistair Cole, *François Mitterrand: A Study in Political Leadership* (London: Routledge, 1994), p. 122.

7. Ibid., p. 162; Dyson and Featherstone, *Road to Maastricht*, p. 130.

8. Dyson and Featherstone, *Road to Maastricht*, pp. 166–167.

9. On the Delors Committee, see ibid., pp. 702–705, 770–773, 741–742; Andrew Moravcsik, *The Choice for Europe: Social Purpose and State Power from Messina to Maastricht* (Ithaca, NY: Cornell University Press, 1998), pp. 261–262, 339–340, 431–432; Niels Thygesen, "The Delors Report and European Economic and Monetary Union," *International Affairs* 65, no. 4 (Autumn 1989), pp. 637–652.

10. Margaret Thatcher, *Downing Street Years* (New York: HarperCollins, 1993), p. 740.

11. Dyson and Featherstone, *Road to Maastricht*, pp. 604–605.

12. Ibid., p. 705

13. See Ken Endo, *The Presidency of the European Commission Under Jacques Delors: The Politics of Shared Leadership* (New York: St. Martin's Press, 1999); Charles Grant, *Delors: Inside the House that Jacques Built* (London: Nicholas Brealey Publishing, 1994), pp. 119–123.

14. Committee for the Study of Economic and Monetary Union, *Report on Economic and Monetary Union in the European Community (The Delors Report)* (Luxembourg: Office of Official Publications of the European Communities, 1989), pp. 18–19.

15. Ibid., pp. 34–40.

16. Nigel Lawson, *The View from No. 11: Britain's Longest-serving Cabinet Member Recalls the Triumphs and Disappointments of the Thatcher Era* (New York: Doubleday, 1993), pp. 893–894; Thatcher, *Downing Street Years*, p. 660; Geoffrey Howe, *Conflict of Loyalty* (New York: St. Martin's Press, 1994); Dyson and Featherstone, *Road to Maastricht*, pp. 601–612.

17. Bulletin EC 6-1989.

18. Bulletin EC 12-1989.

19. Ibid.

20. Quoted in *Le Monde*, December 9, 1989, p. 1.

21. European Commission, *One Market, One Money: An Evaluation of the Potential Benefits and Costs of Forming an Economic and Monetary Union* (Luxembourg: Office of Official Publications, 1990).

22. Thatcher, *Downing Street Years*, pp. 839–862.

23. Bulletin EC S/1-1985.

24. Endo, *Delors*, p. 47.

25. Delors, "Speech to the Parliament," July 6, 1988; OJ-EP, 2-367, July 6, 1988, p. 140.

26. Margaret Thatcher, *Britain in the European Community* (London: Conservative Party Center, 1988), p. 6. Thatcher's description of this speech and denunciation of Delors in her memoirs conveys the depth of her feeling on the matter. See Thatcher, *Downing Street Years*, pp. 742–746.

27. *The Spectator*, July 1990, p. 24.

28. On German unification, see Philip Zelikow and Condoleezza Rice, *Germany Unified and Europe Transformed: A Study in Statecraft* (Cambridge: Harvard University Press, 1995); and Stephen F. Szabo, *The Diplomacy of German Unification* (New York: St. Martin's Press, 1992).

29. The Belgian proposal is reproduced in Finn Laursen and Sophie Vanhoonacker, *The Intergovernmental Conference on Political Union: Institutional Reforms, New Policies, and International Identity of the European Community* (Dordrecht: M. Nijhoff Publishers, 1992), pp. 269–275.

30. The letter is reproduced in ibid., pp. 276–277.

31. Bulletin EC 6-1990.

32. *Economist*, March 23, 1991, p. 15.

33. On the negotiation of the Maastricht Treaty, see Michael J. Baun, *An Imperfect Union: The Maastricht Treaty and the New Politics of European Integration* (Boulder, CO: Westview Press, 1996); J. Cloos, *Le traité de Maastricht: Genèse, analyse, commentaires* (Brussels: Bruylant, 1993); Dyson and Featherstone, *Road to Maastricht*; Anthony Forster, *Britain and the Maastricht Negotiations* (Basingstoke: Palgrave, 1999); David J. Howarth, *The French Road to European Union* (Basingstoke: Palgrave, 2001), pp. 83–144; Laursen and Vanhoonacker, *Intergovernmental Conference*; Colette Mazzucelli, *France and Germany at Maastricht: Politics and Negotiations to Create the European Union* (New York: Garland, 1997); Kathleen McNamara, *The Currency of Ideas: Monetary Politics in the European Union* (Ithaca, NY: Cornell University Press, 1997); Moravcsik, *Choice for Europe*, pp. 379–471; George Ross, *Jacques Delors and European Integration* (Oxford: Oxford University Press, 1995); Wayne Sandholtz, "Choosing Union: Monetary Politics and Maastricht," *International Organization* 47, no. 1 (Winter 1993), pp. 1–39.

34. Dyson and Featherstone, *Road to Maastricht*, p. 691.

35. Quoted in Laursen and Vanhoonacker, *Intergovernmental Conference*, pp. 419–428.

36. Quoted in the *Financial Times*, June 18, 1991, p. 1.

37. Quoted in the *Guardian*, July 7, 1991, p. 12.

38. Quoted in *Agence Europe*, December 6, 1991, p. 1.

39. Quoted in ibid., June 4, 1991, p. 1.

40. Quoted in the *Financial Times*, September 21–22, 1991, p. 3.

41. Quoted in *Agence Europe*, April 18, 1991, p. 1.

42. On EU citizenship, see Cris Shore, *Building Europe: The Cultural Politics of European Integration* (London: Routledge, 2000), pp. 66–112.

43. See Trevor C. Salmon, "Testing Times for European Political Cooperation: The Gulf and Yugoslavia, 1990–1992," *International Affairs* 68, no. 2 (April 1992), pp. 233–253.

44. On the U.S. démarche, see Sophie Vanhoonacker, *The Bush Administration and the Development of a European Security Identity* (Aldershot: Ashgate, 2001), pp. 106–108.

45. Treaty on European Union, text available at http://www.europa.eu.int/abc/obj/ treaties/en/entoc01.htm.

46. Quoted in the *International Herald Tribune*, July 1, 1991, p. 2.

47. Quoted in the *Financial Times*, July 1, 1991, p. 1.

48. On the development of immigration and asylum policy in the EU, see Andrew Geddes, *Immigration and European Integration: Towards Fortress Europe?* (Manchester: Manchester University Press, 2000); and Sharon Stanton Russell, Charles B. Keely, and Bryan P. Christian, *Multilateral Diplomacy to Harmonize Asylum Policy in Europe, 1984–1993* (Washington, DC: Institute for the Study of International Migration, 2000).

49. Quoted in the *Financial Times*, December 12, 1992, p. 3.

50. Quoted in the *Cork Examiner*, June 20, 1992, p. 1.

51. *Le Monde*, September 20–21, 1992, p. 1.

52. Jack Lang, quoted in *Le Monde*, "L'Europe de Maastricht," Special Supplement, August–September 1992, p. 2.

53. Bulletin EC 12-1992.

8

The Challenges
of European Union

The European Union was born into a radically different world than had existed throughout the life of the European Community. A new international system, dominated by the United States, emerged out of the Cold War. Although the European Community never became a third force between the United States and the Soviet Union, the EU saw itself as a possible second force, a badly needed counterweight to Washington. Yet the extent of U.S. power and the EU's weakness became apparent first in the Balkan wars of the late 1990s, then during the Iraq crisis of 2003. The EU's common foreign and security policy made little headway. Efforts to flesh out a defense policy looked promising before falling victim to internal divisions over Iraq.

One of the EU's most pressing challenges—the challenge of eastward enlargement—had an important security dimension reminiscent of the early days of European integration. Both the EU and the countries of Central and Eastern Europe saw enlargement as a means to strengthen European security. Nevertheless, the prospect of enlargement on such a scale, involving so many underdeveloped countries, petrified the EU. The road to accession, begun hesitantly in the early 1990s, proved arduous for both sides. The administrative and technical demands of EU membership dragged the process out for over a decade. As it was, many of the candidate countries seemed ill prepared to join the EU when finally invited to do so, in December 2002.

Implementation of economic and monetary union (EMU) was the other big challenge facing the new EU. Despite unfavorable economic circumstances, a majority of member states met the Maastricht Treaty's convergence criteria and launched the final stage in January 1999 (euro notes and coins were introduced in January 2002). The success of EMU owed a great deal to German chancellor Helmut Kohl. Having nailed his colors to the Maastricht mast, Kohl single-mindedly pushed monetary union regardless of the prevailing economic circumstances. Ironically, Kohl was not in office when EMU came to fruition (he lost the general election of October 1998 to Gerhard Schröder, his Social Democratic opponent). Nor was Jacques Delors, Commission president at the time of the Maastricht Treaty and Kohl's helpmate in the quest for EMU (he retired in 1995).

A new crop of EU leaders came to prominence in the late 1990s. Jacques Chirac, who won the French presidential election in May 1995, was a veteran politician (he had been agriculture minister in the early 1960s). Tony Blair, whose Labour Party won a resounding victory in May 1997, was a relative neophyte. Schröder was little known outside Germany. Delors's successors were politically weak or maladroit, signifying the Commission's declining influence. Meetings of the European Council were often heated, with Chirac unabashedly pushing French priorities. The much-vaunted Franco-German axis lost its luster. Yet the long-standing commonality of Franco-German interest in the EU bound Chirac and Schröder together in a way that excluded Blair, despite the British prime minister's undoubted enthusiasm for European integration.

The EU faced a host of other policy challenges in the 1990s: completing and consolidating the single market, promoting employment, protecting the environment, and preparing the common agricultural policy and cohesion for the onslaught of enlargement. The EU's record was mixed: the single market remained a work in progress; unemployment stayed stubbornly high; sustainable development, the leitmotiv of environmental policy, was easier to proclaim than to achieve; and agriculture and cohesion seemed impervious to reform. Cooperation on justice and home affairs, ranging from immigration and asylum to policing, became increasingly necessary and complicated in light of the growing North-South global divide and the international war against terrorism.

Member states revised the founding treaties of the EU in 1997 (with the Amsterdam Treaty) and 2001 (the Nice Treaty) and launched the Convention on the Future of Europe in 2002. Institutional improvements in the Amsterdam and Nice treaties sought to address public concerns about accountability and transparency in the EU while improving efficiency in anticipation of enlargement. Dissatisfaction with the method and scope of treaty change, in turn, prompted the launch of the convention and the promulgation of a new constitutional treaty. As the EU became more rounded politically, however, the challenge of public estrangement remained formidable in the early twenty-first century.

■ The Challenge of Enlargement

The end of the Cold War raised the prospect of EU enlargement on an unprecedented scale and scope. Three categories of countries sought membership: neutral countries no longer constrained by the Cold War (Austria, Finland, Malta, and Sweden), nonneutral and in some cases NATO members submitting or reactivating membership applications at a time of radically changing international circumstances (Cyprus, Norway, and Turkey), and newly independent Central and Eastern European countries (Bulgaria, Czechoslovakia, Estonia, Hungary, Latvia, Lithuania, Poland, Romania, and Slovenia). Although each country's circumstances were different, there were sufficient similarities between some of the applicants to warrant a common approach by the EU toward them. Austria and the Scandinavian countries were clearly a group apart: economically well developed, politically stable, and well acquainted with the EU's policies and procedures. The Central and Eastern European countries were an equally obvious group: economically underdeveloped, politically unstable (at least during the initial transition to democracy), and unfamiliar with the EU's policies and procedures. Cyprus and Turkey differed from each other economically and politically but were linked because of Turkey's occupation of the northern part of Cyprus and Greece's strong support for Cypriot accession. Finally, Malta, a Mediterranean microstate, was *sui generis*.

The EC was preoccupied with internal developments, notably German unification, EMU, and completion of the single market, when the Cold War came to an end. Member states and the Commission did not want to be bothered with enlargement. To their dismay, Austria and the Scandinavians were dissatisfied with the newly formed European Economic Area and asked to join the EU as soon as possible. The Central and Eastern European countries also wanted early EU accession, which in their case meant the end of the decade at best.

Apart from its timing, member states were equivocal about the prospect of enlargement. France feared a diminution of influence in the EU. Thanks to previous enlargements and to German unification, France's traditional role in the EU seemed under threat. The accession of numerous northern and Eastern European countries would likely shift the political center of gravity in the EU firmly toward Germany. Britain and Denmark, historically Euroskeptical, supported enlargement partly in the hope that it would slow the momentum toward political union. Denmark had a particular interest in restoring Scandinavian solidarity by bringing Finland, Norway, and Sweden into the EU. The poorer member states welcomed the prospect of contributions to the EU budget from wealthy countries such as Austria, Finland, Norway, and Sweden but did not relish the prospect of the Central and Eastern European countries' staking a claim to the EU's redistributive funds.

Regardless of their initial impressions, the Commission and the member states soon realized that enlargement was inevitable. With the Cold War over, the EU could not restrict itself to Western Europe. Other European countries had every right to seek membership in an association that claimed to be open to all the countries of Europe. The EU was hoisted by its own petard, a victim of a long-standing rhetorical claim to pan-European inclusiveness. When the newly independent countries proclaimed their eagerness to rejoin "Europe," they meant joining the EU. For them, membership in the EU was a badge of honor, a stamp of political approval, and a path to prosperity. The EU's preoccupation with internal affairs and concern about the costs of enlargement seemed selfish by comparison.

Austrian and Scandinavian Accession

Most members of the European Free Trade Association (EFTA), a collection of Western European countries not in the EU, considered applying for EU membership at the end of the Cold War. The EU tried to fob them off with the European Economic Area, an association of EU and EFTA members that extended the benefits of the single market to many more consumers and manufacturers and in the process satisfied some of the EFTA countries' main economic reasons for wanting to join the EU. Dissatisfied with what was on offer, most of the EFTA countries applied to join the EU even before concluding negotiations for the European Economic Area in December 1992.[1] The Norwegian, Swedish, and Swiss governments sought EU accession purely on economic grounds, but many interest groups and a large percentage of the population in each country opposed membership for a variety of reasons. Norway's heated debate in the early 1990s about EU accession was almost a repeat of the debate in the early 1970s about EC accession. It had the same outcome. Having again negotiated an accession agreement, a small majority of Norwegians (52.5%) voted against joining the EU in a referendum in November 1994. Rejection of the European Economic Area in a referendum in Switzerland in December 1992 doomed the country's EU application. Advocates of accession narrowly prevailed in Sweden.

Accession was much less contentious in Austria and Finland, which had special strategic interests in joining the EU. Soviet troops withdrew from eastern Austria only in 1955. During the rest of the Cold War, neutral Austria was a liberal democratic outpost in Communist Central Europe. Despite the end of the Cold War, Austria wanted to enhance its security by joining the EU, and even considered applying to join NATO. Having lived in the shadow of the Soviet Union during the Cold War, Finland was even more appreciative of the security dimension of EU membership. Finland would happily have applied to join NATO at the end of the Cold War but could not risk antagonizing Russia by doing so. The neutral applicants were at pains to point out that neutrality would not impede their participation in the common foreign and security policy.

Resolution of the Maastricht ratification crisis, agreement on the post-Maastricht budgetary package, and the applicants' insistence on early membership led to the opening of accession negotiations in 1993. Compared to earlier and later rounds of enlargement, the accession process was relatively swift. After all, many of the agenda items or "chapters" were already included in the European Economic Area. But problems pertaining to social policy, energy, the environment, agriculture, and fisheries still had to be resolved. Social and environmental standards and agricultural subsidies were generally higher in the applicant countries; as for energy policy and fisheries, Norway did not want to relinquish control over its vast reserves of oil and natural gas or over its rich fishing grounds. Other difficulties arose on specific issues such as support for remote and sparsely populated parts of Finland, Norway, and Sweden; truck transit through Austria; the EU's ban on the sale of snuff, to which many Swedes were addicted; and Sweden's state monopoly on the sale of alcohol, which Swedes consumed in great quantity but at considerable expense.

The accession agreements, reached in mid-1994 after hard months of bargaining, included transitional arrangements for certain regulatory matters, a new category of structural funds for Arctic areas, special measures to maintain farmers' incomes in the new member states following the alignment of agricultural prices in the enlarged EU, and the maintenance of higher environmental standards in the applicant countries after their accession. The EU's special concessions to Norway failed to tip the balance in the Norwegian referendum in favor of membership. By contrast, Austria endorsed accession by a majority of 66 percent; Finland by a majority of 60 percent; and Sweden by a majority of 52 percent.

Ratification of the accession agreements was much easier on the EU side, although the Parliament kicked up a fuss because the member states would not countenance major institutional reform in light of enlargement. Indeed, the only institutional change agreed to by the Council in order to facilitate enlargement was the so-called Ioannina Compromise of March 1994, a concession to British and Spanish demands to raise the threshold for a qualified majority.[2] Although denouncing the Ioannina Compromise, which would make decisionmaking in the Council even less efficient, the Parliament had little choice but to approve enlargement, which took place in January 1995. Nevertheless, by raising institutional concerns the Parliament pressured member states to include institutional reform on the agenda of the forthcoming intergovernmental conference.

This was the easiest enlargement for the EU to digest. The three new member states were small demographically and well off economically. Sweden was somewhat Euroskeptical (the results of the country's first elections to the Parliament in September 1995 revealed widespread dissatisfaction with EU membership), but Austria and Finland were relatively enthusiastic new members. Widespread recession in the mid-1990s did not help the image of the EU in the new member states. The EU's arcane legislative system and alien administrative culture shocked Finnish and Swedish politicians and civil servants, who zealously advocated openness and transparency in EU decisionmaking. Finland and Sweden championed higher EU social and environ-

The Fifteen Member States

mental standards and a more liberal EU trade policy. They also promoted a "northern dimension" for the EU, including a rapprochement with Russia and early accession for Estonia, Latvia, and Lithuania, their neighbors across the Baltic Sea.

Far from whetting the EU's appetite for further enlargement, the accession of Austria, Finland, and Sweden highlighted the challenges that lay ahead. Even with the advantage of the European Economic Area, the accession negotiations with Austria, Finland, and Sweden were arduous and time consuming. How much longer and more difficult would the Central and Eastern European negotiations be? The dispute over the threshold for a qualified majority that resulted in the Ioannina Compromise was a harbinger of future disputes over the institutional implications of Central and Eastern European enlargement. Finally, Spain's last-minute threat to block the 1995 enlargement unless the other member states agreed to give Spain a fisheries deal similar to Norway's raised the prospect of similar political blackmail in the run-up to the next enlargement, especially in relation to structural funds. It was little wonder that many EU officials and politicians buried their heads in the sand and hoped that Central and Eastern European enlargement might somehow never happen.

Central and Eastern European Enlargement

Much more so than the accession of Austria, Finland, and Sweden, the accession of Greece, Portugal, and Spain in the 1980s gave some idea of the difficulties likely to be encountered with Central and Eastern European enlargement. Portugal and Spain, newly democratic and economically underdeveloped, took approximately ten years to join the EC (Greece was lucky to have joined sooner in record time). Many more countries wanted to join the EU this time around; they were even poorer and had weaker administrative structures than the Mediterranean applicants of a decade earlier; and the number of EU rules and regulations was considerably larger than before.[3]

Despite the similarities between the two rounds of enlargement, the road to accession for the Central and Eastern European countries was largely uncharted. Member states and the Commission groped for the right path to take. There were major misunderstandings and recriminations between the EU and the applicant states. The applicants accused the EU of foot dragging; the EU accused the applicants of grandstanding. Public opinion on both sides tired of the process, wondering if the means were worth the end and if the end was worth having.

Various European summits provided milestones along the way. As accession finally came into sight, enlargement dominated the EU's agenda. Some member states, more interested in enlargement than others, sought to accelerate the process while in the Council presidency. They had leeway to do so because enlargement was primarily an intergovernmental activity, with the presidency leading the negotiations and coordinating member states' positions. The Commission was relegated to a supporting role: providing information, drafting progress reports; and acting as honest broker. The Parliament was a cheerleader for enlargement, engaging in lofty rhetoric about European unification while dreading the practical impact of accession on everyday parliamentary pursuits.

From assistance to association. Eastern Europe might as well have been on another planet during most of the history of the EU.[4] The existence of the Cold War and the hostility of the Soviet Union toward Western Europe helped cement European integration. The Soviet Union would not allow the EC to establish diplomatic relations with the countries of Central and Eastern Europe, insisting instead that the EC deal with the Council for Mutual Economic Assistance, the Soviet bloc's supposed equivalent to the EC. The EC agreed to recognize that body only in 1988, when reform in Central and Eastern Europe made it obsolete and presaged its members' independence.

In 1989 the Commission assumed responsibility for coordinating Western assistance to Central and Eastern Europe. The EC launched its own aid program (Poland and Hungary Assistance for the Reconstruction of the Economy), known by the acronym PHARE, to complement the member states' assistance efforts in the region. As well as providing urgent humanitarian assistance, PHARE helped recipients develop social-market economies and establish democratic institutions. A separate initiative, led by French president François Mitterrand, resulted in the establishment of the European Bank for Reconstruction and Development. With the EC and its member states as majority shareholders (the United States and other non-EU members were the other shareholders), the bank became a major provider of loans to promote economic development in the former Soviet bloc.

Financial and technical assistance was a welcome and necessary first step for the modernization of Central and Eastern Europe. It complemented a series of bilateral trade and cooperation agreements between the EC and the Central and Eastern European countries. Intended primarily to provide much-needed market access to the EC for Central and Eastern European products, the trade and cooperation agreements pitted the member states' protectionist proclivities against the pervasive rhetoric of pan-European integration. When it came to concrete market access measures, the EC refused to make generous concessions for agricultural products, textiles, and steel, highly sensitive sectors politically for the EC and highly important sectors economically for the Central and Eastern European countries.

Moral pressure for a more generous EC approach and for recognition of the Central and Eastern European countries' entitlement to a closer relationship with the EC led to offers of association with selected ex–Soviet bloc countries. Pushed by Helmut Kohl, whose country had so much to gain from a successful transition in Central and Eastern Europe, in August 1990 the Commission proposed association agreements with Czechoslovakia, Hungary, and Poland, the most economically advanced and strategically important countries in the region. The "Europe agreements" (so named to suggest a unique relationship between the EC and the associated countries) would include free trade, intensive economic cooperation, and an institutionalized political relationship. Member states were reluctant to promise eventual EU membership but acknowledged that the "final objective" for the new associates was to join the EU.

Negotiations for the Europe agreements with Czechoslovakia, Hungary, and Poland took place throughout 1991. The EC drove a hard bargain on market access and movement of people. The agreements took even longer to ratify than to negotiate, as entrenched interests in some member states objected to specific provisions, especially on agriculture. Because the agreements covered areas of mixed member state and EU competence, the Commission implemented interim agreements for some of the areas of EU competence pending member state ratification of the global agreements. The Commission also opened negotiations for Europe agreements with additional countries in the region, eventually concluding ten agreements altogether (including agreements with the Czech Republic and Slovakia following the breakup of Czechoslovakia in January 1993). Negotiation and ratification of the Europe agreements continued into the mid-1990s, further demonstrating the EU's inability to deal expeditiously and generously with its neighbors to the east.

From Copenhagen to Copenhagen. It was only after negotiation of the Maastricht Treaty and resolution of the ratification crisis that the EU began to turn its attention to the challenge of Central and Eastern European enlargement. Spurred by Denmark, which strongly supported enlargement, the European Council declared unequivocally in Copenhagen in June 1993 that "the associated countries in Central and Eastern Europe which so desire shall become members of the European Union." The European Council also endorsed conditions drawn up by the Commission for the accession of new member states. These were the so-called Copenhagen criteria:

- Stability of institutions guaranteeing democracy, the rule of law, human rights, and respect for and protection of minorities
- Existence of a functioning market economy, as well as the capacity to cope with competitive pressures and market forces in the EU
- Ability to take on the obligations of membership, including adherence to the aims of political, economic, and monetary union

The European Council further stipulated that the EU's "capacity to absorb new members, while maintaining the momentum of European integration," would be "an important consideration" in the accession process.[5]

Delors, who was lukewarm about enlargement, finally accepted that it was unavoidable. By then his days as Commission president were numbered (he left office in January 1995). His successor, Jacques Santer, was more amenable to enlargement, which became a priority of his generally lackluster Commission presidency. Kohl was the only leader of a large member state to support enlargement wholeheartedly, at least for the countries closest to Germany. Jacques Chirac, who succeeded Mitterrand as president of France in May 1995, was even less keen on enlargement than Mitterrand had been. John Major supported enlargement in the hope that widening would weaken the EU. That hardly endeared him to the Central and Eastern Europeans, who wanted to join a strong EU and had few qualms about voluntarily sharing sovereignty.

Between 1994 and 1996, as the Europe agreements finally came into effect, the ten Central and Eastern European countries lodged applications for membership. By that time neither they nor the EU were in any doubt about the difficulties ahead. Five years after the fall of the Berlin Wall, Central and Eastern Europe was in bad shape administratively, economically, and environmentally. Countries in the region still faced the daunting legacy of several decades of Communist mismanagement. Although conditions varied from country to country, all struggled with the transition from communism to capitalism and from dictatorship to democracy. The lengthy process of reconstruction and rehabilitation involved an array of legal, banking, and business reforms; the privatization of state-owned companies; agricultural and industrial modernization; major social welfare reform; massive environmental improvement; a revolution in public administration; a new educational system; and a major overhaul of physical plant and infrastructure. The prospect of EU membership provided an incentive for the aspiring member states to persist with painful reforms that were necessary in any case, although the EU model of economic management to which they aspired was not necessarily the most appropriate to their needs.

By the mid-1990s there was an unspoken understanding between the EU and the Central and Eastern European applicants: the EU accepted the inevitability of enlargement, and the applicants accepted the extent of the challenge. Missing from this implicit bargain was a commitment on the part of the EU to restructure its own policies and procedures in anticipation of enlargement. The EU used enlargement as a pretext to reform the common agricultural policy (CAP) and cohesion policy and to streamline its institutional structure. But those efforts, culminating in the *Agenda 2000* negotiations (for policy reform) and the Nice Treaty (for institutional reform), were half-hearted and inadequate. Although insisting on radical reform in Central and Eastern Europe, the EU refused to launch an equally painful but necessary overhaul of its own institutions and policies. The EU wanted enlargement on the cheap, not necessarily in financial terms, but in terms of avoiding politically costly but urgently needed internal reforms.

The EU stepped up its efforts in 1994 to prepare the applicant countries for accession. Based on a Commission report and prodded by the German presidency in the second half of the year, the European Council agreed in Essen in December 1994 to launch a "structured dialogue" between the EU and the applicants. Covering most EU policy areas, the structured dialogue involved regular ministerial meetings between both sides as well as annual meetings of the heads of state and government of current and prospective member states on the margins of the European Council. The first such high-level gathering took place at the Essen summit itself.[6]

The EU also began the process of integrating the candidate countries into the single market. In June 1995 the European Council approved a Commission white paper on how to prepare the candidate countries, sector by sector, for full participation in the single market.[7] The specificity of the white paper left neither the EU nor the candidates in any doubt about the complexity and enormity of the task ahead. Far from simply promulgating new laws, the candidates would have to overhaul their entire administrative, legal, and economic structures. The EU reformed the PHARE program and launched other initiatives in order to help the candidate countries adhere to the EU's single market standards.

Guided by the white paper and assisted by the EU, most of the candidates adopted detailed preaccession plans, or administrative road maps, as part of their overall accession strategies. At the same time the Commission began to gather information and conduct analysis for its formal opinions on the candidates' suitability for EU membership. Published in July 1997 as part of the *Agenda 2000* package, the Commission's opinions reached the following conclusions about the applicants:

- *Democracy and the rule of law:* all had adequate constitutional and institutional arrangements and practices, except Slovakia, which seemed to be sliding back toward authoritarian rule
- *Functioning market economy:* all had made good progress, but structural reforms were still necessary, especially in the financial sector and in social security
- *EU rules and regulations:* all were in the process of absorbing EU rules and regulations and all had a long way yet to go[8]

The most difficult and controversial task for the Commission was to decide which of the candidates to recommend to the European Council for the opening of accession negotiations. The ten candidates were at different levels of development. Some had reformed more thoroughly than others. None wanted to be relegated to a second division of countries slated to join the EU later. The EU and its member states viewed each candidate differently. Because of its size, location, and economic importance, Poland was at the top of the accession queue. The Czech Republic and Hungary, relatively well developed economically, centrally located, and culturally attuned to Western Europe, were well placed for early accession. The Baltic States had strong support from the EU's Scandinavian members, but their propinquity to Russia posed a special strategic challenge. Slovenia, a prosperous and stable former Yugoslav republic, was culturally, economically, politically, and geographically close to Austria, which championed its early accession. Bulgaria and Romania were farther away in every sense from the EU.

The Commission recommended that the EU begin accession negotiations with five countries: the Czech Republic, Hungary, Poland, Estonia, and Slovenia. The choice of the first three was unsurprising. The Commission decided to add Estonia and Slovenia not only on the merits of their cases but also because the Commission wanted to make a sharp distinction between EU and NATO enlargement. Just a week before the Commission released *Agenda 2000*, NATO announced that the Czech Republic, Hungary, and Poland would join the military alliance in 1999. Largely to assuage Russian concerns, the Commission sought to show that EU and NATO enlargements were not congruent. The Commission added Estonia to the list because of its popularity in the EU and added Slovenia because it was obviously ready for membership and because of the political importance of selecting a candidate from southeastern Europe.

The Commission consulted closely with the member states while drafting its opinions and making its recommendations. It was no surprise, therefore, that the European Council endorsed the Commission's findings at the Luxembourg summit in December 1997. The European Council was at pains to point out that the EU would begin entry negotiations with the other candidate countries whenever the Commission deemed that they were ready to start. To emphasize the point, the European Council charged the Commission with preparing annual reports on all the applicants' progress toward accession.[9] Nevertheless, the other candidates felt slighted and feared the emergence in post–Cold War Europe of a new dividing line between them and the enlarged EU. Latvia and Lithuania were especially irked by Estonia's selection for early accession negotiations. The shock of exclusion may have helped them and the other candidates initially relegated to the second division to redouble their reform efforts in order to join the first division as soon as possible.

The EU began accession negotiations with the first five countries in March 1998. The initial stage consisted of a "screening process" to examine in minute detail the extent to which the candidates already met the rules and obligations of EU membership. Substantive negotiations, conducted bilaterally between the EU and each candidate, began in November 1998. The EU organized the vast agenda of the negotiations into about thirty "chapters" or issues corresponding to the EU's policies and programs. Inevitably, negotiators closed the least contentious of them first. As the negotiations progressed, negotiators checked more and more chapters off an accession negotiation scorecard.

In October 1999 the Commission recommended that the EU begin negotiations with the five remaining candidates. Although supposedly based on objective analysis, undoubtedly the Commission succumbed to pressure not only from the candidates, whose leverage was relatively weak, but also from certain member states that advocated a full round of enlargement, primarily for strategic reasons. Instability in the Balkans throughout the 1990s, culminating in the Kosovo War of 1999, was an unnerving backdrop to the enlargement project. The five remaining candidates had made important strides toward meeting the requirements for accession, although Bulgaria and Romania accepted that they were still a long way behind the others. Slovakia, now under democratic government, made rapid economic progress in the late 1990s. The European Council endorsed the Commission's recommendations in Helsinki in December 1999, paving the way for the opening of accession negotiations with Latvia, Lithuania, Slovakia, Bulgaria, and Romania in February 2000.

Despite their late start, the second group of candidates (with the exception of Bulgaria and Romania) soon caught up with the first group in the negotiations. Each country progressed at its own speed, depending on the degree of difficulty of particular agenda items. Although the EU negotiated separately with each country, the relative transparency of the process and publication of the negotiation scorecard pressured the candidates to make progress. None of them wanted to top the list of incomplete chapters. By the end of 2002 only the most contentious issues, such as agriculture and the budget, remained unresolved. Institutional issues (notably the prospective member states' representation in EU institutions) were not included in the accession negotiations but were decided by the existing member states in a separate intergovernmental conference in 2000 that resulted in the Nice Treaty.

The EU was always wary of setting a date for enlargement. The more assertive of the candidates set their sights in the mid-1990s on the year 2000, a nice round number. EU politicians often encouraged them by proclaiming during visits to the capitals of candidate countries their hopes of seeing the EU expand by that time. When the year 2000 came and went, the candidates set their sights on 2002 for accession. Meeting in Göteborg in June 2001 at the end of the strongly pro-enlargement Swedish presidency, the European Council finally decided that countries whose negotiations ended successfully by December 2002 could join in early 2004. That would give both sides a year to

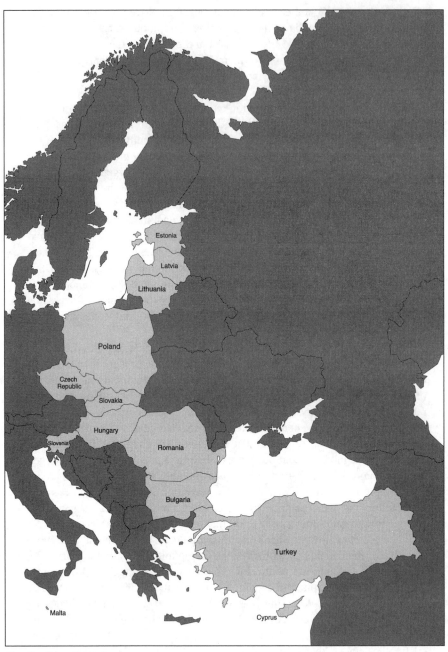

The Candidate Countries

ratify the accession agreements and allow the candidates to become member states in time to participate in the June 2004 elections to the Parliament (thereby possibly increasing the overall turnout for the first time since the original direct elections in 1979).

In a report on enlargement in October 2002, the Commission recommended accession by 2004 for eight of the Central and Eastern European candidates, the exceptions being Bulgaria and Romania, which the Commission recommended for membership in 2007. Nevertheless, the Commission pointed out that most of the candidates had continuing problems with corruption, economic crime, lack of independence of the judiciary, and gaps in implementing the EU's rules and regulations. Although a number of chapters remained to be closed, the Commission was optimistic that the negotiations would end in December 2002 and that the prospective new member states would be fully ready for EU membership by early 2004. An agreement on funding the common agricultural policy during the next budgetary cycle (2007–2013), reached by the European Council in Brussels in late October 2002, removed the last obstacle on the EU's side to a successful conclusion of the negotiations. Despite their dissatisfaction with the EU's offer of smaller agricultural subsidies than farmers in the existing member states would receive, the candidates ended the negotiations at the Copenhagen summit in December 2002.[10] This closed the circle of Central and European enlargement "from Copenhagen to Copenhagen": from the European Council's approval of the EU accession criteria in June 1993 to the European Council's endorsement of the accession agreements almost ten years later.

The long road to accession produced "enlargement fatigue" well before the first candidates joined the EU. Public opinion in the EU and the candidate countries had long ago lost whatever enthusiasm for enlargement it originally possessed. The German government quickly quashed a suggestion, made in August 2000 by the commissioner with responsibility for enlargement, that Germany hold a referendum on the issue. Despite having promised in the previous general election to hold referenda on matters of great public interest, the government was not willing to risk a negative vote on such a sensitive question. Opposition to enlargement accounted in part for the resurgence of the Far Right in Western Europe, notably in Austria, where the extremist Freedom Party formed a coalition government with the Christian Democrats in February 2000. Ireland's rejection of the Nice Treaty in June 2001 looked like another manifestation of anti-enlargement feeling, although the referendum was not about enlargement, and a variety of reasons accounted for a "no" vote. Opinion in the candidate countries, where many people associated enlargement with enduring social dislocation and economic hardship, seemed equally skittish, although ratification of the accession agreements proceeded smoothly.

The Third Mediterranean Enlargement

The EU also negotiated accession agreements with Cyprus and Malta. Cyprus applied to join in July 1990, and the Commission issued a favorable opinion in June 1993. The EU could have negotiated accession with Cyprus at the same time that it negotiated with Austria and the Scandinavian applicants but chose to put Cyprus on the back burner. The EU had an understandable reason: the division of the island into the Turkish-occupied north and the Greek Cypriot south turned the Cypriot application into a poisoned chalice. The EU could be forgiven for wanting to deal with it later rather than sooner.

But the EU could not keep Cyprus on the back burner forever. The European Council's decision in December 1997 to open negotiations with five of the Central and Eastern European candidates plus Cyprus (the so-called 5 + 1 arrangement) incensed Turkey, which disputed the right of the Cypriot government to negotiate on behalf of the entire island. Turkey was in a position to end the partition of the island, subject to the Cypriot government's guaranteeing the rights of what would become a large Turkish minority. Because Turkey also wanted to join the EU (Turkey signed an association agreement in 1964 and applied to join in 1987), the EU had some leverage over the country.

Turkey was an EU applicant unlike any other.[11] The country was desperately poor and politically unstable. It also had a dubious human rights record and discriminated against its minority Kurdish population. As an EU member state, Turkey would be second to Germany in population size. Some Europeans doubted that Turkey was European, pointing out that most of the country lay in the Near East. Moreover, Turks were Muslims, a point that should have been irrelevant but that colored many Europeans' perspective on Turkey's application. Germans complained that Turkish "guest workers" failed to assimilate in Germany and presumed that Turkey would never assimilate in the EU. Although western Europeans had legitimate economic and political reasons to doubt Turkey's suitability in the foreseeable future, many were motivated primarily by anti-Muslim prejudice. All could hide behind deep-rooted Greek hostility toward Turkey.

Turkey's strategic importance was a strong card in an otherwise weak hand. A Western bulwark in a dangerously unstable region, Turkey tried to leverage its strategic position for the promise of EU accession. Turkey also emphasized the threat of Muslim fundamentalism within its borders in order to win a more sympathetic hearing from the EU. Keenly aware of Turkey's strategic value, including Turkey's unofficial alliance with Israel, the United States strongly supported Turkey's EU candidacy. The EU felt that Turkey's application was none of America's business and that U.S. advocacy of it demonstrated a fundamental misunderstanding of the EU's character and accession criteria.

In December 1997, when it agreed to open accession negotiations with the 5 + 1, the European Council did not act on Turkey's long-standing application. As a consolation for Turkey, the European Council announced the launch of the European Conference, an annual meeting of the leaders of all the member states and candidate countries for political consultations. Outraged by the EU's treatment of its application, Turkey boycotted the first meeting of the European Conference, in March 1998. The Turkish government protested so vehemently against its exclusion from the enlargement process and strove so hard to improve its membership prospects that, in December 1999, the European Council relented and officially recognized Turkey as a candidate country. Turkey was again outraged in October 2002 when the Commission recommended that the EU admit eight Central and Eastern European countries, plus Cyprus and Malta, in 2004. The Commission sidestepped the politically charged Turkish question, offering merely to increase preaccession assistance to the country. Nevertheless, EU leaders agreed, at the December 2002 Copenhagen summit, to decide before the end of 2004 whether to open accession negotiations. In the meantime, Turkey strove to make the necessary political and constitutional changes to satisfy the EU.

The EU's willingness to admit Cyprus, regardless of the island's division, robbed Turkey of some leverage over the EU. Nevertheless, it triggered a round of intense diplomatic activity on the Cyprus question in the run-up to the Copenhagen summit in December 2002. Member states were reluctant to bring a divided Cyprus into the EU, but Greece threatened to veto the entire enlargement if Cyprus was not admitted alongside the first wave of Central and Eastern European applicants. Making the best of a bad situation, the EU sought to appease Turkey with additional economic assistance and the promise of eventual accession and appease Greece with the promise of Cypriot accession. The EU's decision not to give Turkey a date for the start of accession negotiations at the Copenhagen summit further strained EU-Turkey relations and damaged prospects for the reunification of Cyprus.

Malta's conservative Nationalist Party applied to join the EC in 1990. Deeply attached to Malta's status as a nonaligned country since independence from Britain, the opposition Labour Party opposed Malta's EU membership. After winning the general election in October 1996, Labour promptly canceled Malta's application. The EU was relieved to have one less application to deal with. The EU was equally nonchalant when the conservatives returned to power in September 1998 and reactivated Malta's application. The Commission reported in February 1999 that Malta could join the accession negotiation already taking place with the 5 + 1. The only problem for the EU was Malta's size: the EU did not relish having another member state approximately the same size as Luxembourg, but without Luxembourg's international standing or tradition of European integration. Nevertheless, Malta moved easily toward

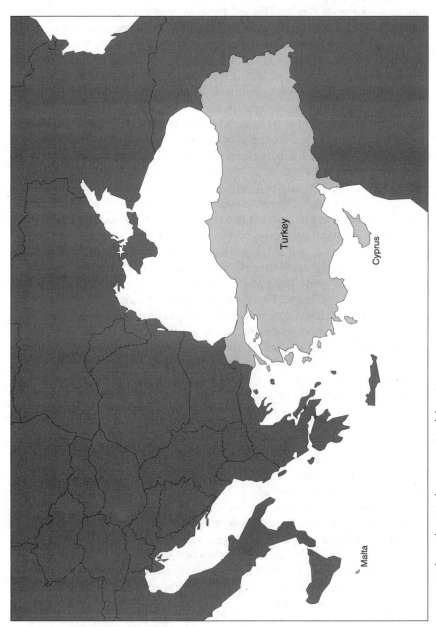

Cyprus, Malta, Turkey: Mediterranean Candidate Countries

EU entry, completing its accession negotiations at the end of 2002. Although a majority approved Malta's membership in a referendum in March 2003, the fiercely anti-EU opposition Labour Party insisted that the issue be decided in the forthcoming general election. Held only a week before the signing of the accession treaties in Athens in April 2003, the governing conservatives easily won reelection, thus ensuring that Malta would join.

▉ Institutional and Political Challenges

The EU enlarged in 1995 without undertaking institutional reform. Nevertheless, the link between enlargement and institutional reform was obvious and unassailable. Numerous memorandums and reports, stretching back to the 1960s, advocated institutional reform in light of imminent enlargement. Yet apart from the introduction of the European Council and the Court of Auditors (a financial watchdog) in the mid-1970s and the Committee of the Regions in the early 1990s, the EU's institutional architecture had remained largely unchanged since the launch of the European Coal and Steel Community, with six member states, in the early 1950s. The only notable alteration to the formula of member states' institutional representation was an increase in the size of Germany's parliamentary delegation as a result of unification, when the German Federal Republic acquired seventeen million more citizens. That was a significant change because it ended the prevailing system of equality of institutional representation among the EU's large member states (Britain, France, Germany, and Italy).

From Amsterdam to Nice

The EU could have undertaken institutional reform in the mid-1990s in response to the accession of three new member states and in anticipation of many more countries joining within the next few years. The Maastricht Treaty mandated an intergovernmental conference in 1996 in order to rectify some of its shortcomings, notably with regard to the common foreign and security policy. Although not convened to negotiate institutional reform, the 1996–1997 conferences gave member states an ideal opportunity to do so.[12] When asked to explain why the conference was taking place, EU officials and politicians usually gave institutional reform as the reason.

Yet there was no talk of radically redesigning the EU's institutional structure or overhauling the EU's decisionmaking procedures. Few were inclined to embark on such an ambitious and politically risky course, especially as Central and Eastern European enlargement was still some years away. In their preparatory reports for the preconference Reflection Group, the Commission, Council, and Parliament called only for minor institutional reform, such as greater use of qualified majority voting and of the co-decision procedure for legislative decisionmaking.

Consisting of representatives of national governments, the Commission, and the Parliament, the Reflection Group met for the first time in Messina, Sicily, in June 1995, the fortieth anniversary of the famous conference of foreign ministers that reanimated European integration. Despite the symbolism surrounding its launch, the Reflection Group contemplated relatively innocuous institutional changes. The purpose of the group was not to negotiate on behalf of the member states but to prepare the conference by drafting a manageable agenda and identifying areas of likely agreement. The actors' different approaches and priorities were evident from the outset, with the Commission, Parliament, and the more supranational-minded member states ranged against the defenders of intergovernmentalism, notably Britain, Denmark, and Sweden. The Reflection Group presented its final report to the European Council in Madrid in December 1995.

It was clear from the Reflection Group's deliberations and final report that "flexibility" or "enhanced cooperation" would become the main institutional issue on the agenda of the conference. The idea of including clauses in the treaties permitting some member states to cooperate more closely in certain policy areas became current for a number of reasons. One was the use of opt-out clauses in the Maastricht Treaty and in the concessions granted to Denmark in order to end the ratification crisis. Another was the likelihood from the perspective of the mid-1990s that the third stage of EMU would proceed with only a minority of member states, if at all. To ensure the success of EMU, participating member states wanting to cooperate more closely in specific economic and fiscal policy areas should be able to do so without being held back by nonparticipants. Britain was the recalcitrant country on everybody's mind. Indeed, widespread frustration with Britain was a principal reason why the idea of enhanced cooperation was so topical at the time. Finally, the prospect of large-scale enlargement in the not-too-distant future intensified interest in enhanced cooperation.

A paper on enhanced cooperation by the combined parliamentary group of Germany's ruling conservative parties stimulated debate in the run-up to the conference. Although written in a personal capacity by two leading members of the group, the paper reflected official German thinking about the EU's future. The paper stated bluntly that "the existing hard core of countries oriented to greater integration and closer cooperation must be further strengthened." It identified the hard core as the original member states minus Italy. That was not conducive to harmonious German-Italian relations, which were already strained because of Germany's criticism of Italy's lax approach to EMU. The paper was equally undiplomatic in its dismissal of Britain's approach to the EU.[13]

The Amsterdam Treaty

The intergovernmental conference began at a special summit in Turin in March 1996. Negotiations proceeded in a desultory fashion until early 1997, when the pace accelerated with a view to reaching a conclusion at the Amsterdam summit in June. Member states dragged out the proceedings largely because of the timing of the British general election. Due to take place no later than May 1997, Britain's partners hoped that the election would see off Major's Conservative government, which held up progress on a range of EU issues. Tony Blair, the Labour Party leader, was an unknown quantity, but he made appropriate pro-European noises and could not have been worse than the current incumbent. They were delighted when Labour won.

The issue of enhanced cooperation became less contentious as the negotiations progressed. A consensus emerged that flexibility should be an option of last resort, a temporary response to specific challenges. In a joint initiative in December 1995, before the conference began, Chirac and Kohl proposed that flexibility take place inside rather than outside the EU, using the EU's institutions, procedures, and mechanisms. That reassured Italy and the non-founding member states. Negotiators quickly agreed to include flexibility in the treaty as long as it was limited in practice so as not to endanger the corpus of EU rules and regulations. Negotiators fleshed out general "enabling" clauses to permit a majority of member states to cooperate more closely and additional clauses specifying how they could do so in certain policy areas. Negotiators also included a provision permitting a member state to block recourse to flexibility on the grounds of "national interest." That provision, redolent of the Luxembourg Compromise, laid to rest British and other concerns about the possible abuse of enhanced cooperation.

Flexibility was an important institutional innovation in the Amsterdam Treaty, although in practice it was so heavily qualified as to be almost impossible to use. Differentiated integration, hitherto an ad hoc arrangement among member states, was now embedded as a key principle in the EU's founding treaties. Because of Britain's change of government, and the likelihood that Stage Three of EMU would start in 1999 with a majority of member states, flexibility was much less salient at the end of the conference than at the beginning. Nevertheless, flexibility remained highly relevant in the context of Central and Eastern European enlargement, which became increasingly pressing toward the end of the decade.

The conference considered three related institutional reforms: extending the use of qualified majority voting in the Council, reallocating votes among member states, and reducing the number of commissioners to one per member state. Although it was far more efficient to make decisions in the Council by voting than by trying to reach consensus, big member states were increasingly unhappy because their relative voting weight had declined over the years as a result of successive enlargements that brought more small countries into the EU. They were especially alarmed by the likely impact of Central and Eastern European enlargement (most of the candidate countries were small). Before agreeing to extend the use of qualified majority voting to various policy areas currently subject to unanimity, big member states demanded either more votes in the Council or the introduction of a double majority combining the traditional requirement of a qualified majority with a new demographic criterion.

The weighting of votes in the Council became bound up with another sensitive political issue: the number of seats per member state in the Commission. The formula of one commissioner per small member state and two commissioners per big member state had not changed since the founding of the EC. Therefore the Commission had grown in size from nine members in 1958 to twenty members in 1996, at the time of the conference. With Central and Eastern European enlargement on the horizon, member states generally agreed that the Commission could not continue to grow at the same rate. Small member states were quite happy to change the formula as long as they continued to be represented in the Commission. Big member states were willing to cut back to one commissioner only in return for extra votes in the Council. France suggested breaking the link between the number of member states and the size of the Commission, perhaps by reducing the Commission to ten or twelve members (France presumed that one of the commissioners would always be French).

EU leaders agreed at the Amsterdam summit in June 1997 to extend qualified majority voting to a few new policy areas, but failed to reallocate votes in the Council and change the size and composition of the Commission. The negotiations demonstrated the political sensitivity of seemingly arcane institutional issues, with national leaders haggling over Council votes and Commission seats until late into the night of the final day of the summit. Too tired to continue, they decided instead to hold another conference before enlargement "to carry out a comprehensive review of the provisions of the treaties on the composition and functioning of the institutions."[14] That was the genesis of the 2000 conference, which resulted in the Nice Treaty.

EU leaders ducked the difficult issue of institutional reform at the Amsterdam summit because enlargement was not pressing enough for them to take tough decisions at the time. Nevertheless, the Amsterdam Treaty contained a number of noteworthy institutional changes. In a major coup for the Parliament, the treaty did away almost completely with the cooperation procedure for legislative decisionmaking and extended and simplified the co-decision procedure. The treaty also incorporated a proposal from the Parliament to cap its size at seven hundred members. At French insistence, member states agreed to enshrine in the treaty an earlier agreement to hold the bulk of the

Parliament's plenary sessions in Strasbourg, despite the location of the Parliament's secretariat in Brussels. That was regrettable, as the Parliament's peripatetic existence (moving monthly between Brussels and Strasbourg) undermined the credibility of the institution.

The Nice Treaty

The EU embarked on another conference in 2000 to tackle the so-called Amsterdam leftovers (extension of qualified majority voting, weighting of Council votes, and size and composition of the Commission).[15] As part of a general institutional reshuffle, member states also addressed the number of seats and votes for the prospective new member states. They did not include Turkey in their calculations. Had they done so, they might have been forced to revise drastically the EU's institutional structure (on the basis of the existing system, Turkey would warrant the second-largest representation in the EU).

The narrowness of the conference agenda was inherently unsatisfactory. The Commission asked a group of "wise men" to draft a report on what the conference should cover. Led by former Belgian prime minister Jean-Luc Dehaene, a Eurofederalist, the report recommended broadening the agenda to include many more issues.[16] Most member states preferred to stick to the institutional implications of enlargement. Their only uncertainty was whether to add flexibility to the agenda. Largely at the urging of the Portuguese presidency in the first half of 2000, member states agreed early in the conference to do so.

Flexibility divided the more integration-minded from the less integration-minded member states, who feared that relaxing the restrictions on recourse to enhanced cooperation would endanger the integrity of the EU and weaken their position in it. Having agreed to include flexibility in the Amsterdam Treaty, however, they had already conceded an important point of principle. That made it easier for them now to allow flexibility to work in practice. Hence the decision to remove the national veto on the use of flexibility and reduce the number of member states allowed to initiate the procedure.

The cleavage between big and small member states, inherent in negotiations about voting weights and Commission size, deepened as the conference progressed. France was the leading proponent of an institutional rebalance in favor of the big member states. France used (or abused) its position as president-in-office, in the second half of 2000, to advance its interests, causing a spectacular row among EU leaders at an informal summit in Biarritz in October 2000, their first detailed discussion of institutional issues since the rancorous Amsterdam summit in June 1997. France claimed that the Biarritz summit cleared the air at the conference. In fact, it led the small member states to dig in their heels and set the stage for a bruising battle on institutional representation at the Nice summit in December 2000.

The discussion of voting weights opened deep divisions among as well as between the big and small member states. France was determined to keep the same number of votes as Germany, a far more populous country. Chirac, a Gaullist, even cited Jean Monnet to bolster his argument that equality between France and Germany in the distribution of Council votes was an inviolable part of the original Franco-German bargain. Schröder conceded the point in return for the addition of a demographic criterion for qualified majority voting. As for the small member states, the Netherlands infuriated Belgium, its less populous neighbor, by demanding more Council votes, thereby ending the traditional parity between both countries.

Rarely did an intergovernmental conference devote so much time to so few issues with so few consequential results. Member states spent most of the conference reiterating well-known positions. As they convened in Nice, EU leaders were far apart on the main agenda items. It looked to two officials involved in the conference "as if eighteen months of preparation had been thrown out of the window and the negotiations [re]started from scratch."[17] In addition to spending two days on other EU business, the European Council spent three days concluding the conference, making the Nice summit the longest in EU history.

The length of the concluding summit and of the conference as a whole hardly justified the effort. The bargain struck in Nice on Council decision-making was especially inglorious. It introduced a triple majority for the enactment of legislative measures: a qualified majority (72 percent) of votes, an absolute majority of member states, and, subject to a specific request by a member state, a qualified majority (62 percent) of the EU's population. EU leaders haggled until the final minutes over the distribution of Council votes. Still refusing to accept fewer votes than the Netherlands, Belgium was finally bought off with the promise of hosting all meetings of the European Council in Brussels. Less controversially and more creditably for the EU, the Nice Treaty also extended the number of policy areas subject to qualified majority voting.

Earlier in the conference the big member states suggested having fewer commissioners than there were member states in the EU and basing the selection of commissioners on a system that would ensure equality among all member states. The small member states were reluctant to agree, fearing that the big member states would skew the system against them. They also resented the big member states' acquisition of far more voting weight in the Council. All agreed in the end to have one commissioner per member state until the EU reached twenty-seven members, when countries would rotate commission appointments according to a system to be worked out later. Although the Amsterdam Treaty capped at seven hundred the size of the Parliament, member states agreed in the Nice Treaty to exceed the cap when reallocating seats in the Parliament in order to accommodate an EU of up to twenty-seven member states. Existing member states grudgingly accepted a reduction in the size of their national delegations in the enlarged EU.

The Nice Treaty succeeded only to a limited extent in preparing the EU institutionally for enlargement. It further complicated an already complex decisionmaking system. Far from simplifying Council decisionmaking, the treaty introduced two new thresholds (number of member states and percentage of EU population) for a qualified majority. The provisions on the size and composition of the Commission constituted an implicit Nice leftover.

The paltry outcome of the conference brought the EU and the process of treaty reform into disrepute. When the Irish electorate rejected the treaty in June 2001 by a convincing margin (64 percent against), it was difficult to lament the treaty's uncertain fate. Although the result raised some doubts about the timing of enlargement, the European Council announced only a week after the referendum that the EU would enlarge regardless of the Irish result, probably in early 2004. Encouraged by other governments and by the Commission, the Irish government pressured the electorate to approve the treaty in a second referendum, in October 2002. Meanwhile the Convention on the Future of Europe, intended to prepare yet another conference, was in session in Brussels. As the purpose of the next conference was to consider the EU's form and structure after enlargement, it was hard to understand why the EU vested such importance in the Nice Treaty. To the relief of the EU establishment and the candidate countries, the Irish electorate endorsed the Nice Treaty at the second attempt by a majority of 63 percent, thanks to a much higher turnout.

The political legacy of Nice was more enduring than the treaty's institutional provisions. The conduct of the conference soured the public's and the politicians' appetite for intergovernmental negotiations on treaty reform. Distrust between big and small member states and bitterness between particular member states was an equally enduring legacy. Small countries, both current and aspirant member states, realized that the EU was moving in an intergovernmental direction dominated by the big member states. France's behavior during the conference was particularly egregious and may have weakened its position in the EU in the long term. France engendered the antipathy not only of the small member states but also of Germany, its traditional partner in the EU.

Other Institutional Reform

Meeting the institutional challenge of enlargement required both treaty-based and non-treaty-based reform. The latter, which could happen without an intergovernmental conference and formal treaty change, held the key to the EU's ability to adapt institutionally to enlargement. Such reform began in response to the resignation of the Commission in March 1999 amid allegations of corruption and mismanagement. It accelerated and spread to other institutions as enlargement became imminent.

The Commission's resignation triggered an institutional upheaval. Building on work begun by the old Commission, Romano Prodi, the new president, launched a "root and branch" overhaul of the Brussels bureaucracy. His ambitious goal was to alter not only administrative procedures and practices but also the culture of the Commission itself. The Prodi reformation included strengthening recently introduced codes of conduct for commissioners and senior officials, denationalizing and slimming down the cabinets, and launching a major shake-up of portfolios and directorates-general (departments). Prodi appointed Commission vice president Neil Kinnock to spearhead the reform effort.[18]

Kinnock unveiled a comprehensive reform strategy in March 2000. Published in the form of a white paper after extensive consultations inside and outside the Commission, the first part identified and described three priorities: long-term planning, financial management and control, and personnel policy. The second part (a separate document) contained a detailed action plan. The Kinnock reforms drew heavily on British and Scandinavian models of public administration that ran counter to the French model on which the Commission was largely based. The French government and many French nationals in the Commission disliked the reform strategy's implicit rejection of the Commission's original organizational principles and ethos, which accentuated a general unease in France about the direction of European integration and the apparent decline of French influence in the EU.[19]

The Commission's reform strategy was a long-term undertaking driven by the Parliament's exposure of corruption and maladministration rather than by anticipation of the disruptive impact of enlargement. Indeed, the white paper on reform hardly mentioned enlargement. Nevertheless, internal reform, which Kinnock compared to a swan gliding along the surface while paddling furiously under the water, helped prepare the Commission for what lay ahead.

National governments began a less far-reaching reform of the Council in 1999, based on the so-called Trumpf-Piris report. The report's guidelines and operational recommendations, which the European Council approved, included strengthening the coordinating role of the foreign ministers, reducing the number of Council configurations, streamlining legislative procedures, and improving preparatory work at all levels. The feasibility of the rotating presidency came increasingly into question as enlargement loomed, but that was an issue requiring treaty change.

Despite having encouraged both the Commission and the Council to undertake reform, the Parliament was slow to put its own house in order. Europarliamentarians acknowledged the need for reform, including better organization of plenary sessions, livelier debates, rationalization of voting procedures, and a reduction in the number of amendments to draft legislation, but were reluctant to do anything about it. Only when Pat Cox became president of the Parliament in January 2002, two years before enlargement, did the Parliament launch a serious reform program. Thereafter the Parliament raced against time to meet the administrative and organizational challenge of enlargement, which threatened to turn the institution into a Tower of Babel.

A More Political Union

Partly in response to the challenge of enlargement but largely in response to the alienation of ordinary Europeans, the EU acquired a sharper political profile throughout the 1990s and into the new millennium. The Maastricht Treaty endowed the EU with political objectives and constitutional characteristics, such as the concept of EU citizenship; the upholding of democracy, human rights, and national identities; and the principle of subsidiarity (the idea that the EU should act outside its specific areas of responsibility only if it could do so more effectively than the member states). The Amsterdam Treaty went farther. It included a key provision stating that the "Union is founded on the principles of liberty, democracy, respect for human rights and fundamental freedoms, and the rule of law, principles which are common to the member states."[20] That short treaty change was highly significant. Whereas the EU and the communities that preceded it were political constructions, member states had not explicitly imbued them with core political values. In the Amsterdam Treaty, member states clearly stated what those values were.

The treaty also included a provision to sanction a member state that deviated from the EU's core values. Should it determine "the existence of a serious and persistent breach . . . of principles mentioned [in the treaty]," the European Council could decide by a qualified majority "to suspend certain of the rights deriving from the application of [the treaty] to the Member State in question, including the voting right of the government of that Member State in the Council."[21] Member states drafted the provision with the Central and Eastern European applicants in mind. Indeed, it was one of the few provisions of the Amsterdam Treaty that owed its origin to impending enlargement.

Not long after the Amsterdam Treaty came into effect, the Christian Democratic Party and the far-right Freedom Party opened negotiations to form a government in Austria. Jörg Haider, leader of the Freedom Party, was a demagogue who exploited latent racism and xenophobia, especially in the context of EU enlargement. Appalled by the prospect of having Haider's party in the Austrian government and emboldened by the Amsterdam Treaty, the other member states threatened unspecified action if the Christian Democrats and the Freedom Party formed a coalition. When the parties went ahead regardless, the other member states introduced mild political sanctions against Austria.

What began with great fanfare in February 2000, when the new Austrian government was formed, ended in embarrassment in September 2000 when the other member states let the matter drop. It was obvious even at the beginning of the imbroglio that Haider was not Hitler and that Austria at the dawn of the twenty-first century could not be compared with Austria in the 1930s. More to the point, it was also obvious that the new Austrian government was not endangering the principles of liberty, democracy, and respect for fundamental human rights. Soon after coming to power, the Austrian government published a program unequivocally endorsing European integration and condemning racism. A committee of "wise men," appointed by the other member states to investigate the political situation in Austria, reported in the summer of 2000 that minority, immigrant, and refugee rights were as well protected there as anywhere in the EU.[22]

As the situation in Austria unfolded, representatives of EU and national institutions negotiated the Charter of Fundamental Rights, a catalog of EU civil and economic rights. Proposed by the German government in 1999 during the celebrations for the fiftieth anniversary of the German constitution, negotiations on the charter proceeded swiftly and relatively smoothly in 2000. The charter was generally uncontroversial, although the British government and some business interests objected to the inclusion of some social rights that could increase labor costs. The European Council "solemnly proclaimed" the charter in Nice in December 2000 but deferred discussion of its constitutional status until the next intergovernmental conference. Although not legally binding, the charter soon became a source of inspiration for the European Court in its development of human rights law.[23]

Politically as well as economically, the new EU was a pervasive presence in the lives of ordinary Europeans. The Austrian affair demonstrated the blur between domestic and EU politics. The launch of the third stage of EMU in January 1999 was an event of great political importance, which many people only appreciated when euro notes and coins began to circulate in January 2002. The changeover to the euro went remarkably well: there were no protests against the demise of national currencies. Europeans generally welcomed the euro and, inasmuch as they knew anything about it, subscribed to the so-called Lisbon strategy for economic modernization proclaimed by the European Council in March 2000. Nor did Europeans seem to mind the establishment of "an area of freedom, security and justice," something called for in the Amsterdam Treaty. Europeans also seemed to want the EU to play a bigger role internationally, both as a peacekeeper in Kosovo and Afghanistan and as a rule maker in commercial, environmental, and other policy areas.

The public backlash. Yet the public's acquiescence in a range of EU activities in the 1990s and early 2000s coincided with a strong backlash against the EU's institutions and way of doing business. There was continuing concern about the supposed democratic deficit. Strictly speaking, the EU's institutions were accountable: people could vote directly for national governments, which formed the Council of Ministers and European Council (of national leaders), and for the Parliament, which had considerable budgetary and decisionmaking power as well as oversight authority. The Commission was unelected but accountable to the Parliament, as the Commission's resignation in March 1999 clearly showed. The European Court and the European Central Bank were unelected, independent, and powerful, but that was the norm for supreme courts and central banks in most liberal democracies. Moreover, in response to the enduring democratic deficit (or to people's perception of it), member states included provisions in the Amsterdam Treaty to strengthen subsidiarity, increase openness and transparency, and involve national parliaments more in EU affairs.

Those measures, which may have improved the quality of EU governance, failed to overcome public unease about the EU. Revelations of wrongdoing in the Commission in 1998 and early 1999 reaffirmed the public's low opinion of the EU's executive body. Under pressure from the Parliament, the Commission agreed to the establishment of a committee of independent experts to inquire into allegations of corruption and cronyism. The committee's report was devastating. Once the Parliament made it clear that the Commission would not survive a vote of censure, the Commission resigned.

The Parliament trumpeted the outcome as evidence of its ability to hold the Commission accountable. Most Europeans were unimpressed. For many of them, the Parliament epitomized all that was wrong with the EU. Parliamentarians' peripatetic existence—moving monthly between Brussels and Strasbourg—and reportedly lavish lifestyles brought the Parliament and the EU as a whole into disrepute. Far from flocking to the polls in the aftermath of the Commission's censure, even fewer voters (49.9 percent) turned out in the June 1999 direct elections to the Parliament than in any of the four previous direct elections.[24] The disgraced Commission's continuation in office for a further six months, until a new Commission finally took over, increased public cynicism about the EU.

Besides disliking the EU's institutions, many Europeans resented what they saw as the EU's intrusiveness and heavy handedness. However exceptional, the Austrian imbroglio added fuel to the fire. Although not an official EU act, the decision by the other member states to impose sanctions against Austria deeply offended many people. Despite acting together, some member states were more zealous than others in advocating and imposing sanctions. The governments of Belgium and France, countries with popular Far Right parties of their own, seized on the Austrian situation for domestic political purposes. Most Europeans despised Haider and his ilk, but many disapproved of what looked like an unwarranted intrusion into Austrian politics and an exploitation of the Austrian situation by some member states.

Fear of referenda. The Austrian affair demonstrated an inevitable consequence of the popular backlash against the EU: member states' fear of holding referenda on EU-related issues. When the Austrian government announced in May 2000 that it would hold a referendum on EU participation unless the other member states came up with a concrete proposal to lift the sanctions, Austria's EU partners soon came to their senses. As the Austrian and other governments knew full well, the outcome of the referendum would have been a huge embarrassment for the EU. The German government, which in its 1998 election manifesto called for more referenda as a matter of principle, shied away from a suggestion that it hold a referendum on enlargement because it feared that the result would go against them. While striving to improve the EU's accountability in so many other ways, national leaders knew that rampant public unease and widespread Eurofatigue made it risky for them to hold referenda on the EU.[25]

The result of the Irish referendum on the Nice Treaty in June 2001 reinforced the point (Ireland was the only member state constitutionally obliged to hold a referendum to ratify the treaty). There were many non-EU-related reasons why Irish voters rejected the treaty, but the result upheld a secular trend throughout the EU of declining popular support for major EU initiatives. The Irish government gave the electorate a chance to redeem itself in a second referendum in October 2002. The government characterized the question as a simple choice between opposing or supporting enlargement, and EU institutions and governments castigated the Irish as ingrates. Whether out of conviction or contrition, more people turned out to vote, and a majority of them endorsed the treaty.

EU leaders had argued that it was undemocratic for Ireland's electorate to torpedo a treaty already ratified by the other member states, especially as the turnout in the first referendum was a paltry 35 percent. Many Irish people, regardless of their position on the treaty, thought that it was undemocratic of the Irish and other EU governments to disregard the result of the first referendum and insist on holding a second one. The EU's handling of the issue reinforced a popular perception that the EU was arrogant and high handed. For their part, national leaders concluded that ordinary Europeans could not be trusted to make momentous decisions about the EU's future.

A key question lurking behind the Irish referendum was how a country that benefited so much from EU membership and that traditionally supported European integration could have swung so far, so fast, against the EU. Few who voted in the referendum chose a position on the merits of the treaty itself. Many in the "no" camp were social conservatives and extreme nationalists who feared the consequences of further integration for Irish identity, neutrality, and society. Others who voted "no," or who deliberately abstained, were not necessarily conservative or nationalistic but, like many EU citizens, disliked the EU institutionally. They shared a widespread feeling that the EU was too remote and unresponsive, too opaque and unaccountable.

A Constitution for Europe

Even as the Irish electorate decided the fate of the Nice Treaty in October 2002, representatives of national and EU institutions met in Brussels in the Convention on the Future of Europe to draft a constitution for the EU. The convention emerged out of dissatisfaction with the Nice Treaty and the process that brought it about. In May 2000, during the conference, Joschka Fischer, Germany's foreign minister, made a speech in Berlin about the nature, organizing principles, and institutional structure of the enlarging EU. Speaking in a personal capacity, although with great authority as foreign minister of the EU's largest member state, Fischer called for a more federal EU. Chirac issued a rejoinder in a historic address to the German parliament in Berlin in September 2001, supporting greater European integration while defending the interests and identities of the member states. Thus began a debate on the future of the EU to which numerous commissioners, Europarliamentarians, and leading politicians in the member states and candidate countries contributed.[26]

The launch of the "post-Nice debate" in the pre-Nice period indicated widespread disillusionment with the narrow focus of the 2000 conference. In a declaration attached to the treaty, member states called for a "deeper and wider debate . . . about the future of the [EU]" as a prelude to yet another conference, in 2004, which would deal specifically with the role of national parliaments in the EU system, simplification of the treaties, the delimitation of competences (responsibilities) between the EU and the member states, and the status of the Charter of Fundamental Rights. The Nice declaration also called for a follow-up declaration by the European Council in Laeken in December 2001 "containing appropriate initiatives for the continuation of the process [of treaty reform]."[27]

Between the Nice summit in December 2000 and the Laeken summit in December 2001, reform-minded member states pressed successfully to broaden the agenda of the next conference. Widespread disappointment with the Nice Treaty, together with the shock of the Irish referendum result in June 2001, helped their case considerably. The Swedish and Belgian presidencies in 2001 campaigned for a broader conference. Despite their different perspectives on European integration—Sweden was somewhat Euroskeptical and Belgium Eurofederal—both countries fretted about the EU's ability to cope institutionally after enlargement and connect with ordinary Europeans. An appreciation of the enormity of enlargement and extent of public alienation from the EU finally convinced the European Council that the next conference could not be conducted like the previous one.

The European Council therefore agreed in Laeken not only to widen the agenda of the conference but also to prepare for it in a novel way. Drawing on the method used to draft the Charter of Fundamental Rights in 2000, the European Council announced that representatives of national governments, national parliaments, the Commission, and Parliament would meet in a convention to prepare the intergovernmental conference "as broadly and openly as possible." The composition of the convention reflected a consensus on the need to diversify participation in the process of EU treaty reform. Thus the convention would consist of fifteen representatives of the national leaders (one from each member state), thirty representatives of the national parliaments (two from each member state), two representatives of the Commission, and sixteen members of the Parliament. The candidate countries would be represented in the same way as the member states, but representatives of the candidate countries would not have a decisionmaking role.[28]

The convention was to have a chairman and two vice chairmen. The European Council selected them in the usual way. Chirac announced that either the chairman would be French or the convention would not take place. He proposed Valéry Giscard d'Estaing, a former president of France, largely because he wanted to remove Giscard from the domestic political scene during the forthcoming French elections. The small member states remembered Giscard's disinterest in them and disdain for the Commission but felt powerless to block the appointment. And so the septuagenarian Giscard, an arch-defender of the interests of big member states, came to personify the future of Europe. The European Council selected the vice chairmen for similar political reasons.

The convention opened in Brussels in February 2002. During the first six months its members conducted wide-ranging discussions about various policy and institutional issues. In addition to the plenary sessions, Giscard organized working groups on topics ranging from economic governance to external relations. The convention got down to business later in the year, after the French and German elections and after the second Irish referendum on the Nice Treaty. The decision to draft a constitution was of greater symbolic than real importance, given that the European Court already interpreted the treaties as constitutional texts. The most controversial institutional proposal was to elect a president of the European Council for a period of up to five years. Giscard and most of the leaders of the big member states saw this as essential for improving the European Council's efficiency and the EU's international standing. Most small countries saw it as further evidence of the big countries' effort to dominate EU affairs. The proposal to elect the president of the Commission went some way to mollify the small countries' concerns, but raised the prospect of competing EU presidencies undermining, rather than enhancing, the EU's role in the world. Another major change sought to help the EU manage its foreign relations: merging the posts of high representative for the common foreign and security policy and commissioner for external relations into the foreign minister of the EU, a position that would straddle the Council and the Commission.

Big and small member states also clashed over the size and composition of the Commission, an issue supposedly resolved in the Nice Treaty. For reasons of legitimacy, the convention proposed that each member state nominate a commissioner; for reasons of efficiency, that only a core group of commissioners have voting rights; and for reasons of equality, that membership in the core group rotate fairly among member states. Another institutional issue supposedly resolved in Nice—the calculation of a qualified majority—proved most contentious in the convention and ensuing intergovernmental conference. Giscard insisted on replacing the cumbersome Nice formula with a simpler system for calculating a qualified majority in the Council: a majority of member states representing at least 60 percent of the EU's population. Led by Spain, the main beneficiaries of the Nice agreement rallied to its defense, threatening to make the 2003–2004 intergovernmental conference a reprise of the Nice debacle.

The draft constitution was far more than a mere tidying up of the existing treaties. Despite unsatisfactory compromises over institutional issues, the constitution was highly significant politically. By incorporating the Charter of Fundamental Rights, the constitution gave the EU the equivalent of a Bill of Rights, an important constitutional component. The draft constitution proclaimed that the EU was based on democracy, the rule of law, and respect for human rights and fundamental freedoms. It outlined the EU's key organizing principles: conferred powers, subsidiarity, proportionality, and loyal cooperation among member states. It also clarified the division of powers or allocation of competences within the EU. Due to British objections, the draft constitution did not include the word *federal,* using instead less-objectionable but inelegant phrases such as *Community way* and *Community method.* Nevertheless, it pointed to a further federalization of the EU while at the same time affirming the EU's unique political nature.

Meeting in Thessalonica in June 2003, the European Council welcomed the draft constitution as "a good basis for starting" the intergovernmental conference, which began in October 2003. Despite their political importance, the convention and the intergovernmental conference failed to spark much interest beyond Brussels, except for a flurry of alarming articles in the British tabloid press. For the most part, few Europeans knew or cared that the convention or intergovernmental conference was taking place. Paradoxically, the convention and intergovernmental conference reinforced a perception prevalent throughout EU history that European integration, and especially political union, was driven by elites. Just as previous treaty changes provided disaffected Europeans with an opportunity to derail the process in national referenda, the outcome of the postconvention intergovernmental conference would do the same thing.

■ Policy Challenges

In the final analysis, Europeans were less interested in the EU's name, constitution, or nature than its performance. As the European Council acknowledged in December 2001, above all people wanted the EU to deliver "more results [and] better responses to practical issues . . . in terms of more jobs, better quality of life, less crime, decent education and better health care. There can be no doubt that this will require [the EU] to undergo renewal and reform."[29] It would also require the EU to meet a formidable array of policy challenges.[30] Some of these, such as maintaining and managing the single market, predated the Maastricht Treaty. Others flowed from the treaty itself. Foremost among these was the final stage of EMU, scheduled to begin in 1999 at the latest, with however many countries that then met the convergence criteria.

EMU was one of most important items on the EU's agenda in the 1990s and the early 2000s. Enlargement was the other. Enlargement would have a major impact on agriculture and cohesion, the EU's two big redistributive policies, but hardly impinged on EMU, for which global economic developments and the ongoing single market program were of more immediate concern. Global political challenges, ranging from Yugoslavia to Afghanistan, had a direct bearing on the EU's emerging foreign, security, and defense policy. In a rapidly changing external environment, the EU's international relations grew more extensive and complex. The terrorist attacks on the United States in September 2001 gave a new impetus to member state efforts to cooperate more closely on justice and home affairs. The fallout from the attacks, especially for the conduct of U.S. foreign policy, posed a particular challenge for the management of U.S.-EU relations.

From Maastricht to Monetary Union

The post-Maastricht phase of EMU began badly even before ratification of the treaty.[31] Rising German interest rates, intended to attract money to help reconstruction in the eastern part of the recently reunited country, pushed up the value of the mark and down the value of other currencies in the exchange rate mechanism of the European Monetary System (EMS). The ratification crisis put weaker currencies under additional pressure. What mushroomed into a major crisis began in August 1992 outside the mechanism with currencies unofficially linked to it. First the Finnish markka, then the Swedish krone collapsed under pressure from huge speculative attacks.

The situation seemed to warrant a general realignment in the exchange rate mechanism. But there had not been a realignment since 1987, giving the EMS the appearance by 1992 of a quasi–currency union. Although governments associated devaluation with political and economic weakness, Italy swallowed its pride and devalued the lire by 7 percent in early September

1992. The British authorities struggled to maintain the value of the pound, which entered the exchange rate mechanism of the EMS in October 1990 at the high rate of 2.95 against the mark. Much to Britain's irritation, Germany's central bank refused to intervene in the currency market to help the pound. Unable any longer to prop up the pound, a chastened Chancellor of the Exchequer pulled sterling out of the exchange rate mechanism on "black Wednesday," September 16, 1992.

Predictions of a "no" vote in the French referendum on the Maastricht Treaty in September 1992 and the narrowness of the eventual outcome intensified pressure on the franc. In a move that revealed Germany's much closer relationship with France than with any other member state, Germany bolstered French efforts to avert a disaster in late September and keep the franc within its exchange rate band. The franc survived; other weak currencies, such as the Spanish peseta, Portuguese escudo, Irish pound, and Italian lire, devalued in late 1992 and early 1993.

The currency crisis peaked in July 1993 when the German Central Bank decided not to make an eagerly awaited cut in interest rates. With international currency transactions increasing at a rapid rate and huge amounts of capital moving freely throughout the EU, the Germans felt unable any longer to support the franc. At an emergency meeting in August 1993, finance ministers decided to relieve pressure by allowing currencies in the exchange rate mechanism to move within a 15 percent band (instead of a 2.5 percent band) around their parity with the mark.

Some central banks lost a lot of money during the currency crisis; some speculators, such as George Soros, the international financier, made a fortune. People who did not understand international finance wondered how EMU could succeed after such an inauspicious beginning. The crisis had a devastating impact in Britain because the EMS, and by implication EMU, became associated with currency turmoil and national humiliation. Yet the currency crisis strengthened the conviction of most EU politicians and officials to press ahead with EMU. The German Central Bank, whose high interest rates exacerbated the crisis, was obliged to act only in Germany's interest. The European Central Bank (ECB), by contrast, would act in the interest of all EMU participants. Nor would there be separate currencies for speculators to attack in a monetary union with a single currency.

Achieving EMU. Stage Two of EMU began without fanfare in July 1994, with the establishment of the European Monetary Institute, whose purpose was to make technical preparations for Stage Three and help coordinate member states' monetary policies. The institute's tasks included specifying the regulatory, organizational, and logistical framework for the proposed European System of Central Banks, including the ECB; drafting a "changeover scenario" from national currencies to the single currency; devising monetary policy instruments and procedures; preparing a cross-border payments system; and compiling reliable statistics. Because the institute was the precursor of the ECB, Kohl insisted on locating it in Frankfurt, home of the German Central Bank and a symbol of sound monetary policy.

The Maastricht Treaty stipulated that Stage Three could begin in January 1997 if a majority of member states met the convergence criteria. It looked in the mid-1990s as if the deadline could not possibly be met. The EU was in recession. High interest rates in Germany pushed up interest rates throughout the EU, increasing the cost of borrowing money and reducing investment. As unemployment rose and consumer spending fell, governments took in less revenue but spent more money on welfare benefits. It was impossible under the circumstances for governments to reduce their deficits and debts to the levels required for participation in Stage Three of EMU. Most member states' inflation rates ranged outside the targeted band of not more than 1.5 percent of the EU's three best performers.

With member states thus diverging from, rather than converging on, the EMU criteria, it was unsurprising that the European Council, meeting in Madrid in December 1995, abandoned the goal of launching Stage Three in 1997. The European Council's decision instead to realize the 1999 deadline also seemed unrealistic. As if to emphasize its resolve, the European Council decided to name the new currency the "euro" and adopted the changeover scenario prepared by the European Monetary Institute on introducing the currency as legal tender throughout the euro zone. What many dismissed at the time as a foolish act of faith looked in retrospect like a bold assertion of political will.

Indeed, the success of EMU only a few years later owed much to the determination of a handful of political leaders, notably Kohl and Santer. Both were in relatively weak positions (Kohl narrowly won the October 1994 elections and lacked a majority in the upper house of parliament; Santer was perceived from the beginning of his presidency as a political lightweight) and ended their careers ignominiously (Kohl accused of accepting illegal party contributions; Santer forced to resign amid allegations of corruption in the Commission). Yet in the mid-1990s Kohl pursued EMU with a passion, arguing relentlessly that it was essential for Germany's and Europe's political and economic well-being. Though far less influential than Kohl, Santer spearheaded the Commission's commitment to EMU and orchestrated the technical measures necessary to ensure the successful launch of the euro.

A change of leadership in Paris also changed the tenor of Franco-German relations, but not the commitment of both countries to see EMU through. Jacques Chirac, elected president in May 1995 at the end of Mitterrand's second term in office, was equivocal about closer European integration and especially about EMU. Violent demonstrations in Paris in December 1995 against government austerity measures reminded the newly elected president of the risks involved in bringing France's public finances into line with EMU standards. Yet the division of authority between the president and prime minister in the French political system allowed Chirac to appear above the fray while his prime minister took the heat for unpopular economic reforms. Moreover, Chirac soon realized that France had little choice but to press ahead with EMU. Making a virtue of necessity and wanting to be seen as a leader of European stature, Chirac jettisoned his earlier misgivings and wholeheartedly endorsed EMU.

Strong political leadership and detailed technical preparations helped smooth the path toward Stage Three. Even so, member states might not have been able to meet the convergence criteria without a welcome improvement in the EU's economic fortunes. As growth rates gradually improved and unemployment peaked in 1996 and 1997, governments were able to reduce public expenditure enough to satisfy the Maastricht criteria. In fact, the criteria were drafted in such a way as to give the member states some wiggle room. Thus the 60 percent reference point for national debt could be exceeded if "the ratio [of debt to GDP] is sufficiently diminishing and approaching [60 percent] at a satisfactory pace." Similarly for budget deficits, the reference point of 3 percent could be missed if the ratio (of deficit to GDP) declined "substantially and continuously and reached a level that comes close to [3 percent]."[32]

With core EU member states such as Belgium and Italy carrying public debts in the range of 120 percent of GDP, the debt criterion would have to be interpreted liberally. The budget deficit criterion was harder for member states to fudge, especially as opponents of EMU insisted on interpreting it strictly. As well as curbing public expenditure, a number of member states made special and sometimes underhanded efforts to meet the 3 percent reference point. France applied a large, once-off payment from the partial privatization of the state-owned telecommunications company toward the country's deficit. The German government wanted to revalue the country's gold reserves and apply the higher balance toward the deficit, but the central bank would not allow it. By contrast, Italy took the courageous step of levying a special tax to help cut the budget deficit. Ultimately, economic recovery tipped the balance for France, Germany, and Italy, the three member states hovering around the 3 percent mark (Greece, with a 4 percent deficit, was not yet in the running).

The seriousness with which governments strove to get their public finances in order testified to their determination to enter the third stage of EMU. In their reports on economic convergence, mandated by the Maastricht Treaty, the Commission and the European Monetary Institute recommended that eleven member states begin Stage Three in January 1999 (Britain and Denmark chose to opt out; Sweden did not want to participate; and Greece joined in January 2001). The European Council endorsed these recommendations without demur at a summit in Brussels in March 1998, thereby avoiding what could have been a bruising political battle over the composition of the euro zone.

Instead the Brussels summit was infamous for a sharp encounter between Chirac and Kohl on a related matter: the presidency of the ECB. Especially because the bank would be located in Frankfurt, Chirac insisted that its first president be French. The governors of the national central banks recommended that the European Council, the body responsible for making the decision, appoint Wim Duisenberg, head of the Dutch Central Bank, to the position. Kohl supported Duisenberg because Duisenberg could be trusted to implement a responsible monetary policy (the Dutch Central Bank was a clone of its German counterpart). What should have been a done deal unraveled at the summit when Chirac objected to the central bankers' efforts to tie the European Council's hands and pushed Jean-Claude Trichet, governor of the French Central Bank, for the job. The dispute ended with a compromise: Duisenberg would be appointed ECB president but step down "of my own free will . . . and not under pressure from anyone," sometime after mid-2002, following the introduction of euro notes and coins. Trichet would then succeed Duisenberg for the remainder of the president's eight-year term in office.[33]

The dispute over Duisenberg's appointment brought out the worst in Chirac and soured his relationship with Kohl. It also raised questions about possible French interference in the operation of the ECB. Yet the members of the ECB's governing board, appointed at the same meeting of the European Council, were experienced, independent-minded central bankers. Duisenberg himself gave a spirited display of independent-mindedness at a hearing in the Parliament only a week after the summit. Thus the Brussels summit was more portentous for the future of Franco-German relations than for the conduct of monetary policy in the EU. Kohl's election defeat in October 1998 cleared the way for a new beginning at the pinnacle of the Franco-German relationship, but Chirac's inflexible defense of French interests, real and perceived, soon alienated Schröder as well.

The third stage. Stage Three of EMU began in January 1999 when exchange rates between participating currencies were locked in place and the ECB, which replaced the European Monetary Institute in Frankfurt in mid-1998, assumed responsibility for monetary policy in the euro zone. The euro itself existed only notionally; it did not begin to circulate for another three years. In the meantime the ECB, the Commission, and national authorities tackled the huge logistical challenge of introducing the new currency and withdrawing the old ones. According to the Maastricht Treaty, the new and old currencies could have circulated alongside each other for up to six months. In the event, national authorities were eager to minimize possible confusion by withdrawing the old currencies almost immediately.

The introduction of euro notes and coins in January 2002 went remarkably well. People snapped up euros from cash machines and banks and exchanged their national currencies more quickly and with far less fuss than expected. There were complaints in some countries of sharp practices by retailers who allegedly used the occasion to raise prices. Otherwise, people easily accepted the euro, being concerned more about the soundness than the color and design of the money in their pockets. Those who traveled across national borders were happy not to have to go to the trouble and expense of changing money.

The ECB faced a difficult task managing monetary policy for a large and disparate zone. As anticipated, a one-size-fits-all monetary policy was far from ideal for a zone that included a booming economy such as Ireland's and a stagnant economy such as Germany's. Given the vast difference in size between the two countries, inevitably the ECB set interest rates more appropriate to Germany's than Ireland's circumstances. Constitutionally obliged to fight inflation, the ECB faced an unexpected risk of deflation in 2002 and 2003 as prices dropped and economic performance faltered in the euro zone as a whole.

The euro began life in January 1999 at 1.18 to the U.S. dollar. Its value dropped steadily until rebounding in late 2002 and 2003, when it regained its original level. Some saw in the decline of the euro evidence that EMU was on shaky ground; others saw it as the market's reaction to initial overvaluation and a reflection of economic fundamentals on both sides of the Atlantic. For EU officials and politicians who envisioned the euro replacing the dollar as the world's leading reserve currency, the drop in the euro's external value was a great disappointment. For manufacturers, it meant that exports from the euro zone were more competitive. For tourists visiting the euro zone, it meant a relatively inexpensive vacation.

The stability and growth pact. EU leaders agreed at the Amsterdam summit in June 1997 to the stability and growth pact, intended to ensure the sustainability of the single currency through the continuation of budget discipline after the launch of Stage Three. At German insistence, the pact included provisions to penalize euro zone countries running "excessive" budget deficits (above 3 percent of GDP). The pact turned into a straitjacket for some countries in 2002 and 2003. Faced with declining revenues and increasing expenditure at a time of renewed recession, they failed to stay within the 3 percent target. Ironically, and to the undisguised delight of its EU partners, Germany was one of the offenders. Schröder's government, narrowly reelected in September 2002, seemed unable or unwilling to do much about it. France, another transgressor, was characteristically unapologetic about its high budget deficit.

It was difficult for the Commission, the guardian of EU orthodoxy, to uphold the stability and growth pact after the Council blocked its effort in

February 2002 to issue a formal "early warning" to Germany and after Prodi announced in October 2002 that the pact was "stupid."[34] Called to account before the Parliament, Prodi explained that the pact seemed unsuited to the straitened economic circumstances of the time. With falling growth and rising unemployment, governments should be in a position to raise spending and borrow money rather than having to abide by the strictures of the pact. The problem with Prodi's pronouncement, and with French and German disregard for the pact, was that it undermined the credibility of EMU, weakened the position of the ECB, and affronted the member states that had taken painful political steps in the 1990s to impose fiscal discipline.

EMU was never intended to be an end in itself but a means toward the greater end of rising productivity, higher growth, and more jobs. By 2002 those objectives seemed elusive. Recession in the United States and uncertainty in the post–September 11 period contributed to a gloomy economic outlook. Nevertheless, Germany's failure to seize the opportunity presented by EMU to undertake badly needed reform blighted prospects in the euro zone. As the engine of the euro zone's economy, Germany had the potential to drive the region out of recession. Instead, Germany burdened itself and the euro zone with its inflexible labor laws, high production costs, and a bloated welfare bill.

Britain remained outside the euro zone, despite Blair's hopes of bringing it in. Apart from not being in the exchange rate mechanism, albeit a mechanism with a wide band margin of 15 percent, Britain easily met the criteria for membership. Gordon Brown, Britain's Chancellor of the Exchequer and Blair's rival within the Labour Party, set criteria of his own for the British economy to meet before accepting the euro. The government promised to hold a referendum before entering Stage Three of EMU. Although Blair argued the case for EMU on economic grounds, he had a compelling political reason to join the euro zone. Despite Britain's size and status, Blair believed that his country would never punch with its full weight in the EU until it adopted the euro.

Market Integration, Modernization, and Employment

Economic and monetary union was one element of a multifaceted approach to promoting growth and employment in the EU. Other elements included the single market program, a revamped social policy, and coordination of member states' employment policies. Completion and consolidation of the single market were fundamental objectives of the new EU and cornerstones of the EU's approach to economic modernization. The single market program of the late 1980s and early 1990s was a political and psychological success but remained a work in progress. Ongoing aspects of it included the enactment of proposals still on the table and of new proposals necessitated by technological and other changes, the transposition of directives into national law, enforcement of single market measures, and liberalization of the energy and telecommunications sectors (excluded from the original single market program).

The rate of single market legislation slowed down in the 1990s either because most of the measures in the 1992 program were already enacted or because of subsidiarity. Some old proposals remained stuck in the decision-making machinery. Foremost among these was the proposal for a European Company Statute to allow enterprises to operate more easily throughout the EU. Introduced by the Commission in 1970, it continued to founder on fundamental conflicts among member states over worker participation in the management of European companies. Nevertheless, there were important breakthroughs in the 1990s involving existing or new proposals, including legislation in the areas of product standards, new technologies, and intellectual property rights.

Member states were obliged to transpose EU directives into national law within a prescribed period and then to enforce them. Without transposition and enforcement, the single market meant little in practice. Regardless of its general political weakness, the Commission pressed member states in the 1990s to improve their mixed records of transposition and enforcement. France, Greece, Italy, and Portugal were consistently among the laggards, with Euroskeptical Britain, Denmark, and Sweden steadfastly at the top of the league.

Hoping to capitalize on the momentum generated by the countdown to the single currency, the European Council endorsed a single market action plan in June 1997. The action plan included specific measures to remove market distortions; improve the enactment, transposition, and enforcement of single market measures; and make the process more relevant to EU citizens. Britain, in the Council presidency in the first half of 1998, pushed the action plan aggressively, "naming and shaming" in order to boost member state compliance and broadening the single market "scoreboard" to include new criteria alongside the more legalistic and quantitative indices used to date.

The Commission was equally forceful in the pursuit of competition policy, a necessary corollary to the single market program. Despite the Commission's vigilance, the problem of national subsidies (state aids) remained acute and continued to distort the single market. Although appreciating that subsidies were expensive, wasteful, and generally unavailing, national governments found it impossible politically to give them up. It was also difficult for the Commission to stamp them out, as legal action proved time consuming and provoked a strong reaction from member states.

The Commission's trustbusters stepped up their investigations in the 1990s into allegations of market abuses and restrictive practices by EU enterprises. Based on a Council regulation of December 1989, the Commission also scrutinized impending mergers that were above a certain financial threshold and met a transnationality requirement. As the number of mergers increased in the early 1990s owing to the single market program, and peaked again in the early 2000s owing to introduction of the euro, the Commission's merger task force became increasingly prominent and powerful. Although it blocked only a small number of mergers, the task force came under severe criticism from certain member states, multinationals, and outside governments for acting hastily and seemingly arbitrarily. The Court of First Instance (the EU's lower court) delivered a devastating blow against the Commission in October 2002 when, twice within a week, it overruled Commission decisions to block major mergers. While putting the Commission on the defensive, the court's rulings emphasized the importance of merger control for market integration in the EU.

Despite the EU's impressive record in the 1990s of staying the course on EMU and consolidating the single market, productivity in the EU remained relatively low and unemployment stubbornly high. The road to EMU, in particular, seemed to exacerbate unemployment, with governments cutting public spending in order to meet the Maastricht criteria during hard times. The Commission turned its attention to unemployment in the late 1980s when it produced the first in a series of annual reports on the subject. The European Council took note of the problem, issuing ritualistic denunciations of unemployment at successive summits. An influential Commission white paper on the challenge of job creation prompted widespread debate in the EU in the mid-1990s.[35]

Responding to rising concerns throughout the EU and eager to increase the Commission's role in coordinating economic policy, Santer proposed in January 1997 a "confidence pact on employment." The purpose of the pact was to boost jobs by strengthening the single market, curbing state aids, improving vocational training, helping small and medium-sized enterprises, and funding Trans-European Networks (transport, telecommunications, and energy infrastructures). Member states agreed during the 1996–1997 intergovernmental conference to modify the EU's objectives to include "a high level of employment." Unemployment rose higher on the EU's agenda when the Socialists in France and Labour in Britain won the elections of May 1997. At the insistence of the new French government, the European Council held a special summit on employment in Luxembourg in November 1997. There the European Council agreed to a "new approach," whereby member states would submit national employment action plans for annual peer review. These would be based on four criteria: employability, entrepreneurship, adaptability of enterprises and individuals, and equal opportunity.

The European Council evaluated member states' annual employment plans for the first time at the Cardiff summit in June 1998. Beginning in 1999, the Commission advised member states on the implementation of their employment policies. The European Council finally reached agreement in December 1998 on a European Employment Pact, which it formally adopted at the Cologne summit in June 1999. This incorporated a number of initiatives: the process agreed upon in Cologne to coordinate economic policy, the Luxembourg process to coordinate employment strategy, and the Cardiff process to improve implementation of the single market program.

The EU's increasing emphasis on employment cast social policy in a new light. Support for old-fashioned social policy, with its intrusive legislation on the workplace, was already on the wane in 1991 when the other member states insisted on adding the social protocol to the Maastricht Treaty in the face of ferocious British opposition. With unemployment high throughout the EU, the social charter seemed a luxury that European business simply could not afford. Governments, including the French one, were unwilling to incur the costs of implementing the social action program. Many quietly acknowledged that the action program risked making European business uncompetitive in the global economy, thereby undermining one of the core objectives of the single market. Even when Labour came to power and agreed to bring the social protocol squarely into the EU (via the Amsterdam Treaty), member states continued to recast social policy as a means of promoting employment rather than making it more costly.

The European Council held a special summit in Lisbon in March 2000 to try to inject new life into economic reform and modernization. EU leaders agreed at the summit that by 2010 the EU should become "the most competitive and dynamic knowledge-based economy in the world capable of sustainable economic growth and more and better jobs and greater social cohesion."[36] In other words, the EU should resemble the United States economically but not socially. Yet the high cost of social welfare in Europe was one of the factors retarding the EU's economic growth along U.S. lines. Thus the much-trumpeted Lisbon objectives contained an apparent contradiction.

The European Council sought to achieve its ambitious goal of a 3 percent rate of annual growth and twenty million new jobs within a decade by implementing the so-called Lisbon strategy through a combination of legislation, benchmarking, and peer pressure. The Lisbon strategy drew on a number of existing initiatives, ranging from completion of the single market, especially for telecommunications and financial services, to better education and training, to exploiting fully the economic potential of the Internet. Emulating the original single market program, the Lisbon strategy set target dates for many of its objectives. The European Council pledged to meet annually in the spring specifically to keep up political pressure for implementation of the Lisbon strategy.

Yet the Lisbon strategy and other initiatives focused political attention on the EU's economic problems without providing adequate solutions. Despite the single market and EMU, the EU and the euro zone remained a collection of dissimilar economies. Growth and job creation varied widely among member states, which faced the additional challenge of global economic uncertainty. Political circumstances made it easier for some member states than others to undertake the painful steps necessary to improve economic performance. The situation was simply not conducive to achieving the laudable Lisbon goals. Although European integration undoubtedly helped the member states economically, the EU seemed unlikely ever to achieve its full potential for growth and job creation.

Agriculture and Cohesion

The common agricultural policy and cohesion policy continued to account for the bulk of EU expenditure in the 1990s and early 2000s. The prospect of Central and Eastern European enlargement affected both directly. Because the candidate countries were poor and had relatively large agricultural sectors, their participation in the CAP and cohesion policy on the same terms as the existing member states could have bankrupted the EU. Enlargement presented an opportunity for radical CAP and cohesion reform, although recipients of generous financial transfers from Brussels wanted to protect their share as much as possible.

Under pressure to curb surpluses and reduce trade-distorting subsidies in order to complete the Uruguay Round of the General Agreement on Tariffs and Trade, the Council agreed to major reform in May 1992. Known by the name of the commissioner for agriculture, the MacSharry reform broke the link between guaranteed prices and overproduction by shifting the basis of subsidies to direct payments to farmers. Ironically, the reformed CAP cost more than the original version because of generous compensation offered to big farmers who otherwise would have experienced a sharp drop in income. Based on the reform package, the Commission concluded an agreement with the United States in October 1992 to reduce export subsidies. Eager to maintain the status quo, France rejected the agreement and, with German support, insisted that the Commission reopen negotiations with the United States. Understandably resentful, the United States nonetheless concluded a new accord with the Commission, which the Council duly endorsed in December 1993, thus facilitating completion of the Uruguay Round.

Widespread concern about food safety, following a number of scares in the mid-1990s, added new pressure for CAP reform. Consumers complained about an agricultural policy that emphasized mass production and paid little attention to the quality of food. At the same time, people became more aware of the damaging environmental consequences of the CAP, which encouraged farmers to produce at all costs. Sensitive to consumer concerns and obliged under the terms of the Amsterdam Treaty to incorporate environmental protection "into the definition and implementation of Community policies and

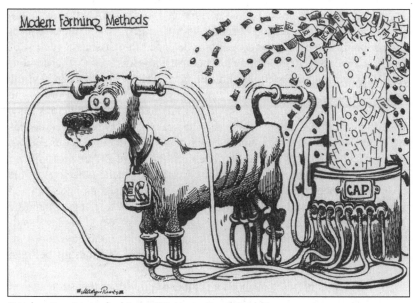

"Modern Farming Methods" © 1991 Martyn Turner/*Irish Times*.

activities . . . with a view to promoting sustainable development," the EU sought to cast the CAP in a more consumer- and environment-friendly light. Under the aegis of *Agenda 2000*, approved by the European Council in March 1999, the EU began to emphasize the importance of organic farming, agri-environmentalism, and rural development.

The main thrust of the agricultural provisions of *Agenda 2000* and of a major CAP agreement of June 2003 was to continue the MacSharry reforms by shifting subsidies from price supports to direct payments. As in the early 1990s, France resisted any reduction of agricultural expenditure, Germany acquiesced in French demands, and the other member states went along with the Franco-German fait accompli. With the imminent conclusion of accession negotiations with the Central and Eastern European countries in late 2002, member states needed to reach an agreement on agricultural expenditure covering the period of the next financial perspective (2006–2013). France and Germany agreed before the opening of the Brussels summit not to cut farm spending but to limit its growth to 1 percent a year after 2006. Faced with a Franco-German accord and eager to conclude the accession negotiations, the other leaders agreed, some against their better judgment, to maintain an exorbitant rate of agricultural expenditure for at least another ten years. The EU therefore missed another opportunity to curb spending on the CAP.

The CAP survived in part because of its residual significance in the history of European integration. France continued to see the CAP as a fundamental element of its original bargain with Germany.[37] At a time of great international change, France desperately defended the CAP as a symbol of enduring Franco-German rapprochement. Sensitive as ever to French concerns, Germany agreed at the Berlin summit in March 1999 and again at the Brussels summit in October 2002 not to upset the apple cart. More to the point, perhaps, the domestic politics of the CAP made it impossible for France and difficult for Germany to countenance radical reform. Despite their declining numbers, farmers were too influential politically for either the French or the German government to confront. The vast majority of EU citizens, with no direct connection to the land, sympathized with the general objectives of the CAP and seemed willing to subsidize farmers at a generous rate. External pressure for CAP reform, emanating from agricultural free traders and the developing world, especially during the Doha Round of World Trade Organization (WTO) negotiations, was insufficient to overcome the entrenched interests of EU farmers or jeopardize the deep-rooted relationship between France and Germany.

The Maastricht Treaty included a number of provisions that strengthened the EU's commitment to cohesion. The most important of these mandated a Cohesion Fund by the end of December 1993 to contribute to projects on the environment and transportation in member states with a per capita GDP of less than 90 percent of the EU average and a program designed to achieve economic convergence. In other words, the Cohesion Fund was intended to help Greece, Ireland, Portugal, and Spain to meet the convergence criteria for participation in EMU. Together with the existing structural funds, the new Cohesion Fund represented a considerable commitment on the part of the EU's net contributors to help the less-developed member states.

As in the case of the provisions on cohesion in the Single European Act, however, it was easier for member states to promise to increase spending on regional development than to make the necessary budgetary arrangements. Just as Delors crafted a post-SEA budgetary package (Delors I) for the period 1988 to 1992, in 1992 he crafted a post-Maastricht budgetary package (Delors II) for the period 1993 to 1999. The second Delors package included generous allocations for cohesion policy, ranging from a doubling of spending on Objective 1 regions (regions with a per capita GDP of less than 75 percent of the EU average) to a large Cohesion Fund.

Economic and political circumstances were hardly propitious in 1992 for an accord on the second Delors package, with the EU in recession, the EMS in crisis, and the fate of the Maastricht Treaty in doubt. Partly to signal the durability of the EU, however, the European Council agreed at the Edinburgh summit in December 1992 to double assistance for the least-developed member states to a whopping thirty billion euros by 1999. It was one of Delors's last political victories. As he and the jubilant leaders of the poorer member states must have known, the battle for the next financial cycle (after 1999) would be overshadowed by the needs of the candidate countries in Central and Eastern Europe.

Agenda 2000, the budgetary package for the post-1999 period, was indeed controversial. By the late 1990s, the situation in the EU with regard to cohesion had changed considerably. Having transformed itself into the Celtic Tiger, thanks in part to immense infusions of well-managed money from the structural funds, Ireland no longer qualified as an Objective 1 region. Yet the Irish government, addicted to "Brussels money," wanted to continue to feed at the EU trough. At the other end of the spectrum, Greece remained relatively impoverished despite receiving huge assistance from the EU. Unlike Ireland, Greece did not use structural funding wisely (and had not benefited from gigantic inward investment). The net contributors to the budget did not want to continue subsidizing a country like Ireland, which was rapidly acquiring one of the highest rates of per capita GDP in the EU, and a country like Greece, which was notorious for squandering its share of the structural funds. With member states tightening their belts for monetary union, and ten poor Central and Eastern European countries knocking at the door, cohesion policy seemed ripe for reappraisal.

Agenda 2000 therefore contained proposals for cohesion policy reform. The Commission proposed keeping spending on cohesion at about one-third of the EU's annual budget for the period 2000–2006, including a large amount for the candidate countries both before and after they joined. The Commission also proposed reducing the structural fund objectives to three, covering low-income countries (where the bulk of the spending would go), declining industrial regions, and the development of human resources. In general, the Commission recommended reducing the proportion of the EU population covered by the structural funds from 51 percent to less than 40 percent.

The crucial European Council meeting on *Agenda 2000*, in March 1999, took place during Germany's presidency. As a relatively new leader, Schröder lacked experience of EU summitry; as president-in-office of the Council, he wanted the summit to end amicably and successfully. Schröder therefore accepted most of the *Agenda 2000* proposals, although he said before the summit that he wanted to reduce EU spending. Because enlargement was not yet pressing, EU leaders deferred difficult budgetary decisions until the negotiations for the next financial package, covering the period 2007–2013, when the demands of the new Central and Eastern European member states would be pressing.

The principle of cohesion policy—the importance of reducing social and economic disparities between richer and poorer countries and regions—was uncontested in the enlarging EU. The problem was how to put that principle into practice. A consensus emerged in the early 2000s that a combination of sound macroeconomic policies, a favorable international economic climate, generous financial transfers from Brussels, and closer coordination in the formulation and implementation of regional policy at the national and European levels was essential for economic development in the poor member states. Cohesion policy covered some of these elements; other EU policies touched on the rest.

Internal Security

Responding to public concern about the social implications of closer integration and globalization, member states strengthened cooperation throughout the 1990s and early 2000s in the area of justice and home affairs. The Amsterdam Treaty contained a number of noteworthy developments in that regard. Thus member states agreed to shift all but police and judicial cooperation out of the intergovernmental pillar on justice and home affairs established by the Maastricht Treaty. They also agreed to bring the Schengen agreement, which facilitated the free movement of people among most member states, into the EU's legal framework. A protocol attached to the treaty provided for Schengen's incorporation into EU law, with special provisions for non-Schengen members Britain, Denmark, and Ireland. In an effort to make the EU more responsive to citizens' concerns, member states pledged, by 2004 at the latest, to create "an area of freedom, security and justice, in which the free movement of persons is assured in conjunction with appropriate measures with respect to external border controls, asylum, immigration and the prevention and combating of crime."[38]

The Amsterdam Treaty included a flexibility clause to allow member states wanting to cooperate more closely on justice and home affairs to use EU institutions, procedures, and instruments. As with similar provisions on foreign and security policy, the treaty allowed a member state to prevent closer cooperation by invoking "important and stated reasons of national policy." That implicit reassertion of the Luxembourg Compromise (the right to veto) testified to some member states' extreme sensitivity on the question of closer cooperation, especially in the area of justice and home affairs.

Having decided to move a number of third pillar issues over to the supranational first pillar, member states remained wary of involving the Commission, the Parliament, and the Court in the remaining third pillar issues: judicial and police cooperation. The fate of EUROPOL, the EU agency for cross-border police cooperation, proved the point. The European Council agreed in June 1993 on a convention to establish EUROPOL. The new body became operational in January 1994, but only on a restricted basis as governments bickered over the role of the European Court. The European Council finally resolved the matter in June 1996 with an agreement allowing the Court to give preliminary interpretations of the EUROPOL convention.

In December 1998, the Council adopted an action plan to bring the area of freedom, security, and justice into existence. Drafted by the Commission, the plan included an explanation of the initiative and a list of measures necessary for its realization. At the same time the Commission and other institutions prepared to implement the Amsterdam Treaty in May 1999. One of the biggest tasks they faced was incorporating the voluminous body of Schengen rules and regulations into the much more voluminous body of EU rules and regulations. Finland identified justice and home affairs as a priority for its presidency during the second half of 1999 and organized a special summit on the subject in Tampere in October. The summit produced the Ten Milestones of Tampere, a set of steps to give concrete meaning to the area of freedom, security, and justice. These included a common asylum and immigration policy; better administrative, judicial, and police cooperation to fight organized crime; and fair treatment of resident third-country nationals.[39]

Drawing on the experience of the single market, in March 2000 the Commission launched the first in a series of biannual "scoreboards" to monitor progress on the creation of the area of freedom, security, and justice and to pressure member states to act. A year later the Commission suggested supplementing EU legislation with a system of peer review for immigration and asylum policy, whereby the Council would adopt multiannual guidelines to be implemented through national action plans and monitored by the Commission. The launch in March 2001 of EUROJUST, the EU body for criminal justice cooperation and coordination, was another example of the impetus provided by Tampere.

As the Commission's willingness to countenance new measures implied, progress on justice and home affairs was extremely mixed. Differences of political interest and administrative capacity among member states ensured unevenness in the enactment and implementation of justice and home affairs measures. The Belgian presidency produced a scathing progress report on the Tampere agenda in December 2001, especially in the area of immigration and asylum. By that time interest in the internal and international dimensions of justice and home affairs focused squarely on global terrorism, following the attacks on the United States in September 2001. The events of September 11 clearly showed the need for close cooperation among member states and other like-minded governments on antiterrorism measures. The most immediate impact of September 11 was to boost cooperation within the EU and between the EU and the United States on issues such as extradition and arrest warrants.[40]

Most Europeans had no idea that the EU was striving to become an area of freedom, security, and justice. Europeans generally took freedom and justice for granted but fretted more about security. Rising street crime in most member states, together with the well-publicized activities of organized criminal gangs, made Europeans feel increasingly insecure in the late 1990s and early 2000s. Although the atrocities of September 11 were directed against the United States, they were mostly planned in Europe. Despite having endured politically inspired terrorism for many years, Europeans appreciated that the new wave of global terrorism was as much a threat to their own countries and societies as it was to the United States.

Economic insecurity in the form of rising unemployment caused further disquiet. It was easy for right-wing demagogues to blame the situation in part on illegal immigration. The success of Far Right parties in Austria, Belgium, Denmark, and France in the early 2000s showed that their message resonated among the electorate. Enlargement was an obvious focus of right-wing concern, as it was easy to exploit popular fears of unrestricted flows into Western Europe of allegedly impoverished and unscrupulous Central and Eastern Europeans. Pandering to such concerns, the EU allowed existing member states a delay of seven years on the applicability to the new member states of the provisions for the free movement of people, a cornerstone of the single market and a basic objective of the EU itself. The EU also worked with the candidate countries to shore up the security of their eastern borders in order to ensure the integrity of the EU's external frontiers.

Insofar as Europeans wanted more integration in the early 2000s, it was certainly in the area of internal security. Accordingly, the EU emphasized "security" more than "freedom" and "justice" in its pursuit of the Amsterdam objectives for justice and home affairs. Even so, many Europeans saw the EU as a poor provider of security or even as a cause of insecurity because it seemed to undermine member states' abilities to act independently. Here was another example of the difficulty that the EU faced in meeting popular expectations and communicating its undoubted achievements.

External Relations

The EU continued in the 1990s and 2000s to be a major actor on the international stage. The EU's weight and stature as an international economic entity were striking. Together with the United States, the EU dominated the WTO. Just as the conclusion of the Uruguay Round of the GATT in the early 1990s depended on the United States and EU's striking a deal on agriculture, the launch of the Doha Round of the WTO a decade later hinged on the United States and EU's reaching agreement on the agenda. The United States and the EU were the principal parties in most cases brought before the WTO dispute settlement body. Yet their cavalier approach to WTO rulings jeopardized not only the dispute settlement mechanism but also the WTO itself.

The EU extended its global economic reach by negotiating or renegotiating a variety of trade and aid pacts. These ranged from the Cotonou agreement of June 2000 with over eighty African, Caribbean, and Pacific countries, which replaced the long-standing (and thrice revised) Lomé agreement, to a free trade agreement with Mexico, which came into effect in March 2001. The EU institutionalized its relationship with the United States first with the Transatlantic Declaration of 1990, then with the New Transatlantic Agenda of December 1995. EU competition policy had a significant international impact. As well as affecting large foreign companies operating, or hoping to operate, in the EU, it was an integral part of many EU trade agreements. The EU became a leading player in international environmental policy, especially after the United States abandoned the field by abruptly rejecting the Kyoto protocol in 2001. Finally, the euro added luster to the EU's international image, although the new currency's initial weakness thwarted its ambition to rival the U.S. dollar as the world's leading reserve currency.

Yet in the realm of foreign policy, security, and defense, the EU remained weak. The common foreign and security policy, an important innovation in the Maastricht Treaty, got off to a slow start. The treaty provided for common positions and joint actions that could be implemented by qualified majority voting if adopted first by unanimity. The distinction between common positions and joint actions was unclear and the decisionmaking process confusing. The Council found it difficult to break the habit of deciding everything entirely by unanimity.

The European Stability Pact, a mechanism to promote good relations among the newly independent countries of Central and Eastern Europe, was one of the EU's earliest and most successful joint actions. It was also an easy issue for the EU to tackle. By contrast, the EU was incapable of preventing Serb atrocities in Bosnia, which ended only after the United States intervened militarily in 1995. Realizing the weakness of the common foreign and security policy even before it became operational, member states called in the Maastricht Treaty for another intergovernmental conference in 1996 to review progress and improve procedures. Public frustration with the EU's ineffectualness in Bosnia focused the EU's attention on the need to develop a more effective means of acting outside its borders.

The Amsterdam Treaty's provisions for the common foreign and security policy were indeed an improvement, but were not as far-reaching as the EU's supranational institutions and supranational-minded member states had hoped for. The provisions included new policy instruments, greater use of qualified majority voting, agreement on "constructive abstention" (by member states not wanting to participate in a particular initiative), and the establishment of a Policy Planning and Early Warning Unit in the Council secretariat. The treaty also established the position of the high representative (or superenvoy) for the common foreign and security policy to represent the EU externally. The EU devised and implemented a number of useful common strategies in the post-Amsterdam period, notably toward Russia, the Western Balkans, and the Mediterranean.

In an inspired move, in June 1999 the European Council appointed Javier Solana the first high representative. Solana's experience as secretary general of NATO, which brought him into close contact with U.S. foreign and defense policymakers, was an invaluable asset for the EU. As intended, Solana personified EU foreign and defense policy cooperation. Yet his authority was moral rather than real. Procedural weaknesses continued to undermine the effectiveness of the EU's external action: Solana was the servant of the presidency; as a senior official he was inferior in rank to the foreign minister of even the smallest member state; and the relationship between his position and that of the commissioner for external relations was unclear.

Once again the situation in the Balkans demonstrated the continuing inadequacy of the common foreign and security policy. The EU was unable to act swiftly and aggressively to halt Serbian assaults on the Muslim population in Kosovo in 1998 and early 1999. The Serbs ended their aggression only when confronted by a sustained NATO bombardment and the threat of a NATO invasion. Although many EU member states participated in the NATO action and in peacekeeping operations in postwar Kosovo, the EU had neither the means nor the will to act decisively in the entire Kosovo affair.

An Anglo-French call in December 1998 for the EU to develop "the capacity for autonomous [military] action" began a process that ended in the establishment of the Rapid Reaction Force in 2003.[41] Britain, the EU's militarily most powerful member state, traditionally eschewed European defense initiatives in favor of close cooperation with the United States. Blair was as Atlanticist as any of his predecessors, but he also favored closer European cooperation on foreign policy and defense, albeit along intergovernmental lines. Having opted out of the euro, Blair saw defense cooperation as a means of giving Britain a leadership role in the EU. Chirac was happy to collaborate with Britain on the pursuit of what was, after all, a long-standing French objective.

Despite some misgivings within the U.S. administration, NATO endorsed the goal of an autonomous EU defense capacity at a summit in Washington in April 1999. Meeting in Cologne two months later, the European Council called for the EU to develop the capacity to undertake military operations independently of NATO, which meant in practice without the United States. According to the Cologne Declaration, this would represent "a new step in the construction of the European Union."[42]

Six months later, at the Helsinki summit in December 1999, the European Council specified exactly what the EU's military capacity would be: a force up to sixty thousand strong, with the necessary command, control, and intelligence capabilities, able to deploy within sixty days and stay in the field for at least a year.[43] The EU established a number of institutions to manage its emerging security and defense policy: the Political and Security Committee, the Military Committee, and the Military Staff. In November 2000 member states held a Capabilities Commitment Conference at which they pledged resources to meet the "headline goals" agreed to at the Helsinki summit. At the same time, the EU effectively took over the structure and responsibilities of the Western European Union, a long-standing organization for intra-European defense cooperation.

The development of a security and defense policy, with the Rapid Reaction Force as its operational arm, preoccupied the EU in the early 2000s. Despite NATO's support of the initiative, the EU and NATO had difficulty sorting out a political-military relationship. Reconciling Turkey, a large NATO member and EU candidate, to the new arrangement was also tricky politically. The biggest challenge, however, was matching the rhetoric of closer security and defense cooperation with the reality of strained member state budgets. Despite their pledges at the capability conference, member states generally reduced military spending during the straitened economic circumstances of the early 2000s.

Despite a commitment to establishing the Rapid Reaction Force, the EU's performance in the realm of foreign, security, and defense policy left a lot to be desired. Even as they called for closer defense cooperation within the EU, Britain and France differed sharply in the 1990s and early 2000s over how to deal with Iraq, which Britain and the United States suspected of harboring weapons of mass destruction. Matters came to a head in March 2003, when the United States and Britain invaded Iraq over the strident opposition of France and Germany. In a fit of pique, the leaders of France, Germany, Belgium, and Luxembourg held a minisummit in late April on defense cooperation, to which Britain and other pro-U.S. member states were pointedly not invited. As the Convention on the Future of Europe came to a close, the EU's fledgling security and defense policy appeared to be in tatters.

Appalled by this turn of events, Solana struggled in the aftermath of the Iraq invasion to repair the damage within the EU and between leading EU member states and the United States. Specifically, he presented a document to the European Council in June 2003 called "A Secure Europe in a Better World." In it, Solana identified three main threats to global security: terrorism, weapons of mass destruction, and the consequences of failed states. Solana advocated a muscular response by the EU toward these threats, possibly including the use of force. This was the basis of the Security Strategy, which the European Council duly adopted.

The new strategy accorded more to the United States than the traditional EU view of post–September 2001 security challenges, although it strongly endorsed the multilateral international system and the fundamental role of the UN. Therefore, it helped to reconcile divergent views within the EU and among the Europeans and Americans while salvaging the EU's incipient security and defense policy. At the same time, the draft constitution included provisions for a permanent president of the European Council and an EU foreign minister, in order to boost the EU's international impact and credibility.

Yet there were limits to establishing a truly effective security and defense policy beyond which most member states were unwilling to go. Neither Britain nor France would countenance stepping down as permanent members of the UN Security Council in favor of a combined EU seat. Few member states wanted to hand over responsibility for national defense to a European supranational authority. Nevertheless, the lessons of the Iraqi debacle were salutary for the EU. Although unwilling and unable to become a superpower like the United States, the EU began to act more responsibly and coherently on the international political stage.

▓ Notes

1. On the 1995 enlargement, see Günter Bischof, Anton Pelinka, and Michael Gehler, eds., *Austria in the European Union* (New York: Transaction Publishers, 2002); Max Jacobson, *Finland in the New Europe* (Westport, CT: Praeger, 1998); Lene Hansen and Ole Waever, *European Integration and National Identity: The Challenge of the Nordic States* (London: Routledge, 2002); Sieglinde Gstöhl, *Reluctant Europeans: Norway, Sweden, and Switzerland in the Process of Integration* (Boulder, CO: Lynne Rienner Publishers, 2002); John Redmond, *The 1995 Enlargement of the European Union* (Aldershot: Ashgate, 1997); Francisco Granell, "The European Union's Enlargement Negotiations with Austria, Finland, Norway and Sweden," *Journal of Common Market Studies* 33, no. 1 (September 1995), pp. 134–148.

2. See *Agence Europe*, March 30, 1994, pp. 1–2.

3. On Central and Eastern European enlargement, see Graham Avery and Fraser Cameron, *The Enlargement of the European Union* (Sheffield: Sheffield University Press, 1998); Stuart Croft, John Redmond, G. Wyn Rees, and Mark Webber, *The Enlargement of Europe* (Manchester: Manchester University Press, 1999); Michael Baun, *A Wider Europe: The Process and Politics of European Union Enlargement* (Lanham, MD: Rowman and Littlefield, 2000); Alan Mayhew, *Recreating Europe: The European Union's Policy Towards Central and Eastern Europe*, 2nd ed. (Cambridge: Cambridge University Press, 2002).

4. See, for instance, Robert Cutler, "Harmonizing EEC-CMEA Relations: Never the Twain Shall Meet?" *International Affairs* 63, no. 2 (Spring 1987), pp. 259–270.

5. Bulletin EC 6-1993.

6. Bulletin EU 12-1994.

7. Commission, "Preparing for Enlargement," COM(95)final.

8. Commission, *Agenda 2000: For a Stronger and Wider Union* (Brussels: Commission, August 1997).

9. Bulletin EU 12-1997.

10. Bulletin EU 12-2002.

11. See Ziya Onis, "Luxembourg, Helsinki and Beyond: Towards an Interpretation of Recent Turkey-EU Relations," *Government and Opposition* 35, no. 4 (Autumn 2000), pp. 463–483.

12. On the Amsterdam intergovernmental conference and treaty, see Geoffrey Edwards and Alfred Pijpers, *The Politics of European Treaty Reform: The 1996 Intergovernmental Conference and Beyond* (London: Pinter, 1997); Anna-Carin Svensson, *In the Service of the European Union: The Role of the Presidency in Negotiating the*

Amsterdam Treaty, 1995–1997 (Uppsala: Acta Universitatis, 2000); Jörg Monar and Wolfgang Wessels, eds., *The European Union After the Treaty of Amsterdam* (London: Continuum, 2001); Finn Laursen, ed., *The Amsterdam Treaty: National Preference Formation, Interstate Bargaining and Outcome* (Odense: Odense University Press, 2002); Bobby McDonagh, *Original Sin in a Brave New World: The Paradox of Europe. An Account of the Negotiation of the Treaty of Amsterdam* (Dublin: Institute for European Affairs, 1998).

13. Christian Democratic Union/Christian Social Union Group in the Lower House, "Reflections on European Policy," Bonn, September 1, 1994.

14. Bulletin EU 6-1997.

15. On the intergovernmental conference and the ensuing Nice Treaty, see Mark Gray and Alexander Stubb, "Keynote Article: The Treaty of Nice—Negotiating a Poisoned Chalice?" in *The European Union: Annual Review of the EU 2000/2001,* ed. Geoffrey Edwards and Georg Wiessala (Oxford: Blackwell, 2001), pp. 5–24.

16. Jean-Luc Dehaene, Richard von Weiszäcker, and David Simon, "The Institutional Implications of Enlargement. Report to the European Commission," October 18, 1999.

17. Gray and Stubb, "Treaty of Nice," p. 13.

18. On Commission reform, see Neill Nugent, *The European Commission* (Basingstoke: Palgrave, 2001).

19. See Desmond Dinan, "Governance and Institutions 2000: Edging Toward Enlargement," in *The European Union: Annual Review of the EU 2000/2001,* ed. Geoffrey Edwards and Georg Wiessala (Oxford: Blackwell, 2001), pp. 25–41.

20. Amsterdam Treaty, text available at http://europa.eu.int/scadplus/leg/en/s50000.htm.

21. Ibid.

22. On the Austrian situation, see Dinan, "Governance and Institutions 2000," pp. 36–41.

23. See Ricardo Alonsa Garcia, "The General Provisions of the Charter of Fundamental Rights of the European Union," Jean Monnet Working Paper 4/02. Available at www.jeanmonnetprogram.org/papers.

24. See Juliet Lodge, ed., *The 1999 Elections to the European Parliament* (Basingstoke: Palgrave, 2001).

25. On the EU and referenda, see Simon Hug, *Voices of Europe: Citizens, Referendums, and European Integration* (Boulder, CO: Rowman and Littlefield, 2002).

26. For an assessment of national contributions to the debate, see Simon Serfaty, ed., *The Finality Debate and Its National Dimensions* (Washington, DC: CSIS Press, 2002).

27. Bulletin EU 12-2000.

28. Bulletin EU 12-2001.

29. Bulletin EU 12-2001, Laeken Declaration.

30. See, for instance, Paul Taylor, *The European Union in the 1990s* (Oxford: Oxford University Press, 1996); Renaud Dehousse, ed., *Europe After Maastricht: An Ever Closer Union?* (Munich: Law Books in Europe, 1994); Andrew Duff, John Pinder, and Roy Pryce, eds., *Maastricht and Beyond: Building the European Union* (London: Routledge, 1994).

31. See Peter B. Kenen, *Economic and Monetary Union in Europe: Moving Beyond Maastricht* (Cambridge: Cambridge University Press, 1995); Desmond Dinan, *Ever Closer Union,* 2nd ed. (Boulder, CO: Lynne Rienner, 1999), pp. 462–476.

32. Treaty on European Union, text available at http://www.europa.eu.int/abc/obj/treaties/en/entoc01.htm.

33. See Lionel Barber, "The Euro: Single Currency, Multiple Injuries," the *Financial Times*, June 10, 1999, p. 10.

34. See the *Financial Times*, October 10, 2002, p. 1.

35. Commission, "Growth, Competitiveness, Employment: The Challenges and Ways Forward into the 21st Century," Bulletin EC S-6/93. See also Helen Drake, *Jacques Delors: Perspectives on a European Leader* (London: Routledge, 2000), pp. 113–143.

36. Bulletin EU 3-2000.

37. See John T.S. Keeler, "Agricultural Power in the European Community: Explaining the Fate of CAP and GATT Negotiations," *Comparative Politics* 28, no. 2 (January 1996), pp. 127–150.

38. Amsterdam Treaty, text available at http://europa.eu.int/scadplus/leg/en/s50000.htm.

39. Bulletin EC 10-1999.

40. See Monica den Boer and Jörg Monar, "11 September and the Challenge of Global Terrorism to the EU as a Security Actor," in *The European Union: Annual Review of the EU 2001/2002,* ed. Geoffrey Edwards and Georg Wiessala (Oxford: Blackwell, 2002), pp. 11–28; and John Occhipinti, *The Politics of EU Police Cooperation: Toward a European FBI?* (Boulder, CO: Lynne Rienner Publishers, 2003).

41. See John Roper, "Two Cheers for Mr. Blair? The Political Realities of European Defense Cooperation," in *The European Union: Annual Review of the EU 1999/2000,* ed. Geoffrey Edwards and Georg Wiessala (Oxford: Blackwell, 2000), pp. 7–24.

42. Bulletin EU 6-1999.

43. Bulletin EU 12-1999.

9

Conclusion

The European Union bears more than a passing resemblance to its long-forgotten precursor, the European Coal and Steel Community. The Coal and Steel Community had a narrow purview and only six member states; the EU covers most areas of public policy and is steadily enlarging to envelop the entire continent of Europe. Nevertheless, they share common traits that recur throughout the history of European integration: the primacy of national interests; the centrality of France and Germany; Britain's semidetachment; the unavoidable involvement of the United States; and the importance of individuals, ideas, and institutions. The political rationale for the Coal and Steel Community—strengthening national and regional security—also underpins today's EU, despite its far greater weight as an economic entity. Most important, practical solutions to concrete and complex challenges, rather than an overarching philosophical framework, shaped both organizations. The result has been an accretion of institutions, power structures, and policies that run the perpetual risk of being incoherent and occasionally unmanageable.

■ National Interests and Supranational Solutions

The Coal and Steel Community epitomized the postwar Western European peace settlement. Although established to resolve a specific economic problem, its prime purposes were political and symbolic. The principle of supranationalism embodied in the High Authority and Court of Justice (the Common Assembly was too weak to mention), balanced by the intergovernmentalism of the Council of Ministers, satisfied French security concerns and helped rehabilitate Germany. The process of European integration contributed to a rapprochement between both countries and, in time, to reconciliation as well.

The launch of the European Economic Community later in the 1950s demonstrated the durability of supranationalism as a solution to practical problems, this time the perceived need for greater trade liberalization and closer economic integration in order to accelerate modernization and growth.

321

Again, however, practical politics were paramount: the six founding members struck a deal in the Rome Treaty that included, at French insistence, arrangements for agriculture subsidies and trade with overseas territories. Without those provisions, French advocates of the EC could not have overcome the resistance of cautious colleagues and suspicious compatriots.

Similarly, a combination of political and economic interests accounts for the emergence of economic and monetary union at key junctures in the history of European integration. France responded to Germany's economic resurgence and diplomatic revival in the early 1970s by floating the idea of Economic and Monetary Union (EMU), which reemerged on the agenda of European integration more than a decade later, thanks to the success of the single market program. The unexpected prospect of German unification at about the same time, following the fall of the Berlin Wall, increased the political salience of EMU. A felicitous combination of economic and political interests, primarily in France and Germany, ensured the conclusion of the Maastricht Treaty and implementation of EMU by the end of the 1990s, but fell short of convincing member states to cede the necessary sovereignty to put the process on a long-term, solid footing.

As in other policy areas, the quest for closer foreign, security, and defense cooperation in the EU represented a practical response to new challenges, not a doctrinaire effort to deepen European integration. The proposed European Defense Community failed in the 1950s because of political opposition in France. The end of the Cold War seemed an opportune time for the new European Union to deepen foreign and security policy cooperation, and the protracted Balkan wars in the 1990s provided an impetus for closer defense cooperation. Nevertheless, sensitivity to national sovereignty proved insurmountable. New challenges in the aftermath of the terrorist attack on the United States in September 2001, and the divisiveness of the Iraq debacle, prompted member states to take a harder look at defense policy cooperation, not for the sake of European integration but for pragmatic security reasons.

Driven by necessity rather than ideology, therefore, what began as a modest common market for coal and steel expanded over the years into an entity touching on almost every aspect of public policy. At the same time, the EU widened as it deepened, with more and more countries wanting to join. The existing member states responded to enlargement in a pragmatic way (only in the case of Greece were they swayed by emotion). The applicant countries, in turn, wanted to join the EU for tangible economic and political reasons, such as market access, eligibility for agricultural subsidies and structural funding, or the consolidation of democracy. For the countries of Central and Eastern Europe, recently dominated by larger neighbors, EU membership had a compelling strategic dimension. Even so, their interest in joining the EU was primarily economic—as long as they could also join NATO.

■ Individuals, Institutions, and Ideas

The seemingly impersonal entity that these countries wished to join was shaped more by individual initiative and involvement than anonymous social and economic forces. The case of Jean Monnet is instructive. His famous method involved building institutions to bind the countries of Western Europe closer together, ultimately transforming the nature of the relationship between them. But institutions were only one side of Monnet's triangular technique: ideas and individuals were the others. Monnet's remarkable life showed how institutions, ideas, and individuals mattered. Monnet was an opportunist who cultivated individuals upon whom he could call to move ideas along. Spring 1950 was the right time to launch a new initiative; supranationalism was an ideal solution to a specific problem; and Robert Schuman was the right person to make it happen. Sometimes Monnet's timing was right, but his ideas were off the mark (his advocacy in the mid-1950s of atomic energy cooperation rather than a common market is a case in point).

Monnet's successors adopted a similar approach. Walter Hallstein thought that he had the right idea (greater supranationalism) and the right time (the need for a new financial agreement), but miscalculated badly (he gave Charles de Gaulle an opening to reassert intergovernmentalism). Jacques Delors became Commission president at an ideal time (member states were eager to reinvigorate economic integration) but initially promoted the wrong idea (economic and monetary union) before championing the right one (completion of the single market). For Monnet and Delors, the EU's most successful supranational leaders, policy goals were instrumental rather than ends in themselves. Lacking a clear vision of the EU's ultimate shape or form, they sought to advance European integration by degrees. Thus they contributed to a situation in which the EU resembled a geological formation, with many layers of initiatives and reforms, taken over the years, deposited on top of each other.

As heads of supranational bodies, Monnet, Hallstein, and Delors stood on weak foundations of political authority. They enhanced their positions by coming from France or Germany, the largest and most influential member states. National governments were the most powerful players throughout the history of the EU; national leaders the most influential individuals; and France and Germany the dominant member states. As European integration intensified and intruded more into everyday political life, national leaders devoted more time to EU affairs. The launch of the European Council in the mid-1970s allowed them to meet regularly to resolve politically sensitive issues and give the EU overall direction.

Frequent contact in the European Council shaped the leaders' impressions of each other, a situation that, in turn, helped shape the outcome of the summits. Although summit communiqués were mostly drafted well in advance, interaction among the summiteers determined their final form and content. What seems in retrospect to have been preordained could have come out otherwise if different interpersonal dynamics had been at play. The long-running saga of the British budgetary question is an obvious example.

De Gaulle's assault against supranationalism in the mid-1960s showed how a powerful individual could shape the direction of European integration. De Gaulle's relationship with Konrad Adenauer further illustrated the importance of individual initiative and action in the EU. Together, they fended off Britain's rival proposal of a free trade area and set the Community on course to implement the customs union and common agricultural policy. The Elysée Treaty, which de Gaulle and Adenauer signed in January 1963, institutionalized the rapprochement between France and Germany at the core of the European Community.

Despite occasional strains in bilateral relations and antipathy between particular leaders, French presidents and German chancellors met regularly under the terms of the Elysée Treaty to resolve disputes and hatch plans for the EU. For instance, Jacques Chirac and Gerhard Schröder used the occasion of the fortieth anniversary of the treaty to reaffirm their countries' commitment to each other at a time of Franco-German tension and to discuss a joint initiative in the Convention on the Future of Europe. Other national leaders also met bilaterally or multilaterally, but none with the same frequency or sense of purpose as their French and German counterparts. The combination of bilateral summitry under the auspices of the Elysée Treaty and multilateral summitry under the auspices of the European Council provided a powerful platform for Franco-German leadership in the EU.

Personal relationships and professional networks oiled the wheels of the EU at every level. As the EU deepened and widened, many more politicians and officials became involved in policymaking and implementation at the European level. Armies of officials in national and regional capitals augmented the corps of Brussels-based bureaucrats. Around them revolved an ever-expanding circle of lawyers, lobbyists, concerned citizens, academics, and students.

Yet "ordinary" Europeans often seemed left out. Europeans were always ambivalent about their singular political experiment. The rapid extension of the EU's policy reach in the early 1990s fueled public fears about legitimacy and democratic control. Europeans complained about the EU's remoteness, the incomprehensibility of decisionmaking, and the unaccountability of the unelected but seemingly all-powerful European Commission, while failing to turn out for European Parliament elections or to take national politicians to task for their votes in the Council of Ministers. These resentments, sometimes allied with anxieties about national identity, increasingly flared into open hostility.

The perception of weak legitimacy widened the gap between the governed and the governing in the EU. The Nice Treaty, an ineffectual attempt at institutional reform, made things worse. The ensuing Convention on the Future of Europe, a novel approach to treaty reform, proposed a number of institutional innovations but failed to catch the public imagination. The EU seemed condemned by its nature and structure, and by the tendency of member states to blame Brussels for their own inadequacies, to remain misunderstood and underappreciated. The EU's poor policy performance exacerbated the problem. With traditional security concerns fading as rallying cries for integration, people generally judged the EU by its ability to deliver greater economic advantage, which it seemed incapable of doing. Together with the challenge of legitimacy, the challenge of meeting economic expectations proved formidable for the EU at the beginning of the new millennium.

Europe Recast

Regardless of the EU's manifest failings, the events of the last fifty years have shown that the proponents of a European union—the EU way—have convincingly won the argument over the future of Europe. No member state has ever seriously contemplated leaving (not even Britain, whose government held a referendum on the issue in 1975, confidently expecting an overwhelming endorsement of membership). Far from wanting to leave, countries have flocked to join. Thus, in the 1990s, the countries of Central and Eastern Europe lined up to share much of their own, recently acquired, fragile sovereignty with the EU and its institutions.

Despite persistent economic problems, Europe today is immeasurably better off than it was at the end of World War II. Standards of living are higher throughout the EU than were imaginable at that time. Europe's welfare states, which developed independently of the EU, are still intact. Responsibility for welfare policies resides at the national level, although the pressure of globalization and constraints of integration are reducing governments' fiscal choices. The evolution of the EU since the 1950s, and especially since the acceleration of integration in the late 1980s, introduced a new kind of politics in Europe.[1] The machinery of EU government is deeply entrenched in the member states' consciousness. Media coverage of the EU, often highly critical, is pervasive and intense.

The EU's existence also reflects a fundamental change in relations among European countries. Alan Taylor's classic book, *The Struggle for Mastery in Europe*, is a salutary reminder of the tenor of intra-European relations in the nineteenth century, when the great powers vied for hegemony, destroying lesser powers without scruple.[2] National leaders enthusiastically followed the dictum of Carl von Clausewitz in treating war as a continuation of politics by other means, a practice that proved ever more suicidal as technology multiplied death and destruction with each new conflict. Realpolitik in Europe reached its zenith (or nadir) between 1914 and 1945, framed by the outbreak of World War I and the end of World War II. Revolution in Russia and the emergence of the Soviet Union, economic collapse and the Great Depression, and the rise of fascism tore Europe apart.

Western Europe has largely overcome, if not forgotten, the effects of those traumatic events. Communism and fascism are discredited beyond repair. Apathy, not extremism, is the chief danger to democracy in Europe today. Small states fret about the intentions of large states but no longer worry about being swallowed up by powerful neighbors. The prospect of EU member states using force against each other is so remote that it is risible. According to Francis Fukuyama, "the end of history" means "the growing 'Common Marketization' of international relations, and the diminution of the likelihood of large-scale conflict between states."[3] Although that may make life duller, historians should welcome it, especially considering the alternative. Intra-EU bargaining in Brussels is today's manifestation of "the continuation of politics by other means." It may be boring, even Byzantine, but it is safe. The battlefields of Jena, Waterloo, Verdun, or Normandy—where seemingly intractable problems were once resolved—have given way to meeting rooms in Brussels, tidily furnished with bottled water. The EU has helped to recast Europe in fundamental ways.

▪ Notes

1. See Alberta Sbragia, ed., *Euro-politics: Institutions and Policymaking in the "New" European Community* (Washington, DC: Brookings Institution, 1992).

2. A.J.P. Taylor, *The Struggle for Mastery in Europe* (Oxford: Clarendon Press, 1954).

3. Francis Fukuyama, "The End of History?" *The National Interest*, no. 16 (Summer 1989), p. 16.

Appendix 1
Abbreviations and Acronyms

BBQ	British Budgetary Question
CAP	common agricultural policy
Coreper	Committee of Permanent Representatives
CSCE	Conference on Security and Cooperation in Europe
EC	European Community
ECB	European Central Bank
Ecofin	Council of Economic and Finance Ministers
ECSC	European Coal and Steel Community
ECU	European currency unit
EDC	European Defense Community
EEC	European Economic Community
EFTA	European Free Trade Area/Association
EMS	European Monetary System
EMU	Economic and Monetary Union
EP	European Parliament
ESPRIT	European Strategic Program for Research and Development in Information Technology
EU	European Union
Euratom	European Atomic Energy Community
EUROJUST	EU body for criminal justice cooperation and coordination
EUROPOL	European police agency
G7	Group of Seven Most Industrialized Countries
GATT	General Agreement on Tariffs and Trade
GDP	gross domestic product
IMF	International Monetary Fund
NATO	North Atlantic Treaty Organization
OECD	Organization for Economic Cooperation and Development
OEEC	Organization for European Economic Cooperation
SEA	Single European Act
VAT	value-added tax
WTO	World Trade Organization

Appendix 2
The Ever-Wider EU, 1957–2004

Original Member States (1957)	1st Enlargement (1973)	2nd Enlargement (1981)	3rd Enlargement (1986)	4th Enlargement (1995)	5th Enlargement (2004)	Remaining Candidate Countries
Belgium	Britain	Greece	Spain	Austria	Czech Republic	Bulgaria
France	Denmark		Portugal	Finland	Poland	Romania
Germany	Ireland			Sweden	Hungary	Turkey
Italy					Estonia	
Luxembourg					Slovenia	
Netherlands					Latvia	
					Lithuania	
					Slovakia	
					Cyprus	
					Malta	

Appendix 3
Major Treaty Changes

Rome (1957)

General: establish the European Community

Institutions: establish the Commission, Council, Parliament, Court, and Economic and Social Committee

Policies: Customs Union (by 1968); Common Agricultural Policy (subject to negotiation); Common Commercial Policy; Competition Policy; Development Assistance Policy; Regional Policy; Social Policy

Single European Act (1986)

General: revitalize the European Community

Institutions: legitimize the European Council (launched in 1975); extend the use of qualified majority voting; strengthen the legislative role of the European Parliament (through the cooperation procedure); establish the Court of First Instance

Policies: complete the single market (by 1992); strengthen cohesion policy; legitimize cooperation on foreign policy (European Political Cooperation); strengthen environmental policy; strengthen research and development policy

Maastricht (1992)

General: launch the European Union

Institutions: extend the use of qualified majority voting; strengthen the legislative role of the Parliament (through the co-decision procedure); establish the Committee of the Regions; introduce the principle of subsidiarity

Policies: Economic and Monetary Union (by 1999); transform European Political Cooperation into the common foreign and security policy; introduce cooperation on justice and home affairs; strengthen environmental policy

■ Amsterdam (1997)

General: limited institutional and policy reform

Institutions: extend the use of qualified majority voting; strengthen the legislative role of the Parliament (extend the applicability of the co-decision procedure); limit the Parliament to seven hundred members

Policies: reform the common foreign and security policy; establish an area of freedom, security, and justice (reform cooperation on justice and home affairs); proclaim the EU's commitment to the principles of liberty, democracy, respect for human rights, and fundamental freedoms

■ Nice (2001)

General: limited institutional reform

Institutions: change the voting weights of the member states and allocate votes to the candidate countries; extend the use of qualified majority voting; change the composition of the Commission to one commissioner per member state until 2007; allocate seats in the Parliament to the candidate countries and increase the Parliament to 732 members

Policies: Reform the Common Commercial Policy

■ Draft Constitutional Treaty (2003)

General: proclaim a constitution for the European Union

Institutions: allow each member state to nominate a commissioner but establish a core group of fifteen commissioners as of 2009; change the criteria for a qualified majority; extend the use of qualified majority voting; elect a president of the European Council; elect the president of the Commission; limit the Parliament to seven hundred members; establish the joint Council-Commission position of EU foreign minister

Policies: reform the common foreign and security policy; reform cooperation on justice and home affairs

Appendix 4
Chronology

1945

February	Yalta conference on postwar settlement
May	End of World War II in Europe
July–August	Potsdam conference on postwar settlement

1946

September	Churchill's "United States of Europe" speech

1947

March	Truman Doctrine announced
	Britain and France sign Dunkirk Treaty (defensive alliance)
May	UN Economic Commission for Europe established
June	Marshall Plan announced
July	Committee on European Economic Cooperation established
October	General Agreement on Tariffs and Trade (GATT) launched
December	International Committee of the Movements for European Unity established

1948

January	Benelux customs union launched
February	Communist coup in Czechoslovakia
March	Brussels Treaty (defensive alliance of France, Britain, and Benelux) signed
April	Marshall Plan (European Recovery Program) enacted
	Organization for European Economic Cooperation (OEEC) established
May	Congress of Europe held in The Hague
June	Berlin Blockade begins

1949

April	NATO treaty signed in Washington, D.C.

	International Ruhr Authority established
May	Federal Republic of Germany (West Germany) established
	Council of Europe launched
	Berlin Blockade ends

1950
May	Schuman Declaration
June	Negotiations begin to establish European Coal and Steel Community (ECSC)
	Outbreak of Korean War
October	Pleven Plan for a European Defense Community (EDC)
November	European Convention for the Protection of Human Rights and Fundamental Freedoms signed

1951
| February | Negotiations begin to establish European Defense Community (EDC) |
| April | Treaty establishing ECSC signed in Paris |

1952
May	Treaty establishing EDC signed in Paris
August	ECSC launched in Luxembourg
September	ECSC Assembly holds first session in Strasbourg

1953
| March | Ad hoc assembly adopts draft treaty for European Political Cooperation |

1954
| August | French National Assembly rejects EDC treaty |
| October | Paris agreement to establish Western European Union |

1955
May	Germany joins NATO
June	Messina Conference on reviving European integration
	Spaak committee holds first meeting
October	Saar referendum
	Monnet launches Action Committee for the United States of Europe

1956
| April | Spaak committee recommends atomic energy community and customs union |

May	Venice Conference approves Spaak committee recommendations
June	Negotiations begin to establish European Economic Community (EEC) and European Atomic Energy Community (Euratom)
October–November	Suez crisis
October	Soviet intervention in Hungary

1957

| January | Saar rejoins Germany |
| March | Treaties of Rome (establishing the EEC and Euratom) signed |

1958

January	Launch of the EEC and Euratom
	Hallstein Commission takes office
March	First plenary session of European Parliament (EP)
May	Collapse of French Fourth Republic
July	Stresa conference on establishing the common agricultural policy (CAP)
September	French endorse Fifth Republic in a referendum
December	De Gaulle elected president of France

1959

| January | First stage of transition to common market begins |
| September | Stockholm Convention establishes European Free Trade Association (EFTA) |

1960

| December | Organization for Economic Cooperation and Development (OECD) established |

1961

July	Association agreement with Greece signed
August	Britain applies to join EC (together with Denmark, Ireland, and Norway)
November	France launches Fouchet Plan for a European political community

1962

| January | Second stage of transition to common market begins |
| April | Fouchet Plan collapses |

July | U.S. president Kennedy outlines "grand design" for transatlantic relations

1963
January | De Gaulle vetoes Britain's application
De Gaulle and Adenauer sign Elysée Treaty
July | Yaoundé Convention between the EC and seventeen African states and Madagascar signed
September | Association agreement with Turkey signed

1965
April | Merger Treaty, fusing the executives of the EC, ECSC, and Euratom, signed
Hallstein introduces controversial budget proposals
July | Empty chair crisis begins

1966
January | EC enters third and final stage of transition to common market
Empty chair crisis ends with Luxembourg Compromise

1967
May | Britain applies a second time to join EC (together with Denmark, Ireland, and Norway)
July | Merger Treaty enters into force
Rey Commission takes office
November | De Gaulle vetoes Britain's application a second time

1968
May | Student and worker riots in Paris
July | Customs union completed eighteen months ahead of schedule

1969
February | Barre memorandum on Economic and Monetary Union (EMU)
April | De Gaulle resigns
July | Britain, Denmark, Ireland, and Norway reactivate membership applications
December | At a summit in The Hague, EU leaders decide to revive the EC

1970
January | Malfatti Commission takes office
April | Agreement to finance EC through "own resources"

June	Accession negotiations with Britain, Denmark, Ireland, and Norway resume
October	Pierre Werner presents plan for EMU
	Foreign ministers adopt Davignon plan for foreign policy cooperation (European Political Cooperation)
November	Foreign ministers hold first European Political Cooperation meeting

1971

January	Second Yaoundé Convention and Arusha agreement enter into force
August	United States announces the suspension of dollar convertibility, formally ending Bretton Woods System

1972

January	Accession treaties signed in Brussels
March	Launch of the monetary "snake"
	Mansholt becomes interim Commission president
September	Norwegians reject EC membership in a referendum
October	At Paris summit, EC leaders agree "to transform the whole complex of . . . relations [between member states] into a European Union" by the end of the decade

1973

January	Britain, Denmark, and Ireland join EC
	Ortoli Commission takes office
July	Conference on Security and Cooperation in Europe (CSCE) opens in Helsinki
October	Arab oil producers quadruple the price of oil and embargo port of Rotterdam
December	EU leaders discuss oil crisis at Copenhagen summit

1974

April	New British government renegotiates membership terms
July	Euro-Arab dialogue opens in Paris
September	EU leaders decide to form European Council
December	EU leaders hold last informal summit in Paris

1975

February	Lomé Convention between EC and forty-six developing countries signed
March	Inaugural meeting of European Council in Dublin concludes renegotiation of Britain's membership terms
	European Regional Development Fund established

June	British referendum on continued EC membership
	Greece applies to join EC
July	Agreement to establish Court of Auditors and strengthen budgetary powers of EP
August	Thirty-five participating states conclude CSCE
December	Tindemans Report on European Union

1976
| July | Accession negotiations with Greece begin |

1977
January	Jenkins Commission takes office
March	Portugal applies to join EC
July	Spain applies to join EC

1978
July	Meeting in Bremen, European Council agrees to establish European Monetary System (EMS)
October	Accession negotiations with Portugal begin
December	Member states decide to launch EMS in January 1978; eight decide to participate in system's exchange rate mechanism

1979
February	Accession negotiations with Spain begin
March	Launch of EMS
May	Accession treaty with Greece signed in Athens
June	First direct elections to EP
September	Spierenburg report on Commission reform
October	Second Lomé Convention signed
November	"Three Wise Men" report on EC reform
	Beginning of British budgetary question

1981
January	Greece joins EC
	Thorn Commission takes office
November	Genscher-Colombo initiative

1982
| February | Greenlanders decide in a referendum to leave EC |

1983
| June | Stuttgart declaration |

1984
February   EP adopts Draft Treaty Establishing the European Union
June   Second direct elections to EP
            At Fontainebleau summit, EC leaders resolve British
                budgetary question
December   Third Lomé Convention signed

1985
January   Delors Commission takes office
February   Agreement on Integrated Mediterranean Programs
March   Dooge Committee recommends intergovernmental conference
                on treaty reform
June   Portugal and Spain sign accession treaties
            Commission publishes white paper on single market
            At Milan summit, EC leaders decide to hold
                intergovernmental conference
September   Intergovernmental conference starts
December   Intergovernmental conference ends

1986
January   Portugal and Spain join EC
February   Foreign ministers sign Single European Act (SEA)

1987
April   Turkey applies to join EC
July   SEA comes into effect
September   Finance ministers strengthen EMS

1988
January   Balladur memorandum on EMU
February   Genscher memorandum on EMU
            At Brussels summit, EC leaders agree on Delors I budget
                package
June   At Hanover summit, EC leaders decide to establish Delors
                committee on EMU

1989
June   Delors report on EMU
            Third direct elections to EP
July   Austria applies to join EC
November   Fall of Berlin Wall

December	At Strasbourg summit, EC leaders decide to hold intergovernmental conference on EMU and adopt Charter of Fundamental Social Rights for Workers

1990

May	Charter for European Bank for Reconstruction and Development signed
June	France, Germany, and Benelux countries sign Schengen Agreement
	At Dublin summit, EC leaders decide to hold intergovernmental conference on political union concurrently with intergovernmental conference on EMU, beginning in December 1990
July	Stage One of EMU begins
	Cyprus applies to join EC
	Malta applies to join EC
October	German unification
	Britain joins exchange rate mechanism of EMS
November	U.S.-EC Transatlantic Declaration signed
December	Intergovernmental conferences begin in Rome

1991

June	Outbreak of war in Yugoslavia
July	Sweden applies to join EC
December	Intergovernmental conference ends at Maastricht summit
	Soviet Union collapses

1992

January	EC recognizes independence of Croatia and Slovenia
February	Foreign ministers sign Treaty on European Union in Maastricht
March	Finland applies to join EU
May	EC and EFTA countries sign agreement for European Economic Area
	Agreement on CAP reform
	Switzerland applies to join EU
June	Danes reject Maastricht Treaty in referendum
September	Britain suspends participation in exchange rate mechanism of EMS
	Currency crisis deepens
	French narrowly approve Maastricht Treaty in referendum
November	Norway again applies to join EU
December	Swiss reject European Economic Area membership in referendum, implicitly rejecting EU membership

At Edinburgh summit, EC leaders agree on Danish opt-outs
from Maastricht Treaty and Delors II budget package
Completion of single market program

1993

February   Accession negotiations with Austria, Finland, and Sweden
                  begin
April   Accession negotiations with Norway begin
May   Danes approve Maastricht Treaty in second referendum
June   At Copenhagen summit, EC leaders agree on EU accession
                  criteria
August   Currency crisis ends
November   Maastricht Treaty comes into effect, and EU comes into being
December   Commission publishes white paper on growth,
                  competitiveness, and employment

1994

March   Dispute over institutional implications of enlargement ends
                  with Ioannina Compromise
                  Hungary applies to join EU
April   Poland applies to join EU
June   Fourth direct elections to EP
                  Accession treaties with Austria, Finland, Sweden, and
                  Norway signed
July   Stage Two of EMU begins
                  European Monetary Institute established
November   Norwegians again reject EC membership in referendum
December   European Energy Charter signed

1995

January   Austria, Finland, and Sweden join EU
                  Santer Commission takes office
June   First meeting of Reflection Group to prepare
                  intergovernmental conference
                  Europe agreements with Estonia, Latvia, and Lithuania signed
                  Romania applies to join EU
October   Latvia applies to join EU
November   Estonia applies to join EU
                  EU and twelve Mediterranean countries sign Barcelona
                  Declaration
December   United States and EU sign New Transatlantic Agenda
                  Reflection Group report on intergovernmental conference

Lithuania applies to join EU
Dayton peace plan for former Yugoslavia signed in Paris
Bulgaria applies to join EU

1996

January	Czech Republic applies to join EU
March	Intergovernmental conference begins in Turin
June	Slovenia applies to join EU
December	At Dublin summit, EU leaders agree on EMU Stability and Growth Pact

1997

June	At Amsterdam summit, EU leaders conclude intergovernmental conference
October	Amsterdam Treaty signed
November	European Council holds special jobs summit in Luxembourg

1998

March	Inaugural session of European Conference (London)
	Accession negotiations with Poland, Hungary, Czech Republic, Estonia, Slovenia, and Cyprus begin
May	At special Brussels summit, EU leaders agree eleven member states will participate in Stage Three of EMU (all except Britain, Denmark, Greece, and Sweden) and choose first president of European Central Bank (ECB)
June	Launch of ECB in Frankfurt

1999

January	Stage Three of EMU (single monetary policy and irrevocably fixed exchange rates among participating currencies) begins
March	Santer Commission resigns
	At Berlin summit, EU leaders agree on *Agenda 2000* budget package
May	Amsterdam Treaty enters into force
June	Fifth direct elections to EP
July	Manuel Marín becomes interim Commission president
September	Prodi Commission takes office
October	At Tampere summit, EU leaders strengthen cooperation on justice and home affairs
December	At Helsinki summit, EU leaders recognize Turkey as candidate for membership

2000

February	Accession negotiations with Latvia, Lithuania, Slovakia, Bulgaria, Romania, and Malta begin
	Intergovernmental conference begins
March	At Lisbon summit, EU leaders launch strategy for economic modernization
September	Danes decide in referendum not to adopt euro
December	Intergovernmental conference ends at Nice summit
	European Council proclaims Charter of Fundamental Rights

2001

January	Greece adopts euro
June	Irish reject Nice Treaty in referendum

2002

January	Euro notes and coins introduced
February	Convention on the Future of Europe begins in Brussels
June	ECSC comes to an end
October	Irish approve Nice Treaty in second referendum

2003

February	Nice Treaty comes into effect
April	Accession treaties with Cyprus, Czech Republic, Estonia, Hungary, Latvia, Lithuania, Malta, Poland, Slovenia, and Slovakia signed in Athens
June	Convention on the Future of Europe ends
September	Sweden decides in a referendum not to adopt the euro
October	Intergovernmental conference begins

2004

May	Historic enlargement of the EU into Central and Eastern Europe
June	Sixth direct elections to EP

Bibliography

Acheson, Dean. *Present at the Creation.* New York: Norton, 1969.

Albert, Michel, and Robert James Ball. *Toward European Economic Recovery in the 1980s: Report to the European Parliament.* New York: Praeger, 1984.

Alphand, H. *L'étonnement d'être, journal 1939–1973.* Paris: Fayard, 1977.

Alting von Geusau, Frans A.M., ed. *The Lomé Convention and the New International Economic Order.* Leiden: A. W. Sijthoff, 1977.

Annan, Noel. *Changing Enemies: The Defeat and Regeneration of Germany.* Ithaca, NY: Cornell University Press, 1997.

Association Georges Pompidou. *Georges Pompidou et l'Europe.* Brussels: Éditions Complexe, 1995.

Avery, Graham, and Fraser Cameron. *The Enlargement of the European Union.* Sheffield: Sheffield University Press, 1998.

Ball, George. *The Past Has Another Pattern.* New York: Norton, 1982.

Baun, Michael J. *An Imperfect Union: The Maastricht Treaty and the New Politics of European Integration.* Boulder, CO: Westview Press, 1996.

———. *A Wider Europe: The Process and Politics of European Union Enlargement.* Lanham, MD: Rowman and Littlefield, 2000.

Beloff, Max. *The United States and the Uniting of Europe.* Washington, DC: Brookings Institution, 1963.

Benoit, Emile. *Europe at Sixes and Sevens: The Common Market, the Free Trade Association and the United States.* New York: Columbia University Press, 1961.

Berger, Vincent. *Monsieur Georges Pompidou et la construction de l'Europe (1962–1972).* Paris: Université de Droit, d'Économie et de Sciences Sociales, 1973.

Beyer, Henri, ed. *Robert Schuman: L'Europe par la réconciliation franco-allemande.* Lausanne: Fondation Jean Monnet pour l'Europe, 1986.

Bieber, R., et al. *1992: One European Market.* Florence: European University Institute, 1988.

Binoche, Jacques. *De Gaulle et les Allemands.* Brussels: Éditions Complexe, 1990.

Bischof, Günter, Anton Pelinka, and Michael Gehler, eds. *Austria in the European Union.* New York: Transaction Publishers, 2002.

Bitsch, Marie-Thérèse. *Histoire de la construction européenne de 1945 à nos jours.* Brussels: Éditions Complexe, 1996.

Bjøl, Erling. *La France devant l'Europe.* Copenhagen: Munksgaard, 1966.

Bloch-Laine, François, and Jean Bouvier. *La France restaurée, 1944–1954: Dialogue sur les choix d'une modernisation.* Paris: Fayard, 1986.

Bloes, Robert. *Le "Plan Fouchet" et le Problème de l'Europe Politique*. Bruges: College of Europe, 1970.

Boltho, Andrea, ed. *The European Economy: Growth and Crisis*. Oxford: Oxford University Press, 1982.

Bossuat, Gérard. *L'Europe occidentale à l'heure américaine: Le Plan Marshall et l'unité européenne, 1945–52*. Paris: Éditions Complexe, 1992.

———. *La France, l'aide américaine et la construction européenne, 1944–1954*. 2 vols. Paris: Comité pour l'Histoire Economique et Financière de la France, 1992.

Bozo, Frederic. *Two Strategies for Europe: De Gaulle, the United States, and the Atlantic Alliance*. Lanham, MD: Rowman and Littlefield, 2001.

Brandt, Willy. *My Life in Politics*. New York: Viking, 1992.

———. *People and Politics: The Years 1960–1975*. London: Collins, 1978.

Brinkley, Douglas, and Richard T. Griffiths. *John F. Kennedy and Europe*. Baton Rouge: Louisiana State University Press, 1999.

Bruce-Gardyne, Jock, and Nigel Lawson. *The Power Game: An Examination of Decision-Making in Government*. Hamden: Archon Books, 1976.

Brugmans, Hendrik. *L'Idée Européenne, 1918–1965*. 2nd ed. Bruges: De Temple, 1966.

Brusse, Wendy Asbeek. *Tariffs, Trade and European Integration, 1947–1957: From Study Group to Common Market*. New York: St. Martin's Press, 1997.

Bührer, Werner. *Western Europe and Germany: The Beginnings of European Integration, 1945–1960*. Washington, DC: Berg, 1995.

Bullen, R., and M. E. Pelly. *Documents on British Policy Overseas*. Series 2, Vol. 1: *The Schuman Plan, the Council of Europe and Western European Integration, 1950–1952*. London: HMSO, 1986.

———. *Documents on British Policy Overseas*. Series 2, Vol. 3: *German Rearmament, September 1950–December 1950*. London: HMSO, 1989.

Bullock, Alan. *Ernest Bevin: Foreign Secretary, 1945–1951*. London: Heinemann, 1983.

Bulmer, Simon, and William Paterson. *The Federal Republic of Germany in the European Community*. Oxford: Oxford University Press, 1992.

Burgess, Michael. *Federalism and European Union: The Building of Europe, 1950–2000*. London: Routledge, 2000.

Butler, David, and Uwe Kitzinger. *The 1975 Referendum*. London: Macmillan, 1976.

Butler, R. A. *The Art of the Possible: The Memoirs of Lord Butler*. London: Hamilton, 1971.

Camps, Miriam. *Britain and the European Community, 1955–1963*. Princeton, NJ: Princeton University Press, 1964.

———. *European Unification in the 1960s: From the Veto to the Crisis*. New York: McGraw-Hill, 1966.

———. *What Kind of Europe? The Community Since de Gaulle's Veto*. Oxford: Oxford University Press, 1965.

Chace, James. *Acheson: The Secretary of State Who Created the American World*. Cambridge: Harvard University Press, 1998.

Charlton, M. *The Price of Victory*. London: British Broadcasting Corporation, 1983.

Chisholm, Michael. *Britain on the Edge of Europe*. London: Routledge, 1995.

Cloos, J. *Le traité de Maastricht: Genèse, analyse, commentaires*. Brussels: Bruylant, 1993.

Cockfield, Arthur. *Creating the Internal Market*. London: Wiley Chancery Law, 1984.

Cogan, Charles G. *The Third Option: The Emancipation of European Defense, 1989–2000*. Westport, CT: Praeger, 2001.

Cole, Alistair. *Franco-German Relations*. Harlow: Longman, 2001.

———. *François Mitterrand: A Study in Political Leadership*. London: Routledge, 1994.

Commission. *Homage à Emile Nöel, Secrétaire Général de la Commission européenne*. Luxembourg: European Communities, 1988.

Connolly, Bernard. *The Rotten Heart of Europe: The Dirty War for Europe's Money*. London: Faber and Faber, 1995.

Coombes, David. *Towards a European Civil Service*. London: Chatham House, 1968.

Corbett, Richard. *The European Parliament's Role in Closer EU Integration*. Basingstoke: Palgrave, 2001.

Cosgrove Twitchett, Carol, ed. *Harmonization in the EEC*. New York: St. Martin's Press, 1981.

Couve de Murville, Maurice. *Une Politique étrangère, 1958–1969*. Paris: Plon, 1971.

Criddle, Byron. *Socialists and European Integration*. London: Routledge, 1969.

Croft, Stuart, John Redmond, G. Wyn Rees, and Mark Webber. *The Enlargement of Europe*. Manchester: Manchester University Press, 1999.

Daddow, Oliver J. *Britain and Europe Since 1945: Historiographical Perspectives on Unification*. Manchester: Manchester University Press, 2003.

Daddow, Oliver J., ed.. *Harold Wilson and European Integration: Britain's Second Application to Join the EEC*. London: Frank Cass Publishers, 2002.

Dahrendorf, Ralf. *From Europe to Europe: A Story of Hope, Trial and Error*. Cambridge: Center for International Affairs, 1996.

Dedman, Martin. *The Origins and Development of the European Union, 1945–1995: A History of European Integration*. London: Routledge, 1996.

De Gaulle, Charles. *Mémoires d'Espoir, suivi d'un choix d'allocutions et messages sur la IVe et la Ve Républiques*. Paris: Plon, 1994.

———. *Memoirs of Hope, Renewal and Endeavor*. New York: Simon and Schuster, 1971.

Dehousse, Renaud, ed. *Europe After Maastricht: An Ever Closer Union?* Munich: Law Books in Europe, 1994.

Deighton, Anne, ed. *Building Postwar Europe: National Decision-Makers and European Institutions, 1948–1963*. London: St. Martin's Press, 1995.

Delanty, Gerard. *Inventing Europe: Idea, Identity, Reality*. New York: St. Martin's Press, 1995.

Dell, Edmund. *The Schuman Plan and the British Abdication of Leadership in Europe*. Oxford: Oxford University Press, 1995.

Délorme, Héléne, and Yves Tavernier. *Les paysans français et l'Europe*. Paris: Armand Colin, 1969.

Delors, Jacques. *La France par l'Europe*. Paris: Grasset, 1988.

Delwit, Pascal. *Les parties socialistes et l'intégration européene*. Brussels: Université de Bruxelles, 1995.

De Ruyt, Jean. *L'Acte unique européen: Commentaire*. 2nd ed. Brussels: Editions de l'Université de Bruxelles, 1987.

Diebold, William, Jr. *The Schuman Plan: A Study in Economic Cooperation, 1950–1959*. New York: Praeger, 1959.

Dinan, Desmond. *Ever Closer Union: An Introduction to European Integration*. 2nd ed. Boulder, CO: Lynne Rienner Publishers, 1999.

Dockrill, Saki. *Britain's Policy for West German Rearmament, 1950–55*. Cambridge: Cambridge University Press, 1991.

———. *Britain's Retreat from East of Suez: The Choice Between Europe and the World*. New York: Palgrave, 2002.

Drake, Helen. *Jacques Delors: Perspectives on a European Leader*. London: Routledge, 2000.

Duchêne, François. *Jean Monnet: The First Statesman of Interdependence*. New York: Norton, 1994.

Duff, Andrew, John Pinder, and Roy Pryce, eds. *Maastricht and Beyond: Building the European Union*. London: Routledge, 1994.

Dyson, Kenneth. *Elusive Union: The Process of Economic and Monetary Union in Europe*. London: Longman, 1994.

Dyson, Kenneth, and Kevin Featherstone. *The Road to Maastricht: Negotiating Economic and Monetary Union*. Oxford: Oxford University Press, 1999.

Eden, Anthony. *Full Circle: The Memoirs of Sir Anthony Eden*. London: Cassell, 1960.

Edwards, Geoffrey, and Alfred Pijpers. *The Politics of European Treaty Reform: The 1996 Intergovernmental Conference and Beyond*. London: Pinter, 1997.

Edwards, Geoffrey, and Helen Wallace. *Council of Ministers of the European Community and the President in Office*. London: Federal Trust, 1977.

Egan, Michelle. *Constructing a European Market: Standards, Regulation, and Governance*. Oxford: Oxford University Press, 2001.

Eichengreen, Barry. *Globalizing Capital: A History of the International Monetary System*. Princeton, NJ: Princeton University Press, 1996.

Ellison, James. *Threatening Europe: Britain and the Creation of the European Community, 1955–1958*. London: Macmillan, 2000.

Ellwood, D. W. *Rebuilding Europe: Western Europe, America and Postwar Reconstruction*. London: Longman, 1992.

Emerson, Michael, et al. *The Economics of 1992: The EC's Assessment of the Economic Effects of Completing the Internal Market*. Oxford: Oxford University Press, 1988.

Endo, Ken. *The Presidency of the European Commission Under Jacques Delors: The Politics of Shared Leadership*. New York: St. Martin's Press, 1999.

Eversen, H. J., and Hans Sperl. *Répertoire de la jurisprudence relative aux traités instituant les Communautés européenes: 1953–1962*. Cologne: C. Heymanns Verlag, 1965.

Fondation Jean Monnet pour l'Europe. *Jean Monnet–Robert Schuman correspondance, 1947–1953*. Lausanne: Fondation Jean Monnet pour l'Europe, 1986.

———. *Temoignages à la memoire de Jean Monnet*. Lausanne: Fondation Jean Monnet pour l'Europe, 1989.

Fontaine, Pascal. *Le Comité d'Action pour les États Unis d'Europe de Jean Monnet*. Lausanne: Centre de Recherches Européennes, 1974.

Forster, Anthony. *Britain and the Maastricht Negotiations*. Basingstoke: Palgrave, 1999.

Friend, Julius W. *Mitterrand*. Boulder, CO: Westview Press, 1999.

———. *The Linchpin: French-German Relations, 1950–1990*. New York: Praeger, 1991.

Fursdon, Edward. *The European Defense Community: A History*. New York: St. Martin's Press, 1980.

Gaddis, John Lewis. *We Now Know: Rethinking Cold War History*. Oxford: Clarendon Press, 1997.

Garton Ash, Timothy. *In Europe's Name: Germany and the Divided Continent*. New York: Random House, 1993.

Geddes, Andrew. *Immigration and European Integration: Towards Fortress Europe?* Manchester: Manchester University Press, 2000.

Genscher, Hans-Dietrich. *Rebuilding a House Divided: A Memoir.* New York: Broadway Books, 1998.

George, Stephen. *An Awkward Partner: Britain in the European Community.* Oxford: Oxford University Press, 1998.

Gerbet, Pierre. *La construction de l'Europe.* Rev. ed. Paris: Imprimerie Nationale, 1994.

Giauque, Jeffrey Glen. *Grand Designs and Visions of Unity: The Atlantic Powers and the Reorganization of Western Europe, 1955–1963.* Chapel Hill: University of North Carolina Press, 2002.

Gilbert, Mark. *Surpassing Realism: The Politics of European Integration Since 1945.* Lanham, MD: Rowman and Littlefield, 2003.

Gill, Christopher. *In Their Own Words: The Advocates of European Integration.* East Haddon: S.E.K. Publishers, 1996.

Gillingham, John. *Coal, Steel and the Rebirth of Europe, 1945–1955.* Cambridge: Cambridge University Press, 1991.

———. *European Integration, 1950–2002: Superstate or New Market Economy?* Cambridge: Cambridge University Press, 2003.

Girão, José A. *Southern Europe and the Enlargement of the EEC.* Lisbon: Economia, 1982.

Girault, René. *Pierre Mendès-France et le rôle de la France dans le monde.* Grenoble: Presses Universitaires de Grenoble, 1991.

Goldstein, J., and R. Keohane. *Ideas and Foreign Policy: Beliefs, Institutions and Political Change.* Ithaca, NY: Cornell University Press, 1993.

Gorman, Lyn, and Marja-Liisa Kiljunen. *The Enlargement of the European Community: Case Studies of Greece, Portugal, and Spain.* London: Macmillan, 1977.

Grant, Charles. *Delors: Inside the House that Jacques Built.* London: Nicholas Brealey Publishing, 1994.

Greenwood, Seán. *Britain and the Cold War, 1945–1951.* New York: St. Martin's Press, 2000.

Griffiths, Richard T. *Economic Development of the EEC.* Cheltenham: E. Elgar, 1997.

———. *The Netherlands and the Integration of Europe, 1945–1957.* Amsterdam: NEHA, 1990.

———. *Socialist Parties and the Question of Europe in the 1950s.* Leiden: E. J. Brill, 1993.

Gros, Daniel, and Niels Thygesen. *European Monetary Integration: From the European Monetary System Towards Monetary Union.* London: Longman, 1992.

Gstöhl, Sieglinde. *Reluctant Europeans: Norway, Sweden, and Switzerland in the Process of Integration.* Boulder, CO: Lynne Rienner Publishers, 2002.

Guyomarch, A., H. Machin, and E. Ritchie. *France in the European Union.* London: Macmillan, 1988.

Haas, Ernst. *The Uniting of Europe: Political, Social, and Economic Forces.* Stanford, CA: Stanford University Press, 1958.

Haines, C. Grove, ed. *European Integration.* Baltimore: Johns Hopkins University Press, 1957.

Hallstein, Walter. *United Europe: Challenge and Opportunity.* Cambridge: Harvard University Press, 1962.

Hanrieder, Wolfram. *Germany, America, and Europe.* New Haven: Yale University Press, 1989.

———. *West German Foreign Policy, 1945–63: International Pressure and Domestic Response.* Stanford, CA: Stanford University Press, 1967.

Hansen, Lene, and Ole Waever. *European Integration and National Identity: The Challenge of the Nordic States*. London: Routledge, 2002.

Harper, John Lamberton. *America and the Reconstruction of Italy, 1945–1948*. Cambridge: Cambridge University Press, 1986.

Healey, Denis. *The Time of My Life*. London: Penguin Books, 1990.

Heath, E. *The Course of My Life. My Autobiography*. London: Hodder and Stoughton, 1998.

Heisenberg, Dorothee. *The Mark of the Bundesbank: Germany's Role in European Monetary Cooperation*. Boulder, CO: Lynne Rienner Publishers, 1999.

Heller, Francis H., and John R. Gillingham. *The United States and the Integration of Europe: Legacies of the Postwar Era*. New York: St. Martin's Press, 1996.

Hendricks, Gisela. *The Franco-German Axis in European Integration*. London: Edward Elgar, 2001.

Hitchcock, William. *France Restored: Cold War Diplomacy and the Quest for Leadership in Europe, 1944–1954*. Chapel Hill: University of North Carolina Press, 1998.

Hogan, Michael. *The Marshall Plan: America, Britain, and the Reconstruction of Western Europe, 1947–1952*. Cambridge: Cambridge University Press, 1987.

Holmes, Martin. *European Integration: Scope and Limits*. Basingstoke: Palgrave, 2001.

Horne, A. *Macmillan*. Vol. 1: *1894–1957*. London: Macmillan, 1988.

———. *Macmillan*. Vol. 2: *1957–1986*. London: Macmillan, 1989.

Howarth, David J. *The French Road to European Union*. Basingstoke: Palgrave, 2001.

Howe, Geoffrey. *Conflict of Loyalty*. New York: St. Martin's Press, 1994.

Hug, Simon. *Voices of Europe: Citizens, Referendums, and European Integration*. Boulder, CO: Rowman and Littlefield, 2002.

Humphrey, Don D. *The United States and the Common Market: A Background Study*. New York: Praeger, 1962.

Institut Charles de Gaulle. *De Gaulle en son siècle*. 6 vols. Paris: Plon, 1991–1992.

Ionescu, Ghita. *The New Politics of European Integration*. London: St. Martin's Press, 1972.

Jacobson, Max. *Finland in the New Europe*. Westport, CT: Praeger, 1998.

Jenkins, Roy. *European Diary, 1977–1981*. London: Collins, 1989.

———. *Life at the Center: Memoirs of a Radical Reformer*. New York: Random House, 1991.

Jobert, Michel. *L'Autre Regard*. Paris: Grasset, 1976.

Jouve, Edmond. *Le Général de Gaulle et la construction de l'Europe*. Paris: Libraire Générale de Droit et de Jurisprudence, 1967.

Kaiser, Wolfram. *Using Europe, Abusing the Europeans: Britain and European Integration, 1945–1963*. London: Macmillan, 1996.

Kaplan, Jacob J., and Günther Schleiminger. *The European Payments Union: Financial Diplomacy in the 1950s*. Oxford: Clarendon Press, 1989.

Kay, John, ed. *1992. Myths and Realities*. London: London Business School, 1989.

Kenen, Peter B. *Economic and Monetary Union in Europe: Moving Beyond Maastricht*. Cambridge: Cambridge University Press, 1995.

Killick, John. *The United States and European Reconstruction, 1945–1960*. Edinburgh: Keele University Press, 1997.

Kindleberger, Charles P. *Marshall Plan Days*. Boston: Allen and Unwin, 1987.

Kipping, Matthias. *Zwischen Kartellen und Konkurrenz: Der Schuman-Plan und die Ursprünge der Europäischen Einigung, 1944–1952*. Berlin: Duncker and Humblot, 1996.

Kissinger, Henry. *The White House Years*. Boston: Little, Brown, 1979.
Kitzinger, Uwe. *Diplomacy and Persuasion*. London: Thames and Hudson, 1973.
Kolodziej, Edward. *French International Policy Under de Gaulle and Pompidou: The Politics of Grandeur*. Ithaca, NY: Cornell University Press, 1974.
Kotlowski, Dean J., ed. *The European Union: From Jean Monnet to the Euro*. Athens: Ohio University Press, 2000.
Kramer, Alan. *The West German Economy, 1945–1955*. New York: Berg, 1991.
Krause, L. B., and W. S. Salant, eds. *European Monetary Unification and Its Meaning for the United States*. Washington, DC: Brookings Institution, 1973.
Kruse, D. C. *Monetary Integration in Western Europe: EMU, EMS and Beyond*. London: Butterworths, 1980.
Kuisel, Richard. *Capitalism and the State in Modern France: Renovation and Economic Management in the Twentieth Century*. Cambridge: Cambridge University Press, 1981.
Kusterer, Hermann. *Der Kanzler und der General*. Stuttgart: Neske, 1995.
Küsters, H. J. *Die Gründung der europäischen Wirtschaftsgemeinschaft*. Baden-Baden: Nomos, 1982.
Lacouture, Jean. *Pierre Mendès-France*. New York: Holmes and Meier, 1984.
Lamb, R. *The Macmillan Years, 1957–1963: The Emerging Truth*. London: John Murray, 1995.
Large, D. C. *Germans to the Front: West German Rearmament in the Adenauer Era*. Chapel Hill: University of North Carolina Press, 1996.
Laursen, Finn, ed. *The Amsterdam Treaty: National Preference Formation, Interstate Bargaining and Outcome*. Odense: Odense University Press, 2002.
Laursen, Finn, and Sophie Vanhoonacker, eds. *The Intergovernmental Conference and Political Union: Institutional Reform, New Policies and International Identity of the European Community*. Maastricht: EIPA, 1992.
———. *The Ratification of the Maastricht Treaty: Issues, Debates and Future Implications*. Maastricht: EIPA, 1994.
Lawson, Nigel. *The View from No. 11: Britain's Longest-serving Cabinet Member Recalls the Triumphs and Disappointments of the Thatcher Era*. New York: Doubleday, 1993.
Lefèvre, Sylvie. *Les Relations économiques franco-allemandes de 1945 à 1955: De l'occupation à la coopération*. Paris: Comité pour l'histoire économique er financière de la France, 1998.
Lerner, Daniel, and Raymond Aron, eds. *France Defeats the EDC*. New York: Praeger, 1957.
Lindberg, Leon. *The Political Dynamics of European Economic Integration*. Stanford, CA: Stanford University Press, 1963.
Lipgens, Walter. *Die Anfänge der europäischen Einigungspolitik*. Stuttgart: Klett, 1977.
———. *A History of European Integration*. Vol. 1: *1945–1947: The Formation of the European Unity Movement*. Oxford: Clarendon Press, 1982.
Lipgens, Walter, ed. *Documents on the History of European Integration*. Vols. 1–3. Berlin: Walter de Gruyter, 1986–1988 (vol. 3 edited with Wilfried Loth).
Lodge, Juliet, ed. *The 1999 Elections to the European Parliament*. Basingstoke: Palgrave, 2001.
Lord, C. *Absent at the Creation: Britain and the Formation of the European Community, 1950–1952*. Aldershot: Dartmouth, 1996.
Loth, Wilfried. *Der Weg nach Europa, Geschichte der europäischen Integration 1939–1957*. 3rd ed. Göttingen: Vandenhoeck and Ruprecht, 1990.

Loth, Wilfried, and Robert Picht. *De Gaulle, Deutschland und Europa.* Opladen: Leske and Budrich, 1991.

Loth, Wilfried, William Wallace, and Wolfgang Wessels. *Walter Hallstein: The Forgotten European?* New York: St. Martin's Press, 1998.

Lucarelli, Bill. *The Origin and Evolution of the Single Market in Europe.* Aldershot: Ashgate, 1999.

Ludlow, N. Piers. *Dealing with Britain: The Six and the First British Application to the EEC.* New York: Cambridge University Press, 1997.

Ludlow, Peter. *The Making of the European Monetary System.* London: Butterworths, 1982.

Luif, P. *On the Road to Brussels: The Political Dimension of Austria's, Finland's, and Sweden's Road to Accession to the European Union.* Vienna: Austrian Institute for International Affairs, 1995.

Lynch, Frances M.B. *France and the International Economy: From Vichy to the Treaty of Rome.* London: Routledge, 1997.

Maclean, Mairi, and Jean-Marc Trouille. *France, Germany and Britain.* Basingstoke: Macmillan, 2000.

Macmillan, H. *At the End of the Day, 1961–1963.* London: Macmillan, 1973.

———. *Pointing the Way, 1959–1961.* London: Macmillan, 1972.

———. *Riding the Storm, 1956–1959.* London: Macmillan, 1971.

———. *Trades of Fortune, 1945–1955.* London: Macmillan, 1969.

Maier, Charles S., ed. *The Cold War in Europe: Era of a Divided Continent.* 3rd updated and expanded ed. Princeton, NJ: Markus Wiener, 1996.

Maillard, Pierre. *De Gaulle et l'Allemagne. Le rêve inachevé.* Paris: Plon, 1990.

Maravall, José. *The Transition to Democracy in Spain.* New York: St. Martin's Press, 1982.

Marjolin, Robert. *Memoirs, 1911–1986: Architect of European Unity.* London, Weidenfeld and Nicolson, 1986.

Martin, S., ed. *The Construction of Europe.* Dordrecht: Kluwer, 1994.

Massigli, René. *Une comédie des erreurs, 1943–1956: Souvenirs et refléxions sur une étape de la construction européene.* Paris: Plon, 1978.

Mayes, D., ed. *The European Challenge: Industry's Response to the 1992 Programme.* Hemel Hempstead: Harvester Wheatsheaf, 1991.

Mayhew, Alan. *Recreating Europe: The European Union's Policy Towards Central and Eastern Europe.* 2nd ed. Cambridge: Cambridge University Press, 2002.

Mazzucelli, Colette. *France and Germany at Maastricht: Politics and Negotiations to Create the European Union.* New York: Garland, 1997.

McAllister, Richard. *From EC to EU: A Historical and Political Survey.* New York, 1997.

McDonagh, Bobby. *Original Sin in a Brave New World: The Paradox of Europe. An Account of the Negotiation of the Treaty of Amsterdam.* Dublin: Institute for European Affairs, 1998.

McKay, David. *Rush to Union: Understanding the European Federal Bargain.* Oxford: Clarendon Press, 1996.

McNamara, Kathleen. *The Currency of Ideas: Monetary Politics in the European Union.* Ithaca, NY: Cornell University Press, 1997.

Mélandri, Pierre. *Les États-Unis et le défi européen 1955–1958.* Paris: PUF, 1975.

———. *Les États-Unis face à l'unification européene, 1945–1954.* Paris: Pedone, 1980.

Menon, Anand, and Vincent Wright, eds. *From the Nation State to Europe: Essays in Honour of Jack Hayward.* Oxford: Oxford University Press, 2001.

Menudier, Henri. *Le couple franco-allemand en Europe*. Asnières: Publications de l'Institut d'allemand d'Asnières, 1993.

Middlemas, Keith, ed. *Orchestrating Europe: The Informal Politics of European Union, 1973–1995*. New York: Fontana Press, 1995.

Miller, James Edward. *The United States and Italy, 1940–1950: The Politics and Diplomacy of Stabilization*. Chapel Hill: University of North Carolina Press, 1986.

Milward, Alan. *The European Rescue of the Nation State*. 2nd ed. London: Routledge, 2000.

———. *The Frontier of National Sovereignty: History and Theory, 1945–1992*. London: Routledge, 1993.

———. *The Reconstruction of Western Europe, 1945–1951*. Berkeley: University of California Press, 1984.

———. *The UK and the European Community*. Vol. 1: *The Rise and Fall of a National Strategy, 1945–1963*. London: Whitehall History Publishing in association with Frank Cass, 2002.

Monar, Jörg, and Wolfgang Wessels, eds. *The European Union After the Treaty of Amsterdam*. London: Continuum, 2001.

Monnet, Jean. *Memoirs*. Garden City, NY: Doubleday, 1978.

Moon, Jeremy. *European Integration in British Politics, 1950–1963: A Study of Issue Change*. Aldershot: Gower, 1985.

Moravcsik, Andrew. *The Choice for Europe: Social Purpose and State Power from Messina to Maastricht*. Ithaca, NY: Cornell University Press, 1998.

Morgan, Annette. *From Summit to Council: Evolution of the EEC*. London: Chatham House, 1976.

Mowat, R. C. *Creating the European Community*. Tonbridge: Blandford Press, 1973.

Nöel, Gilbert. *Du pool vert à la politique agricole commune*. Paris: Economica, 1988.

Nugent, Neill. *The European Commission*. Basingstoke: Palgrave, 2001.

Occhipinti, John D. *The Politics of EU Police Cooperation: Toward a European FBI?* Boulder, CO: Lynne Rienner Publishers, 2003.

Offner, Arnold A. *Another Such Victory: President Truman and the Cold War, 1945–1953*. Stanford, CA: Stanford University Press, 2002.

O'Neill, Francis. *The French Radical Party and European Integration*. London: Gower, 1981.

Ovendale, R., ed. *The Foreign Policy of the Labour Governments, 1945–1951*. Leicester: Leicester University Press, 1984.

Owen, Geoffrey. *From Empire to Europe: The Decline and Revival of British Industry Since the Second World War*. London: HarperCollins, 1999.

Padoa-Schioppa, Tommaso et al. *Efficiency, Stability and Equity: A Strategy for the Evolution of the Economic System of the European Community*. Oxford: Oxford University Press, 1987.

Parsons, Craig. *A Certain Idea of Europe*. Ithaca, NY: Cornell University Press, 2003.

Pattison de Ménil, Lois. *Who Speaks for Europe? The Vision of Charles de Gaulle*. London: Nicolson and Weidenfeld, 1977.

Pelkmans, Jacques, and Alan Winters. *Europe's Domestic Market*. London: Routledge, 1988.

Peyrefitte, Alain. *C'était de Gaulle*. Vol. 1: *La France redevient la France*. Paris: de Fallois/Fayard, 1994.

———. *C'était de Gaulle*. Vol. 2: *La France reprend sa place dans le monde*. Paris: de Fallois/Fayard, 1997.

Pinto-Lyra, Rubens. *La gauche en France à la construction européene*. Paris: Librairie Générale de Droit et de Jurisprudence, 1978.

Poidevin, Raymond. *Histoire des débuts de la construction européenne, mars 1948–mai 1950: Actes du Colloque de Strasbourg 28–30 novembre 1984*. Brussels: Bruylant, 1986.

———. *Robert Schuman, homme d'état, 1886–1963*. Paris: Imprimerie nationale, 1986.

Pompidou, Georges. *Pour rétablir une vérité*. Paris: Flammarion, 1982.

Pond, Elizabeth. *The Rebirth of Europe*. Washington, DC: Brookings Institution, 2002.

Preeg, Ernest H. *Traders and Diplomats: An Analysis of the Kennedy Round of Negotiations Under the General Agreement on Tariffs and Trade*. Washington, DC: Brookings Institution, 1970.

Pryce, Roy, ed. *The Dynamics of European Integration*. London: Croom Helm, 1987.

Redmond, John. *The 1995 Enlargement of the European Union*. Aldershot: Ashgate, 1997.

Redmond, John, and Glenda G. Rosenthal. *The Expanding European Union: Past, Present, Future*. Boulder, CO: Lynne Rienner Publishers, 1998.

Riddell, Peter. *The Thatcher Government*. London: Martin Robertson, 1983.

Rodríguez-Pose, Andrés. *The European Union: Economy, Society and Polity*. Oxford: Oxford University Press, 2002.

Rollat, A. *Delors*. Paris: Flammarion, 1993.

Ross, George. *Jacques Delors and European Integration*. Oxford: Oxford University Press, 1995.

Roussel, Eric. *Charles de Gaulle*. Paris: Broché, 2002.

Ruane, Kevin. *The Rise and Fall of the European Defense Community: Anglo-American Relations and the Crisis of European Defense, 1950–55*. Basingstoke: Macmillan, 2000.

Rueff, Jaques. *Combats pour l'ordre financier*. Paris: Plon, 1972.

———. *The Monetary Sin of the West*. London: Macmillan, 1972.

Sandholtz, Wayne. *High-Tech Europe: The Politics of International Cooperation*. Berkeley: University of California Press, 1992.

Schaad, Martin P.C. *Bullying Bonn: Anglo-German Diplomacy on European Integration, 1955–61*. New York: St. Martin's Press, 2000.

Schaetzel, Robert. *The Unhinged Alliance: America and the European Community*. New York: Harper and Row, 1975.

Schain, Martin, ed. *The Marshall Plan: Fifty Years After*. Basingstoke: Palgrave, 2001.

Scheinman, Lawrence. *Atomic Energy Policy in France Under the Fourth Republic*. Princeton, NJ: Princeton University Press, 1965.

Schmid, Carlo. *Erinnerungen*. Berne: Scherz Verlag, 1979.

Schmidt, Hans A. *The Path to European Union: From the Marshall Plan to the Common Market*. Baton Rouge: Louisiana State University Press, 1962.

Schulze, Max-Stephan, ed. *Western Europe: Economic and Social Change Since 1945*. London: Longman, 1999.

Schuman, Robert. *Pour l'Europe*. Paris: Nagel, 1963.

Schwabe, Klaus, ed. *Die Anfänge des Schuman-Plans, 1950–1951*. Baden-Baden: Nomos, 1988.

Schwartz, Thomas Alan. *America's Germany: John J. McCloy and the Federal Republic of Germany*. Cambridge: Cambridge University Press, 1991.

———. *Lyndon Johnson and Europe: In the Shadow of Vietnam*. Cambridge: Harvard University Press, 2003.

Schwarz, Hans-Peter. *Konrad Adenauer: A German Politician and Statesman in a Period of War, Revolution and Reconstruction.* Vol. 1: *From the German Empire to the Federal Republic, 1876–1952.* Oxford: Berghahn Books, 1995.

———. *Konrad Adenauer: A German Politician and Statesman in a Period of War, Revolution and Reconstruction.* Vol. 2: *The Statesman.* Oxford: Berghahn Books, 1997.

Serfaty, Simon, ed. *The Finality Debate and Its National Dimensions.* Washington, DC: CSIS Press, 2002.

Serra, Enrico, ed. *Il Rilancio dell'Europa e i Trattati di Roma.* Brussels: Bruylant, 1989.

Servan-Schreiber, J. J. *The American Challenge.* New York: Atheneum, 1968.

Shore, Cris. *Building Europe: The Cultural Politics of European Integration.* London: Routledge, 2000.

Simonian, Haig. *Privileged Partnership: Franco-German Relations in the European Community, 1969–1984.* Oxford: Clarendon Press, 1985.

Smets, P. F., ed. *La Penseé européenne et atlantique de Paul-Henri Spaak.* Brussels: J. Goemmaere, 1980.

Smith, Brendan P.G. *Constitution Building in the European Union: The Process of Treaty Reform.* The Hague: Kluwer Law International, 2002.

Smith, M. L., and Peter M.R. Stirk. *Making the New Europe: European Unity and the Second World War.* London: Pinter Publishers, 1990.

Soutou, Georges-Henri. *L'alliance incertaine: Les rapports politico-stratégiques franco-allemands, 1954–1996.* Paris: Fayard, 1996.

Spierenburg, Dirk, and Raymond Poidevin. *The History of the High Authority of the European Coal and Steel Community: Supranationality in Operation.* London: Weidenfeld and Nicolson, 1994.

Spinelli, Altiero. *The Eurocrats: Conflict and Crisis in the European Community.* Baltimore: Johns Hopkins University Press, 1966.

Stanton Russell, Sharon, Charles B. Keely, and Bryan P. Christian. *Multilateral Diplomacy to Harmonize Asylum Policy in Europe, 1984–1993.* Washington, DC: Institute for the Study of International Migration, 2000.

Steinherr, Alfred. *Thirty Years of European Monetary Integration from the Werner Plan to EMU.* London: Longman, 1994.

Stevens, Anne, with Handley Stevens. *Brussels Bureaucrats? The Administration of the European Union.* London: Palgrave, 2001.

Stikker, Dirk U. *Men of Responsibility: A Memoir.* New York: Harper and Row, 1965.

Stirk, Peter M.R. *A History of European Integration Since 1914.* New York: Pinter, 1996.

Stirk, Peter M.R., and David Weigall, eds. *The Origins and Development of European Integration: A Reader and Commentary.* London: Pinter, 1999.

Svensson, Anna-Carin. *In the Service of the European Union: The Role of the Presidency in Negotiating the Amsterdam Treaty, 1995–1997.* Uppsala: Acta Universitatis, 2000.

Szabo, Stephen F. *The Diplomacy of German Unification.* New York: St. Martin's Press, 1992.

Talbot, Ross B. *The Chicken War.* Ames: Iowa State University Press, 1978.

Taylor, A.J.P. *From the Boer War to the Cold War: Essays on Twentieth-Century Europe.* London: Penguin Books, 1995.

Taylor, Paul. *The European Union in the 1990s.* Oxford: Oxford University Press, 1996.

Thatcher. Margaret. *Downing Street Years*. New York: HarperCollins, 1993.

Thody, Philip Malcolm Waller. *Europe Since 1945*. London: Routledge, 2000.

———. *The Fifth French Republic: Presidents, Politics and Personalities*. London: Routledge, 1998.

Trachtenberg, Marc. *A Constructed Peace: The Making of the European Settlement, 1945–1963*. Princeton, NJ: Princeton University Press, 1999.

Tratt, J. *The Macmillan Government and Europe: A Study in the Process of Policy Development*. London: Macmillan, 1996.

Triffin, Robert. *Europe and the Money Muddle: From Bilateralism to Near-Convertibility*. New Haven: Yale University Press, 1957.

———. *The Future of the European Payments System*. Stockholm: Almquist and Wiksell, 1958.

———. *Monetary Reconstruction in Europe*. New York: Carnegie Endowment for International Peace, 1952.

Triffin, Robert, ed. *EMS: The Emerging European Monetary System*. Brussels: National Bank of Belgium, 1979.

Tsoukalis, Loukas. *The Politics and Economics of European Monetary Integration*. London: Allen and Unwin, 1977.

Tsoukalis, Loukas, ed. *Greece and the European Community*. Farnborough: Saxon House, 1979.

Tugendhat, Christopher. *Making Sense of Europe*. New York: Columbia University Press, 1988.

Ungerer, Horst. *From EPU to EMU: A Concise History of European Monetary Integration*. Westport, CT: Quorum Books, 1997.

Uri, Pierre. *Partnership for Progress: A Program for Transatlantic Action*. New York: Harper and Row, 1963.

Urwin, Derek. *Community of Europe: A History of European Integration Since 1945*. 2nd ed. London: Longman, 1995.

Vaïsse, Maurice. *La grandeur. Politique étrangère du général de Gaulle, 1958–1969*. Paris: Fayard, 1997.

Varsori, Antonio, and Elena Calandri, eds. *The Failure of Peace in Europe, 1943–1948*. Basingstoke: Palgrave, 2002.

Viner, Jacob. *The Customs Union Issue*. New York: Carnegie Endowment for International Peace, 1950.

Von der Groeben, Hans. *The European Community: The Formative Years*. Luxembourg: Office for Official Publications of the European Communities, 1987.

Wall, Irwin M. *France, The United States, and the Algerian War*. Berkeley: University of California Press, 2001.

———. *The United States and the Making of Post-War France, 1945–1954*. Cambridge: Cambridge University Press, 1991.

Wallace, Helen, William Wallace, and Carole Webb, eds. *Policy-Making in the European Communities*. London: Wiley, 1977.

Werts, Jan. *The European Council*. Amsterdam: North-Holland, 1992.

Wexler, Imanuel. *The Marshall Plan Revisited*. Westport, CT: Greenwood Press, 1983.

Wilcox, Francis Orlando, and H. Field Haviland. *The Atlantic Community: Progress and Prospects*. New York: Praeger, 1963.

Wilkes, George, ed. *Britain's Failure to Enter the European Community, 1961–1963: The Enlargement Negotiations and Crises in European, Atlantic, and Commonwealth Relations*. London: Frank Cass, 1997.

Williams, Charles. *Adenauer: The Father of the New Germany*. New York: Wiley, 2000.

Willis, F. Roy. *France, Germany and the New Europe, 1945–1967*. Rev. and expanded ed. Stanford, CA: Stanford University Press, 1968.

Willis, F. Roy, ed. *European Integration*. New York: New Viewpoints, 1975.

Wilson, Harold. *Memoirs: The Making of a Prime Minister, 1916–1986*. London: Weidenfeld and Nicolson, 1986.

Winand, Pascaline. *Eisenhower, Kennedy, and the United States of Europe*. New York: St. Martin's Press, 1993.

Wood, Stephen. *Germany, Europe and the Persistence of Nations: Transformation, Interests and Identity, 1989–1996*. Aldershot: Ashgate, 1998.

Wright, Jonathan. *Gustav Stresemann: Weimar's Greatest Statesman*. Oxford: Oxford University Press, 2002.

Wurm, Clemens, ed. *Western Europe and Germany: The Beginnings of European Integration*. Oxford: Berg, 1995.

Young, Hugo, *This Blessed Plot: Britain and Europe from Churchill to Blair.* Woodstock: Overlook Press, 1999.

Young, John W. *Britain, France and the Unity of Europe, 1945–1951*. Leicester: Leicester University Press, 1984.

———. *France, the Cold War and the Western Alliance, 1944–1949*. New York: St. Martin's Press, 1990.

Zelikow, Philip, and Condoleezza Rice. *Germany Unified and Europe Transformed: A Study in Statecraft*. Cambridge: Harvard University Press, 1995.

Index